INTRODUCTION TO THE
LAW OF REAL PROPERTY

Third Edition

**An Historical Background of The
Common Law of Real Property
And Its Modern Application**

By

CORNELIUS J. MOYNIHAN

*Late Judge of the Superior Court of Massachusetts
Professor of Law
Boston College Law School; Suffolk University Law School*

SHELDON F. KURTZ

*Percy Bordwell Professor of Law
The University of Iowa College of Law*

WEST
GROUP

A THOMSON COMPANY

Mat #18503883

American Casebook Series, and the West Group symbol are registered trademarks used herein under license.

COPYRIGHT © 1982, 1988 WEST PUBLISHING CO.
COPYRIGHT © 2002 By WEST GROUP
     610 Opperman Drive
     P.O. Box 64526
     St. Paul, MN 55164–0526
     1–800–328–9352

All rights reserved
Printed in the United States of America
ISBN 0–314–26031–5

TEXT IS PRINTED ON 10% POST CONSUMER RECYCLED PAPER

Preface

This book is a revised edition of the classic Moynihan's Introduction to the Law of Real Property that has been used by countless law students, lawyers, and courts for over the last 60 years. The basic structure of the text has been largely retained but edited and updated with references to newer Restatements, the Uniform Probate Code and the Uniform Trust Code. This edition also includes a more detailed treatment of the Rule Against Perpetuities.

In the United States little has changed in the basic classification system of estates in land since the American Revolution. Essentially all present interests are classified as either life estates or fee simple estates, including the fee simple determinable and the fee simple on condition subsequent. All future interests, whether created as legal estates in land or as equitable estates in trust, are classified as one of three types of reversionary interests, vested or contingent remainders or as one of two types of executory interests. This book provides the reader with the historical background explaining how and why this classification system developed. It also provides the reader with the necessary tools to distinguish one interest from another and an explanation of the importance of the distinction even though that importance is diminishing.

While the estates in land system may not be the most exciting area of the law to some, it is perhaps that area of legal study on which history has had, and continues to have, its greatest impact. Furthermore, without a thorough understanding of that history, it is difficult to understand and appreciate the modifications to that system that have been adopted in many states. However, no attempt is made here to reflect all of these changes by exhaustive citations to state cases and statutes. These changes may (1) affect the classification of present and future interests, such as treating all defeasible fees the same or requiring the recording of certain documents to enforce reversionary interests, or (2) abolish or modify the Rule in Shelley's Case, the Doctrine of Worthier Title, the Rule of Destructibility with respect to contingent remainders, or the Rule Against Perpetuities. Thus, no competent lawyer would rely on this book for more than putting the estates in land system into its proper historical setting without further researching applicable state law variations. On the other hand, all law students will find here the multitude of rules from which the current estates in land system is derived and more than enough information to successfully navigate a first-year property course. Furthermore, we believe this book is a wonderful introduction into one of the most important areas of our shared legal heritage.

The prefaces to the prior editions have aptly noted the contribution of many of the great works of property and future interests laws to the development of this book and the authors continue to be indebted to the authors of those works. Furthermore, to the names of Pollack, Maitland, Simpson, Gray, Tiffany, Casner, Powell, Simes and Smith, should be added Waggoner, Langbein and Halbach, who through their work on various restatement projects have furthered our understanding of the laws in this area. Anyone writing in this field is necessarily indebted to all of them.

SHELDON F. KURTZ

Iowa City, Iowa

Summary of Contents

*

Table of Contents

Page

*

INTRODUCTION TO THE
LAW OF REAL
PROPERTY
Third Edition

*

Chapter 1

HISTORY, TENURE, AND SEISIN

INTRODUCTION

It would be economical in terms of time and effort if we could begin the study of the law of real property by proceeding directly to a consideration of that law as it is in our own day and place. Unfortunately, such a short cut is not practical. A thorough understanding of the modern land law of the United States is impossible without a knowledge of its historical background as that law has been a millennium in the making. During this long period great changes have been effected by means of legislation and judicial decisions, as well as by the development of new social systems and customs. This process of change has been one of evolution, not revolution. The imprint of the past is still discernible in the present. In this branch of the law more than in any other perhaps, we can time and again profitably invoke the often quoted statement of Mr. Justice Holmes: "Upon this point a page of history is worth a volume of logic."[1] And, if the aridity of legal history tends to be irksome, we might recall Mr. Justice Cardozo's statement that this is a field "where there can be no progress without history."[2]

§ 1. The Norman Settlement

We begin in England with the Norman Conquest (1066). The Norman arrow, shot perhaps at random, that pierced the eye socket

---

1. New York Trust Co. v. Eisner, 256 U.S. 345 at 349, 41 S.Ct. 506 at 507, 65 L.Ed. 963 at 983 (1921).

2. Cardozo, The Nature of the Judicial Process 54 (1921). *See also* Wyzanski, History and Law, 26 U. Chi.L.Rev. 236 (1959).

of Harold, the Saxon king, decided not only the Battle of Hastings but deflected the course of development of English law for centuries to come. The Conquest, while preserving the framework of the Old English state, gave to England a new dynasty, a new ruling class and a new system of land holding.

William, the Conqueror, operated on the principle of political legitimacy. Tenuous as his claim to the English throne may have been, his successes in battle put beyond dispute his assertion that he was the legitimate successor of Edward the Confessor and, therefore, entitled to the rights and prerogatives of an English king. Consequently, those who had opposed him at Hastings and in the later uprisings forfeited their lands.[1] The Saxon nobility, who had formed the backbone of the opposition, were for the most part wiped out or driven into exile. Their lands became available for distribution to William's men as a reward for services and the distribution itself served as a means of establishing a new Norman aristocracy.

It is a tribute to the extraordinary administrative ability of William that this vast redistribution of English lands was carried out in an orderly manner. The whole process was controlled by the firm hand of the King. Immense holdings were granted, as might be expected, to his kinsmen and to his closest associates in the great project of the Conquest. William gave almost one-fourth of England to ten of his principal followers[2] and made grants to lesser barons of the smaller fiefs or holdings of English earls and thegns. Normally, the grants were not of a compact territorial unit but consisted of manors scattered through several counties.

The peasant occupants of village lands probably were left undisturbed for the most part in their little holdings but they acquired new lords to whom they had to render the ancient dues. Continuity with the past was preserved through the principle applied by the Conqueror that every earl, bishop, abbot, and baron

---

§ 1

1. *See* the writ of William I to the Abbot of Bury St. Edmunds ordering the abbot to turn over to the king the lands of the abbey tenants "who stood in battle against me and were slain" at Has-tings. The writ is set out in Douglas and Greenaway, 2 English Historical Documents 918 (Oxford Univ. Press, 1953).

2. *Id.* at 22.

to whom he gave land held it with the same rights and privileges as his English predecessor in title had on the day when King Edward the Confessor "was alive and dead."[3]

The larger baronial estates, or honours as they came to be called, were normally created out of the holdings of numerous Englishmen. As many as eighty English estates, situated in different regions, might be combined to compose a single lord's honour. In the course of the Norman settlement several thousand smaller estates were compressed into fewer than two hundred major honours. The lords of these honours were the men who, with William, established the new English state.

§ 2. The Introduction of Feudal Tenure

From a legal standpoint one of the significant aspects of the Norman plantation was the introduction into England of the most highly organized type of feudal tenure—military tenure. Feudalism is a generic term that may be used to describe the social structure of Western Europe in the Middle Ages. It had for its central core the relationship of lord and vassal (not then a word of opprobrium) bound together by a bond of personal loyalty and owing mutual aid and assistance. The relation was usually evidenced by the solemn ceremony of homage wherein the vassal knelt before the lord, acknowledged himself to be his lord's man and swore fealty to him. It was frequently accompanied by a grant of land from the lord to the vassal, the land to be held of the lord by the vassal as tenant.[1] Normally, by the terms of the grant specific services were imposed

3. This curious expression comes from Domesday Book, the record of the great survey of England made by William's order in 1086. See § 4, infra.

§ 2

1. Land was not the only subject matter of a feudal grant. It was customary throughout Western Europe in the Middle Ages for great and petty lords to obtain vassals bound to render military service by granting to such vassals a monetary annuity. The feudal bond was created by the rendition of homage by the grantee to the grantor. These grants

numbered in the thousands. See Lyon, From Fief to Indenture (1957).

In the medieval period status, not contract, was the usual basis of rights and duties. It is interesting to observe that by the twentieth century there had been some retreat from contract back to status as the source of rights and obligations. See, e.g., Javins v. First National Realty Corp., 428 F.2d 1071 (D.C.Cir. 1970), cert. denied 400 U.S. 925, 91 S.Ct. 186, 27 L.Ed.2d 185 (1970) (landlord held impliedly to warrant the habitability of rental housing units).

on the tenant and these services were considered to be a burden on the land itself.

Military tenure was known in Normandy and the Conqueror used it to build a military organization adequate to maintain the Crown against rebellion from within and invasion from without. Most of the lords and barons to whom he granted English lands held them under an obligation to supply a specified quota of knights to the king whenever they should be required. The number of knights to be furnished was in each case fixed by the terms of the charter evidencing the grant and, therefore, initially depended on the will and necessities of the king. This number bore no constant relation to the size or value of the honour granted. The lay lords who received grants of the king were accustomed in their own countries to the institution of tenure, or land holding, in return for military service to a lord.[2] On the other hand, the bishops and abbots to whom William gave lands, or confirmed older grants, on condition of knight service were not so accustomed. On these ecclesiastical tenants-in-chief he also imposed the duty of finding a stipulated number of knights for royal service.[3] This innovation of the Conqueror, induced by the military necessities of the times, yielded an additional 800 knights, in round numbers, for the king's service. In all, the quota of knights demanded of the lay and ecclesiastical baronage amounted to approximately 5000 men.

§ 3.   The Creation of Sub–Tenures

The expense to the tenants-in-chief of maintaining as part of their households the prescribed quota of knights must have been

2. A person holding land directly under the king was called a tenant in chief (in Latin, tenant *in capite*). By the year 1086 there were approximately fifteen hundred tenants in chief. As to tenure in Normandy, *see* Tabuteau, Ownership and Tenure in Eleventh–Century Normandy, 21 Amer.J.Legal Hist. 97 (1977).

3. The Constitutions of Clarendon (1164), purporting to embody established feudal customs, provided in Cl. XI: "Archbishops, bishops and all benef-iced clergy of the realm, who hold of the king in chief, have their possessions from the lord king by barony and are answerable for them to the king's justices and officers; they observe and perform all royal rights and customs and, like other barons, ought to be present at the judgments of the king's court together with the barons, until a case shall arise of judgment concerning mutilation or death." Douglas & Greenaway, 2 English Historical Documents 721 (Oxford Univ. Press, 1953).

considerable. Moreover, the constant presence in the household of a number of armed men, inclined to be disorderly at times, was a matter of concern particularly to the ecclesiastical tenants. Slowly at first but with increasing frequency the tenants-in-chief made allotments of lands to their knights who thereupon became tenants of their lords. The amount of land given in return for the obligation to supply the service of one knight (the knight's fee of feudal records) varied. It depended on the bargain made by the lord and his prospective tenant. A particular tract might be made up of a number of knight's fees and, in later times, might be subdivided into fractional parts of a knight's fee. In some cases the number of knights enfeoffed, that is, given land, by the tenant in chief exceeded the quota owed for the king's service and in other cases the number was less.[1]

All tenure implied some service due from the tenant to the lord. However, the service fixed at the creation of the tenure might be and often was nonmilitary in nature. The king "compensated" his important administrative and household officials with a grant of land and to such tenures was attached the duty of rendering specific services necessary to the functioning of the royal household. The service prescribed required the performance of such duties as those of marshal, steward, butler, or chamberlain. These were tenants of dignity and rank, but this type of tenure also embraced tenants who served the king in his chamber, his pantry, and his kitchen. The Conqueror, for example, gave half a hide of land (about 60 acres) in Gloucestershire to his cook. The greater tenants in chief, whose households were often royal establishments in

§ 3

1. In 1166 Henry II ordered each of his tenants in chief to answer what amounted to a questionnaire on the number of knights enfeoffed on the tenant's estate and the number required by his *servitium debitum*. The purpose of this survey may have been to provide a basis for an increase in the feudal assessment which in most cases had been fixed in the Conqueror's reign. The returns of the tenants in chief (*Cartae Baronum*) show in many cases the enfeoffment of more knights than required for the king's service. The return of the Archbishop of York explains how this came about: "For our predecessors enfeoffed more knights than they owed to the king, and they did this, not for the necessities of the royal service, but because they wished to provide for their relatives and servants." Douglas and Greenaway, 2 English Historical Documents 907 (Oxford Univ.Press, 1953). *See also* 3 Holdsworth, History of English Law 42–43 (3rd ed. 1927).

miniature, also gave lands to some of their retainers subject to the obligation to render a prescribed personal service to the lord. Such tenures, whether held of the king or of an intermediate lord, became known as serjeanty tenures.[2]

Moreover, many a small landholder found it advisable in an unruly age to place himself under the protection of some powerful earl or abbot by becoming his man. He hoped thereby to gain as an ally "a mightier friend than the law could be."[3] He surrendered his lands to the lord to be received back from him subject to the duty of rendering military or other service. By this process the tenurial system was further expanded.

§ 4. The Domesday Book

In the last year of his reign William, the Conqueror, ordered a comprehensive and detailed survey of most of the land in England. The primary purpose of the survey was fiscal in nature. William desired precise, up-to-date information as to contributions made by each estate to the Danegeld, a direct tax levied throughout the country. But in addition he sought an accurate and complete picture of the results of the redistribution of English lands that had taken place in the twenty years that had elapsed since the Norman invasion.

The great survey was carried out through commissioners who were sent into most of the shires to receive the sworn verdicts of selected jurors as to the property holdings of each tenant, the source of the tenant's title, the extent and value of his holdings, the composition of the estate, and any changes in the size of the estate since the Conquest. The entire project was accomplished with a ruthless Norman efficiency that shocked the easy going Saxons.[1] The information obtained was rearranged and summarized accord-

2. Serjeanty tenure is further described in § 6, *infra*.

3. Maitland, Domesday Book and Beyond 70 (1897).

§ 4

1. The Anglo–Saxon Chronicle after relating that William at his Christmas Council in 1085 had "much thought and very deep speech" with his council "about this land, how it was set and by what men" goes on to tell us: "Then he sent his men all over England into every shire and had them find out how many hundred hides there were in the shire, or what land and cattle the king himself had in the country, or what dues he ought to have in twelve months from the shire. Also he had a record made of how much land his archbishops had, and his

ing to the holdings in each county of the king's tenants-in-chief and to that extent the survey became a statistical record of feudal tenures. The rearranged summary or digest was compiled in two volumes which became popularly known as the Domesday Book.[2] The two volumes, originally kept in the king's treasury, are still preserved in the Public Record Office in London—the finest extant legal record of any medieval kingdom.

Although the Domesday Book tells us little of the kinds of tenure and the services due from the tenants, it does make clear that the principle of dependent tenure had been firmly established as the basic form of English land holding.[3] At the end of the Conqueror's reign there was little place in English law for the man who, in the words of Domesday Book, had been free "to go with his land to whatever lord he would."

§ 5.   Legal Relations of Lord and Tenant

In addition to the personal relationship arising from the feudal bond between lord and tenant there existed a legal relationship

bishops and his abbots and his earls— and though I relate it at too great length—what or how much everybody had who was occupying land in England, in land or cattle, and how much money it was worth. So very narrowly did he have it investigated, that there was no single hide nor a yard of land, nor indeed (it is a shame to relate but it seemed no shame to him to do) one ox nor one cow nor one pig was there left out, and not put down in his record: and all those records were brought to him afterwards." Douglas and Greenaway, 2 English Historical Documents 161 (Oxford Univ. Press, 1953).

2. One explanation for the name of the book is that the records were deemed by the populace to be as conclusive as the day of judgment. See, 2 Holdsworth, History of English Law 163 (1927). For a brief description of the Domesday inquisition and translated excerpts from the book, see, Douglas and Greenaway, 2 English Historical Documents 847–878 (1953). Maitland's essays

on the subject (Domesday Book and Beyond) are a highly specialized treatment.

Almost eight hundred years later (in 1874), another survey of land ownership in Great Britain was made. The compilation was, of course, called "The New Domesday Book." See Spring, Landowners, Lawyers, and Land Law Reform in Nineteenth Century England, 21 Amer.J.Legal Hist. 40, 50 (1977).

3. "The general theory that all land tenure, except indeed the tenure by which the king holds land in demesne, is dependent tenure, seems to be implied, not only by many particular entries, but also by the whole scheme of the book. Every holder of land, except the king, holds it of (de) some lord, and therefore every acre of land that is not royal demesne can be arranged under the name of some tenant-in-chief. Even a church will hold its land, if not of the king, then of some other lord." Maitland, Domesday Book and Beyond 151 (1897).

which, to use modern terms, rested partly in contract and partly in property. The lord owed protection and warranty to the tenant[1] and the tenant owed services to the lord. Both parties also had rights centered in the land that were the subject of the tenure. If B holding land under O was in actual occupancy, then B was said to be tenant in demesne and obviously had property rights consisting of a general right to possess, use, and enjoy the land. But B's lord, O, who in turn may have held of the king, also held the land—not in demesne but in service. Not only B but the land itself owed the service stipulated when the tenure between O and B was created. This service attached to the land and ran with it. B could not transfer the land free from this feudal obligation. If B transferred the land to C the parties were free to agree between themselves as to how the service would be discharged, but O's right to the service could not be eliminated. If the service was not forthcoming O had the remedy of distress (the right to seize any chattels found on the land whether owned by B or C) and in some cases a remedy against the land itself.[2]

So also, the service owed to the king from a tenant-in-chief bound the tenement regardless of the number of sub-tenures created or of the sub-divisions made of the land.

The same piece of land, then, could be the subject of property rights in different persons in the sense that several persons could have proprietary interests centered in the land. And, since a single parcel could be the subject of several tenures with a different service attaching to each tenure, the adjustment of the rights of the

§ 5

1. The doing of homage by a tenant created an implied obligation on the part of the lord to warrant the title to the lands conveyed to the tenant. If the tenant was later ousted by one having a better title, the lord was required to give him a tenement of equal value. In any proceeding against the tenant by one claiming title to the land the tenant could call upon his lord to defend the title. The advantage to the tenant of being able to call in (vouch to warranty) a powerful lord to assume the defense of his title helps to explain the creation of

tenures by commendation. See § 3, *supra*. In the thirteenth and later centuries express warranties were commonly inserted in charters of feoffment.

2. In early feudal times a deliberate refusal on the part of the tenant to render the services due to the lord amounted to felony and the lands on conviction of the tenant reverted or escheated to the lord. Cessation of services soon ceased to be a felony but the Statute of Gloucester (1278) gave the lord the remedy of forfeiture of the land for wilfully withholding the services.

persons in the feudal hierarchy became an increasingly complex process.[3]

Viewing the system of tenure as a whole it appeared as a pyramidal structure. At the top of the pyramid was the king who alone was always lord and never tenant. Directly under him were the tenants-in-chief; beneath these were tenants of lower social standing holding the smaller parcels into which an honour or barony was sub-divided. At the broad base were the peasants actually tilling the soil (the tenants paravail). All persons having an intermediate place in this structure held the land in a dual capacity—they were tenants of those above them and lords (mesne lords) with respect to those holding under them.

§ 6. The Classification of Tenures

Inasmuch as lord and tenant were free to fix between themselves at the time of the creation of a new tenure the kind and amount of services due from the tenant, a wonderful variety of tenures developed. By the thirteenth century the land law was becoming private property law and less a branch of public law involving governmental, military, and jurisdictional aspects. The king's courts, administering a centralized legal system, assumed the task of reducing the variety of tenures to a manageable classification and by the time of Edward I's reign (1272–1307) the great division of tenures into free and unfree had been established and the list of free tenures had become fixed under four major headings.[1]

The distinction between free and unfree tenures indicates the connection between personal status and tenure that obtained in the medieval land law and still existed at the end of the thirteenth century. The principal test applied by the judges in any given case

3. "It is no impossibility that Edward should hold in villeinage of Ralph, who holds in free socage of the Prior of Barnwell, who holds in frankalmoin of Earl Alan, who holds by knight's service of the king." 1 Pollock and Maitland, History of English Law 239 (2d ed. 1898) (hereinafter cited as Pollock & Maitland).

§ 6

1. For a detailed discussion of the distinction between free and unfree tenure, see 3 Holdsworth, History of English Law 29–34 (3rd ed. 1927) (hereinafter cited as Holdsworth); 1 Pollock & Maitland 368–373.

to determine the nature of the tenure as free or unfree was the character of the services required to be rendered by the tenant: were the services definite and certain or were they dependent on the will of the lord as to quantity or manner of performance; were they of a servile nature or worthy of a free man? The legal consequence of the tenure being free or unfree was important. The tenant of land holding in free tenure was protected by the king's courts and had the benefit of the real actions; the unfree tenant had his remedy against those disturbing his possession only in his lord's court.

FREE TENURE

Free tenures were classified under four main divisions:

    A.   Tenure by knight service;

    B.   Serjeanty;

    C.   Frankalmoin;

    D.   Free and common socage.

A few words may be said about each of these tenures.

A. *Tenure by Knight Service*

This was the typical tenure of feudalism and most of the tenants-in-chief of the king held their lands by this tenure. Originally the most honorable form of tenure, tenure by knight service gave to the tenant in the twelfth century not only land ownership but a voice in the great council and jurisdiction over his sub-tenants.[2] The obligation to render military service by supplying the specified quota of properly armed and equipped knights for the king's host meant actual military service in the first century after the Conquest. In theory, the required period of service was forty days and then only within the kingdom. As the art of war developed it was becoming increasingly clear that an army of paid professional soldiers was more efficient than a hastily summoned motley assort-

---

2. Attendance at the king's court by tenants-in-chief and at the lord's court by under-tenants was an auxiliary service attaching to most tenures. In medieval times the word "court" was not restricted to a tribunal presided over by a professionally trained judge sitting with or without a jury. As to suit at court, *see* 1 Pollock & Maitland 586–594.

ment of non-professionals. Consequently, Henry II (1154–1189) encouraged his tenants-in-chief to make a monetary payment instead of providing knights. This monetary payment, known as scutage, was made to the king by the tenants-in-chief, who, in turn, proceeded to levy scutage on their own tenants who owed the duty of supplying knights for the king's service. From the middle of the twelfth to the latter part of the thirteenth century military tenure supplied knights, or the money to hire knights, for the royal army, but the tendency to treat scutage as merely another form of direct tax became more pronounced. Because of the splitting of knights' fees into fractional parts and the very complexities of tenure itself, it proved an inefficient form of tax and gradually fell into disuse. With the decay of the feudal system military tenure had become inadequate to supply either the men or the money to furnish the sinews of war. As Maitland so well put it: "But in truth, the whole system is becoming obsolete. If tenure by knight service had been abolished in 1300, the kings of the subsequent ages would have been deprived of the large revenue that they drew from wardships, marriages and so forth; really they would have lost little else."[3]

B. Serjeanty Tenure

Serjeanty means service and is derived from the medieval Latin word "serientia." It designates a type of tenure characterized by the obligation to perform a personal service definite as to time and usually localized as to place of performance. The services were heterogeneous in nature ranging from honorable to menial. They related to solemn occasions of state, performance of duties in the royal or seignorial household, military service, royal sporting activities, and the rendering at stated times of supplies or specific articles.[4] Many officers of state, members of the royal household, important officials attached to the households of magnates, and humbler tenants held their lands by serjeanty in the twelfth and thirteenth centuries.

3. 1 Pollock and Maitland 276.
4. For a description of the services due from different serjeanty tenants, see Kimball, Serjeanty Tenure in Medieval England 69–129(1936); 3 Holdsworth, History of English Law 46–51(3rd ed. 1927).

The wide variety of services due from serjeanty tenants and the similarity of some of the services to those due from other classes of tenants made it difficult to distinguish this tenure in many cases from knight service or socage tenure. The element of personal service seems to have been its one distinguishing feature. When the practice of retaining hired servants developed in the fourteenth century the services due from serjeanty tenants were in many cases commuted to a payment of rent and the tenure was converted into socage.

Eventually, serjeanty tenure became divided into grand serjeanty and petty serjeanty. The former name was reserved for serjeanty tenures held directly of the king and requiring the performance of some honorary ceremonial service. Petty serjeanty became socage tenure in effect and involved services of a humbler nature— such as to provide military supplies or articles of small value.[5] A few vestiges of grand serjeanty remain to the present day in England in connection with coronation ceremonies, but as a whole this form of tenure had no important impact on the land law.

C. Frankalmoin Tenure

Frankalmoin, meaning free alms, was a tenure arising from a gift of lands to a church, religious body, or ecclesiastical official in return for services of a religious nature, such as saying Masses or prayers, but with no secular obligation.[6] No lay person could hold by frankalmoin. The mere fact that land was held by an ecclesiastical tenant, such as a bishop or abbot, did not make the tenure frankalmoin. Many prelates and ecclesiastics held lands by knight service. The strictly religious nature of the service and the absence of any secular duty was the chief quality of frankalmoin.

5. Although serjeanty tenures were held of the crown and of mesne lords in the twelfth and thirteenth centuries, by the latter part of the fifteenth century serjeanty tenure could be held only of the king. Since wardship was incident to grand serjeanty, but not to petit serjeanty, Littleton writing about 1481 could describe the latter class as "socage in effect." Littleton, Tenures § 160. As to wardship, see § 7, infra.

6. If the services required of the grantee were specific in nature—such as saying mass for the grantor on certain days or a specific number of times a year—the tenure was called tenure by divine service. However, this tenure was another type of frankalmoin.

Grants of land to be held in frankalmoin could not be made, except by the king or with his permission, after the Statute Quia Emptores (1290) and as a result this form of tenure became of slight importance.

D. Free and Common Socage

The services due from a man holding by socage tenure were normally of an agricultural or monetary nature. He was bound to perform specified agricultural work on the lord's own lands, or to render annually to the lord a definite quantity of agricultural products, or, more often, to pay a periodic rent in money. This money rent might be nominal or substantial. But whatever service was due it was fixed and definite, not dependent on the will of the lord as to amount or quantity. In this quality of definiteness lay the distinguishing feature between socage tenure and unfree tenure. Eventually, this form of tenure became the great residual tenure. A free tenant who did not hold by military service or by serjeanty or by frankalmoin was deemed to hold in socage. Originally it was not as dignified a form of holding as military tenure but because it was freer from oppressive financial burdens than the more aristocratic tenures it had distinct advantages for the tenant when knighthood ceased to be in flower. It was destined to become, as we shall see later, the one surviving form of tenure.[7]

UNFREE TENURE

Unfree tenure has for its background the manorial organization that dominated so much of life in medieval England. The manor was an agricultural, governmental, and fiscal unit, usually co-extensive in territory with the ancient village, composed of lands held by the lord and by tenants of different classes. A portion of the manorial lands was held of the lord by free tenants in socage or by knight service. The remaining lands (demesne lands) were retained

---

7. Two special varieties of socage tenure, both of them influenced by local custom, were gavelkind tenure and burgage, or borough English, tenure. Gavelkind prevailed in the county of Kent and was subject to special rules, the most important being that on the death of the tenant the land descended to all of the sons equally. Burgage tenure existed in a few places (such as in a portion of Nottingham) by special custom. On the death of the tenant the land descended to the youngest son—the precise opposite of the general common-law rule of primogeniture.

by the lord in his own possession and enjoyment and consisted of the manor house with its appurtenances, scattered strips of arable land in the open fields, and the pasturage and waste lands. The labor force required to work these demesne lands of the lord was supplied by a servile class of manorial inhabitants, called villeins. The villein was a serf but not a slave. Against his lord he had no rights except security of life and limb, but against third persons he had the rights of a free man. He could not leave the manor and his time and his labor were at the arbitrary command of the lord; his humble cottage or hovel, as well as his little strip in the common fields, he held at the will of the lord.

Not only did the lord supervise the agricultural economy of the manor; he also, through the manorial courts over which he presided in person or through his bailiff, adjudicated controversies among his tenants and regulated much of their daily lives.[8] The villein tenant received whatever protection to which he was entitled from the manorial and not the royal courts.

Such was the manor in thirteenth century England. In the next century an evolutionary process began that in time would change the personal status of the villein into that of a free man, and would convert his precarious tenure into that of a substantial property owner. A growing scarcity of agricultural labor, greatly accentuated by the plague of the Black Death (1348–1349), forced most lords to substitute a money rent for labor service by the villein tenants.[9]

---

8. The lord's rights of jurisdiction were exercised by means of two courts: the Court Baron for free tenants and the Court Customary for villein tenants. In most manors the court exercised not only civil jurisdiction but also criminal jurisdiction of minor offenses. Actions of detinue, debt, covenant, and tort for defamation were common. As proof that the age of chivalry was over, consider this case from one of the Courts Baron: "It is found by inquest (the jury of tenants) that Rohese (Rose) Bindebere called Ralph Bolay thief, and he called her whore. Therefore both in mercy 3d. (fined three pence each). And for that the trespass done to the said Ralph ex-

ceeds the trespass done to the said Rohese, as has been found, therefore, it is considered that the said Ralph do recover from the said Rohese 12 d. for his taxed damages." And sad to relate, a manorial court found it necessary to issue the following rule: "It is ordered that all women in the vill hold their tongues and not scold or defame anyone." 2 Holdsworth 383.

9. The decline in the value of money which resulted from the importation to Europe of gold and silver from the new world inured to the benefit of the fourteenth century villein tenants' successors. In Maitland's striking phrase, the increase in the value of the land

Gradually, the obligations of the villein tenants became fixed by manorial customs so that their land holding became a definite type of customary tenure, no longer dependent on the lord's will.[10]

This customary tenure evolved into a unique type of land holding which later became known as copyhold tenure. The rights of such tenants were evidenced by the records of the manorial courts. They had the right to transfer their lands upon payment of a fine to the lord but such transfers could not be made by the common-law methods of feoffment and grant available to tenants holding by a free tenure.[11] Copyhold lands were transferable only by surrender and admittance. The tenant could, by custom, surrender the lands to the lord of the manor to the use of a person designated by the tenant, and the lord was bound to admit such person into the tenancy. The surrender and admittance were recorded on the rolls of the manorial court and a copy of the rolls was delivered to the new tenant as evidence of his title. Hence, the tenant was said to hold by copy of court roll and the form of holding was labeled copyhold tenure.

The freehold of lands originally held by an unfree tenure was in the lord, not the tenant. Thus, a copyhold tenant could not maintain a real action in the royal courts to protect his interest. In fact, until the fifteenth and sixteenth centuries the tenant's only remedy was in the manorial courts. The courts of equity, and later the common-law courts, however, became active in regulating and supervising the manorial courts and the customary tenant was given protection against the lord of the manor and against third persons. Yet copyhold tenure continued to bear the marks of its origin even at the period of its ultimate development, and because

during the seventeenth century was "an unearned increment, the product of the American mines." 3 Holdsworth 212.

10. Brief mention may be made of a peculiar form of manorial tenure known as tenure in ancient demesne. This was restricted to tenants of manors which had belonged to the Crown in the time of Edward the Confessor and William the Conqueror. These tenants stood midway between free and villein tenants and had special privileges and obli-

gations. Traces of this tenure persisted into the twentieth century. See Mertenns v. Hill, (1901) 1 Ch. 842. It was converted into socage tenure in 1926. Law of Property Acts, 1922 and 1925. Proof that a particular parcel of land was held in ancient demesne was established by resort to Domesday Book and the records of that book were conclusive.

11. See generally ch. 6, infra.

of its unsuitability to modern life it was the subject of considerable legislation in the nineteenth century. Statutes were enacted providing for compulsory enfranchisement of the land at the option of either lord or tenant.[12] It was finally abolished as of January 1, 1926 by the Law of Property Act, 1922, which converted it into free and common socage.[13]

§ 7. The Incidents of Free Tenures

In addition to the particular services required to be rendered by the tenant to his lord in accordance with the terms stipulated at the creation of the tenure, there were further rights given to the lord and obligations imposed on the tenant, known as incidents of tenure. These incidents derived from the feudal relationship, apart from any express agreement of the tenant. By the fifteenth century the services due from the various tenants had for the most part been commuted into fixed money rents which decreased in value as the purchasing power of money declined. But some of the profitable incidents of tenure were tied to the land itself and, therefore, became more valuable as land values increased. As a consequence, such incidents had a more significant effect on the development of the land law than the ancient tenurial services or their monetary equivalents.

The principal incidents were homage and fealty, relief and primer seisin, wardship and marriage, aids, fines for alienation, and escheat.

Homage and Fealty

Homage was the feudal ceremony whereby the tenant, kneeling unarmed before the lord, solemnly acknowledged himself to be the man of the lord. It was a necessary incident to tenure by knight service and became obsolete when that tenure ceased to be military in fact. Fealty was the oath sworn by the tenant to be faithful to his

12. For a detailed treatment of the history of copyhold tenure, see 7 Holdsworth 296–312.

13. For a brief explanation of the scope of the Law of Property Act, 1922, 1925 see Cheshire and Burn, Modern Law of Real Property 4–7, 81–86(13 ed.1982). A few incidents, e.g., the tenants' rights of common of pasturage of beasts, continue to attach to lands formerly copyhold unless lord and tenant agree to their extinction.

lord. Like homage it fell into disuse and was no longer exacted in practice after the end of the feudal period. The duty of allegiance owed to the king as supreme lord overshadowed and eventually eliminated the fealty owed to other lords.

Relief and Primer Seisin

A relief was a sum payable to the lord by the heir of a deceased tenant for the privilege of succeeding to his ancestor's lands, sort of a feudal inheritance tax. Inheritance was a privilege to be paid for, not an unconditional right. While the relief was originally an incident of military tenure, it was later extended to socage and serjeanty tenures. In the case of socage tenure, the amount of the relief became fixed at one year's rent and in that of serjeanty tenure at one year's value of the land. As early as Magna Carta (1215), the relief payable by the heir of a military tenant was set at 100 shillings for a knight's fee. Payment of the relief by the heir of a subtenant entitled him to immediate possession but on the death of a tenant-in-chief the king by royal prerogative was entitled to first seisin (*primer seisin*) of all the deceased tenant's lands, not only those held directly of the king but also those held of mesne lords. Only after an official inquest to determine heirship, the doing of homage, and the payment of the relief was the heir admitted to seisin or possession.

Wardship and Marriage

Upon the death of a tenant holding by knight service or grand serjeanty leaving as his heir a male under 21 or a female under 14, the lord was entitled to wardship of both the person and the lands of the heir. The lord had a right to the rents and profits of the lands with no duty to account at any time to the heir. This profitable guardianship continued during the male heir's minority or until the female heir married or attained the age of 16. The custody of the ward's person imposed on the lord a duty to maintain and educate the ward but also gave him the right to arrange a suitable marriage for the ward and to pocket the profit from the arrangement. The heir might refuse the tendered marriage but in that event the lord had a right to the value of the marriage, that is, to that sum which the prospective spouse's family was willing to pay for the match. If the heir married without the consent of the lord, the lord was entitled to double the value of the marriage. In early feudal times the lord had a legitimate interest in the marriage of his female ward to insure that she did not marry an enemy of his, but the extension of this right of marriage to male wards indicates that both wardship and marriage soon found the real basis for their continued existence in their pecuniary value to the king and the mesne lords. As early as the thirteenth century they were looked upon as valuable rights to be bought and sold and as late as the seventeenth century they were an important source of royal revenue.[1]

Socage tenure was free from the burdensome aspects of wardship and marriage that applied to military tenures. Guardianship of the infant socage tenant was given to his nearest relative who was incapable of inheriting the land, and the guardian in socage was accountable at the end of the guardianship to his ward for the profits derived from the land as well as for any profits accruing from the ward's marriage.[2]

Aids

Aids were originally financial contributions made to the lord by the tenant to assist the lord in times of emergency and arose out of the close personal bond inherent in the early tenures. But what had been once a matter of benevolence on the part of the tenant crystallized into an obligation. The chief aids due from a military tenant were to ransom the lord's person if taken prisoner, to help in the expense of making his eldest son a knight, and to assist in providing a dowry for his eldest daughter on her marriage. Statutes in the thirteenth and fourteenth century fixed the amounts of the

---

§ 7

1. So important to the Crown were the revenues from feudal dues that in 1540 a special administrative and judicial tribunal, the Court of Wards and Liveries, was set up by Parliament (32 Henry 8 ch. 46) to supervise the collection of those dues. The records of this Court show that in the period 1610–1613 sales of wardships averaged about one hundred and twenty-three per year and that by 1640 the average annual revenue from sales of wardships and

marriages was over 39,000£. Bell, The Court of Wards and Liveries 57, 114 (1953).

2. Oddly enough, the term "guardian in socage" still appears in the New York statutes (N.Y. Dom. Rel. Law § 80 (McKinney 1999)) although tenure has long ceased to exist in that state. In Combs v. Jackson, 2 Wend. 153 (N.Y. 1828), common-law guardianship in socage was recognized with respect to lands granted in socage prior to the American Revolution.

latter two aids and tenants in socage were subject to these statutory aids. Aids were abolished in 1660.

Fines for Alienation

Prior to 1290 the tenant could not alienate or transfer his fee without a license from the lord of the fee who exacted a fine or monetary payment for the license. By the beginning of the thirteenth century tenants other than tenants-in-chief had the power, within rather vague limits, to convey their lands to others, but seignorial rights in the land were still sufficiently strong to preserve to the lord a financial return on the transaction.[3] The Statute Quia Emptores, enacted in 1290, granted to "every freeman" the right to alienate without paying a fine to his lord. This statute was construed as not affecting the rights of the king, hence tenants *in capite* continued to be subject to fines for alienation until 1660 when legislation was adopted abrogating most of the tenurial incidents.

Escheat

On the death of the tenant without heirs the land returned or escheated to the lord of the fee. Moreover, if the tenant was convicted of a felony his lands also escheated or fell back to the lord on the theory that the tenant's blood had been so corrupted as to lose its inheritable quality.[4] In the event of escheat for a felony the Crown was entitled to hold the felon's lands for a year and a day and to waste them—a right which the lord of the fee usually bought

---

3. The Great Charter of 1217 provided; "No free man shall henceforth give or sell so much of his land as that out of the residue he may not sufficiently do to the lord of the fee the service which pertains to that fee." Although the Charter did not distinguish between tenants-in-chief and mesne tenants, in fact such a distinction was drawn in the thirteenth century and the king's right to prohibit tenants-in-chief and serjeanty tenants from alienating was recognized. In 1327 it was provided by statute that where lands held directly of the king were alienated without his license they would not be held forfeited but the

transfer would be subject to a reasonable fine. 3 Holdsworth 78–87.

4. Felony originally meant a serious breach of the feudal bond created by the tenant's homage. Only later did it come to include grave crimes of various kinds. Magna Carta (1215) settled the right of the feudal lord to escheat for felony. ch. 32. But if the tenant committed high treason the lands of the traitor were forfeited to the Crown. This right of forfeiture was based on royal prerogative, not on tenure, and it undercut the feudal lord's right of escheat in high treason cases.

off or compounded for in later times. Escheat for a felony was abolished by statute in 1870 and escheat for failure of descending heirs was abrogated in 1925.[5]

§ 8.   Statutes Affecting Tenure

After it had become established that a mesne tenant could alienate or transfer his interest in the land, subject to the payment of a fine to the lord of the fee, the alienation might be made by substitution or by sub-infeudation. If B holds land under O and conveys his entire interest in the land to C, C now holds as tenant under O and B drops out of the tenurial picture. It is true that so long as the services required of the tenant were of some importance the lord of the fee would have a personal interest in the identity of the tenant. In time, however, the incidents of tenure became much more valuable than the particular services so that it made no practical difference to the lord whether B or C was his tenant. Hence, the lords had no strong objection to alienation by substitution. But the practice of alienation by sub-infeudation was definitely objectionable from the viewpoint of the lords. By sub-infeudation a new tenure was created. Thus, B, holding lands under O, conveys to C the whole or a portion of his holding so that C holds the land so conveyed under B. B has now become a mesne lord and a new tenure has been created between B and C. This will have little effect on the services due to O since the latter can still look to the land for their rendition, but it may seriously minimize the value of the incidents of tenure due to O. For example, suppose that in making the conveyance to C, B reserved as the only services to be performed by C the payment of a penny a year rent. In the event of B dying without heirs, O's right of escheat would only entitle him to the annual rent of a penny. B's seignory would escheat to O, not the land itself; and B's seignory would become almost valueless. Likewise, if B died leaving an infant heir, O's right of wardship and marriage would be of inconsequential value as C's commitment was limited to a penny a year.

---

5. Escheat exists in the United States in the sense that if a person dies intestate with no descending, ascending or collateral heirs, the property passes to the state.

In order to protect the interests of the lords against alienations by sub-infeudation the Statute Quia Emptores was enacted in 1290.[1] This statute gave mesne tenants the right to alienate their lands without payment of a fine to the overlord but the transferee would hold not under the transferor but under the transferor's lord. The statute provided that "from henceforth it shall be lawful to every free man to sell at his own pleasure his lands and tenements or part of them, so that the feoffee shall hold the same lands or tenements of the chief lord of the same fee, by such service and customs as his feoffor held before."[2] Free alienation by substitution was granted but alienation by sub-infeudation was forbidden. The important result of this statute was to prevent the creation of new tenures and, from today's perspective, this statute is the historical underpinning for the proposition that land is freely alienable. Over a period of time, as mesne lordships fell in and as existing tenures were dissolved by death of the tenant without heirs, by escheat for felony, or by forfeiture for treason, the cumulative effect was to break down the pyramid of tenures and bring them directly under the king. This process was further aided by the presumption applied by the courts that in the absence of proof to the contrary a tenant is deemed to hold directly of the king. The statute was applicable only to conveyances of an estate in fee simple. Since the statute did not purport to bind the king, freedom of alienation was not given to his tenants in capite. The king continued to exact a fine for alienation from his tenants in capite until his right was abolished in 1660.

It is not profitable to discuss in detail the steps by which the strictly feudal system of tenure evolved into the present type of land ownership. Some of the changes have already been mentioned. Many of the services required to be rendered by the tenant were commuted into money payments. With the decline in the value of

§ 8

1. 18 Edw. 1, ch. 1. The name of the statute derives from its two opening Latin words, meaning "Because purchasers. * * * " English statutes were written in Latin or French until the fifteenth century.

2. The statute also provided that where the tenant conveyed only a part of the land the feoffee (transferee) must render to the lord of the fee a proportionate part of the services attached to the tenure. Inevitably, this led to a fragmentation of the services among numerous landholders.

money, many rents became so insignificant as not to be worth collecting. Homage and fealty became meaningless formalities never observed in practice. However, the incidents of marriage, wardship, aids, and fines for alienation were burdensome exactions still imposed on many landholders to the benefit of the king. These incidents were not unfair under feudal conditions but when feudalism disappeared and a strong central government was otherwise able to give adequate protection to life and property their continuation served only the purpose of increasing the royal revenue. In the seventeenth century they were felt to be intolerable and Parliament afforded relief by enacting the Tenures Abolition Act in 1660.[3] This statute converted tenure by knight service into tenure of free and common socage. It abolished the incidents of wardship, marriage, aids, primer seisin, fines for alienation, homage and scutage. It did not affect in any way frankalmoin or copyhold tenure. It did not abolish the honorary services attached to grand serjeanty. As a result of the statute, practically all lay free tenure became socage tenure. The obligations of that tenure were usually to pay a rent and a relief amounting to one year's rent. (It will be recalled that a relief was a sum payable by an heir of full age on succeeding to his ancestor's lands.) In place of the revenues of which the Crown was deprived by the Tenures Abolition Act, there was granted to the king a hereditary tax on beer and other beverages.[4] Thus, the landholders were enabled to unload their burden onto the people at large.

At the beginning of the twentieth century the situation with respect to tenure in England may be summarized as follows: most land was held in common socage, a substantial part was held by

3. 12 Charles 2, ch. 24. The statute was retroactive to 1645. The abolition of military tenures and the Court of Wards and Liveries had long been an issue between king and parliament. Negotiations between the contending parties had broken down in 1610 over the question of the amount of annual revenue to be granted to the king as compensation for giving up wardships and marriages. James I's price of 200,000 pounds per annum was unacceptable to the House of Commons. Bell, The Court of Wards and Liveries 133–149 (1953).

4. In addition to the tax on beer and "strong waters" the statute also provided for the following taxes: "For every Gallon of Coffee made, and sold to be paid by the maker Fower (four) pence; For every Gallon of Chocolate Sherbert and Tea made and sold, to be paid by the maker thereof Eight pence." V Statutes of the Realm 261–262.

copyhold, and a small amount in frankalmoin. The peculiar customs applicable to gavelkind and borough English affected the law of descent in some localities. The incidents of relief and escheat still remained. But by the end of the first quarter of the century a series of sweeping reform statutes completed the process of simplification that had begun with Quia Emptores in 1290.[5] All tenure was reduced to a single form—common socage. Copyhold, frankalmoin and the customary tenures of gavelkind, borough English and ancient demesne were abolished. Escheat was replaced by a right of the Crown to take the property of a deceased tenant who died intestate and without heirs. Of the incidents of tenure only the right of relief remains to a mesne lord and as a practical matter relief would be payable at the present time only in the very rare case of an existing intermediate tenure. In England today land is still theoretically held in tenure, not owned absolutely, but, with respect to the tenant's enjoyment of the land, tenure is an innocuous theory.[6]

5. This reform legislation consisted of nine acts beginning with the Law of Property Act, 1922 (12 & 13 Geo. 5, ch. 16) and went into effect for the most part on January 1, 1926. The principal statutes are set out in 20 Halsbury, Statutes of England 331 et seq (2d ed. 1950).

6. The titles to thousands of manorial lordships still exist in England and can be readily purchased through a firm of London real estate agents. The going price is about $6,000. The lordship carries with it the title of "Lord of the Manor of _____" but usually nothing more. *See* N.Y. Times, Aug. 12, 1982 at A14, col. 1.

Feudalism for Sale: Britain Offers Titles of the Past

By STEVEN RATTNER

Special to The New York Times

LONDON, Aug. 11—For people who feel a craving for a touch of aristocracy, Strutt & Parker, a firm of British real estate agents, has the solution. For prices starting at about $6,000, they will sell anyone the right to call himself—or herself—Lord of the Manor.

Lingering traditions are common in Britain, but one of the longest lingering and least known are the 65,000 lordships of the manor, a title dating to feudal times, when the lord of the manor was a sort of municipal government, enforcing rules and levying fees.

Unlike peerages, which carry the right to sit in the House of Lords, lordships of the manor have no special privileges but, unlike peerages, they can be bought and sold. Nor can a lord of the manor call himself Lord Smith, although he may style himself John Smith, Lord of the Manor of North Fambridge, or wherever.

"It satisfies a bit of fantasy," said Cecil Humphery–Smith, a heraldic expert, who owns a "few dozen." For the buyers, "it ties them to tradition when all around them things are changing," he said.

To all appearances, that attraction is on the rise. For decades there was only

§ 9. Tenure in the United States

There can be no doubt that lands in the original American colonies were held in tenure. Some of the early royal grants of lands specified that the lands should be held in free and common socage and reserved nominal services, such as the annual rendering of "two beaver skins" stipulated in the grant to William Penn. Since Quia Emptores did not bind the king he could grant to his tenants-

an occasional transfer of a lordship of a manor. But in the past year, Strutt & Parker has encountered a horde of potential buyers as it has auctioned and sold 22 such titles.

Americans Among New Owners

Among the new owners are a handful of Americans, including Denis Woodfield, director of treasury services at Johnson & Johnson in New Jersey, who became Lord of the Manor of Hamptonet nearly two years ago.

"It is a neglected part of English history that has always fascinated me," said Mr. Woodfield in a telephone interview. Did he ever use his title? "Of course not," he responded indignantly. "I'd be laughed at."

But Mr. Woodfield has visited his manor, which lies west of London in Berkshire. The local inhabitants to whom he explained his position evinced "an extreme lack of interest," he reported. "At the pub, the response was polite interest by the publican who asked if I would care for another beer," he said.

Like Mr. Woodfield, many lords of the manor buy the titles because of the historical documents that come along with them and because the price often directly reflects the importance of the papers. For example, the Manor of Orton Longueville in Cambridgeshire, now being offered by Strutt & Parker, comes with more than 100 indentures, wills, mortgages, assignments and other manorial records, the oldest dating back to the 17th century.

Lordships of the manor began 900 years ago when the kings of England started giving their followers large blocs of land and vast powers in an effort to promote allegiance to the crown. From the start, the title could be sold along with the manor houses and surrounding estates to which they were attached.

By the late 19th century, the break-up of the great estates had substantially diminished the hold of the lords of the manors, whose powers had always been limited to their own lands. Then, in 1925, Parliament abolished the last of the manorial governing and taxing powers and also made it possible for the title to be retained when the manor house was sold off, or vice versa.

"It's quite something to be able to draw up a chart that runs right back to the Norman Conquest," said Leslie Retford, a schoolteacher who recently became lord of the manor of Pleshey. "I bought it from a man whose family had had it since 1720."

Some Titles Carry Mineral Rights

A few lordships of the manor still carry with them mineral rights, and, occasionally, the right to hold markets and fairs and perhaps to collect fees from stalls.

At an auction of titles last June, Dora Borrier paid the equivalent of $5,600 to be Lord of the Manor of Barrow, which carried with it minerals rights and the opportunity to collect 13 cents in rent for each telegraph pole on common land.

in-chief the right to sub-infeudate and this power was expressly given to some of the proprietaries. The Penns, for example, made grants of lands to be held of them in free and common socage. The service reserved was usually an annual payment of a small sum of money which was called a quit rent.[1] In New England, quit rents were exceptional and long before the Revolution land was held completely free of any feudal service or incidents. After the Revolution, lands were deemed to be held in tenure of the state as sovereign in place of the Crown. Several states passed statutes, or enacted constitutional provisions, declaring lands to be owned allodially and abolishing tenure.[2] In the remaining states it would seem that lands are still held in tenure of the state as overlord. In those states in which tenure exists Quia Emptores is in force, except in South Carolina and, perhaps, in Pennsylvania.[3]

From the practical standpoint it is not important today whether lands are owned allodially or are held in tenure. If tenure exists in a particular state and Quia Emptores is deemed to be in force there can be no sub-infeudation. If tenure exists and Quia Emptores is not in force a rare question might conceivably arise as to the nature of the rent reserved on a conveyance in fee. The right of escheat was in its origin a consequence of feudal tenure but in all

§ 9

1. In the charters granted to Lord Baltimore and to Penn they were given the right to erect manors and to hold therein courts-baron and courts-leet. Perhaps the closest approach to a successful attempt to set up a manorial system took place in New York. Some of the grants made by Colonial governors to the great proprietors purported to confer manorial privileges. The proprietors in turn made to settlers numerous conveyances in fee reserving in the deeds a perpetual rent payable in wheat, "fat hens" and a day's service "with carriage and horses" and a fine for alienation. In the 1840s these perpetual rents resulted in resentment, rioting, litigation and legislation. The story is told briefly and well in Sutherland, Tenantry on the New York Manors, 41 Corn. L. Q. 620 (1956).

2. See, e.g., Conn. Gen. Stat. Ann. § 47–1 (West 1978). The Constitution of New York formerly provided: "All lands shall forever remain allodial so that the entire and absolute property is vested in the owners, according to the nature of their respective estates." N.Y. Const. (1938) Art. I, § 10. This innocuous sentence was deleted in 1962 on the recommendation of the Temporary Commission on the Revision and Simplification of the Constitution. N.Y. Leg. Doc. (1959) No. 58. The commission's report describes the provision as an "historic relic" dealing with "allodial tenures"! Id. 53.

3. As to Pennsylvania, See, Chestnut, Effect of Quia Emptores on Pennsylvania and Maryland Ground Rents, 91 U. Pa. L. Rev. 137 (1942); Gray, Rule Against Perpetuities, §§ 24–28(4th ed. 1942).

states there are statutes to the effect that title to lands of a person dying intestate and without heirs shall vest in the state or a political subdivision thereof. Escheat has become an incident of sovereignty in place of an incident of tenure.

§ 10. The Effects of Tenure

If the doctrine of tenure had ceased to have vitality at the close of the medieval period its long range effects would probably not have been significant.[1] But due to the lack of an adequate tax structure the incidents of tenure continued to exist as a primary source of royal revenue and the attempts of land owners to circumvent these burdens, and the counter-moves to prevent such evasions, had a profound effect on the development of real property law.[2] The Statute of Uses,[3] perhaps the most important single statute in the long history of the land law, was directed at attempts to evade the feudal dues by conveyances to uses. The Rule in Shelley's Case[4] and the Doctrine of the Worthier Title[5] were judicial responses to attempts by landowners to escape the incidents of tenure, particularly the feudal inheritance tax–the relief. In this struggle over tenurial incidents the law of real property became distorted and tortured. The medieval doctrine of tenure left to later ages a legacy of complexity and confusion which only the slow passage of time has been undone by courts and legislatures. But, even today we continue to be plagued by doctrines which many argue should long ago have been laid to rest.

§ 11. The Meaning of Seisin

Seisin was a concept of vast importance in the medieval land law. Most of that law concerned itself with seisin, remedies to

§ 10

1. This statement is subject to the qualification that the theory that all land is ultimately derived from the sovereign is a product of the institution of tenure. This theory was transplanted to American law and even today in some states the original source of a good record title to land must be a grant or patent from the sovereign. See 3 American Law of Property, §§ 12.15, 12.16 (1952).

2. In fact, much of modern estate planning is motivated by a desire to avoid or minimize income and death taxes.

3. See ch. 8, infra.

4. See ch. 6, infra.

5. See id.

recover seisin, and the consequences of loss of seisin. The concept of seisin affected the law of descent, the doctrine of estates, modes of conveyancing, the forms of action, and principles of the law of future interests. While seisin is largely inconsequential today, its influence has been too pervasive to be ignored; it explains much of the old law and some of the modern. For example, a widow's right to dower depended at common law on seisin of the lands by the husband during the marriage. This is still the law in some states.[1] A brief discussion of seisin is, therefore, necessary.

The word "seisin" has in it an implication of seizure and violence but more properly it connotes peaceful possession. "The man who is seized is the man who is sitting on land; when he was put in seisin he was set there and made to sit there."[2] Originally, seisin meant simply possession and the word was applicable to both land and chattels. Prior to the fourteenth century it was proper to speak of a man as being seised of land or seised of a horse. Gradually, seisin and possession became distinct concepts. A man could be said to be in possession of chattels, or of lands wherein he had an estate for years, but he could not be said to be seised of them. Finally, seisin came to mean, in relation to land, possession under claim of a freehold estate.[3] The tenant for years had possession but not seisin; seisin, rather, was in the reversioner who had the fee.

§ 12. The Significance of Seisin

It is a familiar process in our legal thinking of today to distinguish sharply between possession and ownership. Ownership, we say, is a legal concept, a bundle of legal relations; but possession is a matter of physical fact. O may own a parcel of land but B may be in possession of it. In fact, that is commonly the case in the landlord-tenant relationship.

§ 11

1. See, e.g, Iowa Code §§ 622.211–212.

2. 2 Poll. & Mait. 30.

3. The concept of seisin was also extended to some kinds of intangible rights. The lord of the fee was said to be seised in service while the feudal tenant was seised in demesne. And a man could be seised of an advowson, that is, the right to present a clergyman to a benefice. This illustrates the early common-law process of reification of rights— "thing-making."

In the medieval common law, ownership and possession were not so sharply distinguished. Rather, they blended into each other and merged in the concept of seisin. Seisin is possession, but a peculiar possession—possession of land by a man holding a freehold estate therein. Thus, seisin is much more than possession—it is the basis of ownership in so far as the common law admits of ownership of land.[1] The holder of a freehold estate was entitled to possession in fact but was also responsible to perform one or more of the feudal incidences of tenure.

Much of the law of the medieval period was concerned with remedies to protect seisin. If O was seised of Blackacre in fee simple and B entered and ousted O, claiming a freehold estate therein, B now had seisin and O was disseised. O could recover seisin by making a peaceable entry for that purpose.[2] If such self-help was not practical O could, as early as 1166, bring an assize of novel disseisin against his disseisor to recover seisin. This legal action was summary in nature, and judgment was entered in the King's court on a verdict returned by a jury of neighbors summoned by the sheriff as directed by the writ. No question of ownership could be litigated, the sole issue being whether the defendant had ousted the plaintiff wrongfully and without judgment. The action would lie only between disseisee and disseisor.

If O's ancestor had been seised of the land but on his death and before O entered as heir B wrongfully took possession, O could not use the remedy of novel disseisin. A new remedy ultimately was fashioned to take care of this situation—the action known as the assize of mort d'ancestor. In the thirteenth century numerous forms of writs of entry were provided to deal with various fact situations—such as descent of the seisin from the disseisor to his heir, the death of the disseisee, and a transfer of seisin by the disseisor to a third person. Finally, the highest and most solemn

§ 12

1. See Maitland, The Mystery of Seisin, 3 Select Essays in Anglo–American Legal History 591 (1909).

2. Prior to 1381 a disseisee could have made a forcible entry in order to recover seisin but a statute enacted in that year made such an entry a crime. The statute was the forerunner of American statutes forbidding a forcible entry and detainer of land. See, e.g. Ill. Comp. Stat. Ann. ch. 57, ¶ 1 (West 1991); Mass. Gen.Laws Ann. ch. 184, § 18 (West 1991).

form of action was the writ of right, an action proprietary in nature but actually deciding the question of the older and better seisin between the litigants.[3]

This system of real actions amounted to "a graduated hierarchy of actions" which reflected the relativity of right to seisin.[4] O's seisin may be better than B's but inferior to that of C and C in turn may have to yield to a stronger claim of D. The judgment in a particular action binds only the parties and stands only until someone else in another action establishes a better claim. Thus, the right to seisin is relative—just as in the modern law title or ownership is relative, not absolute.

If we compare the position of the disseisee with that of the disseisor the contrast is striking. Since B, the disseisor, had seisin (even though wrongfully) he could convey an estate in fee simple to a third person which would be valid against everyone except O, the disseisee. On the other hand, O was no longer the tenant and he had no estate; he merely had a right of entry which in time was turned into a right of action and this right, like a chose in action, was non-assignable although it could be released to the disseisee. O had nothing which he could alienate. Until O re-entered or recovered seisin after judgment in a real action B was more "owner" than O. On B's death the fee descended to his heir and his widow was entitled to dower. If B died without an heir the land escheated to the lord of the fee. If O died leaving an heir the right of entry descended to the heir but if O died without an heir there was no escheat because there was a tenant (B) who could render the feudal services due to the lord.

3. For a good summary of the development of the real actions, see, Concise History of the Common Law 354–362 (5th ed. 1956).

4. 2 Pollock & Maitland 74: " 'Possessoriness' has become a matter of degree. At the bottom stands the (action or assize of) novel disseisin, possessory in every sense, summary and punitive. Above it rises the mort d'ancestor, summary but not so summary, going back to the seisin of one who is already dead.

Above this again are writs of entry. * * * The writs of entry are not so summary as are the assizes, but they are rapid when compared with the writ of right; the most dilatory of the essoins (excuses for a continuance) is precluded; there can be no battle (trial by battle) or grand assize. Ultimately we ascend to the writ of right. Actions are higher or lower, some lie 'more in the right' than others."

The concept of seisin was so fundamental to the operation of the feudal system that it was a strict rule that seisin could never be in abeyance or suspended. There always had to be a person seised to whom the lord of the fee could look to the discharge of the feudal obligations and on whom the demandant in a real action may have his writ served. If a freehold estate in land was to be conveyed it had to be by a transfer of the seisin; if land is to descend it had to descend to the heir of the last person seised, for seisin was the stock of descent. And, no limitation of an estate was allowed if the effect would be to put the seisin in abeyance.

§ 13. The Decline of Seisin

The development of the action of ejectment in the latter part of the fifteenth century eventually made obsolete the real actions and the technicalities of seisin with which they were inextricably bound.[1] In ejectment the emphasis was on possession and although the right to possession ultimately depended on title, seisin became more and more an incident of ownership. By the time of Elizabeth ejectment had displaced the real actions as the standard action to try title.[2] The rout of seisin as a cardinal doctrine in English land law was completed by the reform legislation of the nineteenth century. The Dower Act (1833)[3] provided that a widow should have dower even though her husband was not seised during coverture. The Inheritance Act (1833)[4] changed the rule that descent of land must be traced from the person last seised. In 1837 the right of entry of a disseisee was made devisable[5] and in 1845 it was made transferable by deed.[6]

§ 13

1. Although the successful plaintiff in ejectment recovered a judgment for possession of the land, ejectment was classified as a personal, not a real, action because it originated as a special form of the action of trespass. *See* Plucknett, Concise History of the Common Law 573 (5th ed. 1956); 1 Walsh, Commentaries on Law of Real Property § 5(f) (1946).

2. In contrast with the real actions, ejectment was a safe, simple and expeditious remedy. In a real action the plain-

tiff proceeded at his peril: if he selected the wrong writ from among the numerous writs of entry or if there was a variance between writ and pleading or pleading and proof the mistake was fatal.

3. 3 & 4 Wm. 4, ch. 105, § 3.

4. 3 & 4 Wm. 4, ch. 106, § 2.

5. 7 Wm. 4 & 1 Vict., ch. 26, § 3.

6. 8 & 9 Vict., ch. 106, § 6.

In the United States the doctrine of seisin, although of some importance in the post-Revolutionary period, was never in force to the same extent as in England.[7] Statutes regulating the law of descent and the effectiveness of future interests, as well as those abolishing dower and curtesy, reduced its vitality. The rule that an owner who has been disseised has no title which he can convey to a third person has, except in a handful of jurisdictions, been rejected by the courts or abrogated by statute.[8] The law of disseisin has been absorbed in the law of adverse possession.[9] Although the word "seisin" appears in modern statutes with a fair degree of frequency, it is usually treated as synonymous with "ownership".[10] A similar construction is given to the term when used by an unwary testator lured by the sound of the word "seized" who is likely unaware of its meaning.[11] The modern warranty deed usually contains among the covenants for title a covenant of seisin, but in the majority of states this covenant is equivalent to the covenant of right to convey an indefeasible fee simple and is not satisfied by a common-law seisin in the grantor.[12]

7. For details, See, P. Bordwell, Seisin and Disseisin, 34 Harv.L.Rev. 717, 725–740 (1921).

8. *See, e.g.,* Mass. Gen. Laws Ann. ch. 183, § 7(West 1991). The rule persisted in New York until changed by statute in 1941 N.Y. Real Prop. Law § 260 (McKinney 1989). It still obtains, for example, in Connecticut. Loewenberg v. Wallace, 147 Conn. 689, 166 A.2d 150 (1960). Conn. Gen. Stat. Ann. § 47–21 (West 1995)provides; "Any conveyance or lease, for any term, of any building, land or tenement, of which the grantor or lessor is ousted by the entry and possession of another, unless made to the person in actual possession, shall be void."

9. Under the law of adverse possession if a person (A) enters against an owner of land (O) who fails to timely sue A within whatever period is provided by the state's statute of limitations to recover possession from the wrongdoer and A's possession is actual, open, continuous, exclusive and under claim of right, then O's title is lost and the title vests in A.

10. Dial v. Dial, 378 Ill. 276, 38 N.E.2d 43 (1941); Mass.Gen.Laws Ann. ch. 237, § 4 (West 1988). Sometimes "seisin" and "possession" are equated.

11. *See* Dalton v. Eash, 411 Ill. 296, 103 N.E.2d 483 (1952). Contra, Leach v. Jay, 9 Ch.D. 42 (1878).

12. "Possession does not satisfy a covenant of seizin. Such covenant means that the grantor, at the time of the conveyance, was lawfully seized of a good, absolute and indefeasible estate of inheritance in fee simple and had power to convey the same. N.Y. Real Prop. Law § 253 (McKinney, 1989)." Hilliker v. Rueger, 228 N.Y. 11, 15, 126 N.E. 266, 267 (1920). *Contra*, Raymond v. Raymond, 64 Mass. (10 Cush.) 134 (1852) (covenant of seisin satisfied by an actual seisin in grantor).

In sum, although a knowledge of the concept of seisin is necessary for an understanding of the historical basis of present-day law, the concept itself is no longer a vital force in that law.

Chapter 2

FREEHOLD ESTATES

§ 1. The Theory of Estates

By the end of the thirteenth century English land law had begun to work out the doctrine of estates as the primary basis to classify various interests in land. The word *"estate"* is of feudal origin and derived from the Latin word *"status."* It speaks to us of a time when landholding was inseparably connected with a man's political and personal status in the community.

The theory of estates, a peculiarity of Anglo–American law, is based on the concept of ownership measured in terms of time. "Proprietary rights in land are ... projected upon the plane of time. The category of quantity, of duration, is applied to them."[1] The maximum allowable interest, the estate in fee simple, is of potentially infinite duration; a life estate or an estate for years, on the other hand, is an estate of finite duration. The owner of a fee simple could carve out and convey estates of lesser duration and, therefore, retain some interest in the land, or the owner could carve out estates of differing duration and at the same time grant these estates to different persons. However, at any given time the aggregate duration of all interests, if more than one, in any parcel of land, had to sum to infinity.

In medieval times the only estates fully recognized by the law and given protection in the King's courts were the freehold estates–

§ 1
1. 1 Pollack and Maitland, History of English Law 10 (2d ed. 1898).

33

the fee simple, the fee tail, and the life estate. These were the estates to which seisin[2] attached. The later common law recognized the existence of nonfreehold estates, the most important of these being the terms of years, the historical antecedent of the leasehold estate today. When the common law was fully developed, an estate could be defined as an interest in land which is presently possessory (so-called "present interests") or would be possessory were it not for the existence of a prior possessory interest in another (so-called "future interests").[3]

The catalog of estates as finally evolved by the common law was as follows: the fee simple absolute, the fee simple determinable, the fee simple on condition subsequent, the fee simple subject to an executory interest, the fee tail,[4] the life estate (including the marital estates[5]), the estate (or term) for years, periodic estates, estate at will, and estate at sufferance. Since these estates are the principal basis of the classification of rights in land today, they will be discussed in some detail in this and the next chapter.

§ 2.   The Fee Simple

An estate in fee simple[1] was, and still is, the largest estate known to the law. It denotes the maximum of legal ownership, the greatest possible aggregate of rights, powers, privileges, and immu-

2. *See* ch. 1, §§ 11–13, *supra.*

3. The Restatement adopts a broader definition of the word "estate." It described it as "an interest in land which (a) is or may become possessory; and (b) is ownership measured in terms of duration." Restatement of Property, § 9 (1936) (Reprinted with the permission of The American Law Institute.)

4. Prior to 1290, there was also the fee simple conditional. *See generally* ch. 2, § 5, *infra.*

5. *See* § 11, *infra.*

§ 2

1. There is more than one kind of fee simple, although all of them share, in common, the potential of infinite duration. The most common is the fee simple absolute, although more often than not it is, as here, simply referred to as the fee simple. The other fee simple estates—the fee simple determinable, the fee simple on condition subsequent, and the fee simple subject to an executory interest—are all estates of potentially infinite duration. However, they contain within the terms of the grant language of either a limitation or condition evidencing an event on which the estate could terminate. Thus, in the more common fee simple or fee simple absolute, the word "absolute" evidenced that the estate was not subject to any such limitation or condition.

nities which a person may have in land.[2] It is an estate of potentially infinite duration in the holder and the holder's successors who acquire the holder's interest in the property either by conveyance, devise, or inheritance. The three hallmarks of the estate are that it is alienable, devisable, and descendible.[3]

The concept of the estate in fee simple was developed in the period between the Conquest and the enactment of the Statute Quia Emptores in 1290[4] by which time restrictions on the right of

2. The fact that a person owns a fee simple does not mean that other persons may not have any rights in the same property. Other persons may have some limited interest in the land such a right to use the land or an easement. For example, today it is common for the interest of a landowner in fee simple to be subject to an easement in favor of a power company or telephone company.

3. Littleton, in his famous treatise "Of Tenures" written in the 15th Century began his book by defining the fee simple as follows: "Tenant in fee simple is he which hath lands or tenements to hold to him and his heirs forever."

It may be helpful to mention some of the great earlier books in English legal literature which contributed to the development of Anglo–American law. You may not rush out to read them but at least you will know they exist. The principal treatises are: Glanvill, *De Legibus et Consuetudinibus Regni Angliae* (c. 1187). This was the first treatise on the common law. It is translated from the Latin in G.D.G. Hall, The Treatise on the Laws and Customs of the Realm of England Commonly Called Glanvill (1965).

The next treatise appeared in the 13th Century: Bracton, *De Legibus et Consuetudinibus Angliae*. It is translated from the Latin in S.E. Thorne, Bracton On the Laws and Customs of England (Vols. III & IV, 1977). Then came Littleton, Tenures (c. 1481; Waumbaugh's ed. 1903); Coke on Littleton

(1628; the formal title is "The First Part of the Institutes of the Laws of England; or A Commentary on Littleton"; commonly cited as Co. Litt.); Blackstone, Commentaries on the Laws of England (1765); there are numerous American editions.

Coke on Littleton was the leading text book on property law for over two hundred years. There were, for example, at least twenty-two copies of the book in colonial Virginia. Blackstone's Commentaries, much less technical than Coke, was far more popular. It has been called "perhaps the most stylish and readable contribution ever made to English legal literature." J.H. Baker, An Introduction to English Legal History 166 (2d 3d. 1979).

For an excellent brief discussion of the influence of these works, *see* T. Plucknett, Concise History of the Common Law 255–289 (5th ed. 1956).

4. In the era immediately after the Conquest a gift of land to a tenant conferred on the donee only a life estate and the land reverted to the lord of the fee upon the tenant's death. Whether the heir of the deceased tenant would be permitted to succeed to the land depended on the lord's will. In any event the heir had to make a monetary payment before being granted the privilege. By the late 1100s, it would seem, succession by the heir had become the usual situation and the lord was entitled to exact from the heir only a reasonable relief.

the tenant to alienate or transfer the land during his lifetime were largely eliminated.[5] When the principle of inheritability was admitted, a gift to a man and his heirs clearly gave the donee an estate that would endure during the donee's life and would continue after his death by descent to his heir. But the form of the gift "to B and his heirs" also seemed to give the heir an interest in the land. Could B convey to a third person and thereby defeat the heir apparent's expectancy? The law of the twelfth century hesitated over this question. However by 1225, it was decided that at least where the ancestor (B in the gift to "B and his heirs") had conveyed to another and warranted the title for himself and his heirs, the heir could not, after the ancestor's death, upset the conveyance.[6] Thus, from the thirteenth century on, the phrase "and his heirs" in a conveyance to "B and his heirs" merely indicated that B was given an estate in fee simple; B's heirs took no interest in their own right under the conveyance.

Today, we describe the phrase "and his heirs" as words of limitation, not words of purchase. Words of limitation are those words defining or denoting the quantum of interest given to the

Where the donor intended that the land descend to the donee's heir the form of the gift specified that the grant was to the donee and his heirs. Such expression of intention was effective to insure the right of the heir to inherit the land.

5. Restrictions on alienation had a two-fold source: the rights of the lord of the fee, and the rights of the heirs of the tenant. Since gifts of land were feudal in nature, the lord had, especially in the case of military tenures, a legitimate interest in the tenant's identity. Until the 13th Century, the lord had a right of control over alienations by his tenant but the law was changing. In the middle 1200s, the consent of the lord was no longer needed for an alienation by the tenant who held land to himself and his heirs but the lord could still exact a fine for the alienation. Quia Emptores eliminated this seignorial incident in the case of the mesne tenant by granting him the right "to sell at his own pleasure his lands or tenements or part of them." But tenants-in-chief of the Crown continued to be subject to the requirements of the payment of fine for alienation until 1660 when this last vestige of feudal restraint on alienation of free tenures was abolished by the Tenures Abolition Act, 12 Charles 2, c. 24. For a discussion of the tenant's power of alienation in the medieval period, see 3 Holdsworth, History of English Law 73–87.

6. D'Arundel's Case, Bracton's Note Book, case 1054. Since the heir was bound by the ancestor's warranty made to the ancestor's grantee, he was debarred from claiming the land. Although the doctrine of warranty thus contributed to the formulation of a rule of free alienability, other factors, such as the rule of primogeniture (descent to the eldest son) and a growing policy in favor of free alienation, also influenced the final result.

grantee.[7] Words of purchase, on the other hand, are those words that identify the grantee. In the conveyance, "B and his heirs," for example, B is the word of purchase; "and his heirs" are the words of limitation. Put another way, words of purchase indicate the person who takes; words of limitation indicate the nature of the interest that is taken. A purchaser, in this context, is any person acquiring an estate in any way other than by descent. The term is not restricted to a grantee who pays value for the conveyance. A donee or a devisee under a will takes by purchase; an heir who inherits land does not acquire by purchase.[8]

Since an estate in fee simple was an estate of general inheritance, it was necessary at common law for the creation of such an estate that the conveyance use words of general inheritance. Furthermore, with the verbal ritualism so characteristic of the period, only the words "and his heirs" were sufficient for this purpose.[9] Substitute words were ineffective. Thus, a conveyance to "B and his heirs" gave B a fee simple (assuming, of course, that the grantor had a fee simple to convey); a conveyance to "B forever" or "B and his assigns" or even to "B in fee simple" merely gave B a life estate.[10]

The phrase, "and his heirs" however was not necessary to create a fee simple by a devise in a will. Thus, if testator (T) devised land to "B," and T had a fee simple in the land, B acquired a fee

---

7. See Lusk v. Lusk, 694 So.2d 4 (Ala.1997).

8. The distinction between words of purchase and words of limitation is a constantly recurring problem in the construction of wills and trusts, and, as should be expected, their meaning is highly dependent on context. See, e.g., Smith v. Groton, 147 Conn. 272, 160 A.2d 262 (1960)(in a conveyance to my children and their legal representatives, phrase legal representatives were words of limitation); Fatheree v. Gregg, 20 Ill.2d 620, 170 N.E.2d 600 (1960)(in a gift to B or the heirs of B's body, phrase "heirs of the body" are words of purchase; In re Parant's Will, 39 Misc.2d

285, 240 N.Y.S.2d 558 (N.Y.Sur.Ct. 1963)(phrase "and her children" words of purchase, not limitation); Commerce Union Bank v. Warren County, 707 S.W.2d 854 (Tenn.1986)("heirs" are words of purchase).

9. As stated by Littleton: "If a man would purchase lands or tenements in fee simple, it behoveth him to have these words in his purchase, To have and to hold to him and to his heirs; for these words, his heirs, makes the estate of inheritance." Co. Litt. § 1.

10. Id. See also Restatement of Property, § 27, comment b (1936).

simple under the devise.[11]

As might be expected, there were some exceptions to the general common-law rule with respect to conveyances of a fee. For example, if the grantor conveyed land to a trustee for the benefit of another, the trustee acquired a legal estate of that quantum as would enable the trustee to carry out his duties as trustee despite the absence of the word "heirs" in the conveyance. And, since a corporation can have no heirs, a conveyance to a corporation gave it a fee simple absent some expression of a contrary intent. Also, where joint tenants[12] held title in fee simple, a release of the interest of one joint tenant's interest to the other was effective to pass that interest in fee without the use of the word heirs.[13] Lastly, a conveyance to the heirs of a named person who was deceased at the time of the conveyance (e.g., O conveys Blackacre to B's heirs) could create a fee simple in such heirs or heir even though the phrase "and his heirs" was not included in the conveyance.[14]

While heirs did not take as purchasers under a conveyance to "B and his heirs", if B owned the property until his death, B's heirs[15] could only succeed to the property by descent[16] prior to

---

11. Until 1540 with the adoption of the Statute of Wills, devises of property were not recognized by the common-law courts, although wills could be recognized in the courts of equity. Thus, the various rules applicable to conveyances, such as the use of the phrase "and his heirs" to create a fee simple developed prior to 1540 did not apply to wills and the courts wisely decided to limit the rules to conveyances. See 1 Amer. Law of Prop., § 2.5 (A.J. Casner ed. 1952)(hereinafter cited as ALP).

12. See ch. 9, infra.

13. See Restatement of Property, § 29 cmt. e (1936). Conversely, a conveyance by one tenant in common to his cotenant required the use of the word "heirs" to carry the fee.

14. Restatement of Property, § 30 (1936).

15. Under the common-law inheritance system known as "primogeniture"

the eldest male son or his representative was the preferred heir to all other children, with daughters taking equally only in the absence of a male line. Primogeniture was abolished in England in 1925. See Administration of Estates Act, 1925, 15 & 16 Geo. 5, c.23. Primogeniture never received a foothold in the United States where inheritance among children runs to both daughters and sons. However, even though abolished in England generally, primogeniture was still used, until just recently, to govern the descent of the English crown. Primogeniture did not apply throughout England. For example, lands held in gravelkind tenure and in burgage tenure were subject to special customs. Gavelkind lands descended to all sons equally; burgage lands (a/k/a "borough English") to the youngest son only (the exact reverse of primogeniture).

In the United States property of an intestate (a person who dies without a

adoption of the Statute of Wills in 1540. Thus, B's heirs clearly had an expectancy in the property during B's life. After the adoption of the Statute of Wills,[17] generally enabling property owners to dispose of their lands by will to anyone, B's heirs were no longer assured that when B died they would succeed to the property. That statute cemented the third characteristic of the fee simple—devisability. Importantly, even if B's heirs succeeded to the property upon B's death because B died intestate, they succeed as successors of B, not as purchasers from B's grantor.

§ 3. Modern Law—Creation and Characteristics of Fee Simple

The common-law rule requiring words of general inheritance to create a fee simple by conveyance has been abolished by statute in most states and in some by case law.[1] However, the common-law rule continues to apply to conveyances predating a statutory repeal in a particular state,[2] and is sometimes applied in those states having no statute affecting it.[3] Because abrogation of the common-law rule is typically prospective only, it can be important to know

will) descends equally to all children or to their representatives.

16. A person who dies without a will is called an "intestate" and that person's property passes by descent in accordance with the laws of intestate succession. A person who dies with a valid will is called a "testator" and the recipients under the will take by devise or bequest.

17. 32 Hen. 8 c. 1 (1540).

§ 3

1. See Cole v. Winnipisseogee Lake Cotton & Woolen Mfg. Co., 54 N.H. 242 (1874); Dennen v. Searle, 149 Conn. 126, 176 A.2d 561 (1961). It is thought that the common-law rule continues to apply in Maine and South Carolina. See 1 ALP, § 2.4 (1952).

2. See Ivey v. Peacock, 56 Fla. 440, 47 So. 481 (1908); Elwell v. Miner, 342 Mass. 450, 174 N.E.2d 43 (1961).

3. See Cole v. Steinlauf, 144 Conn. 629, 136 A.2d 744 (1957)(dictum that deed to "B and his assigns forever" gives B only a life estate); Grainger v. Hamilton, 228 S.C. 318, 90 S.E.2d 209 (1955). The dictum in Cole v. Steinlauf was repudiated in Dennen v. Searle, supra note 1. The Restatement, despite some criticism, takes the position that in the absence of a statute, the common-law rule applies. Restatement of Property, § 27 (1936). For the Reporter's justification of this position, see 2 Powell, Real Property, ¶ 180 (1950); compare 1 ALP, § 2.4 (1952). The Restatement (§ 27 cmts. c, d and f) states that the following conveyances are effective to create a fee simple in the grantee: "to B and heir," to B or his heirs," and "to B and his eldest heirs."

when abrogation occurred in order to make an accurate assessment of the current state of the title of any particular parcel of land.

Modern deeds usually follow a standardized form and when properly drafted rarely raise a question as to the kind of estate created. But wills, and deeds involving gratuitous transfers, are often drafted by lay persons and often raise problems of construction because of the failure to use language clearly indicating the estate intended to be given. Although it was never required in the case of a will that words of inheritance be used in order to give the devisee a fee simple in the devised lands, it was necessary for the testator to indicate in some way his intention to give a fee simple. There was at common law no presumption that the testator intended to give the donee a fee simple. Thus, a devise of Blackacre "to B," without more, gave B only a life estate. This common-law rule has been changed by statute in most states. The statutes, in effect, create a presumption that the testator intended that the donee take a fee simple unless the will indicates an intention to give him a smaller estate.[4]

In numerous wills cases, problems of construction arise as to the nature of the estate created in the devisee. As the court in *Bramley v. White*[5] observed, "[A]lthough words of inheritance are not necessary to create an absolute estate by will and it is not essential that the words 'for life' or their precise equivalent be used in order to create a life estate, in the absence of words of either sort descriptive of the quantity of an interest given, a testator's intent must be determined by construction." The problem often arises in the case where a testator devises his real and personal property to his wife with power to use and enjoy the property as she wishes, and then adds that any of the property remaining at her death is to go to his children or other designated persons. Does the wife take a fee simple in the real property and an absolute interest in the personal property or only a life estate?[6] Most courts seem to have

---

4. *See, e.g.,* Mass. Gen. Law. Ann. C. 191 § 18: "A devise shall convey all the estate which the testator could lawfully devise in the land mentioned, unless it clearly appears by the will that he

intended to convey a less estate." *See generally* ALP § 2.4 (1952).

5. 281 Mass. 343, 346–347, 183 N.E. 761, 762 (1933).

6. "The fact that a donee has the power to sell or otherwise dispose of

held in this and similar cases that the first donee takes a life estate.[7] Basically the question is one of the testator's intent as manifested by the language of the will viewed in its entirety and in the light of circumstances surrounding the testator at the time the will was executed.

The constructional problem, however, is complicated by a so-called rule of repugnancy. Under this rule, if a fee simple in land or an absolute interest in personal property is given to one person, together with a general power of disposal by deed or will, a gift over to another person of what remains undisposed of on the death of the first taker is void on the alleged ground that the gift over is repugnant to and inconsistent with the interest of the first taker.[8] Although the rule has been criticized as illogical and frustrative of the donor's intent, it is accepted in many jurisdictions.[9]

property given by will does not in itself prevent the gift being construed as a life interest." *Id.* at 348, 183 N.E. at 762.

7. *See, e.g.,* Bell v. Killian, 266 Ala. 12, 93 So.2d 769 (1957); In re Estate of Smythe,132 Cal.App.2d 343, 282 P.2d 141 (1955); Burley v. Maguire, 127 Conn. 242, 16 A.2d 358 (1940); Hanks v. McDanell, 307 Ky. 243, 210 S.W.2d 784 (1948); Rolland v. Hamilton, 314 Mass. 56, 49 N.E.2d 436 (1943); Krause v. Krause, 113 Neb. 22, 201 N.W. 670 (1924); Stanton v. Guest, 285 Pa. 460, 132 A. 529 (1926). *Contra,* Seifert v. Sanders, 178 W.Va. 214, 358 S.E.2d 775 (1987).

8. *See, e.g.,* Ide v. Ide, 5 Mass. 500 (1809); Sweet v. Arnold, 322 Ill. 597, 153 N.E. 746 (1926).

9. *See, e.g.,* Kelley v. Meins, 135 Mass. 231 (1883); Sterner v. Nelson, 210 Neb. 358, 314 N.W.2d 263 (1982). For a detailed discussion, *see* Simes & Smith, The Law of Future Interests §§ 1481–1491 (2nd ed. 1956).

The rule was applied to personal property in the case of Fox v. Snow, 6 N.J. 12, 76 A.2d 877 (1950). Testatrix bequeathed her husband a bank account with any balance in the account at his death to be "held by my niece . . . absolutely and forever." The court held that bequest to the husband to be general in form and coupled with an absolute power of disposal. Thus, the court found the gift over to the niece void. In a forceful dissent, Justice Vanderbilt attacked the doctrine as a technical rule, lacking any sound principle to support it, that defeated the plain intent of the testatrix without serving any public policy.

The rule seems inconsistent with the ability to create a fee simple subject to an executory interest. *See, e.g.,* In re Estate of Price, 73 Wash.App. 745, 871 P.2d 1079 (1994). It has been abrogated by statute in Ohio, New Jersey, New York and West Virginia. *See* Ohio Rev. Code § 2131.07 (West 1953); N.J.S.A. 3A:3–16 (West 2001); N.Y. EPTL § 6–5.5 (McKinney 1966); W. Va. Code § 36–1–16 (1931). It has been rejected in Texas. Johnson v. Stark, 585 S.W.2d 900 (Tex.Civ.App.1979).

On the flip side, it has been held that where an estate is granted for life but the life tenant is empowered to dispose of the property as the life tenant sees fit, the coupling of the life estate and power of disposition does not elevate the life

Today, the fee simple has the same formal characteristics as it had at common law after the enactment of the Statute of Wills in 1540; it is an estate of general inheritance—alienable, devisable, and descendible—and of potentially infinite duration. Attempts by transferors of land to curtail the inheritability or alienability of the fee simple are invariably struck down by the courts.[10] Thus, if T devises Blackacre to "B and her heirs on her father's side of the family" B takes an estate in fee simple and the attempt to restrict the descent to the paternal side of the family is ineffective.[11] Furthermore, there is a very strong policy favoring the free and unfettered alienability of land; thus, attempted restraints on alienation of a fee simple are invalid.[12]

While the fee simple estate still represents the ultimate in ownership of law, the right of an owner in fee simple to make such use of the land as the owner pleases is subject to a number of limitations, including rights of adjacent owners[13] and governmental control.[14] Moreover, in many cases, easements and restrictive covenants affect the use of land.

estate to a fee simple such that the life tenant can dispose of the property by will. *See, e.g.,* Caldwell v. Walraven, 268 Ga. 444, 490 S.E.2d 384 (1997).

10. Littleton stated: "A man cannot crate a new kind of inheritance" and modern courts agree with him. See, Co. Litt. 27.

11. *See* Johnson v. Whiton, 159 Mass. 424, 34 N.E. 542 (1893); Beeman v. Stilwell, 194 Iowa 231, 189 N.W. 969 (1922).

12. *See* White v. Brown, 559 S.W.2d 938 (Tenn.1977). For a thorough treatment of restraints on alienation, 6 ALP, §§ 26.1–26.47 (1952); 6 R. Powell, The Law of Real Property, ¶¶ 839–843 (P. Rohan rev. 1981); Restatement (Second) of Property (Donative Transfers) §§ 3.1–45 (1983).

13. The rights of adjacent owners could include the right to be free of a nuisance and rights to lateral and subjacent support. "Lateral support refers to the vertical stability offered to one piece of land by adjacent land ... [and] the common law right to lateral support is violated when the defendant excavates his land too close to the property line, or without taking necessary support precautions, and the plaintiff's land gives way into the defendant's excavation ...

Subjacent support ... referred to the duty imposed on a property owner to provide support to a property owner *above* him." Kurtz and Hovenkamp, American Property Law, 3rd ed. 760–61 (1999)

14. The most common government control is zoning although there are numerous other government regulations that affect the use of land, such as landmark preservation and laws relating to clean air and water.

Review Problems

1. O (grantor)[15] deeds Blackacre to B and his heirs. B has a fee simple absolute.

2. O deeds Blackacre to B. Under the English common law, B has only a life estate because the phrase "and his heirs" does not appear in the deed. Today, B takes whatever estate O has such that, if O has a fee simple absolute, so does B. The same results occur both today and under the English common law had O conveyed either to B in fee simple or to B forever.

3. T (testator) devises Blackacre to B forever. Assuming T had a fee simple absolute, so does B. The phrase "and his heirs" was not necessary to devise a fee simple. Obviously, if T devises Blackacre to B and his heirs, B also has a fee simple.

4. O deeds Blackacre to the heirs of B. Under the English common law and assuming B was dead at the time of the conveyance, B's heir took a fee simple absolute. This was an exception to the rule that the phrase "and his heirs" was necessary to create a fee simple absolute.

§ 4. The Qualified Fees

The fee simple could also be qualified[1] or defeasible. A qualified fee simple is one subject to a limitation (the "fee simple determinable"), or a condition subsequent (the "fee simple subject to a condition subsequent"), or an executory interest ("the fee simple subject to an executory interest).[2]

The fee simple is an estate of potentially infinite duration. Similarly, a fee simple determinable is an estate of potentially infinite duration. However, unlike the fee simple absolute, the fee simple determinable[3] could come to an end or expire automatically

---

15. Throughout this book, O refers to a living grantor; T refers to a testator.

§ 4

1. According to Blackstone, a qualified fee was a fee to which some qualification was attached such that the estate would end if the qualification occurred, or would continue infinitely if it never occurred. See Blackstone Commentaries, (10th ed. 1787) 109–110.

2. It also included the "fee simple conditional." See § 5, infra.

3. This estate is also known as the "fee simple subject to a special limitation."

upon the happening or non-happening of an event stated as a limitation in the conveyance or will creating the estate. Thus, suppose O, who owns Blackacre in fee simple absolute, conveys Blackacre to "B and his heirs *so long as Blackacre is used for residential purposes and if Blackacre is not so used, it shall revert to O and his heirs.*"[4] B has a fee simple determinable. The estate granted to B is a fee simple that is an estate of general inheritability and might last infinitely. Yet it is determinable because it might expire on the occurrence of the stated limitation, namely the use of the land for non-residential purposes. B's estate automatically ends if the land is used for nonresidential purposes. If B's estate ends, title automatically reverts to O who again owns Blackacre in fee simple absolute. During the existence of B's estate, O retains a future interest which is called a "possibility of reverter."[5] Typically, the fee simple determinable arises through the use of the following phrases: "so long as," "while," "until," or "during."[6] Thus, if O conveys Blackacre to "B and his heirs *until Blackacre is no longer used for residential purposes* and if not so used Blackacre shall revert to O and his heirs" B has a fee simple determinable and O has a possibility of reverter. The possibility of reverter is alienable and in most jurisdictions is devisable and descendible.[7] The possibility of reverter, whether acquired by alienation, descent or devise, continues to be called a possibility of reverter in the hands of the grantor's successor.

A fee simple subject to a condition subsequent[8] exists when the fee simple is subject to a stated condition subsequent (rather than a limitation) which, if it occurs, invokes a power in the grantor to

4. Do you remember that "B" is the word of purchase and "and his heirs" the words of limitation that establish a fee simple. It is the additional words of limitation *"so long as Blackacre is used for residential purposes"* evidencing O's intent that B's estate might not last infinitely which create the fee simple determinable.

5. Remember, a future interest is an interest in property where the right to possession is postponed because some one else has a present interest in the property. Thus, here, O's possibility of reverter is a future interest while B's fee simple determinable is a present interest. For a more thorough discussion of the possibility of reverter, *see* ch. 4, § 3, *infra*.

6. Restatement of Property, § 44 cmt. l (1936).

7. *See generally* 1 ALP, § 4.70 *et. seq.*

8. This estate may also be called a "fee simple on condition subsequent."

terminate the estate granted on the happening of the condition, *if the grantor so chooses.* The grantor, however, need not exercise the power of termination, in which case the grantee's estate continues. In other words, the grantee's estate does not automatically end when the condition occurs; it continues until the grantor exercises the power to take back the property. For example, suppose O, the owner of Blackacre in fee simple absolute, conveys Blackacre to "A and his heirs upon the condition that[9] if A or A's successors cease to use Blackacre for residential purposes, O or O's successors shall have the right to re-enter and possess Blackacre." A has a fee simple subject to a condition subsequent and O has a right of entry for condition broken (or a power of termination).[10] On the happening of the stated condition, that is, on the breach of the condition against using the property for non-residential purposes, the estate continues in A until O effectively exercises the right of entry for condition broken by making an entry or bringing and action to recover the land.[11] The breach of the condition does not cause an automatic termination of the granted estate. The power of termination in many states is inalienable;[12] in others, statutes make the interest alienable.[13] Typically, the interest is both devisable and descendible. The interest in the hands of transferee continues to be called a power of termination.

9. Other phrases which are often used to create the fee simple subject to a condition subsequent are: "provided that" and "but if."

10. *See* Restatement of Property, § 45 (1936).

11. At common law it was necessary for the grantor to make an actual entry on the land in order to terminate the fee simple on condition subsequent. Today, the grantor may bring an action without first making an entry although some jurisdictions require that the grantor give notice of his election to terminate before bringing the action. *But see* Storke v. Penn Mutual Life Ins. Co., 390 Ill. 619, 61 N.E.2d 552 (1945).

While conceptually, the fee simple determinable terminates automatically when the limitation occurs suggesting the grantor has no need to bring an action for possession, rarely would the grantee of the terminated estate voluntarily leave the property. Thus, it is practically necessary where the limitation has occurred for the grantor to sue for possession.

12. An exception arose for the power of termination incident to a reversion which is fairly typical in the landlord-tenant relationship where the landlord has both a reversion when the tenancy comes to an end and a power of termination when tenant breaches a condition in the lease such as non-payment of rent.

13. *See generally* Restatement of Property, § 160 (1936).

The basic difference between the fee simple determinable and the fee simple on condition subsequent is that the former automatically expires by force of the limitation contained in the granting instrument if it occurs, whereas the fee simple on condition subsequent continues despite the breach of the stated condition subsequent until it is divested or cut short by the exercise of the power of termination. Clearly, therefor, a cause of action for possession begins to run in favor of the holder of the possibility of reverter immediately upon the happening of the limitation set forth in the instrument creating the fee simple determinable.[14] Conceptually, the cause of action for possession should not begin to run against the holder of a power of termination until the power of termination is exercised. This is because, prior to that time, continued possession by the holder of the fee simple on condition subsequent is not wrongful.[15] However, by statute and decision in many states the cause of action for possession runs on both the possibility of reverter and right of entry for condition broken from the moment the limitation or condition occurs. Thus, if the holder of the future interest fails to sue for possession in a timely manner,[16] the grantee wrongfully in possession could acquire a title by adverse possession.

Many states have statutes that terminate both possibilities of reverter and rights of entry for condition broken where the holder of these interests fail to periodically file in the local land records office a statement of intent to enforce the holder's interest should the limitation or condition defeating the grantee's estate occur, Others have statutes that restrict the time in which the holder of such interest may enforce it.[17]

---

14. *See* Storke v. Penn Mutual Life Ins. Co., 390 Ill. 619, 61 N.E.2d 552 (1945); School District v. Hanson, 186 Iowa 1314, 173 N.W. 873 (1919).

15. *See* City of New York v. Coney Island Fire Dept., 259 A.D. 286, 18 N.Y.S.2d 923 (N.Y.App.Div.1939).

16. Each state by statute provides a time period in which causes of action for possession against a wrongful possessor can be brought. Holders of a cause of action who fail to bring their action in a timely manner are forever barred to the effect that the wrongful possessor acquires a title by "adverse possession" so long as the possession was actual, open, exclusive, continuous and under claim of right.

17. *See, e.g.,* Iowa Code § 614.24 (failure to timely file extinguishes estate); Ill. Rev. Stat. Ch. 110, §§ 13–102–3 (enforcement action must be brought within fixed period of time).

The fee simple determinable and the fee simple on condition subsequent were largely used by grantors to control the use of land by their grantees. Their use has waned substantially with the advent of both zoning laws and restrictive covenants as devices better suited to control the use of land.

In many cases, the language used in a deed may be ambiguous and thus open to construction through the litigation process to determine whether a fee simple determinable or fee simple on condition subsequent was created. Over the years the courts have developed a constructional preference for the fee simple on condition subsequent.[18]

Lastly, there is the fee simple subject to an executory interest (also called the fee simple subject to an executory limitation). This estate exists when the fee simple is subject to a condition subsequent which, if it occurs, causes that interest to be divested in favor of a person, other than the grantor or the grantor's successors. For example, suppose O, the owner of Blackacre in fee simple absolute, conveys Blackacre to "B and his heirs but if B uses the property for commercial purposes, then to C and his heirs." B has a fee simple subject to an executory interest. C has an executory interest.[19] Here, if B's estate terminates by the happening of the condition subsequent, B's estate automatically ends. C does not have to exercise any power of termination. Of course, if the condition occurs and B does not voluntarily vacate the property, C will have to bring an action of ejectment against B.

Review Problems

1. O, who owns Blackacre in fee simple absolute, conveys Blackacre to "B and his heirs *so long as Blackacre is used for residential purposes and if Blackacre is not so used, it shall revert to O and his heirs.*" B has a fee simple determinable. Since a fee simple determinable is an estate of potentially lesser duration than the fee simple absolute in that it could be lost because of the

---

18. *See* ch. 4, § 5, *infra.*

19. The executory interest is a shifting executory interest. Prior to the Statute of Uses (1536), C's estate was an

invalid common-law estate, although if created by a "use" it would be recognized in the courts of equity. *See* ch. 7, *infra.*

occurrence of a limitation, O did not grant to B all that O had. O retained an interest. It is called a possibility of reverter. Similarly, if O conveys Blackacre to B and his heirs until Blackacre is no longer used for residential purposes, B has a fee simple determinable and O has a possibility of reverter.

2. O, the owner of Blackacre in fee simple absolute, conveys Blackacre to "A and his heirs upon the condition that if A or A's successors cease to use Blackacre for residential purposes, O or O's successors shall have the right to re-enter and possess Blackacre." A has a fee simple subject to a condition subsequent. Since a fee simple on condition subsequent is an estate of potentially lesser duration than the fee simple absolute in that it could be lost because of the occurrence of a condition, O did not grant to A all that O had. O has a right of entry for condition broken (or a power of termination).

3. O, the owner of Blackacre in fee simple absolute, conveys Blackacre to "B and his heirs but if B dies without any surviving children, then to C and his heirs." B has a fee simple subject to an executory interest. C has an executory interest. In this case O has nothing as the sum of B's interest and C's interest equals a fee simple absolute in that if B's estate terminates, it inures to C in fee simple absolute.

§ 5. The Fee Simple Conditional and the Fee Tail

Prior to 1285 a gift of land to "A and the heirs of his body" created a fee simple conditional in A, and since the grantor conveyed away less than the grantor had, the grantor retained a possibility of reverter. The courts construed this conveyance as if it were to A and his heirs on the condition that A have an heir of his body.[1] The courts also held that, upon the birth of issue to A, the condition had been fulfilled and that A then had the power to alienate the land in fee simple. But, the courts did not go so far as to hold that A acquired a fee simple for himself. Thus, if A had issue but later died without any issue who survived him and A had

§ 5

1. Heirs of the body are synonymous with issue and descendants. De-

scendants are the children, grandchildren, and so forth, of a decedent.

not alienated the land to another during his life, the land reverted to the grantor even though A had surviving collateral relatives.[2] This construction of a gift to "A and the heirs of his body" was undoubtedly influenced by the judicial bias in favor of free alienability of land, but it ran counter to the intention of many donors. Such gifts were commonly made to subsidize marriages and it was the donors' intention that upon failure of issue that the lands should revert to them. By this construction of the gift as a fee simple conditional, the donee was frequently able to defeat the rights of both his issue and the donor.[3]

In 1285 Parliament afforded relief to donors by enacting the statute De Donis Conditionalibus.[4] The effect of this statute was to abolish the fee simple conditional and to create a new kind of estate of inheritance—the estate in fee tail. The estate in fee tail was so called because it was an estate of inheritance the descent of which was cut down (in Latin, "*talliatum*"; in French, "*taille*") to the heirs of the body of the donee.

After De Donis, a gift of land to "B and the heirs of his body" created an estate in fee tail in B. This estate would last so long as there were any lineal descendants of B living and upon failure of such issue the land would revert to the donor or his heirs. Thus, B's estate might end at B's death. But, it might end years or even

2. Collateral relatives (e.g., siblings and cousins) are related to a decedent through a common ancestor, such as parents and grandparents.

3. For example, if the holder of the fee simple conditional wanted to acquire a fee simple absolute in the land, the holder could, upon birth of issue, convey the land to a friend (perhaps an attorney). This conveyance would transfer a fee simple absolute to the transferee who, in turn, could reconvey that estate to the transferor. Thus, by this simple devise, the holder of a fee simple conditional could convert his estate into a fee simple absolute.

4. 13 Edw. 1 c. 1. The opening Latin words of the statute may be translated "Concerning gifts of land made upon condition" etc.

The statute, after reciting the grievances of donors by reasons of the courts' construction of a gift to a man and the heirs of his body as a conditional fee simple, provided: "... that the will of the giver according to the form in the deed of gift manifestly expressed shall be from henceforth observed, so that they to whom the land was given under such condition shall have no power to alien the land so given, but that it shall remain unto the issue of them to whom it was given after their death, or shall revert unto the giver or his heirs if issue fail ..."

centuries after B's death when B's line of lineal descendants became extinct and, thus, there were no descendants of B on the planet. For example, suppose in 1720, O conveys to B and the heirs of his body. B dies in 1750 survived by Child C who dies in 1795 survived by Grandchild GC who dies in 1845 survived by Great-grandchild GGC who dies in 1906 without any surviving descendants. Under these facts, B's line of descendants is finally extinguished (i.e., becomes extinct) in 1906 and B's fee tail estate would only then come to an end *even though B actually died in 1750.*

B, the tenant in tail, could convey the land to a third person but B's grantee acquired only an estate for B's life because the restrictions imposed by De Donis prevented B from making any conveyance that would cut off the rights of B's issue or the reversioner. Thus, even though B conveyed to C, C acquired only an estate measured by B's life. Upon B's death, C's estate was extinguished and the property passed to B's heir of the body, if any, for life. If B had no living descendants at his death, or if B did but at some future point in time, B's line of descendants became extinct, the property reverted to the grantor or his heir who had the reversion.

The restrictions on B were burdensome and Parliament was petitioned to repeal the statute but refused. The most likely reason for such refusal was that the estate in fee tail was not subject (beyond the tenant's lifetime) to forfeiture for treason or attainder for felony and was not liable for the debts of the former tenants in tail. But, the courts sanctioned methods to evade the statute. In 1472 the courts permitted the rights of the issue of the tenant in tail to be extinguished by a fictitious law suit called the common recovery and in the following century permitted the rights of reversioners to be similarly extinguished.[5] Subsequent cases slowly evolved the principle that, through various actions known as fines, the fee tail could be converted into a fee simple. Finally, in 1833 fines and recoveries were abolished in England by statute and a

---

5. Taltarum's Case, Y.B. 12 Edw. 4 c. 19. Familiarity with the esoteric learning of fines and recoveries is not necessary for today's law student. For a brief description of both fines and recoveries, *see* Plucknett, Concise History of the Common Law 613–615, 617–622 (5th ed. 1956).

tenant in tail in possession was permitted by the statute completely to dock or bar the entail by a deed recorded in the Court of Chancery and convey the land to a third person in fee simple.[6]

Since the fee tail was an estate of inheritance it could not be created by an inter vivos conveyance at common law without the use of the word "heirs" in the limitation.[7] This strict rule did not apply to limitations in a will. The intention of the testator, if clearly expressed in the will, would be given effect despite the absence of the word "heirs." The words "of the body" were those commonly used in both deeds and wills to show the intention to create a fee tail rather than a fee simple but other words having the same meaning were equally effective.[8]

It was permissible for the grantor of a fee tail to restrict the inheritance (by proper words in the limitation) to a particular group of lineal descendants of the grantee. There could be an estate in tail male or in tail female and either one of these could be a fee tail general or a fee tail special. Thus, a grant to a man and the heirs male of his body created a "fee tail male." A grant to a man and the heirs female of his body created a "fee tail female."[9] If the grant was to a donee and the heirs of his body by a particular spouse, the estate was a "fee tail special"; if no particular spouse was designated, it was a "fee tail general." If the tenant in tail of a fee tail special survived the particular spouse and no issue had been born to the marriage, the estate was called the fee tail with possibility of issue extinct.

6. Fines and Recoveries Act, §§ 15, 40. The estate tail can no longer be created in England as a legal estate. Under the sweeping reform legislation of 1925, the only estates capable of being created as legal estates are the fee simple absolute in possession and the term of years absolute. The estate in tail and the life estate can exist only as equitable estates. A tenant in tail may nevertheless disentail and enlarge his equitable interest into a legal fee simple. See Cheshire and Burn, Modern Law of Real Property 250–256(13th ed. 1982).

7. Co. Litt. 20 a.b. A conveyance to B and his issue gave B a life estate. As to modern law, see § 6, infra. The problem arising from a gift of land by will (devise) to "B and his issue" is also treated in § 6.

8. See § 7, infra.

9. Estates in fee tail female were, in fact, rarely created but estâtes in tail male were an integral part of the English family settlement and were, therefore, very numerous from the sixteenth to the nineteenth centuries.

Review Problems

1. In 1280 O, the owner of Blackacre in fee simple absolute, conveys Blackacre to B and the heirs of his body. B has a fee simple conditional and O, who conveyed away less than he had, retained a possibility of reverter. If B died without surviving issue, Blackacre would revert to O. If during life B had issue, B was capable of alienating the property and conveying a fee simple absolute to his grantee. If he did not alienate the land upon the birth of issue, then upon B's death the fee simple conditional passed to his descending heir as a fee simple conditional, or if none, B's estate terminated and the property reverted to O.

2. In 1310, O, the owner of Blackacre in fee simple absolute, conveys Blackacre to B and the heirs of his body. B has a fee tail and O, who conveyed away less than he had, retains a reversion. O dies in 1350 leaving H as his sole heir. B dies in 1400 survived by a child C. At that point C has a fee tail and H has a reversion. In 1425 C dies without any surviving lineal descendants. C is survived by H. This results in the termination of the fee tail, and title to the property reverts to H who takes a fee simple absolute.

3. In 1400 O, the owner of Blackacre in fee simple absolute, conveys Blackacre to B and the male heirs of his body. B has a fee tail male and O, who conveyed away less than he had, retains a reversion.

4. In 1400 O, the owner of Blackacre in fee simple absolute, conveys Blackacre to B and the female heirs of his body. B has a fee tail female and O, who conveyed away less than he had, retains a reversion.

5. In 1400 O, the owner of Blackacre in fee simple absolute, conveys Blackacre to B and the heirs of his body with C. B has a fee tail special and O, who conveyed away less than he had, retains a reversion. B and C never have children before C dies survived by B. B has a fee tail special with possibility of issue extinct and O has a reversion. At B's later death, the property reverts to O.

§ 6. Modern Law—The Fee Tail in the United States

The estate tail had a hostile reception in the United States. While widely recognized during the colonial period, opposition to it developed in the post-revolutionary era on the ground that it was incompatible with American social conditions.[1] This opposition arose partly from the association of the fee tail with the rule of primogeniture (descent of land to the eldest son to the exclusion of all other children) and partly from the employment of the fee tail in England as a legal device to keep ancestral lands in the family for use as a basis of social and political power.

Beginning in the late eighteenth century and extending into the twentieth, state after state enacted legislation abrogating the fee tail and creating a statutory substitute so that at the present time only four jurisdictions, Delaware, Maine, Massachusetts and Rhode Island (as to deeds) recognize the estate as it existed at common law. The statutory provisions relating to the fee tail are not uniform but they may be grouped under three main headings:

A. The most common form of statute converts what would have been a fee tail at common law into a fee simple. Thus, if O, the owner of Blackacre in fee simple, conveys Blackacre to "B and the heirs of his body" B has a fee simple. This is the result in about twenty-seven jurisdictions.[2]

B. In the next largest group of states (eight in all) the statutes substitute for the fee tail a life estate in the grantee or devisee and a remainder in fee simple in his issue.[3] Thus, in these states in a grant to "B and the heirs of his body" B has a life estate

§ 6

1. See Morris, Primogeniture and Entailed Estates in America, 27 Colum. L. Rev. 24 (1927) (treating of the Colonial period).

2. The California statute is fairly typical: "Estates tail are abolished, and every estate which would be at common law adjudged to be a fee-tail is a fee simple; and if no valid remainder is limited thereon, is a fee simple absolute." Cal. Civ. Code Ann. § 763 (West 1983). Statutes of this kind, or statutes so construed as to reach the same result, exist in: Alabama, Arizona, District of Columbia, Georgia, Indiana, Kentucky, Maryland, Michigan, Minnesota, Mississippi,

Montana, Nebraska, New Hampshire, New Jersey, New York, North Carolina, North Dakota, Oklahoma, Pennsylvania, South Dakota, Tennessee, Vermont, Virginia, West Virginia, Wisconsin and Wyoming. The Texas Constitution forbids recognition of the fee tail(Art. 1, § 26) and in Hawaii the estate has been held not to exist. See, Restatement of Property, § 104 (1936).

3. Statutes of this type exist in Arkansas, Colorado, Florida, Illinois, Kansas, Missouri, and New Mexico. Georgia is also included in this group as to limitations which would under English law create a fee tail by implication.

and B's issue have a remainder which will be a fee simple when it becomes possessory.[4]

C. In three states, Connecticut, Ohio and Rhode Island (as to wills only) statutes provide that an estate given in fee tail shall be an estate in fee simple to the issue of the donee in tail. These statutes have the effect of giving the donee a fee tail for his lifetime only and on his death his issue take in fee simple. Thus, in those states, a conveyance to "B and the heirs of his body" gives B an estate in fee tail for his life and on his death his children take in fee simple. Since B has an estate in fee tail for life (rather than a life estate), conceptually B should be able to defeat the rights of B's issue by conveying the property to a third person in fee simple.[5] However, it appears that, with the possible exception of Rhode Island, B cannot convey an estate greater than an estate measured by B's own life.[6]

In the four states which still recognize the fee tail in its common-law form, Delaware, Maine, Massachusetts, and Rhode Island (when created by deed), a tenant in tail in possession has the power to convey in fee simple by an ordinary deed and thereby bar the entail and all reversions, remainders and executory interests expectant thereon. A creditor of a tenant in tail in possession can, except in Delaware, subject the estate to his claim as though it were owned by the debtor in fee simple.[7] But the tenant in tail has no power to dispose of the estate by will. Oddly enough, it is not clear whether on the tenant's death, the estate will descend to all of his children equally or the rule of primogeniture will apply so as to give it exclusively to the eldest son. According to the Restatement of Property,[8] upon the death of the tenant in tail the land descends to

---

4. On the question of the necessity of B's issue surviving B in order to take, see 2 Powell, Real Property, ¶ 198 (1950).

5. With the abolition of fines and recoveries, a tenant in tail could convey a fee simple by deed. In Rhode Island, however, he can only convey an estate for his own life.

6. See St. John v. Dann, 66 Conn. 401, 34 A. 110 (1895); Guida v. Thomp-

son, 160 N.E.2d 153 (Ohio Com.Pl. 1957). But see Restatement of Property, § 88–96 (1936).

7. In Delaware the creditor of the tenant in tail can cause to be sold on execution only an estate for the life of the tenant in tail. Hazzard v. Hazzard, 29 Del. 91, 97 A. 233 (1916).

8. Restatement of Property, § 85 cmt. b (1936). Even the Restatement would criticize any conclusion that pri-

all of the surviving descending heirs, although it suggests that primogeniture might still apply in Massachusetts, Delaware and Maine. In any event, modern equal protection theory would suggest that gender discrimination resulting from any preference for sons over daughters would be unconstitutional.

In Iowa, Oregon, and South Carolina, De Donis is not deemed to be in force because, unlike the Statute of Uses, it was not a so-called received common-law statute. Thus, in those states a conveyance to A and the heirs of his body (or an equivalent limitation) creates a fee simple conditional in A.[9]

Even though the fee tail is largely of historical interest, occasionally a modern case arises where the results are affected by whether a fee tail existed in the chain of title. For example, in *Robins Island Preservation Fund, Inc. v. Southold Development Corporation*[10] the resolution of the dispute centered on whether two New York statutes[11] properly resulted in the conversion of a fee tail into a fee simple of lands held in the 18th century by a resident of New York who was a loyalist during the American Revolution and from whom the plaintiff claimed a title.

§ 7.   Construction Problems—Meaning of Death Without Issue

It is not unusual in a conveyance or a bequest to one person to simultaneously create a gift over to another person if the first person dies without issue. Thus, O, the owner of Blackacre in fee simple absolute, devises Blackacre "to B and his heirs *but if B dies without issue* then to C and his heirs." The phrase "die without issue" is ambiguous. It may mean that C is to take only if the entire line of B's descendants (children, grandchildren, etc.) runs

mogeniture would apply because such a result would be "an undesirable survival of a form of inheritance not suited to present ideas."

9. *See* 1 ALP §§ 2.11–2.12. In Iowa, upon birth of issue the estate in fee simple conditional ripens into a fee simple absolute in the hands of the grantee unlike the common law under which the grantee was merely empowered to con-

vey a fee simple absolute. *See* Prichard v. Department of Revenue, 164 N.W.2d 113 (Iowa 1969).

10.   959 F.2d 409 (2d Cir.1992).

11. The statutes were the New York statutes providing for the forfeiture of lands of loyalists and the statute converting the fee tail into a fee simple.

out, whenever that occurs, much like the termination of a fee tail. Or, the phrase may mean that C is to take if, and only if, at the time of B's death B leaves no issue surviving him.[1] Put another way, the problem is whether the words "die without issue" should be construed to mean indefinite failure of issue or definite failure of issue, that is, failure of issue at an undefined point of time or failure of issue at a definite point of time, namely B's death.

If the indefinite failure of issue construction is adopted, B has a fee tail and C has a remainder in fee simple. Although in form the limitation to B and his heirs facially appears to give B a fee simple, the additional conditional phrase "if he die without issue" cuts down B's interest to one which will last only as long as B has lineal descendants—a period which corresponds with the duration of a fee tail. Thus, the indefinite failure of issue construction of the words "die without issue" gives the limitation the same legal effect as if it read "to B and the heirs of his body, then to C and his heirs."

On the other hand, if the phrase "die without issue" is given the definite failure of issue construction, that is, if it is taken to mean failure of issue at the time of B's death only, then B has a fee simple subject to a shifting executory interest in C. C will take only in the event that B dies leaving no lineal descendant surviving him. If B dies leaving a child, C will not take even if the child should die a month later leaving no issue. Of course, if B dies without issue who survive B, C will also take.

At a relatively early date the English courts established a preference for the indefinite failure of issue construction with the result that in the limitation under discussion B takes a fee tail by implication and C takes a remainder in fee simple.[2] This construc-

---

§ 7

1. There is also another possibility, that B might die without ever having had issue. Under this construction B's estate is not defeated if B has a child but later dies without any surviving issue. *See* Bullock v. Seymour, 33 Conn. 289 (1866); Tolley v. Wilson, 371 Ill. 124, 20 N.E.2d 68 (1939).

2. *See* St. John v. Dann, 66 Conn. 401, 34 A. 110 (1895). A similar result

occurred with a devise to "B for life but if B shall die without issue then to C and his heirs." Here, B would also take a fee tail with a remainder in C in fee. Machell v. Weeding, 8 Sim. 4, 59 Eng. Rep. 2 (1836). In this case Shadwell, V. C. stated: "I consider it to be a settled point that, whether an estate be given in fee or for life, or generally, without any particular limit as to its duration, if it be followed by a devise over in case of the

tion was historically understandable because until the Statute of Uses (1536)[3] executory interests were not recognized as valid common-law estates, and if C were to take at all C would have to take by way of remainder on the expiration of B's interest.[4] After executory interests became valid, however, the same constructional policy was continued. But, since the preference for the indefinite failure of issue construction amounted only to a rebuttable presumption, language in a deed or will indicating that the grantor or testator intended that the gift over should take effect at the death of the first taker without issue[5] or on the death of another named person or within a designated period was given controlling weight.[6]

Influenced by the English precedents, a considerable number of United States courts at an earlier date adopted the indefinite failure of issue construction. But in about thirty states there are statutes[7] establishing a preference for the definite failure of issue construction and a similar result has been reached in a few jurisdictions without the aid of a statute. At the present time, therefore, in

---

devisee dying without issue, the devisee will take an estate tail." But a similar limitation in a deed would give B a life estate since in a conveyance by deed the word "heirs" was at English common law necessary to create a fee tail. *See* Simes & Smith, The Law of Future Interests § 522 (2nd ed. 1956).

3. 27 Hen. 8, ch. 10. This statute is discussed in detail in chaps. 8 & 9, *infra.* The common-law preference for indefinite failure of issue was also consistent with the idea of when heirs of the body (the phrase typically associated with the creation of the fee tail) would expire.

4. There could be no remainder after a fee simple. The subject of remainders is treated in ch. 5, *infra.* For a thorough discussion of the English common-law preference, *see* 1 Simes & Smith, The Law of Future Interests § 522 (2nd ed. 1956); Warren, Gifts Over on Death Without Issue, 39 Yale L.J. 332 (1930).

5. For example, if T devised Blackacre to B and his heirs but if B died without issue surviving him, then to C,

T's intent of fixing B's death as the point in time to determine whether B died with or without issue would control. If B died with issue, the property, at B's death, passed to B's successors (B's heirs if B died intestate or those takers of the property designated in B's will). If B died without surviving issue, the property would pass to C.

6. The often cited case of Pells v. Brown, Cro.Jac. 590, 79 Eng.Rep. 504 (1620) affords a good illustration. There O devised land to "Thomas and his heirs forever, and if Thomas died without issue, leaving William his brother, then to William and his heirs." The court held that definite failure of issue was intended by the testator and, therefore, Thomas took a fee simple subject to an executory interest in William.

7. For a list of these statutes, *see* 5 ALP § 21.50 (1952); 1 Simes & Smith, The Law of Future Interests § 526 (2nd ed. 1956).

most jurisdictions there is a constructional preference for definite failure of issue.[8]

It would not be accurate, however, to say that the constructional problem no longer exists since the statutes do not apply to deeds or wills taking effect prior to the statutes so that as to such instruments the former rule in the particular jurisdiction could govern.[9]

A further constructional problem may also arise in the case of a will where there is a limitation such as "to B and his heirs but if B die without issue to C and his heirs." What is the import of the words "if B die?" Do they mean "die before the testator dies?"; or "die before or after the testator without issue?"

If the words mean "die before the testator" then the gift to C is substitutional. If B survives the testator C will not take even if B dies later leaving no issue. But if the words mean "die before or after the testator without issue," the gifts to B and C are successive and C could take if B dies before or after the testator without issue. The latter is the usual construction but the language of a particular will may show that the testator intended the gift over to take effect only if B predeceased the testator.[10]

In the typical "die without issue" gift or devise, there is no independent gift to the issue of the named ancestor. Thus in a gift to B and his heirs but if B dies without issue then to C and his heirs, B's issue are not takers under the terms of the instrument. Thus, if B dies with issue, B could devise the property to another in

8. The Restatement of Property rejects the common-law presumption of indefinite failure of issue. Restatement of Property, § 266 (1936). The common-law presumption also applied to dispositions of personal property even though there can be no fee tail in personalty. *See* Simes & Smith, The Law of Future Interests, § 523 (2nd ed. 1956).

9. For example, in Hayes v. Hammond, 336 Mass. 233, 143 N.E.2d 693 (1957) the indefinite failure of issue construction was applied to a limitation in a will executed before 1888, the effective date of the Massachusetts statute estab-

lishing a preference for the definite failure of issue construction.

10. *See* Goldberger v. Goldberger, 34 Del.Ch. 237, 102 A.2d 338 (1954). *See also* Dorfman v. Allen, 386 Mass. 136, 434 N.E.2d 1012 (1982).

For a comprehensive treatment of this topic and related problems, *see* 5 ALP, §§ 21.49–21.57 (1952); 3 Powell, Real Property ¶¶ 340–344 (1952); Simes & Smith, The Law of Future Interests §§ 521–551 (2nd 1956); Restatement of Property, §§ 268–269 (1936).

his will. B could devise the property because his estate was not divested as the condition (die without issue) did not occur. In some cases, however, a gift over on the death of named ancestor has been held to create an implied gift in the ancestor's issue if the ancestor dies with issue.[11] For example, suppose T, the owner of Blackacre, devises Blackacre to B for life, but if B dies without issue, to C and his heirs. B dies with issue. There is an implied gift to B's issue.[12]

Review Problems

1. O, the owner of Blackacre in fee simple absolute, devises Blackacre "to B and his heirs *but if B dies without issue* then to C and his heirs." Under the English common law, B had a fee tail and C had a vested remainder.[13] The English courts analogized the phrase "die without issue" to that event which caused the termination of a fee tail, namely, the extinction of B's entire line of lineal descendants. Once fee tails are extinguished, the rationale for the analogy fails and courts then construed the conveyance as creating a fee simple in B subject to an executory interest in C.

2. T, the owner of Blackacre in fee simple absolute, devises Blackacre to B for life, but if B dies without issue, to C and his heirs. B dies with issue. There is an implied gift to B's issue.

3. T, the owner of Blackacre in fee simple absolute, devises Blackacre to B and his heirs but if B dies without issue then to C and his heirs. B survives T. In a jurisdiction adopting the substitutional construction, B has a fee simple absolute since the only way B's estate could have been divested would have been had he died without issue in T's lifetime. In a jurisdiction adopting the successive construction, B has a fee simple subject to an executory interest in C. If B later dies without issue who survive him, C has a fee simple absolute. If B later dies with issue who survive B, then B's estate ripens into a fee simple absolute and passes to B's devisees or, if B died intestate, to B's heirs. There is no gift from T to B's issue.

---

11. *See* Restatement (Second) of Property, (Donative Transfers) § 25.9 cmt. c (1988).

12. *Id.*

13. *See* ch. 5, *infra.*

§ 8.   Construction Problems—Gift to B and His Children—The Rule in Wild's Case

If testator devises Blackacre "to B and his children" and at the testator's death B has no children what interest does B take, and what interest, if any, do B's after-born children take? Basically, the problem is whether the words "and his children" are to be taken as either words of limitation indicating the size of the estate given to B (and, thus are the equivalent of either "and his heirs" or the "heirs of his body,") or words of purchase indicating a gift also to B's after-born children themselves. The English courts, and a few United States courts, have held that, in the absence of an expressed contrary intent by the testator, the words "and his children" are words of limitation and B takes a fee tail. This rule of construction is the so-called first Rule in Wild's Case.[1] It stems from a dictum in that case: "If A devises his lands to B and to his children or issues (sic), and he hath not any issue at the time of the devise, that the same is an estate tail." This peculiar construction of the word "children" (which normally means issue in the first generation only) was in part due to the popularity of the fee tail in England at the time, and in part due to a desire to have the children take more than the life estate which would have been the maximum they could have taken as purchasers by way of remainder, because of the absence of words of inheritance or their equivalent.

In the United States there is no sound reason for applying a rule of construction that the testator is presumed to have intended to create a fee tail. Therefore, the first resolution in Wild's Case has been generally repudiated. However, there are cases in some jurisdictions which adopt it even though a local statute converts the fee tail into some other estate.[2] The preferable view, and the one most frequently held, is that B takes a life estate and the children a remainder.[3] The first resolution in Wild's Case applied only to devises of land since at common law in a conveyance by deed it was necessary to use words of inheritance in order to create a fee tail.

§ 8

1. 6 Co. 16 b, 1 Eq.Cas.Abr. 181 (1959).

2. *See* Simes, Handbook of the Law of Future Interests, § 108 (2nd ed. 1966).

3. Restatement of Property, § 283 (1936).

A second rule of construction is derived from a second resolution or dictum in Wild's Case. The second resolution was that if, at the time the devise to B and his children takes effect, B has living children, then B and his children take concurrent interests as joint tenants for life. This second resolution has generally been adopted as a rule of construction in so far as it presumes that the testator intended that B and his children take as co-tenants, but today they would usually take as tenants in common in fee simple.[4] A few jurisdictions hold that B takes a life estate with a remainder in fee simple in the children.[5] Where the gift is by deed some courts prefer the latter construction as more consistent with the donor's intent that all of B's children take an interest, whenever born.[6]

§ 9. Life Estates

An estate for life is an estate which is not terminable at any fixed or computable period of time and has its duration measured by the life or lives of one or more persons. Unlike the fee simple and fee tail it is not an estate of general inheritance[1], but like these two estates it was classified at common law as a freehold estate.

Life estates may be created by deed or by will (under the older terminology these were called conventional life estates); or they may be created by operation of law, in which case they were called legal life estates. Whether a particular life estate is a conventional or a legal one makes no difference other than in the mode of creation, but the distinction does provide convenience of classification for purposes of our discussion.

4. *See, e.g.,* In re Parant's Will, 39 Misc.2d 285, 240 N.Y.S.2d 558 (N.Y.Sur. Ct.1963). The second resolution applies to personalty as well as to land.

5. For a detailed treatment of the topic, *see* 5 ALP, §§ 22.22–22.26; Simes & Smith, The Law of Future Interests § 691–702 (2nd ed. 1956).

6. *See, e.g.,* United States v. 654.8 Acres of Land in Roane County, Tenn., 102 F.Supp. 937 (E.D.Tenn.1952).

§ 9

1. While not an estate of general inheritance, today if duration of the life estate is measured by the life of someone other than the life tenant and the life tenant predeceases such other person, then the balance of the terms can pass through the deceased life tenant's estate to the life tenant's heirs (if the life tenant died intestate) or the successors named in the life tenant's will.

§ 10.　Creation of Life Estates by Deed or Will

A life estate arises when the conveyance or will expressly limits the duration of the created estate in terms of the life or lives of one or more persons, or when the instrument, viewed as a whole, manifests the intent of the transferor to create an estate measured by the life or lives of one or more persons. The simplest and most common form of limitation is "to B during his life" or "to B for life" but no words of art are necessary and a life estate can result from other limitations of a similar nature. Thus, if O, the owner of Blackacre in fee simple absolute, conveys Blackacre "to B until he dies," or "to B for his use during his natural life," or "to B and at his death to go to B's children," in each case B takes an estate for his own life. At common law a conveyance "to B" without more only gave B a life estate, but under modern law B would normally take a fee simple because of the widespread existence of statutes creating a presumption that a conveyor intends to pass his entire estate to the conveyee.[1]

It is not unusual to find in a will, in addition to the language giving an interest to the designated beneficiary, further provisions specifying the powers of disposition the beneficiary shall have or restricting his powers of disposition. These additional provisions raise a problem of construction as to the estate intended to be given to the beneficiary. Thus, if T devises Blackacre "to B with the right to use or dispose of Blackacre as B sees fit" B could be held to have a fee simple in the absence of other language in the will indicating a contrary intent.[2] But if T devises Blackacre "to B with power to sell or mortgage if B finds it necessary" B has only a life estate.[3] Here the restricted power of disposition, being inconsistent with a fee simple, indicates the testator's intent to limit B's interest to a life estate. If the estate given to the beneficiary is expressed to be for life, the addition of a power to convey in fee will not, by the weight of authority, enlarge the estate into a fee simple. Thus, T devises Blackacre "to my wife, W, to have, to hold and to use the same as she sees fit during her lifetime. I give my wife power to sell

§ 10
1. See § 3, *supra* note 1.
2. See Benz v. Fabian, 54 N.J.Eq. 615, 35 A. 760 (1896).

3. See Restatement of Property, § 108 cmt. e (1936); 2 Powell, Real Property, ¶ 202(3).

any part or all of my real estate, also power to mortgage or assign as she sees fit or deems proper." W takes a life estate with a power to sell or mortgage.[4] This is not the equivalent of a fee simple since W has no power to devise the land and it is not inheritable by her heirs.[5]

An estate which is measured by the life of the grantee is called simply a life estate. An estate which is measured by the life of a person other than the grantee is called an estate pur autre vie. Thus, O conveys Blackacre to B "to have and to hold during the life of C." B has an estate pur autre vie.[6] Today, if B dies in C's lifetime, B's estate passes to the devisees under his will or to his heirs. If C dies in B's lifetime, then B's estate comes to an immediate end.

Suppose O conveys Blackacre to B for life and B, in turn, conveys to C for life. Here C's estate ends if B dies in C's lifetime since C cannot take a greater estate than B had. Upon the termination of the estates of both B and C because of B's death, the property reverts to O. If C dies in B's lifetime, C's estate also ends because the effect to B's conveyance to C was to grant to C an estate measured by the life of B and C, whoever died first. Thus, if C dies in B's lifetime, C's estate ends and B, who conveyed to C less than B had, takes the reversion. Of course, at B's later death the property reverts to O.

4. Langlois v. Langlois, 326 Mass. 85, 93 N.E.2d 264 (1950). It should be noted that this was a "home-made" will. In some states there are statutes providing that when a life tenant is given a power to dispose of the fee the estate is to be regarded as a fee simple in favor of creditors, purchasers and mortgagees. For a list of these statutes, see 2 Powell, Real Property, ¶ 202(3) nn. 78, 79.

5. *But see* White v. Brown, 559 S.W.2d 938 (Tenn.1977) where the court held that a devise to Evelyn White of decedent's home "to live in and not to be sold" devised a fee simple to Evelyn. The court also held the attempted restraint on alienation was void.

6. At common law if B died before C the property was regarded, until C died, as without an owner, hence the first person to take possession (called the common occupant) was entitled to the estate. This conclusion resulted from the fact that the estate pur autre vie was not an estate of inheritance and could not descend to the heirs of the life tenant, and not being personal property it could not pass to the administrator. But if the conveyance was to "B and his heirs for the life of C," then on the death of B during C's lifetime the heir of B took, not by descent but as "special occupant." This common-law rule was abolished in England by statute and is the subject today of statutory regulation in most states.

An estate pur autre vie may be created with more than one measuring life. Thus, O conveys "to B to have and to hold for the lives of A, B and C." B gets a life estate which will endure until the death of the survivor of the three named persons.[7]

A life estate, as well as a fee simple, may be one on special limitation (that is, determinable),[8] or subject to a condition subsequent[9] or executory limitation.[10] Whether a devise by a testator to his wife "so long as she remains a widow" (there being no gift over on the wife's death) creates a defeasible fee simple or a defeasible life estate often presents a difficult problem of construction. The Restatement favors the determinable life estate construction,[11] but recent cases indicate a trend toward holding that the devisee-spouse takes a fee simple defeasible on her marriage.[12] Thus, if the spouse does not remarry, the spouse's estate passes to the devisees under her will, or absent a will, to her heirs.

Review Problems

1. O, the owner of Blackacre in fee simple absolute, conveys to B for life. B has a life estate and O has a reversion. B's estate

---

7. In a few states there are statutes limiting the number of the measuring lives to two when the life estate is followed by a remainder. See 6 ALP, §§ 25.92–25.98.

8. See Bekins v. Smith, 37 Cal.App. 222, 174 P. 96 (1918) (to B so long as she lives and conducts religious services).

9. See, e.g., Knowles v. South County Hospital, 87 R.I. 303, 140 A.2d 499 (1958) (to B for life provided he lives on the farm at least three months each year, and "grows at least a peck of Indian maize, or Rhode Island Johnycake corn, on the ear.")

10. See, e.g., In re Estate of Audley, 256 Wis. 433, 41 N.W.2d 378 (1950).

11. Restatement of Property, § 108, cmt. bb (Supp.1948). See also Restatement (Second) of Property (Donative Transfers), § 6.3 (restraints on remarriage of testator's widow valid)(1983).

12. See, e.g., Dickson v. Alexandria Hospital, Inc., 177 F.2d 876 (4th Cir. 1949); Ramsey v. Holder, 291 S.W.2d 556 (Ky.1956); Kautz v. Kautz, 365 Pa. 450, 76 A.2d 398 (1950); In re Mattison's Estate, 122 Vt. 486, 177 A.2d 230 (1962). Cf. Bowman v. Brown, 394 Pa. 647, 149 A.2d 56 (1959) ("to my wife as long as she sees fit to remain on the premises and keep said premises in repair and pay taxes on same" held to give wife determinable life estate). A gift to a woman "during widowhood" is usually held to create a determinable life estate and the Restatement takes the position that a devise to a wife defeasible on her remarriage is normally an equivalent limitation. Restatement of Property, § 108, n. 9 (1936). Cf. Taylor v. Farrow, 239 S.W.2d 73 (Ky.1951); Lewis v. Searles, 452 S.W.2d 153 (Mo.1970).

ends at B's death. At B's death, O, or O's successors in interest, have a fee simple absolute.

2. B has a life estate in Blackacre. B conveys the life estate to C. C has a life estate pur autrie vie. C's estate ends if B dies in C's lifetime at which time the property reverts to B's grantor who has the reversion. If, on the other hand, C dies in B's lifetime, C's estate continues in C's heirs or devisees until such time as B dies when the estate ends and the property reverts to B's grantor.

3. T, the owner of Blackacre in fee simple absolute, devises Blackacre to his wife "so long as she remains a widow." This conveyance could be construed as granting W either a fee simple determinable or a determinable life estate. If the former, W's estate is not lost if W never remarries and W has an interest at her death which is descendible and devisable. If the latter, in all events W's estate ends at her death (and might end earlier should she remarry). Upon the termination of W's estate the property reverts to the successors of T.

§ 11. Life Estates Created by Operation of Law

Legal life estates, or life estates created by operation of law, arose out of the marital relationship. The various kinds of legal life estates were: A. Tenancy in fee tail after possibility of issue extinct; B. The husband's estate by the marital right; C. Curtesy; D. Dower.

A. Tenancy in Fee Tail After Possibility of Issue Extinct

A tenant in fee tail special, upon the death of the designated spouse without issue, has only a life estate in the land. Thus, O conveys Blackacre to B and the heirs of his body by his wife, Mary. Mary dies leaving no issue who survive B. It is obvious that there can never be issue capable of inheriting the estate. On B's death the land must, by virtue of De Donis, revert to O. Hence, B may be properly said to have, after the death of Mary, only a life estate. But if the original conveyance had created a fee tail general, instead of a fee tail special, there could not be tenant in tail after possibility of issue extinct. Since the fee tail estate exists today in only a few jurisdictions, a life estate resulting from a tenancy in tail after possibility of issue extinct is rarely found in modern law.[1]

B. Estate by the Marital Right

At common law the husband had, by right of marriage, a life estate in all lands of which his wife was seised of a freehold estate (an estate of inheritance or for life) at any time during the marriage and prior to birth of issue. This estate, also known as the husband's estate jure uxoris, was probably a product of the concept that the husband was guardian of the wife. It entitled the husband to the use and occupation of the land, as well as the rents and profits, free from any claim of the wife. He could convey his estate without her consent, and the land was liable to execution for his debts, but the purchaser obtained an estate that could not outlast the marriage. Actually, the estate was not measured by the life of the husband but was one which continued until the marriage was dissolved by death or divorce, or until issue was born alive of the marriage. Upon the birth of issue alive, the husband acquired an estate by the curtesy initiate in his wife's inheritable estates which estate lasted until his death.[2] If he survived his wife, this estate by the curtesy initiate became, on his wife's death, an estate by the curtesy consummate. The estate by the curtesy initiate differed from the estate by the marital right in that the husband now held for his own life and had sole seisin in himself whereas prior to birth of issue his estate was substantially an estate during the joint lives of husband and wife, and both were jointly seised.

Although the husband had rights in his wife's equitable estates similar to those given to him in her legal estates, it was through

§ 11

1. It will be recalled that some states statutes abrogating the fee tail have the effect of substituting a life estate in the conveyee for the common-law fee tail. See § 2.6, supra. In a sense, a life estate so created can be said to be a life estate created by operation of law although the phrase is not usually applied to this situation.

2. Technically, the estate by the curtesy initiate existed only in the wife's estates of inheritance which the issue of the marriage were capable of inheriting. Thus, it would exist in the wife's estate in fee simple or in fee tail general but not in a fee tail special if the husband was not the named spouse. The estate by the marital right, but not an estate by the curtesy initiate, could exist in lands in which the wife had only a life estate.

courts of equity that married women first obtained some ameliora-
tion of the harsh rules of the common law.[3] The reforms inaugurat-
ed by the chancellors in the seventeenth century were carried to
completion in the nineteenth century by legislation abolishing the
husband's estate by the marital right and the estate by the curtesy
initiate. These statutes, commonly called Married Women's Property Acts, generally gave to married women the same rights in their
real and personal property which they would have if unmarried,
subject in some jurisdictions to the husband's estate by the curtesy
consummate or to a requirement that the husband must join in a
conveyance of the wife's lands to make the transfer fully effective.[4]

C. Tenancy by the Curtesy

At common law, a tenancy by the curtesy was a life estate to
which the husband was entitled in all lands of which his wife was
seised in fee simple or in fee tail at any time during the marriage
provided that there was issue born alive capable of inheriting the

3. This result was achieved through
two devices—the doctrine of the wife's
equity to a settlement, and the recognition of the validity of a trust for the
wife's sole and separate use. At the end
of the seventeenth century it became
established that if the husband sought
to reach his wife's equitable assets he
would be allowed to do so only if he
consented to an adequate settlement out
of those assets for her separate use and
benefit. This settlement usually took the
form of a new trust for the separate use
of the wife and the issue; the terms of
this new trust being determined by the
Court of Chancery. This doctrine of the
wife's equity to a settlement was supple-
mented in the eighteenth century by
rulings that property could be conveyed
or devised to third persons as trustees
for the benefit of a married woman for
her separate and exclusive use free from
the control of her husband. Later it was
held that lands could be conveyed directly to a married woman, without the intervention of trustees, for her "sole and
separate use" and in such case equity
would protect the property from the

claims of her husband and his creditors.
Although at law the husband in such a
case acquired a life estate in the land, in
equity he was treated as a trustee for his
wife. Property interests of the wife so
protected in equity were called a married woman's separate equitable estate
or her "sole and separate" estate. See 1
ALP, §§ 5.50–5.56.

4. See, e.g., Mass. Gen. Laws Ann.
ch. 209, § 1 (West 1998); N.Y. Dom. Rel.
Law § 50 (McKinney's 1999). At the
present time in Massachusetts a husband may elect to claim curtesy only in
lands owned by his wife at the time of
her death in fee simple or in fee tail.
The estate of curtesy is identical with
the widow's estate of dower. The term
"curtesy" is abolished and the term
"dower" is applied to the interest taken
by the husband. Mass. Gen. Laws Ann.
ch. 189, § 1 (Supp. 1987). In New York
curtesy is abolished with respect to estates of wives dying after August 31,
1930. N.Y. Real Prop. Law § 189
(McKinney's 1989).

estate.[5] On the birth of such issue the husband's tenancy by the marital right was enlarged to an estate for his own life which he held "by curtesy of the law of England."[6] Although the husband's estate for his life was called curtesy initiate prior to his wife's death and curtesy consummate after her death, he had a present life estate in both situations and there was no substantial difference between the two types of curtesy.[7]

In modern American law curtesy is obsolescent as a source of life estates. Curtesy initiate was swept away by the Married Women's Property Acts. Curtesy consummate, or more simply curtesy, has been completely abolished in almost all states.[8]

D. Dower

At common law a widow was entitled on the death of her husband to a life estate in one-third of the lands of which he had been seised at any time during the marriage of an estate in fee simple or in fee tail, provided that the estate was one capable of being inherited by issue of the marriage.[9] During the husband's lifetime the wife had a protected expectancy, called inchoate dower. No conveyance by the husband, even to a bona fide purchaser for value, would be effective to defeat the wife's right to dower, nor could creditors of the husband impair her right. On the husband's death the widow was entitled to have assigned or set off to her the

---

5. "The time when the issue was born is immaterial, provided it were during the coverture; for, whether it were born before or after the wife's seisin of the lands, whether it be living or dead at the time of the seisin, or at the time of the wife's decease, the husband shall be tenant by the curtesy." Blackstone, Comm. 128.

6. In contrast to the more restricted rights of a husband in his wife's lands under Norman and French law. For the historical development of curtesy, see 1 ALP, §§ 5.58–5.59.

7. Curtesy attached to the wife's equitable estates in fee, at least where not excluded by the terms of the conveyance to the wife.

8. The apparent last hold out was Massachusetts. See Mass. Gen. Laws Ann. ch. § 189, § 1 (West 1991). However, both widows and widowers are entitled to "dower" being a life estate in one-third of the deceased spouse's lands.

9. If the husband's estate was one in fee simple or in fee tail general there would be no problem of the capacity of the issue to inherit. But if lands were given in fee tail special to a man and a named wife, his second wife would not be entitled to dower because no issue of the second marriage could inherit the estate.

specific lands to be held in dower and her dower then became consummate.[10] Once dower had become consummate her status was the same as that of any other life tenant.

Since seisin by the husband of an estate of inheritance was a pre-requisite to dower, his widow was not entitled to dower in lands in which he had a reversion or remainder expectant upon an estate of freehold. And since the concept of seisin applied only to legal estates, dower did not attach to equitable interests.[11] Moreover, the husband's seisin must have amounted to beneficial ownership. If he held legal title as trustee for another, his widow had no dower in the lands thus held.[12]

At a time when land was the principal source of wealth dower was a fairly adequate device for assuring to the widow some measure of support after the death of her husband.[13] In an agrarian economy it was an acceptable form of social and economic security for the widow. Partly for this reason and partly because it was a familiar institution, common-law dower existed in the United States in the colonial and post-Revolutionary period. In the nineteenth century it was frequently broadened to include equitable estates. By the twentieth century common-law dower had become of diminishing importance and it was abolished in a large majority of the states.[14]

10. In comparing curtesy and dower it should be noted that: 1. birth of issue was a pre-requisite to curtesy but not to dower—the widow was entitled to dower even if no issue resulted from the marriage; 2. the husband's estate by the curtesy was a life estate in *all* of the lands of which the wife was seised of an appropriate estate during the marriage but the widow's estate in dower was a life estate in only one-third of the husband's lands; 3. the husband's estate by the curtesy initiate commenced on the birth of issue, but the wife's right to dower became an estate only on the assignment of her dower lands to her; 4. unlike the husband's estate by the curtesy initiate, the wife's inchoate right of dower could not be independently transferred to a third person although it

could be released to a conveyee of the husband's estate.

11. This rule was changed by the Dower Act in 1833. 3 & 4 Will. 4, c. 105, § 3. Dower was abolished in England in 1925 by the Law of Property Act, 15 Geo. 5, c. 23, § 45(c).

12. For a thorough discussion of dower, *see* 2 ALP, §§ 5.1 to 5.49.

13. It should be remembered that at common law the wife was not an heir of her husband and that a land owner had no power of devise (except by custom in a few localities) prior to 1540.

14. *See, e.g.,* N.Y. Real Property Law § 190 (McKinney 1989) (as to realty acquired by the husband since September 1, 1930).

Dower and curtesy typically were derivative estates and, therefore, the interest of the surviving spouse could not outlast the basic estate from which the dower or curtesy derived. Thus, if the husband acquires a title in fee simple which was defective because of a superior title in a third person, the wife's dower rights were subject to the same infirmity.[15] Similarly, if the basic estate was a fee simple determinable or a fee simple on condition subsequent, the fact that it was a fee simple defeasible would not initially have prevented dower or curtesy, but the happening of the specified event which caused the expiration or termination of the fee simple would also end the dower or curtesy interest.[16]

E. Rights of Surviving Spouses Today

As noted, both the common-law estates of dower and curtesy are largely obsolete today, although some vestiges of them in a modified form can appear in some states. In lieu of these obsolete estates, the states have adopted statutes that equalize the rights of both widows and widowers, create rights for surviving spouses in both real and personal property, extend protection to the surviving spouse from disinheritance by will and permit surviving spouses to claim shares of a deceased spouse's property in lieu of claiming under a will. In many states, surviving spouses may also claim a share in property transferred away by the deceased spouse while living if transferred in a form under which the deceased spouse retained some economic benefits in the transferred property. The most comprehensive and most nuanced of these statutes are those in the Uniform Probate Code.

Under the Uniform Probate Code, if the decedent died intestate the surviving spouse is entitled to the entire estate (both real and personal) unless the decedent also was survived by issue or a parent. If the decedent was survived by issue the surviving spouse still is entitled to the entire estate if the surviving spouse is also the

---

15. If the husband acquires the fee simple subject to an option in a third person to buy the land, the wife's dower interest is also subject to the option. *See* Forte v. Caruso, 336 Mass. 476, 146 N.E.2d 501 (1957); Matlack v. Arend, 2 N.J.Super. 319, 63 A.2d 812 (1949).

16. Restatement of Property, 54 and Monograph on Dower and Curtesy as Derivative Estates, Appendix to volume 1.

ancestor of all such issue and the spouse has no other issue.[17] If the spouse is either a step-ancestor of decedent's descendants or has descendants who are not descendants of the decedent, or if decedent had surviving parents, the surviving spouse takes less than the entire estate.[18]

The surviving spouse is also entitled to reject the provisions of a deceased spouse's will and claim a forced share of the decedent's estate. The size of this share ranges from 3% to 50% depending on the length of the marriage.[19] In addition, the spouse's share attaches not only to decedent's property owned at death but to property transferred by the decedent during life where the decedent retained substantial economic benefits or control in or over the property, such as revocable trusts, life insurance and so forth.[20] This share, however, is reduced by property owned by the spouse at the decedent's death that is derived by the spouse from the decedent.[21]

§ 12.　Characteristics of a Life Estate

A tenant for life of a possessory estate has a right to the undisturbed possession of the land[1] and to the income and profits thereof. His use and enjoyment of the premises is limited by the

17. Unif. Prob. Code § 2–102.

18. *Id.*

19. Unif. Probate Code § 2–202. For marriages under one year, the surviving spouse is entitled to up to $50,000.

20. Unif. Probate Code §§ 2–205–2–207.

21. Unif. Probate Code § 2–209. Other states have comprehensive elective share statutes. *See, e.g.,* N.Y. EPTL, § 5–1.1 (McKinney 1999) Del. Code Ann. tit. 12, § 902.

§ 12

1. The prevailing view is that the life tenant can recover from a third party wrongdoer only the damages sustained as to his life estate and not full damages to the fee. *See* Zimmerman v. Shreeve, 59 Md. 357 (1882); Tinkham v. Wind, 319 Mass. 158, 65 N.E.2d 14 (1946); *Contra*, Rogers v. Atlantic, Gulf & Pacific Co., 213 N.Y. 246, 107 N.E. 661 (1915). The matter is now regulated by statute in New York so as to allow the life tenant to recover for all damage done to the realty only if all living persons having an interest in the land are made parties to the action. N.Y. Real. Prop. Act. Law § 833 (McKinney 1979). The Restatement adopts the view that the life tenant is restricted to recovery of damages to his life estate, the damages being measured by the difference between the value of the life estate before the trespass or other wrongful conduct and its value after the wrongful conduct. Restatement of Property, § 118 (1936).

law of waste, that is, he is under a duty to refrain from any act which will diminish the value of the reversion or the remainder if such act is also, under all of the circumstances, an unreasonable use of the premises.[2] On the termination of the life estate for a reason other than the tenant's own act or default, the life tenant or the life tenant's estate is entitled to emblements, that is, to cultivate and harvest annual crops previously planted.[3]

A life estate is alienable and the life tenant can convey the estate to a third person, or mortgage it, or lease it for a term of years not greater than the duration of the life estate. But the life tenant cannot (apart from the now obsolete common-law doctrine of tortious feoffment) convey a greater estate than the life tenant had.[4] Sometimes the deed or will creating the life estate contains language purporting to restrict the life tenant's power to convey the estate. The courts have been more willing to allow some forms of restraint on the alienation of a legal life estate than they have been in the case of a fee simple. Since, as a practical matter, a life estate is not readily saleable because of its uncertain duration, a restraint on its transfer may be thought to be less objectionable than it would be if the estate were a fee simple. Yet the validity of the restraint depends largely on the type of restriction. Thus, in most jurisdictions a disabling restraint on alienation of the life estate ("to B for life but without power to sell until B reaches the age of thirty") is void. But a restraint in the form of a forfeiture of the estate on attempted alienation ("to B for life but if B ceases to live on the land or conveys it, then to C") is held valid in nearly all jurisdictions. The forfeiture restraint is less objectionable since, apart from its deterrent effect on the life tenant, it does not render the land unmarketable in the hands of the holder of the future

2. The above statement is admittedly a broad generalization. It is intended primarily as a caveat that the rights of the owner of a possessory life estate must be balanced with the rights of the owner of a future estate in the same land. For a discussion of the law of waste, see 5 ALP, §§ 20.1–20.14; 5 Powell, Real Property, ¶¶ 636–646.

3. A life tenant also has the privilege of taking estovers, that is, to cut timber reasonably necessary for repairs to fences and structures and as fuel for fires. See Zimmerman v. Shreeve, 59 Md. 357 (1882).

4. A conveyance by a person owning an estate for his or her own life which purports to give the grantee a fee simple transfers to the grantee an estate for the life of the grantor.

interest. So also, a promissory restraint is treated like a forfeiture restraint and is held valid ("to B for life, B hereby agreeing not to convey her estate").[5]

Since a life tenant has a limited interest in the land, the life tenant owes certain duties to the owner of the future interest in the land, the remainderman or the reversioner. The life tenant is obligated to preserve the land and structures in a reasonable state of repair but is not bound to make expenditures for that purpose in excess of the profits, rent, or income received by the life tenant. Failure to discharge this duty amounts to permissive waste for which the life tenant is liable to the owner of the future interest.[6] The life tenant, however, is under no duty to make extraordinary repairs, or to rebuild structures damaged or destroyed without fault, or to make improvements. If the life tenant voluntarily makes improvements the life tenant cannot call on the owner of the future interest to contribute to the cost. The life tenant must pay the carrying charges on the property to the extent of the gross income, or the fair rental value if the life tenant personally occupies the property. Therefore, the life tenant must pay the interest on any mortgage or other incumbrance to which the life estate and the future interest are subject but the life tenant is not personally obligated to make payments on the principal.[7] The life tenant has a

---

5. It should be noted that we are here discussing restraints on alienation of a legal life estate only. The matter of restrictions on the transfer of an equitable life estate under a trust involves the problem of spendthrift trusts. As to the latter, see IIA A.W. Scott, The Law of Trusts, §§ 150–162 (4th ed. 1987).

For an excellent exposition of restraints on alienation of various types of estates, see Restatement (Second) of Property (Donative Transfers), §§ 3.1–4.5 (1983).

6. See Beliveau v. Beliveau, 217 Minn. 235, 14 N.W.2d 360 (1944). As to the remedies available to the owner of the future interest, see 1 ALP, § 2.24; Restatement of Property., §§ 129, 131 (1936).

7. However, if both the life estate and the future interest are subject to a mortgage and the principal of the mortgage debt becomes due and is paid by the owner of the future interest, the latter has a lien on the life estate to enforce payment out of that estate of a proportionate part of the sum paid. The burden of payment should be apportioned between the life estate and the future interest in accordance with their respective values, under the view taken by the Restatement. Restatement of Property, § 132 (1936). Accord Matter of Colligan's Estate, 202 Misc. 728, 110 N.Y.S.2d 638 (N.Y.Sur.Ct.1952) (under New York statute).

duty to pay current taxes levied on the property.[8] Assessments by a municipality or other public authority (frequently called betterment assessments) for public improvements specially benefitting the property must be borne wholly by the life tenant where the life of the improvement does not exceed the probable duration of the life estate. But where the special assessment is one for an improvement of a permanent or quasi-permanent nature, it must be apportioned between the owner of the life estate and the owner of the future interest in accordance with the respective values of the two estates.[9]

Although a life tenant is free, in the absence of a valid restraint in the creating instrument, to sell the interest, a life estate is not as a practical matter a marketable commodity. The life tenant, therefore, is faced with a difficult situation when the land is unproductive or the carrying charges exceed or substantially diminish the income. Can the life tenant maintain judicial proceedings to compel a sale of the fee simple over the objections of the owner of the future interest, or when the owner of the future interest is unascertained or a minor? In many states there are statutes which, under specified conditions, authorize a court to order a sale of the complete ownership of the land for reinvestment.[10] Apart from statute,

8. Taxes are normally assessed on the realty as a unit and not on the basis of the separate estates of the life tenant and the reversioner or remainderman. An unpaid tax usually constitutes a lien on the entire property and this lien is enforceable by a sale of the fee simple, thus destroying both the life estate and the future interest.

9. The problem of valuation of a life estate may arise in a number of other situations: e.g. apportionment of damages recovered for an injury to the land by a third person; apportionment of the award when the property has been taken by eminent domain proceedings; valuation for estate or inheritance tax purposes. The basic problem of valuation is that of determining the present value of an annuity equal to the expected annual net income of the property to be re-

ceived by the life tenant. The process involves the use of mortality tables to determine the life expectancy of the life tenant, an estimate of future annual earning capacity expressed in terms of a percentage of the value of the fee simple, and the use of a "discount rate" to obtain the present value of the future earning capacity. As to the details, see 5 Powell, Real Property, ¶ 666.

10. The statutes usually provide that the court, on the petition of the life tenant or owner of an interest in the land, may appoint a trustee or referee with authority to sell and convey the land in fee simple if the court decides that such sale is necessary or expedient. See, e.g., N.Y. Estates, Powers & Trust Law § 7–2.4 (McKinney 1992). After such a sale has been made the life tenant is entitled to receive during life the

the present trend of judicial authority recognizes a power to order a sale when necessary for the protection of the persons interested, particularly when the owners of the future interest are minors or unascertained.[11]

income of the proceeds. Spring v. Hollander, 261 Mass. 373, 158 N.E. 791 (1927).

11. *See, e.g.,* Cauffiel v. Cauffiel, 39 Del.Ch. 190, 161 A.2d 432 (1960). For a thorough discussion, *see* Simes & Smith, The Law of Future Interests, §§ 1941–1946 (2nd ed. 1956, Supp. 1985).

Chapter 3

NONFREEHOLD ESTATES (LANDLORD AND TENANT)

§ 1. Introduction

The relation of landlord and tenant normally arises from a contract whereby the owner of an estate in land transfers a possessory interest (other than a freehold) in the whole of the land, or in a designated space in the land, or in a building on the land, to a transferee in return for a consideration which is usually the payment of, or agreement to pay, rent. From the property perspective, the essence of the transaction is the creation of a right to possession in the transferee or tenant. Depending on the nature of the particular interest transferred, the estate of the transferee-tenant is classified as an estate for years, a periodic estate, or an estate at will. These three estates form the core of the modern landlord and tenant relationship.

For historical reasons the English common law drew a sharp distinction between these three estates and the more important feudal estates of fee simple, fee tail, and the life estate. It denied that the tenant for years or of a periodic estate or at will was seised of a free tenement and grouped these estates under the heading of non-freehold estates. The estate for years originally performed a social and economic function different from that of the fee simple, the fee tail, and the life estate. These latter estates were family estates in the sense that they provided the necessary economic support for the family unit. By contrast the term of years was used in the thirteenth century principally as a money lending device designed to evade the Church's prohibition of usury. The borrower, rich in land but short of cash, would give the lender a long term lease of a portion of his lands and out of the lands the lender would recoup both principal and profit.[1] Probably because of this difference of function, the common law set the term of years apart from the older estates and held that the lessee for years was not seised of a free tenement.[2] Thus, the fee simple, the fee tail, and the life estate were "freehold" estates but the estate for years was "non-freehold."

The consequence of this refusal to view the tenant for years as seised of a free tenement was that the tenant was denied the benefit of the real actions (in which the successful plaintiff recovered a judgment for possession of the land)[3] and the tenant's only remedy against a stranger to the title who dispossessed the tenant was an action for damages. But the rise of the agricultural or husbandry lease in the fourteenth and fifteenth centuries made imperative additional protection for the lessee and in 1499 he was given the judicially created remedy of ejectment by which the tenant could recover possession from one who ousted him.[4] Although the action of ejectment finally gave the lowly termor or

---

§ 1

1. To illustrate, suppose B wanted to buy O's land but borrowed money from A to do so. Instead of giving A a mortgage on the land (as B would do today), B would ask A how long A would need to receive the rents and profits from the land to reimburse A for the loan. Suppose A said 5 years. B would then have O deed the property to A for 5 years, and then to B and his heirs.

2. See Plucknett, Concise History of the Common Law 570–574 (5th ed. 1956). Cf. A.W.B. Simpson, A History of the Land Law 71–77(2d ed. 1986).

3. See also ch. 1, § 12, .

4. The position of the tenant for years at early common law was well described by Professor Kales: "In the

feudal scheme of society the term for years seems to have had no place. No feudal dues or services were exacted from tenants for years. The possession did not count for anything from the feudal point of view. The relation between the landlord and tenant was only that produced by a personal contract. * * * From the feudal point of view the tenant for years had no estate at all, but only a personal claim against the freeholder to occupy according to the agreement. The tenant only came to have an estate or right of property, when the law began to give him a remedy whereby he might specifically enforce the contract by securing and retaining the possession which was promised." A. M. Kales, Estates, Future Interests and Illegal Conditions and Restraints in Illinois § 21 (1920).

tenant for years a better remedy than the real actions available to the owners of freehold estates, the common law had already classified the estate for years as personal property. To distinguish it from other chattel interests it was called a chattel real. Since it was personal property, on the death of a tenant for years the unexpired term passed not to the tenant's heir but to the executor or administrator of the tenant's estate.[5]

At the present time the term for years is viewed as an interest in land, an estate, but the lease or rental agreement creating the interest is both a conveyance and a contract and the contractual element in the transaction may be more important than the property component.[6]

5. Under modern statutes real and personal property normally pass to the same persons when the owner dies intestate.

Statutes which use the words "real property", "real estate" or "lands, tenements and hereditaments" without indicating their intended applicability to leaseholds invite litigation over the question whether an estate for years is included in the statutory coverage. The answers given in the decisions have not been uniform since policy considerations in a particular case may outweigh legal history. See, e.g., Stagecrafters Club, Inc. v. District of Columbia Div. of American Legion, 110 F.Supp. 481 (D.C.Cir.1953) (leasehold held subject to sale on execution as personal property); Harbel Oil Co. v. Steele, 83 Ariz. 181, 318 P.2d 359 (1957) (mortgage of leasehold held mortgage of real property); Pierce v. Pierce, 4 Ill.2d 497, 123 N.E.2d 511 (1954) (partition available to joint owner of leasehold although partition statute referred to "lands, tenements, and hereditaments"). Cf. Ampco Printing—Advertisers' Offset Corp. v. New York, 14 N.Y.2d 11, 247 N.Y.S.2d 865, 197 N.E.2d 285 (N.Y. 1964) (tax on rent not a tax on real property). See also Zinn, The Real Estate Lease in Kansas: Some Problems of Characterization, 17 Kan. L. Rev. 707 (1969); Comment, 25 N.C.L.Rev. 516 (1947).

6. The modern trend is to emphasize the contractual nature of a lease and to minimize its property aspect. This is especially evident in tenancies of residential premises. See, e.g., Javins v. First National Realty Corp., 428 F.2d 1071 (D.C.Cir.1970), cert. denied 400 U.S. 925, 91 S.Ct. 186, 27 L.Ed.2d 185 (1970). For an extreme view, see Young v. Garwacki, 380 Mass. 162, 402 N.E.2d 1045 (1980) where the court said: "We have also attacked the theory on which the tenant's status classification depends. In the line of cases creating and applying the implied warranty of habitability, we have overthrown the doctrine of caveat emptor and the notion that a lease is a conveyance of property." 380 Mass. at 168, 402 N.E.2d at 1049.

Compare the language of the New York Court of Appeals in 219 Broadway Corp. v. Alexander's, Inc., 46 N.Y.2d 506, 414 N.Y.S.2d 889, 387 N.E.2d 1205 (N.Y.1979): "Thus, it can be said, and we would be remiss not to . recognize, that a lease achieves two ends, to wit: the conveyance of an estate in real property from lessor to lessee, and the delineation of the parties' rights and obligations pursuant thereto." 46 N.Y.2d at

§ 2. The Various Types of Tenancies

The various types of non-freehold estates recognized today are:

A. The estate (or term) for years;

B. The periodic estate;

C. The estate (or tenancy) at will;

D. The tenancy at sufferance; and

E. Statutory tenancies.

A. *The Estate (or Term) for Years*

An estate for years is any estate having a duration for a fixed or computable period of time, usually expressed in terms of a unit of a year or of a multiple or fraction of a year. Thus, a lease for one thousand years creates an estate for years; so also does a lease "for two weeks commencing July 1 next year." Typically the estate for years has a fixed beginning date and a fixed ending date set forth in the lease.[1] The requirement of definiteness of duration, however, is satisfied if the estate has a certain ending date even though its commencement in possession is stated to depend on the happening of a specified event. The stipulated event may be the completion of a building by the lessor on the land subject to the lease.[2] But if the termination date is indefinite the estate does not meet the tradi-

---

509, 387 N.E.2d at 1206. The court further stated: "While, as previously noted, a lease is often chameleonic in both character and function, its fundamental purpose remains to serve as a vehicle for the conveyance of an interest in real property. Until this end is achieved, any rights or obligations of the parties which may be embodied in the lease remain dormant." 46 N.Y.2d at 511, 387 N.E.2d at 1207.

§ 2

1. Restatement (Second) of Property (Landlord & Tenant) § 1.4 (1977).

2. In such a situation the validity of the lease may be challenged on the ground that the interest of the lessee is contingent and may not vest or fail within the twenty-one year period of the Rule against Perpetuities. See ch.8 § 11, *infra.* In Wong v. Di Grazia, 60 Cal.2d 525, 35 Cal.Rptr. 241, 386 P.2d 817 (1963) the court upheld the validity of a ten year lease to commence upon the erection by the lessor of a described building on the premises. The court construed the lease as requiring construction within a reasonable time and a reasonable time was held to be less than twenty-one years. The court disapproved a contrary holding in Haggerty v. Oakland, 161 Cal.App.2d 407, 326 P.2d 957 (1958). As to the concept of the Rule against Perpetuities, see Simes & Smith The Law of Future Interests § 1242 (2d ed. 1956).

tional requirement for an estate for years.[3] This requirement of certainty of duration relates to the maximum period of duration. The estate for years may, like an estate in fee simple or a life estate, be defeasible by reason of being subject to a special limitation, a condition subsequent, or an executory interest.[4] In fact, most leases create estates for years on condition subsequent by reason of the presence in the instrument of a clause giving the lessor a right of re-entry or power of termination on breach by the lessee of any of the specified conditions set out in the lease.[5]

1. Leases and the Statute of Frauds

Leasehold estates are commonly created by an agreement in writing signed by both landlord and tenant. The agreement usually

---

3. *See* Farris v. Hershfield, 325 Mass. 176, 89 N.E.2d 636 (1950); Idalia Realty and Development Co. v. Norman, 232 Mo. 663, 135 S.W. 47 (1911); Restatement of Property, § 19 (1936). *Cf.* Elm Farm Foods Co. v. Cifrino, 328 Mass. 549, 105 N.E.2d 366 (1952). Leases "for the duration" of the war, or until the cessation of hostilities have caused a split in the courts as to their effectiveness in creating an estate for years. Holding to the traditional view are: Lace v. Chantler, (1944) 1 K.B. 368, 1 All. Eng. L. Rep. 305; Stanmeyer v. Davis, 321 Ill.App. 227, 53 N.E.2d 22 (1944). *Contra,* Rupp Hotel Operating Co. v. Donn, 158 Fla. 541, 29 So.2d 441 (1947); Watkins v. Cohen, 91 N.E.2d 708 (Ohio Com.Pl.1949). *See* 32 Cal. L. Rev. 199 (1944).

4. In Loitherstein v. I.B.M. Corp., 11 Mass.App.Ct. 91, 413 N.E.2d 1146 (1980) the parties executed a lease for a term of ten years with an option in the lessee to terminate the lease at the end of the fifth year by giving a twelve month written notice to that effect and the payment of a specified "termination charge." The court said: "A lease for a term of years may properly be made subject to termination at a specified time, upon the occurrence of an event or events within the control of the party

electing to terminate. Such a provision creates a conditional limitation on the leasehold estate." 413 N.E.2d at 1148. More accurately, the provision creates a special limitation and the estate of the lessee is a determinable estate for years. *See* 2 R. Powell, The Law of Real Property ¶ 245 (P. Rohan rev. 1977).

Apart from statute, there is no maximum limit on the duration of an estate for years but in a minority of jurisdictions there are statutes regulating the length of all leases or of leases of particular kinds of property, such as agricultural lands or city and town lots. *See, e.g.,* Cal. Civ. Code § 717 (West 1982)(lease of land for agricultural purposes limited to 51 years); *id.* § 718 (lease of city or town lot restricted to 99 years). In Massachusetts a term for 100 years or more having 50 years unexpired is treated as a fee simple for purposes of dower, descent and distribution, levy on execution, and sale by executors and administrators. Mass. Gen. Laws Ann. ch. 186, § 1 (West 1991).

5. At times a lease may contain both a special limitation and a power of termination. *See, e.g.,* Ghoti Estates, Inc. v. Freda's Capri Restaurant, 332 Mass. 17, 123 N.E.2d 232 (1954).

specifies the parties and the premises being leased, states the duration of the estate created and the rent, and recites the covenants or promises undertaken by each of the parties. But, to what extent is a writing required? Prior to the English Statute of Frauds (1677) an estate for years, regardless of the length of the term, could be created by oral agreement coupled with entry into possession by the lessee. The Statute of Frauds required that transfers of interests in land (other than leases "not exceeding the term of three years from the making thereof") be evidenced by an instrument in writing signed by the grantor.[6] Therefore, after the Statute became effective most leases for a period of three years or less continued to be valid. The Statute did not require that the writing be signed by the grantee or lessee.

All of the states have statutes modeled on the English Statute of Frauds' provisions regulating the creation of estates in land. Most of the state statutes, however, allow oral leases for one year or less, rather than the three-year period of the English statute.[7] Only a few states have retained the language of the English Statute: "from the making thereof." Therefore, under the usual American statute an oral lease for one year is valid even though the term is to begin at some time (e.g. three months) in the future.[8] Some statutes require that the lease be signed by the lessee in order to be enforceable against him.[9]

An oral lease for a period longer than permissible under the local Statute of Frauds is not usually held invalid for all purposes.

6. 29 Car. 2, c. 3. If the lease for more than three years was not in writing it was to be given the effect of a tenancy at will, thereby making it terminable by either party without notice.

7. For a complete listing of the statutes in the several states, see Restatement (Second) of Property (Landlord & Tenant) § 2.1, Statutory Note (1977). In the majority of the New England states the statutes contain no exception for short term leases and provide, in effect, that an oral transfer of any estate in land creates only a tenancy at will. See, e.g., Mass. Gen. Laws Ann. ch. 183, § 3 (West 1991): "An estate or interest in land created without an instrument in writing signed by the grantor or his attorney shall have the force and effect of an estate at will only * * *."

8. See Restatement (Second) of Property (Landlord and Tenant) § 2.1 cmt. f (1977); Cf. R. Schoshinski, American Law of Landlord and Tenant, § 2.5 (1980).

9. Since a lease is a conveyance of an interest in real property it must be delivered by the lessor in order to be effective. 219 Broadway Corp. v. Alexander's, Inc., 46 N.Y.2d 506, 414 N.Y.S.2d 889, 387 N.E.2d 1205 (1979).

Upon entry into possession by the lessee the relation of landlord and tenant arises. Only the agreement as to duration is invalidated and other provisions of the lease such as the amount and time of payment of rent, and mode of termination, are given effect. Most courts have held that a periodic tenancy arises from the payment of rent on a periodic basis as provided in the oral lease.[10] Moreover, an oral lease may be enforceable in equity, despite the failure to comply with the Statute of Frauds, on the basis of the doctrine of part performance. Entry into possession and payment of rent by the lessee do not take the case outside the Statute, according to the better and prevailing view. However, where the parties have rendered substantial performance in compliance with the terms of the oral lease, such as making major improvements to the premises as required by the lease, full effect is given to the lease.[11]

Under the Uniform Residential Landlord Tenant Act, if the landlord neither signs nor delivers a written lease to the tenant but accepts rent without reservation, the lease agreement is as effective as if it had been signed.[12] If the tenant neither signs nor delivers a written lease to the landlord, acceptance of possession and payment of rent without reservation validates the lease.[13] However, under this law, the lease term cannot be longer than one year.[14]

The common law drew a distinction between the status of the lessee prior to lessee's entry into possession under the lease and after the entry. Prior to his entry the lessee had a contractual right to an estate for years but not an estate. Until actual entry the lessee's interest, known as an *interesse termini* (interest in a term), would not enable him to maintain an action of trespass against a third party. In modern law, the concept of *interesse termini* serves no useful purpose and is frequently ignored by the courts although

---

10. *See* Schoshinski, *supra* note 8, § 2.25. *Cf.* Restatement (Second) of Property (Landlord and Tenant) § 2.3 (1977).

In the few states having statutes providing that an oral lease creates only a tenancy at will, the periodic payment of rent will not affect the nature of the tenancy. *See, e.g.,* Chase v. Aetna Rub-

ber Co., 321 Mass. 721, 75 N.E.2d 637 (1947).

11. *See* Schoshinski, *supra* note 8, § 2.5.

12. URLTA, § 1.402.

13. *Id.*

14. *Id.*

traces of the doctrine may be found in an occasional case.[15] Characterization of the tenant's interest as a contract right rather than an estate can effect the landlord's damages if the tenant reneges on the agreement prior to the commencement date of the lease. For example, suppose L leases Blackacre to T for $500 a month for a term of two years to commence in ninety days. Thirty days later T notifies L that T will not take possession and will not comply with the lease. Typically if a tenant wrongfully terminates a lease during the term, landlord can sue for unpaid rents. Here, since the term had not yet commenced, L can only sue for actual damages measured by the difference, if any between the promised rent and the property's fair rental value.[16]

2. Delivery of Possession to the Lessee

Suppose that at the time fixed for the commencement of the lessee's estate the premises are wrongfully occupied by a third person, such as a former tenant improperly holding over. The lessee can normally recover possession in an action against the holdover occupant and can also recover damages from him, but what are the lessee's rights against the lessor? The answer depends on whether the court is willing to imply a covenant on the part of the lessor to deliver possession to the lessee on the date specified in the lease for the beginning of the lessee's term. The American courts are divided on the question. Many of them adopt the so-called English rule which obligates the landlord to deliver actual possession of the leased premises to the tenant.[17] But a substantial number follow the so-called American rule that requires only that the lessor give

---

15. *See, e.g.,* Simon v. Kirkpatrick, 141 S.C. 251, 139 S.E. 614, 54 A.L.R. 1348 (1927). The doctrine of *interesse termini* was abolished in England by the Law of Property Act, 1925, 15 Geo. 5, c. 20, § 149(1)(2) and a term of years takes effect without entry into possession by the lessee.

16. *See* Malani v. Clapp, 56 Hawaii 507, 542 P.2d 1265 (1975).

17. *See, e.g.,* Hannan v. Dusch, 154 Va. 356, 153 S.E. 824 (1930). This view is adopted by the Uniform Residential

Landlord and Tenant Act, § 2.103 (1972) (enacted in 14 states) and, in general, by the Restatement (Second) of Property (Landlord and Tenant) § 6.2 (1977). The Restatement takes the position that the landlord has a reasonable time to evict the third person before the landlord is in default. There are statutes in fourteen states requiring the landlord to deliver possession. The statutes are listed in a Statutory Note to § 6.2 of this Restatement.

the lessee the legal right to possession.[18] In these latter jurisdictions the lessee's only remedy, in the absence of an express covenant in the lease that the lessor will deliver possession to the lessee, is against the wrongful occupant.[19] Neither the English nor the American rule create rights in the lessee against the landlord where a wrongdoer ousts the lessee after the lessee takes possession of the leased premises.[20]

3. Is it a Lease, a License or an Easement?

It often becomes necessary to distinguish between leasehold interests and other interests having similar aspects but different legal consequences. Thus, a particular transaction may, arguably, create an estate for years, a license, or an easement.[21] Depending on how the transaction is classified, different legal incidents attach to the relationship. If, for example, O, owner of a building, gives to B for a specified term the exclusive right to erect and maintain an advertising sign on the roof or the wall of the building, the nature of B's interest determines whether the privilege given to B is revocable, whether possessory remedies are available to B, and the tort liability of O and B to third persons for the condition of the premises.[22] In this and analogous situations, the test usually ap-

---

18. See, e.g., Snider v. Deban, 249 Mass. 59, 144 N.E. 69 (1924). The rule that there is no duty on the landlord to deliver possession is sometimes referred to as "the New York rule" because of early decisions in that state adopting this viewpoint. But New York now provides by statute that in the absence of contrary agreement "there shall be implied in every lease of real property a condition that the lessor will deliver possession at the beginning of the term." N.Y. Real Prop. Law § 223-a (McKinney, 1968).

19. For a comprehensive treatment of this subject, see Weissenberger, The Landlord's Duty to Deliver Possession: The Overlooked Reform, 46 U.Cinn.L.Rev. 937 (1977).

20. But see § 3, infra (landlord's covenant of quiet enjoyment).

21. A license is usually defined as a revocable privilege to do an act or series of acts on land in the possession of another. A common type of license is the use of a seat in a movie theatre. Cf. Restatement of Property, §§ 512, 514, 519 (1936). An easement is an interest in land in the possession of another consisting of the privilege of making a limited use of the land. An easement is not revocable at the will of the grantor. See Restatement of Property § 450 (1936); Baseball Pub. Co. v. Bruton, 302 Mass. 54, 18 N.E.2d 362, 119 A.L.R. 1518 (1938). A common type of easement is a right of way across the land of another to reach a public road.

22. The advertising sign cases are fairly numerous. See, e.g., Gaertner v. Donnelly, 296 Mass. 260, 5 N.E.2d 419 (1936); Lewis v. Baxter Laundries, 254

plied by the courts in determining the nature of the interest created is the intention of the parties with respect to conferring a possessory right on the recipient of the interest.

The distinctive feature of an estate for years is the right of the tenant to exclusive possession of a defined physical area for the duration of the specified term. Whether such a right of possession has been given to the transferee is often not easily determined because of ambiguous language in the creating instrument, the restricted rights imposed on the transferee by the terms of the agreement, or the circumstances of the transaction.[23]

4. Leases and the Recording Acts

Since a lease creates an estate in land it may be subject to the provisions of a recording statute in the state where the land is located. The recording statutes are, in general, designed to give protection to third parties subsequently acquiring interests in the land for value and in good faith. There is considerable variation in the recording acts as to what leases are required to be recorded.

Mich. 216, 236 N.W. 239 (1931); Bridge Hardware Co. v. Disosway & Fisher, Inc., 199 Misc. 259, 101 N.Y.S.2d 863 (N.Y.Sup.Ct.1950). Absent a clearly expressed intention to create a tenancy, the courts usually hold that the arrangement amounts to a license. Occasionally, the transaction is held to create an easement. See, e.g., Baseball Pub. Co. v. Bruton, note 21, supra.

23. It may, for example, be difficult to determine whether a non-transient occupant of furnished rooms is a tenant or a lodger. See Roberts v. Casey, 36 Cal.App.2d Supp. 767, 93 P.2d 654 (1939); Davis v. Francis Scott Key Apartments, Inc., 140 A.2d 188 (Mun. App.D.C.1958); Comment, Tenant, Lodger, and Guest: Questionable Categories for Modern Rental Occupants, 64 Yale L.J. 391 (1955). For a thorough discussion of the distinction between leases and other arrangements, see 1 American Law of Property [hereinafter referred to as "ALP"], § 3.10, Schoshinski, supra note 8, §§ 1.3–1.7.

In the past few years a new development in vacation housing has been the creation of time sharing arrangements, so-called "time shares". For example, a developer in a resort area erects an apartment type multi-unit building and transfers to a number of persons the exclusive right to use a dwelling unit in the building for a week or a month or other agreed interval of time during a specified period of each year. The arrangement may grant the purchaser an anomalous kind of fee simple estate in a specific unit, with the exclusive right of occupancy limited to designated time periods, or it may transfer an estate of "interval ownership" for a specified number of years, or it may give the "purchaser" only a contract right, without ownership, to use a unit which is to be designated by the seller, during an interval in each year. See, e.g., In re Sombrero Reef Club, Inc., 18 B.R. 612 (Bkrtcy.S.D.Fla.1982). Statutes in many states regulate the sale of time-sharing rights.

Some statutes provide for the recording of all leases but most of them require only the recording of leases having a specified duration. Many states call for the recording of leases having a term of more than one year; other jurisdictions specify leases for more than three years and a few require recording only if the lease term is in excess of seven years.[24] An unrecorded lease is valid between its immediate parties even though there was a failure to comply with an applicable recording act, but the lease is not enforceable against a subsequent transferee of the premises for value and in good faith without notice of the lease. The meaning of "notice" depends on the language of the particular statute and the judicial construction given to it. If the lease is a short-term lease which is not required to be recorded, a subsequent purchaser of the premises takes subject to the lease regardless of notice of it.

A lease, unlike a deed, is often a lengthy document. A lease of valuable business property, for instance, may well run over a hundred pages in length. It is obvious that if such a lease must be recorded in its entirety in the registry or recording office such offices will be unnecessarily burdened with papers that are of no legitimate interest to third persons. Moreover, the parties to the lease may desire to keep certain information confidential, such as the amount of rent specified in the lease. In response to this problem, statutes have been enacted in many states allowing the parties to record, instead of the entire lease, a memorandum or "notice of lease."[25] These statutes specify the contents of the notice of lease and usually require that it state the names of the parties, the date of commencement and duration of the term, a description of the premises as set out in the lease, and any rights to renew or extend the lease. Some statutes expressly allow the inclusion of additional material. The recorded notice of lease is given the same effect as if the lease had been recorded and operates to give constructive notice of the lease.[26]

24. A complete listing of all of the pertinent statutes is set out in Restatement (Second) of Property (Landlord and Tenant) § 2.1, Statutory Note (1977).

25. See, e.g., Conn. Gen. Stat. Ann. § 47–19 (West 1995); Mass. Gen. Laws ch. 183, § 4 (West 1991); N.Y.Real Prop. Law. § 291–C (McKinney 1989).

26. Mister Donut of America, Inc. v. Kemp, 368 Mass. 220, 330 N.E.2d 810 (1975) (holding that a recorded notice of lease gives to third persons constructive

B. The Periodic Tenancy

A periodic estate is a tenancy which will continue for a year or a fraction of a year and for successive similar periods unless terminated by either party by proper notice.[27] There are various kinds of periodic tenancies but the most common are those from year-to-year and from month-to-month. By its nature, the periodic tenancy is continuous and of indefinite duration. Thus, if the tenancy is from month-to-month it is a single, continuous tenancy until terminated, not a tenancy for one month which comes to an end at the expiration of the month and is renewed for the following month.[28]

Although historically the periodic estate was derived from the tenancy at will, its general characteristics are similar to those of the estate for years. The interest of the tenant is assignable, the tenant is liable for permissive waste, and the death of either landlord or tenant does not terminate the tenancy.[29] Unlike the estate for years which terminates without notice at the end of the specified term,[30] the periodic estate continues until terminated by the giving of proper notice by either party. The common law required a six months' notice to terminate a tenancy from year-to-year, and for lesser periods a notice equal to the period. Thus, for a tenancy from month-to-month the notice of termination must be a month's notice. In all cases the notice must terminate the estate at the end of a period, not at some intermediate day. Thus, if a month-to-month tenancy runs from the first day of each month, notice on May 15, to terminate on June 15, would be improper. If the parties

notice of an option to lessee to purchase the premises contained in the lease although not mentioned in the notice of lease).

27. Restatement (Second) of Property (Landlord and Tenant) § 1.5 (1977; Restatement of Property, § 20 (1936).

28. See Wagner v. Kepler, 411 Ill. 368, 104 N.E.2d 231 (1951). Accord, Spiritwood Grain Co. v. Northern Pac. Ry. Co., 179 F.2d 338 (8th Cir.1950) (tenancy from year-to-year). Occasionally, a statute eliminates the continuity factor and converts what would normal-

ly be a periodic estate into one for a fixed period. See, e.g., Conn.Gen.Stat. Ann. § 47a–3d (West 1994) (oral lease for indefinite term at monthly rental creates tenancy for one month only). Cf. Restatement (Second) of Property (Landlord & Tenant) § 1.5 cmt. c; § 17.1 cmt. i (1977).

29. Restatement (Second) of Property (Landlord & Tenant), § 1.5 cmt. f (1977).

30. No notice is necessary to terminate an estate for years as the lease itself fixes the date of termination.

by agreement specify the period of notice, their agreement will be given effect.[31] Statutes in many states regulate the length of notice required to terminate such tenancies,[32] and it is not uncommon for states to provide less than six months notice to terminate a year-to-year periodic tenancy.

Under the common law, the notice to terminate a periodic tenancy could be oral or written, unless the lease otherwise provided. Statutes in most states, however, require the notice to terminate to be in writing.[33]

A periodic tenancy may be created by express agreement of the parties, by a letting for an indefinite time with rent payable at periodic intervals, by holding over with the assent of the lessor after the expiration of an estate for years, or by entry into possession under an invalid lease.

A common method of creating such tenancies is by inference on a general letting when the rent is payable periodically. In earlier times, if L let property to T and no duration of the tenancy was expressed but an annual rent was reserved and paid, the English law treated the tenancy as one at will. But in the seventeenth century the courts began to infer that the parties intended by such transaction to create a tenancy from year-to-year.[34] Since the latter tenancy, unlike a tenancy at will, could not be terminated by either party without proper notice, it gave protection to both parties against a sudden termination of the tenancy.[35] Since no definite term was specified, the reservation and payment of a periodic rent afforded the basis for the conclusion that a periodic tenancy was intended. Most state courts have adopted this view.[36] In modern

---

31. *See, e.g.,* Israel v. Beale, 270 Mass. 61, 169 N.E. 777, 68 A.L.R. 588 (1930) (tenancy from year-to-year terminable on two months' notice prior to end of a year).

32. For a collection of these statutes, *See* 1 ALP, § 3.90 (1952); 2 Powell, Real Property, § 255 (1950); Restatement (Second) of Property (Landlord and Tenant) § 1.5, Statutory Note (1977).

33. *See* Restatement (Second) of Property (Landlord and Tenant), § 1.5, Statutory Note (1977). *See also* URLTA § 4.301 (written notice required)

34. 7 Holdsworth, History of English Law 243–245 (1926).

35. Blackstone remarked that "courts of law have of late years leaned as much as possible against construing demises where no certain term is mentioned to be tenancies at will; but have rather held them to be tenancies from year-to-year so long as both parties please, especially where an annual rent is reserved." Bl.Com.II, 147.

36. *See, e.g.,* 28 Mott St. Co. v. Summit Import Corp., 34 A.D.2d 144,

times rent is usually paid on a monthly basis when the subject of the tenancy is residential property, and, therefore, a letting on an indefinite basis with the rent payable monthly will, in the absence of statute, result in a tenancy from month-to-month.[37] In a number of states, however, statutes prevent the normal inference from being made and create a tenancy at will.[38]

Periodic tenancies frequently result from a holding over by a tenant after the expiration of an estate for years. If, after the expiration of the term fixed by the lease, the tenant remains in possession, the landlord may elect either to treat him as a trespasser[39] and have him ejected by summary process or recognize him as a tenant. If the landlord elects to recognize the occupant as a tenant, as by accepting rent from him, many courts hold that the new tenancy is from year-to-year if the original term was for one year or longer.[40] Some courts take the view that the new periodic tenancy is governed by the manner in which rent was payable under the original lease. Thus, if a monthly rental was reserved the holdover tenancy is from month-to-month. The Restatement adopts the view that the period of the new periodic tenancy for the holdover tenant is determined by the manner in which "the rent was computed under the lease that has terminated."[41] Thus, if rent

310 N.Y.S.2d 93 (1970), aff'd, 28 N.Y.2d 508, 319 N.Y.S.2d 65, 267 N.E.2d 880 (1971); Elliott v. Birrell, 127 Va. 166, 102 S.E. 762 (1920).

37. See, e.g., Bhar Realty Corp. v. Becker, 49 N.J.Super. 585, 140 A.2d 756 (1958).

38. For a collection of these statutes See 2 Powell, Real Property, § 254, n. 20. In Maine and Massachusetts the Statute of Frauds has been construed as permitting the creation of periodic estates only by written agreement. In those two states an oral letting for an indefinite time, even though the rent is paid periodically, creates a tenancy at will. Davis v. Thompson, 13 Me. (1 Shep.) 209 (1836); Ellis v. Paige, 18 Mass. (1 Pick) 43 (1822).

39. More accurately, the former tenant is a tenant at sufferance, not a trespasser.

40. See, e.g., A. H. Fetting Mfg. Jewelry Co. v. Waltz, 160 Md. 50, 152 A. 434 (1930). For an excellent discussion of the holdover problem, See 1 ALP, §§ 3.33–3.36. In Maine and Massachusetts the tenant holding over with the landlord's consent is a tenant at will. See note 45 supra.

In numerous jurisdictions there are statutes controlling the obligations of a holdover tenant. See Schoshinski, American Law of Landlord and Tenant, § 2.23 (1980).

41. Restatement (Second) of Property (Landlord & Tenant), § 14.4 cmt. f (1977).

is computed on a monthly basis and paid monthly, a month-to-month tenancy arises; if rent is computed on an annual basis but is paid monthly, a year-to-year tenancy arises.

Where a lease for years is unenforceable (usually because of failure to comply with the Statute of Frauds) but the lessee enters into possession and pays rent on a periodic basis in accordance with the terms of the lease agreement, typically a periodic tenancy results. The provisions of the lease, except as to duration, are normally held to be applicable to the periodic tenancy and regulate the amount and time of payment of rent as well as the other obligations of the parties.[42]

C. The Tenancy at Will

An estate (or tenancy) at will is an estate which is terminable at the will of either landlord or tenant and has no other specified period of duration.[43] Such a tenancy is properly an estate since the tenant has an exclusive right to possession and may maintain an action of trespass or ejectment against persons interfering with his possessory interest. Its duration is dependent on the will of both parties and, unlike the periodic estate, no formal notice of a prescribed length of time is required for its termination.

A tenancy at will may be created by an express agreement between the landlord and tenant that the tenant shall hold possession so long as both parties agree.[44] Such explicit agreements are relatively infrequent and more often a tenancy at will is inferred in situations where the holding is indefinite and a periodic tenancy cannot be presumed.[45] Thus, if property is let for an indefinite time and no rent is reserved, the natural inference is that the parties intended a tenancy at will.[46] An agreement that the tenant shall

---

42. But see URLTA, § 1.402 (lease created with a one year term).

43. Restatement of Property § 21 (1936); Restatement (Second) of Property (Landlord and Tenant) § 1.6 (1977).

44. See Say v. Stoddard, 27 Ohio St. 478 (1875).

45. See, e.g., Farris v. Hershfield, 325 Mass. 176, 89 N.E.2d 636 (1950)

(written agreement for letting at $25.00 a month, no duration specified). In Massachusetts an oral letting on a monthly rental basis creates a tenancy at will. In most other states the facts of the case would normally require the inference of a tenancy from month-to-month.

46. Lepsch v. Lepsch, 275 App.Div. 412, 90 N.Y.S.2d 157 (4th Dept.1949) (divorced wife given right and privilege

hold possession at the will of the landlord creates a tenancy at will since it is implied that the tenancy also is terminable at the will of the tenant. Does an agreement that the premises shall be held at the will of the tenant create only a tenancy at will? For example, if O conveys to B "for as many years as desired by B" does B get a tenancy at will or a determinable life estate? Lord Coke stated that "when the lease is made to have and to hold at the will of the lessee, this must also be at the will of the lessor"[47] and his pronouncement has influenced some courts to hold that a tenancy at will results from such a transfer.[48] Other courts have taken the view that the transferee receives a determinable life estate or a determinable fee simple depending on the language of the instrument.[49]

At common law a tenancy at will could be terminated by either party, without formal notice, by expressing an intention to treat the tenancy as ended. In the event of termination by the landlord, the tenant was allowed a reasonable time to remove his personal property and was entitled to emblements.[50] Since the relation assumes the assent of both parties to a continuance of the tenancy, the death of either landlord or tenant terminates the estate.[51] So also, a conveyance of the reversion by the landlord ends the tenancy at will. A lease for years made by the landlord to a third person has the same effect and it is immaterial that the lease was made for the purpose of putting an immediate end to the tenancy.[52] An assignment by the tenant terminates his estate but, according to the modern view, a sublease by the tenant is effective between the parties thereto.[53]

of occupying former husband's home rent free until parties otherwise mutually agreed).

47. Co.Litt. § 55a.

48. See Foley v. Gamester, 271 Mass. 55, 170 N.E. 799 (1930); Shorter v. Shelton, 183 Va. 819, 33 S.E.2d 643 (1945).

49. See Thompson v. Baxter, 107 Minn. 122, 119 N.W. 797 (1909); Putnam v. Davis, 103 N.H. 121, 166 A.2d 469 (1960); Garner v. Gerrish, 63 N.Y.2d 575, 483 N.Y.S.2d 973, 473 N.E.2d 223

(N.Y.1984). The Restatement is in accord with this position. Restatement (Second) of Property (Landlord and Tenant) § 1.6 cmt. g, Illus. 5, b (1977).

50. Emblements are growing crops, such as corn or beans.

51. Restatement (Second) of Property (Landlord & Tenant), § 1.6 (1977).

52. See Curtis v. Galvin, 83 Mass. (1 Allen) 215 (1861).

53. See Anderson v. Ries, 222 Minn. 408, 24 N.W.2d 717 (1946), 31 Minn.

Because the ability of a tenancy at will to abruptly terminate at either party's will gave economic security to neither landlord nor tenant, statutes in most states require that either party desiring to terminate shall give the other written notice of a specified length of time, usually thirty days or a period equal to the interval between rent days. These statutes have generally been construed as not prescribing an exclusive mode of termination; therefore the estate comes to an end on the death of either party and on conveyance or lease by the landlord.[54] The estate at will even as modified by statute may not be the precise equivalent of a periodic estate.

D. The Tenancy at Sufferance

A tenancy at sufferance is a possessory interest in land which exists when a person who had an estate in land wrongfully continues in possession after the termination of such estate. The difference between a tenant at will and a tenant at sufferance is that the possession of the tenant at will is rightful from the date of entry; the tenant at sufferance is one who takes possession rightly but at some point wrongfully remains in possession.[55] A tenant for the life of another, a periodic tenant, or one for years or at will who wrongfully retains possession after the expiration of his estate becomes a tenant at sufferance. Since the tenant's original entry was rightful, a tenant at sufferance is not liable in an action of trespass until after entry by the landlord.

L.Rev. 620 (1947); Public Service Co. of New Hampshire v. Voudoumas, 84 N.H. 387, 151 A. 81 (1930). *See generally* § 8.

54. *See* Chester A. Baker, Inc. v. Shea Dry Cleaners, Inc., 322 Mass. 311, 77 N.E.2d 223 (1948); Seavey v. Cloudman, 90 Me. 536, 38 A. 540 (1897). *Contra*, Gretkowski v. Wojciechowski, 26 N.J.Super. 245, 97 A.2d 701 (1953) (statutory requirement of notice held to prevent termination of estate on death of landlord). A list of the statutes requiring notice to terminate a tenancy at will is contained in Restatement (Second) of Property (Landlord & Tenant) § 1.6, Statutory Note (1977). In some states the common-law rule that a conveyance by the landlord terminates the tenancy at will is modified by statute. *See, e.g.,* Mass. Gen. Laws Ann. ch. 186, § 13 (West 1991)(tenancy at will of property occupied for dwelling purposes "shall not be terminated by operation of law by the conveyance, transfer or leasing of the premises by the owner or landlord thereof.")

55. "There is a great diversity between a tenant at will and a tenant at sufferance; for tenant at will is always by right; and tenant at sufferance entreth by a lawful lease, and holdeth over by wrong. A tenant at sufferance is he that at the first came in by lawful demise, and after his estate ended continueth in possession and wrongfully holdeth over." Co.Litt. § 57b.

In view of the minimal interest of the tenant at sufferance, why is that interest still included in the catalogue of estates? The main justification seems to be that it lends support to the doctrine that the landlord may at his election convert the tenancy at sufferance of the holdover tenant into a periodic tenancy, or, in some states, into a tenancy for a definite period. In a few jurisdictions the interest of the tenant at sufferance has been enlarged by statutes requiring that the landlord give written notice, usually thirty days, before commencing an action against the tenant to recover possession.[56]

E. Statutory Tenancies

In recent years there has developed a form of tenancy unknown to the common law: a tenancy that, apart from express agreement, is terminable at will by the tenant but is terminable by the landlord only under limited circumstances. For example, a tenant of public housing cannot be evicted except for cause and after the landlord follows a procedure prescribed in the public housing regulations.[57] In effect the tenant has a determinable life estate. Similarly, a tenant who occupies rent control housing may have an estate that is more expansive than the traditional common-law tenancies.[58] Some statutes give the residential tenant the right to continue occupancy despite the termination of the duration of the term specified in the lease.[59] These anomalous modern tenancies may be conveniently grouped under the heading of "Statutory Tenancies."

---

56. *See, e.g.*, Mich.Comp.Laws Ann. § 554.134 (1948); Mass.Gen.Laws Ann. ch. 186, § 13 (West 1991). The Massachusetts statute is restricted to a tenancy at sufferance of residential property resulting from a tenancy at will being determined by operation of law or by act of the landlord other than by the statutory notice to quit. The purpose of the statute is to prevent the landlord from evicting the tenant immediately after he, the landlord, has terminated the tenancy at will by leasing to a third person.

57. *See, e.g.*, Spence v. Reeder, 382 Mass. 398, 416 N.E.2d 914 (1981); Joy v. Daniels, 479 F.2d 1236 (4th Cir.1973).

58. *See* Gentile v. Rent Control Bd. of Somerville, 365 Mass. 343, 312 N.E.2d 210 (1974); Guerriera v. Joy, 64 N.Y.2d 747, 485 N.Y.S.2d 979, 475 N.E.2d 446 (N.Y.1984).

59. N.J. Stat. Ann. 2A:18–61.1 (West Supp. 1986). For a comparable development in French Law giving the tenant security of tenure, *see* Note, Landlord and Tenant in French Law; A Recent Statute, 3 Oxford J. of Legal Studies, 425 (1983).

§ 3. Obligations of the Landlord—The Common–Law View

Because a lease is both a conveyance and a contract, the obligations of the parties to a lease are a product of both property and contract law. The common law itself imposed few duties on the landlord. At common law, the landlord had the obligation to give the tenant a legal right to possession (and in some jurisdictions actual possession itself).[1] In addition, landlord impliedly promised (according to the prevailing view) that the tenant would have "quiet enjoyment" of the leased premises. This promise meant that the tenant's possession would be free from interference by the landlord, or by third persons acting under the landlord's authority, or by the holder of a paramount title. In other words, landlord's principal obligation was to assure the tenant a right to possession and then to leave the tenant alone. Landlord did not, apart from a few exceptions, impliedly warrant that the premises were fit for their intended use. Furthermore, under the traditional law the landlord had no duty to maintain the premises in a fit condition for their intended use,[2] unless the landlord expressly promised to do so. In brief, until the late twentieth century the common law gave little protection to the tenant whether the tenancy was residential or commercial, inviting the quip that at common law the tenant had but one right—the right to pay rent. The governing rule was that of caveat emptor.[3]

§ 3

1. § 2A *supra.*

2. A nineteenth century English judge could blandly assert: "Fraud apart, there is no law against letting a tumble down house * * *." Robbins v. Jones, 15 C.B.(N.S.) 221, 240, 143 Eng. Rep. 768, 776 (1863). And his American counterpart would agree. *See* Royce v. Guggenheim, 106 Mass. 201, 202–203 (1870); Daly v. Wise, 132 N.Y. 306, 30 N.E. 837 (1892). An exception existed in the case of a lease of a furnished dwelling for a short period of time. *See* Ingalls v. Hobbs, 156 Mass. 348, 31 N.E. 286 (1892). But this exception applied only with respect to the condition of the

premises at the beginning of the tenancy and did not cover defects which arose later. *See* Davenport v. Squibb, 320 Mass. 629, 70 N.E.2d 793 (1947). For a discussion of the recognized exceptions, *see* Borders v. Roseberry, 216 Kan. 486, 532 P.2d 1366 (1975).

3. "It is well settled that there is no implied covenant in a lease of this kind [lease of a dwelling house] that the premises are fit for habitation. The doctrine *caveat emptor* applies, and the rule is the same in reference to a lease of a dwelling house as to a conveyance of real estate of any other kind." Stevens v. Pierce, 151 Mass. 207, 209, 23 N.E. 1006 (1890).

It was, therefore, of paramount importance for the parties to a lease, especially the tenant, to have the agreement expressly state the respective rights and obligations of each party. Inevitably, over the course of time, as the nature of rental property and the needs and expectations of lessor and lessee changed, leases became more complex. In a modern lease of space in an office building, for example, there will be numerous covenants spelling out the obligations of the landlord and tenant. The lessor may promise to furnish heat, light, air conditioning, elevator service, janitorial service, repairs, window cleaning, and, perhaps, parking facilities. Landlord will normally reserve the right to terminate the lease in the event of the tenant's default in payment of the agreed rent, as well as in the event of the tenant's breach of any of the other lease covenants and conditions to be observed by tenant. The lease will normally define the rights of the parties in the event of accidental destruction of, or damage to, the premises, e.g. by fire; and it will specify the effect on the lease of a taking by eminent domain. In addition to covenanting to pay the specified rent, the tenant may agree to use the premises only for the stated purpose and, moreover, may covenant not to use any part of the building "for any purpose reasonably objectionable to the landlord."[4] Tenant will usually covenant not to assign or sublet the lease without the landlord's consent and will undertake to surrender the premises at the end of the term in good condition, apart from normal wear and tear. Thus, the modern lease is a highly complex transaction in which the contractual element is a substantial, if not the predominant, component.

Yet courts until the late twentieth century refused to apply modern principles of contract law to leases. The law as applied to leases has been to a large extent "a matter of history that has not forgotten Lord Coke."[5] Thus, the principle of the mutual dependen-

4. See Cooley v. Bettigole, 1 Mass. App.Ct. 515, 301 N.E.2d 872 (1973).

5. Gardiner v. William S. Butler & Co., 245 U.S. 603, 605, 38 S.Ct. 214, 62 L.Ed. 505 (1918). Lord Coke (1552–1634) deserves more than a footnote in any property book. Sir Edward (commonly called Lord Coke but actually not

a lord) was successively Solicitor–General, Attorney–General, Chief Justice of the Common Pleas, Chief Justice of the King's Bench, and parliamentary leader. Master of the common law and expert on the Year Books, his famous work on Real Property (Coke on Littleton) is still the authoritative exposition of post-feu-

cy of promises that is normally applicable to bilateral contracts was not historically applied to leases.[6] For example, if the lessor covenants in a lease of non-residential property to make repairs, a breach of this covenant will not ordinarily relieve the tenant of the obligation to pay rent, although it will give rise to a cause of action for breach of contract.[7] Similarly, a breach by the lessee of the covenant to pay rent or a breach of any other covenant in the lease will not give the lessor the right to terminate the lease in the absence of a statutory provision, or of a clause in the lease, conferring such right.[8]

An exception to the rule of the independency of lease covenants in leases was made in cases of wrongful eviction of the tenant by the landlord. The unfairness of allowing the landlord to collect rent after wrongfully ousting the tenant impelled the courts to resort to the contract doctrine of failure of consideration.[9] An actual eviction takes place when the landlord wrongfully deprives the tenant of

dal land law. On his death his widow, after thirty-six years of stormy married life, wrote: "We shall never see his like again, praises be to God." The thousands of law students in America who, until the middle 1800s, were forced to master the technicalities of Coke on Littleton, were inclined to agree. For a full scale treatment, see Bowen, The Lion and the Throne (1956).

6. One of the reasons assigned for the independency of covenants in leases is that the law as to leases had become settled before the doctrine of the mutual dependency of promises in bilateral contracts had evolved in the late eighteenth century. See 6 S. Williston, Contracts § 890 (3d ed. 1962). Moreover, since a lease operated to give the lessee an estate in the land he was viewed as having received the principal thing bargained for, with the covenants being treated as ancillary or incidental. See 1 ALP, § 3.11.

7. See Stone v. Sullivan, 300 Mass. 450, 15 N.E.2d 476 (1938); Stewart v. Childs Co., 86 N.J.L. 648, 92 A. 392 (1914); Graham Hotel Co. v. Garrett, 33

S.W.2d 522 (Tex.Civ.App.1930). It is possible, of course, that a serious breach of the landlord of his assumed duty to make repairs may enable the tenant to avail himself of the defense of constructive eviction. See Reste Realty Corp. v. Cooper, 53 N.J. 444, 251 A.2d 268 (1969).

8. tenBraak v. Waffle Shops, Inc., 542 F.2d 919 (4th Cir.1976); Brown's Adm'rs. v. Bragg, 22 Ind. 122 (1864). In most jurisdictions at the present time there are statutes allowing the landlord to terminate the lease for non-payment of the reserved rent. For a list of these statutes, see Restatement (Second) of Property (Landlord and Tenant) § 12.1, Statutory Note (1977).

9. See Morse v. Goddard, 54 Mass. (13 Metc.) 177 (1847); Fifth Avenue Building Co. v. Kernochan, 221 N.Y. 370, 117 N.E. 579 (1917). Corbin points out that the rule as to the effect of an eviction "gave the courts an opportunity to infiltrate the law of contracts into the law of landlord and tenant." 3A Corbin, Contracts § 686 (1960).

possession of the whole or a part of the leased premises. If the eviction is total the lessee's obligation to pay rent is suspended during the period the tenant is deprived of possession. Tenant may sue to recover possession or may treat the lease as terminated and sue for damages for breach of the lessor's covenant of quiet enjoyment. If the eviction is partial only, tenant may continue in possession of the remainder of the premises without liability to pay any rent for use and occupation although tenant is still bound by any other covenants of the lease.[10] Where the partial eviction is not by act of the landlord but by paramount title (a title in a third person superior to that of the landlord) the rent is apportioned and the tenant is liable for the fair rental value of the retained land.

The defense of eviction as a remedy available to a tenant was enormously expanded when in the early nineteenth century the courts developed the doctrine of "constructive" eviction.[11] A constructive eviction occurs when the landlord by conduct of omission or co-mission and in contravention of an express or implied provision of the lease substantially deprives the tenant of the beneficial use and enjoyment of the premises. It is irrelevant that there is no ouster by the landlord. The landlord's conduct is deemed to be equivalent to depriving the tenant of physical possession.[12]

10. One reason assigned for the suspension of the entire rent is that the landlord may not apportion his own wrong. Smith v. McEnany, 170 Mass. 26, 48 N.E. 781 (1897). The court in this case also suggested that the rule may be partly due to the ancient common law view of rent as something issuing out of the land and charged on every part of the land. The Restatement rejects the rule totally abrogating the tenant's obligation to pay rent in the case of a partial eviction. Restatement (Second) of Property (Landlord and Tenant) § 6.1 cmt. h (1977). For a helpful explanation of the common-law concept of rent, see Humbach, The Common Law Conception of Leasing: Mitigation, Habitability and Dependence of Covenants, 60 Wash. U.L.Q. 1213, 1226–1233 (1983).

11. See Dyett v. Pendleton, 8 Cow. 727 (N.Y.1826).

12. The older cases frequently stated that in order to establish a constructive eviction the tenant must show that the conduct of the landlord which deprived the tenant of the beneficial use of the premises was "intentional". See, e.g., Hopkins v. Murphy, 233 Mass. 476, 124 N.E. 252 (1919). But modern courts hold that the actual intention of the landlord is immaterial if his acts of commission or omission have the effect of depriving the tenant of the beneficial use and enjoyment of the premises. See Blackett v. Olanoff, 371 Mass. 714, 358 N.E.2d 817 (1977).

Where all of the elements of a constructive eviction have been met, the tenant may terminate the lease and extinguish his liability for future rent. Tenant may also recover damages for the landlord's breach of the covenant of quiet enjoyment. Moreover, tenant may obtain equitable relief by way of injunction or specific performance.[13]

In order to take advantage of the defense of constructive eviction, the landlord must have either by an act or by an omission failed to perform some duty that landlord was otherwise obligated to perform (such as the duty to make repairs). Furthermore, as a result of such failure tenant must be substantially deprived of the use and enjoyment of the property. Additionally, the tenant must (1) give notice to the landlord of the condition that substantially interferes with tenant's use and enjoyment of the premises, (2) provide the landlord with a reasonable opportunity to correct the problem, and (3) if not corrected, surrender possession of the property within a reasonable time after the wrongful act, or omission to act, of the landlord.[14]

A typical case of constructive eviction arises from the failure of the lessor to furnish heat or other similarly important services in breach of a covenant by the landlord in the lease to provide such services and the tenant's removal from the premises because of such breach following notice to landlord and landlord's failure to correct the breach within a reasonable time period.[15]

13. *See* Charles E. Burt, Inc. v. Seven Grand Corp., 340 Mass. 124, 163 N.E.2d 4 (1959)(allowing tenant to obtain a declaratory judgment that landlord's omissions were of sufficient consequence that if tenant removed from the premises tenant could defend landlord's action for rent by claiming a constructive eviction.).

14. What is a reasonable time is usually a question of fact. *See* The Automobile Supply Co. v. The Scene–In–Action Corp., 340 Ill. 196, 172 N.E. 35, 69 A.L.R. 1085 (1930); Westland Housing Corp. v. Scott, 312 Mass. 375, 44 N.E.2d 959 (1942). Abandonment is essential to provide evidence of the "substantiality"

of the landlord's interference with tenant's use and enjoyment.

15. *See* The Automobile Supply Co. v. The Scene–In–Action Corp., n. 14; Charles E. Burt, Inc. v. Seven Grand Corp., note 13, *supra*. For an interesting case involving the distinction between an actual eviction and a constructive eviction, *see* Barash v. Pennsylvania Terminal Real Estate Corp., 26 N.Y.2d 77, 308 N.Y.S.2d 649, 256 N.E.2d 707 (1970) (failure of landlord to carry out agreement to supply a continuous flow of fresh air to law office in 29 story office tower with sealed windows, during evenings and weekends).

The doctrine of constructive eviction has served as a bridge in modern times to the acceptance of the mutual dependence of covenants in leases. The courts usually speak in terms of "constructive eviction" (the language of property law) but in reality they are applying contract principles of dependency of performance.[16] Some decisions expressly state that those promises in the lease which go to the "whole consideration" of the lease, if not performed, will excuse performance by the other party.[17] The trend appears to be toward an open recognition of the doctrine of mutual dependency of promises where the promised performance was viewed by the parties as an essential or, at least, a significantly important part of the agreement.[18]

§ 4. Obligations of the Landlord—The Modern View

A. *The Residential Tenancy*

Since the 1970s, there have been significant changes in the obligations of landlord of residential tenancies. The old common-law rules that had their source in a rural agricultural society were found to be unsuited to an urban society faced with a critical housing shortage. Courts and legislatures came to recognize that a long term lease of farm land and a short term lease of an apartment in a high rise building in a city should not be forced into the same legal mold. Furthermore, to require a tenant to vacate premises in

---

16. For a helpful discussion of this topic, *see* Hicks, The Contractual Nature of Real Property Leases, 24 Baylor L.Rev. 443 (1972). The author asserts: "One can find ten constructive eviction cases for every one relying on the theory of mutually dependent covenants." *Id.* at 461.

17. *See, e.g.,* Medico–Dental Building Co. of Los Angeles v. Horton & Converse, 21 Cal.2d 411, 132 P.2d 457 (1942) (covenant by lessor against competition); University Club of Chicago v. Deakin, 265 Ill. 257, 106 N.E. 790 (1914) (covenant by lessor against competition); Ringwood Associates Ltd. v. Jack's of Route 23, Inc., 166 N.J.Super. 36, 398 A.2d 1315 (1979) (unreasonable refusal of lessor to assent to assignment or sublease by lessee).

18. *See* the cases cited in note 17, *supra.* The Restatement adopts the view of the dependence of promises in leases whether the promise was made by the landlord or by the tenant, when the promise was "a significant inducement" to the other party to enter into the lease. Restatement (Second) of Property (Landlord and Tenant) §§ 7.1, 13.1 (1977). For a thorough critique of the application of the dependency doctrine to leases, *see* Humbach, The Common Law Conception of Leasing: Mitigation, Habitability, and Dependence of Covenants, 60 Wash.U.L.Q. 1213, 1271–1287 (1983).

order to claim a constructive eviction where there may be little or no alternative habitable housing appears draconian. To meet the needs of modern residential tenants courts fashioned new doctrines and legislatures provided new remedies.[1]

The principal change has been the abandonment of the classic common-law rule that the landlord owes the tenant no duty to put the premises in a habitable condition at the beginning of the tenancy and no duty to maintain the premises in a condition fit for habitation during the tenancy. The courts have substituted an implied warranty of habitability that results in a duty on the part of the landlord to put and maintain the residential unit in a condition that meets the standards set out in the relevant state and municipal housing codes or sanitary regulations, or that makes the premises fit and habitable. The leading case of *Javins v. First National Realty Corp.*[2] not only repudiated the old common-law rule of *caveat emptor* in the residential landlord-tenant field but broke new ground in allowing the tenant to set up the breach of the warranty of habitability as a defense to the landlord's action to evict the tenant for non-payment of rent.

Although *Javins* was not the first case to announce the rule of an implied warranty of habitability in residential tenancies,[3] it was influential in persuading other courts to adopt the concept. Courts in numerous other states have also held that a landlord impliedly warrants that the housing unit let to the tenant is in habitable condition at the inception of the tenancy and will be maintained in

§ 4

1. For an excellent over-view of the revolution in residential landlord-tenant law, *see* Glendon, The Transformation of American Landlord–Tenant Law, 23 B.C.L.Rev. 503 (1982).

2. 428 F.2d 1071 (D.C.Cir.1970), *cert. denied*, 400 U.S. 925, 91 S.Ct. 186, 27 L.Ed.2d 185 (1970).

3. Both Minnesota and Wisconsin had earlier recognized an implied warranty of habitability. *See, e.g.,* Delamater v. Foreman, 184 Minn. 428, 239 N.W. 148 (1931); Pines v. Perssion, 14 Wis.2d 590, 111 N.W.2d 409 (1961). The *Pines* holding was later undermined by Posnanski v. Hood, 46 Wis.2d 172, 174 N.W.2d 528 (1970). Furthermore, even in the District of Columbia where the facts of Javins occurred, the D.C. Court of Appeals had held that a lease of premises that were uninhabitable as of the first day of the lease was an illegal lease where the local housing code stated that leases of premises in violation of the Code were illegal. *See* Brown v. Southall Realty Corp., 237 A.2d 834 (D.C.Ct.App. 1968).

that condition throughout the tenancy.[4] Moreover, many states have enacted comprehensive statutes in the area, many of them based on the Uniform Residential Landlord and Tenant Act.[5] Other states, while not enacting comprehensive codes, have passed statutes requiring landlords to maintain rented premises in a habitable condition. Overall, by judicial decision or by statute the overwhelming majority of states have abandoned the traditional common-law attitude of *laissez-faire* in residential tenancies and substituted a policy requiring landlords to maintain the residential premises in a "habitable" condition.[6]

In the absence of clarifying legislation, a question may arise as to the kind of residential property to which the implied warranty is applicable.[7] Does the warranty apply to all rented residential prop-

4. *See, e.g.*, Green v. Superior Court of San Francisco, 10 Cal.3d 616, 111 Cal.Rptr. 704, 517 P.2d 1168 (1974); Lemle v. Breeden, 51 Hawai'i 426, 462 P.2d 470 (1969); Jack Spring Inc. v. Little, 50 Ill.2d 351, 280 N.E.2d 208 (1972); Mease v. Fox, 200 N.W.2d 791 (Iowa 1972); Steele v. Latimer, 214 Kan. 329, 521 P.2d 304 (1974); Boston Housing Auth. v. Hemingway, 363 Mass. 184, 293 N.E.2d 831 (1973); Kline v. Burns, 111 N.H. 87, 276 A.2d 248 (1971); Marini v. Ireland, 56 N.J. 130, 265 A.2d 526 (1970); Pugh v. Holmes, 486 Pa. 272, 405 A.2d 897 (1979); Kamarath v. Bennett, 568 S.W.2d 658 (Tex.1978); Birkenhead v. Coombs, 143 Vt. 167, 465 A.2d 244 (1983); Foisy v. Wyman, 83 Wash.2d 22, 515 P.2d 160 (1973); Teller v. McCoy, 162 W.Va. 367, 253 S.E.2d 114 (1978). *See also* Tonetti v. Penati, 48 A.D.2d 25, 367 N.Y.S.2d 804 (2d Dept. 1975).

5. For a list of these statutes, *see Glendon, supra* note 1 at 523, n. 134. For a thorough survey and analysis of recent housing legislation, *see* Cunningham, The New Implied and Statutory Warranties of Habitability in Residential Leases: From Contract to Status, 16 Urb.L.Ann. 3 (1979). The Uniform Residential Landlord and Tenant Act (URL-

TA) was published in final form in 1972 and is a comprehensive housing code. For its text, *see* 7A U.L.Ann. 503–559 (1978).

6. Although the *Javins* court and others which have embraced the concept of implied warranty purport to base it on contract law and reject the notion of a lease as primarily a conveyance, Professor Glendon correctly points out that the concept "does not belong to the domain of contract but to that of regulation." *Glendon, supra* note 1 at 548. And, the view that the independence of promises in leases was a consequence of treating the lease as a conveyance rather than a contract has been vigorously disputed. *See* McGovern, Dependent Promises in the History of Leases and Other Contracts, 52 Tul.L.Rev. 659, 679 (1978). Professor McGovern states: "Rarely has a proposition about legal history been so often asserted with so little evidence to support it. If medieval lawyers regarded a lease as a conveyance rather than a contract, they never said so." *Id.* at 679.

7. For a helpful discussion of the scope of the implied warranty, *see* Stoebuck and Whitman, The Law of Property § 6.38, 3rd ed. (2000); H. Hovenkamp

erty or only to property containing multiple apartments? Most courts have given a broad scope to the warranty and hold that it applies to all rented housing, whether part of a multiple family building or a single family residence.[8]

The courts are not wholly in agreement as to the scope of the warranty in relation to relevant housing codes. They are in accord that the implied warranty is at least co-extensive with the pertinent health and housing codes and that a substantial failure to comply with those codes is a breach of the landlord's obligation as to fitness for occupancy.[9] But the language of some of the cases indicates that the court would find a breach of the warranty even in the absence of a code violation where in fact the premises are unfit for human occupancy.[10] The warranty covers not only the physical condition of the premises but also includes "facilities vital to the use of the premises for residential purposes" and requires "that these essential facilities will remain during the entire term in a condition which makes the property livable."[11]

The landlord also has obligations with respect to the condition of so-called common areas of the premises (entry ways, hallways, stairways, elevators and other areas available to the tenants of a multi-unit building) retained in the control of the landlord. Most

& S. Kurtz, The Law of Property, § 9.8 (2001).

8. See, e.g., Javins v. First National Realty Corp., supra note 2; Boston Housing Auth. v. Hemingway, supra note 4; Mease v. Fox, 200 N.W.2d 791 (Iowa 1972)(applicable to single family home); Restatement (Second) of Property (Landlord & Tenant) § 5.5(1) (1977). But in Kline v. Burns, supra note 4, the New Hampshire court seems to limit the warranty to rental of "an apartment as a dwelling unit." Id. at 92, 276 A.2d at 251.

9. See Winchester Management Corp. v. Staten, 361 A.2d 187 (D.C.App. 1976); Restatement (Second) of Property (Landlord & Tenant) § 5.5(1) (1977).

10. Green v. Superior Court of City and County of San Francisco, 10 Cal.3d 616, 111 Cal.Rptr. 704, 517 P.2d 1168

(1974); Boston Housing Auth. v. Hemingway, 363 Mass. 184, 293 N.E.2d 831 (1973); Marini v. Ireland, 56 N.J. 130, 265 A.2d 526 (1970).

11. Boston Housing Auth. v. Hemingway, 363 Mass. 184, 199, 293 N.E.2d 831 (1973); Kline v. Burns, 111 N.H. 87, 92, 276 A.2d 248, 252 (1971). "Essential" facilities would usually include, e.g., heat, hot water, electricity, and elevator service in a high rise apartment building. In Trentacost v. Brussel, 82 N.J. 214, 412 A.2d 436 (1980) the court held that the implied warranty of habitability obligates the landlord to furnish reasonable safeguards to protect the tenants from foreseeable criminal activity on the leased premises and common areas.

courts hold that the landlord has a common-law duty to exercise reasonable care to maintain common areas in a reasonably safe condition for the use of the tenant, his family, and persons using the areas in right of the tenant.[12] This duty extends to common areas in both residential and business premises.[13]

Under the implied warranty of habitability, the tenant has numerous remedies to remedy a landlord's breach. Where the landlord fails to maintain the premises in a "habitable" condition and the breach is a material one, the tenant can terminate or rescind the rental agreement, sue for damages, and assert a right to an abatement of the rent. Tenant's right to terminate the lease, when not based on statute, is said to rest on the ground that the implied agreement of the landlord to maintain the premises in habitable condition and the tenant's promise to pay rent are mutually dependent and, therefore, failure of the landlord to perform excuses performance by the tenant.[14] As with constructive eviction, in order to exercise the remedy of lease termination the

---

12. Restatement (Second) of Property (Landlord & Tenant) § 17.3 (1977). In the Reporter's Note to this section it is stated that the rule holding the landlord accountable for dangerous conditions in a common area which he knows about or could have discovered by the exercise of reasonable care "is supported by the great weight of authority." § 17.3 at 200. A minority of jurisdictions applied the so-called Massachusetts rule which held that the duty of the landlord was only to use reasonable care to maintain the common areas in as good condition as they were in, or appeared to be in, at the beginning of the particular tenancy. McCarthy v. Isenberg Brothers, Inc., 321 Mass. 170, 72 N.E.2d 422 (1947). This peculiar Massachusetts view was abandoned in King v. G. & M. Realty Corp., 373 Mass. 658, 370 N.E.2d 413 (1977) and the Restatement rule was adopted.

13. The issue of the landlord's duties with respect to common areas usually arises in the context of a tort action for personal injuries suffered by the tenant or others due to the defective condition of a common area. For a thorough analysis, see Browder, The Taming of a Duty—The Tort Liability of Landlords, 81 Mich.L.Rev. 99 (1982). See generally Prosser and Keeton, The Law of Torts (5th ed. 1984).

14. The *Javins* case and the other cases cited *supra* note 4 adopt this view. See also Restatement (Second) of Property (Landlord & Tenant) §§ 5.4(1), 5.5(1)(4), 10.1) (1977). The Uniform Residential Landlord and Tenant Act § 4.101(a) spells out in detail the procedure for termination. The courts, in fashioning remedies for the tenant, purport to apply principles of contract law; whether they have done so consistently with normal contract rules is a matter of dispute. See Humbach, The Common Law Conception of Leasing: Mitigation, Habitability, and Dependence of Covenants, 60 Wash.U.L.Q. 1213 (1983); Abbot, Housing Policy, Housing Codes, and Tenant Remedies: An Integration, 56 B.U.L.Rev. 1 (1976).

tenant must vacate the premises after notice to the landlord of tenant's intention to do so. On vacating, tenant ceases to be liable for future rent. Tenant will, however, be liable for the fair rental value of the premises in their defective condition during any past period of occupancy[15] and may be entitled to collect damages for the period of his occupancy while the premises were not habitable. Some courts hold that for breach of the implied warranty, tenant may also seek specific performance or repair the property and then deduct the cost of the repair from future rent.[16]

Because of a local housing shortage, the tenant as a practical matter may well find it preferable to forego the right to terminate the tenancy, despite violations of the sanitary or housing code, and to assert a right to an abatement of the rent. Statutes imposing a duty on the landlord to maintain residential premises in a habitable condition usually do not expressly provide for rent abatement or reduction in the event of breach by the landlord but authorize the tenant to assert the breach as a defense in recoupment or as a counterclaim when sued for rent or eviction by the landlord.[17] Apart from statute, the courts have implemented the warranty of habitability by allowing the tenant to use a breach of the warranty defensively when sued by the landlord for rent or for possession of the premises on the ground of non-payment of rent.[18] The end result is tantamount to the tenant being able to withhold rent for breaches of the warranty. It also gives the tenant an abatement of the rent in almost all cases since the tenant is obligated only to pay

15. *See, e.g.*, Boston Housing Auth. v. Hemingway, 363 Mass. 184, 201, 293 N.E.2d 831, 844 (1973).

16. *See, e.g.*, Pugh v. Holmes, *supra* note 4. The "repair and deduct" remedy is of little utility to tenants faced with high cost repairs.

17. *See, e.g.*, Uniform Residential Landlord and Tenant Act § 4.105(a). Some statutes provide that on petition of the tenant alleging code violations the court may authorize the tenant to pay into court "the fair value of the use and occupation of the premises." Mass. Gen. Laws Ann. ch. 111, §§ 127C, 127F, 127H

(West 1996); *cf.* N.Y. Real Prop., Acts. Law Art. 7–A (McKinney 1979) (authorizing court to allow rent withholding). Mass. Gen. Laws Ann. ch. 239, § 8A (West 1988)(impliedly authorizes the tenant to withhold rent in case of sanitary code violation even without prior court authorization).

18. *See* Green v. Superior Court, Javins v. First National Realty Corp., Jack Spring, Inc. v. Little, *supra* note 4. Berman & Sons, Inc. v. Jefferson, 379 Mass. 196, 396 N.E.2d 981 (1979).

the fair rental value of the premises in its "uninhabitable condition."[19]

When the tenant seeks to recover damages for breach of the warranty of habitability (or a rent reduction equal to the damages) the courts have used different formulas for measuring the damages. One common formula is to calculate damages as the difference between the promised rent and the property's fair rental value in its uninhabitable condition. Another formula (which presupposes that the tenant made a good bargain by promising to pay rent for habitable premises at a bargain price) calculates damages as the difference between the property's as warranted value and its fair market value in its uninhabitable condition.[20] Other courts adopt a formula by which the agreed rent is reduced by a percentage equal to the total diminution of use and enjoyment by reason of the breach of warranty.[21]

In a few states statutes expressly authorize the court to appoint a receiver, on petition of the tenants of the non-complying premises, to take control of the property, collect the rents and make necessary repairs.[22] These statutes may amplify the courts' normal equity jurisdiction.[23]

19. In Berman & Sons, Inc. v. Jefferson, *supra* note 17, the court said: "We hold that the tenant's obligation abates as soon as the landlord has notice that premises fail to comply with the requirements of the warranty of habitability. The landlord's lack of fault and reasonable efforts to repair do not prolong the duty to pay full rent." 379 Mass. at 198, 396 N.E.2d at 983.

20. *See* Mease v. Fox, *supra* note 8. This measure is applicable only if the tenant remains in possession. If tenant vacates the premises, then damages are limited to the difference between the "as warranted value" and the lower "promised rent."

21. *See, e.g.,* Pugh v. Holmes, supra note 4; McKenna v. Begin, 5 Mass.App. Ct. 304, 362 N.E.2d 548 (1977); Academy Spires Inc. v. Brown, 111 N.J.Super. 477, 268 A.2d 556 (1970); Park West Management Corp. v. Mitchell, 47

N.Y.2d 316, 418 N.Y.S.2d 310, 391 N.E.2d 1288 (1979). *Compare* Boston Housing Auth. v. Hemingway, 363 Mass. 184, 203, 293 N.E.2d 831, 845 (1973) ("The measure of damages (for breach of warranty) would be the difference between the value of each apartment as warranted and the rental value of each apartment in its defective condition.") The Restatement adopts the "proportional value" rule but concedes that it may not be the majority rule. Restatement (Second)of Property (Landlord & Tenant) § 11.1 and Reporter's Note to the Section, p. 361 (1977). For a helpful discussion of the various formulas, *see* Stoebuck & Whitman, The Law of Property, 3rd Ed. (2000) at 319–325; Hovenkamp & Kurtz, The Law of Property, 5th ed. (2000) at 291.

22. *See, e.g.,* Conn. Gen. Stat. Ann. §§ 47a–14a-g (West 1994); Mass. Gen. Laws Ann. ch. 111, §§ 127I (West 1996).

In many states, tenants who either successfully assert an implied warranty defense or complain to local housing authorities about unhabitable premises can be protected from retaliation by their landlords by use of the retaliatory eviction defense. For example, suppose T is a month-to-month tenant who successfully defended a rent action on the grounds that the premises were unhabitable. If L later serves T with a notice to terminate the month-to-month tenant and then sues T for possession, T might defend on the grounds that L's motive in terminating the tenancy was to retaliate against T for T's prior successful defense.[24] If T can establish such a retaliatory motive, the notice of termination is deemed invalid and the tenancy continues.

B. The Commercial Tenancy

In contrast to the protected position of the residential tenant under modern law, the commercial tenant's rights remain substantially the same as at common law. Generally the commercial tenant takes the premises in the condition in which they actually exist at the commencement of the tenancy and the law will not imply a warranty that they are fit for the intended use.[25] Most courts have

23. In Perez v. Boston Housing Auth., 379 Mass. 703, 400 N.E.2d 1231 (1980) the court upheld the appointment of a temporary receiver to take over the functions of the statutory board of managers of the Boston Housing Authority and to assume control of the management of all the housing units, numbering over 15,000, owned and operated by the Authority. The trial judge found rampant and appalling violations of the state sanitary code and incompetent management on the part of the board members. The court found both a statutory and equitable basis for the appointment of the receiver.

24. See, e.g, Robinson v. Diamond Housing Corp., 463 F.2d 853 (D.C.Cir. 1972).

25. An exception has been recognized when the lease is one of space in a building under construction or alteration and the lease restricts the lessee to a specified use. Woolford v. Electric Appliances, Inc., 24 Cal.App.2d 385, 75 P.2d 112 (1938); J. D. Young Corp. v. McClintic, 26 S.W.2d 460 (Tex.Civ.App. 1930). Moreover, a landlord is under a duty to disclose to the tenant "latent" defects in the premises of which he is, or reasonably should be, aware. A latent defect is one not discoverable on a reasonable inspection. A landlord is liable for a personal injury sustained because of such defect by the tenant or by a person on the premises in his right. See Prosser and Keeton, The Law of Torts § 63 (5th ed. 1984). Restatement (Second) of Property (Landlord & Tenant) § 17.1 (1977). As to the so-called "public use" exception, see Restatement (Second) of Property (Landlord & Tenant)

refused to expand the concept of implied warranty of habitability so as to include an implied warranty of fitness for use in the case of a lease of property for business purposes.[26] The public policy considerations that led progressive courts to expand the rights of the residential tenant were not found to be applicable to leases of commercial or business properties. The commercial tenant has been left to protect his interests by such express covenants as he can negotiate in an arms length business deal with the landlord. Not only does he take the premises as he finds them (subject to the few recognized exceptions) but the landlord is under no duty, apart from express agreement, to maintain the premises in a condition suitable for use by the tenant.

The breach of an express covenant by the landlord will, of course, give the tenant an action for damages. Furthermore, constructive eviction may afford the tenant the right to terminate the lease.[27] Moreover, the growing trend toward abandoning the doctrine of the independence of lease covenants even in commercial leases may enlarge the remedies of the tenant so as to include rent abatement on breach by the landlord.[28]

§ 17.2 (1977) (landlord who leases property for purpose involving admission of public is liable for injuries to person injured by defect in premises existing when tenancy began).

26. Buker v. National Management Corp., 16 Mass.App.Ct. 36, 448 N.E.2d 1299 (1983); Cameron v. Calhoun–Smith Distributing Co., 442 S.W.2d 815 (Tex. Civ.App.1969). *But cf.* Reste Realty Corp. v. Cooper, 53 N.J. 444, 251 A.2d 268 (1969); Earl Milliken, Inc. v. Allen, 21 Wis.2d 497, 124 N.W.2d 651 (1963).

27. *See* § 3 *supra*, notes 16 & 17 and accompanying text, *supra*, for a discussion of constructive eviction.

28. *See, e.g.*, Teodori v. Werner, 490 Pa. 58, 415 A.2d 31 (1980) (commercial tenant entitled to rent abatement on breach by landlord of non-competition promise in lease); Restatement (Second) of Property (Landlord & Tenant) §§ 5.5(3)(4), 5.4, 7.1 (1977)(defining remedies available to tenant on land-

lord's breach of a promise which was a "significant inducement to the making of the lease").

A covenant by the landlord to make "all outside repairs" has been construed as an implied agreement to indemnify the lessee against loss sustained by him as a result of a breach by the landlord. Great Atlantic & Pacific Tea Co., Inc. v. Yanofsky, 380 Mass. 326, 403 N.E.2d 370 (1980) (landlord required to indemnify tenant for amount of settlement paid to customer of lessee who sustained personal injury as a result of landlord's failure to make promised outside repairs).

Even though a landlord has not promised in the lease to make repairs to the premises, he may be liable by statute in tort for personal injuries suffered by the tenant, or a third person, as a result of an unsafe condition of the premises where the tenant has given him written

Strict adherence to common-law rules may be changing even here. In *Davidow v. Inwood North Professional Group–Phase I*[29] the court held that a commercial lease contained an implied warranty by the landlord that the premises were suitable for their intended purposes. The court refused to treat landlord's duty to repair and tenant's obligation to pay rent as independent lease covenants reasoning that the policies favoring implied warranties in residential leases have equal force in many commercial tenancies.

§ 5. Obligations of the Tenant

Apart from obligations based on any express promises contained in the lease, including the obligation to pay rent, the common law imposed few duties on the tenant. The principal legal obligation of the tenant, whether the tenancy was one of a residential, agricultural or commercial nature, was to abstain from the commission of "waste." The somewhat nebulous concept of waste required the tenant to refrain from conduct in the use and enjoyment of the premises that was injurious to the landlord's reversionary interest. Waste can be either voluntary or permissive. Voluntary waste consists of affirmative action by the tenant resulting in injury to the property, or an impermissible substantial alteration of the property. Permissive waste consists of neglect by the tenant of a duty imposed by law with respect to the property, such as a duty to make minor repairs. The traditional common-law view was that the tenant for years had a rather vague obligation to preserve structures on the land from deteriorating due to the elements when this could be done by the making of "ordinary" repairs.[1] Tenants at will were not subject to such an obligation.[2] However, the doctrine

notice of the condition. *See* Mass. Gen. Laws Ann. ch. 186, § 19 (West 1991).

29. 747 S.W.2d 373 (Tex.1988).

§ 5

1. *See* Suydam v. Jackson, 54 N.Y. 450, 454 (1873) (lessee under implied obligation to repair a leaking roof over one story extension of building; duty extends to "ordinary repairs").

2. "While a tenant at will impliedly agrees to use the premises in a tenant-like manner, he is not liable for a mere omission or failure to act. He is liable for voluntary, but not for permissive waste." Means v. Cotton, 225 Mass. 313 at 319, 114 N.E. 361 at 363 (1916). In Gade v. National Creamery Co., 324 Mass. 515, 87 N.E.2d 180 (1949) a commercial tenant at will was held liable for voluntary waste in overloading the floor of a store room so as to cause its collapse.

of permissive waste no longer seems applicable to residential tenants in view of the landlord's obligation, flowing from the implied warranty of habitability, to maintain the premises in a condition fit for use. Commercial tenants, by contrast, would seem to continue to be subject to a duty to refrain from permissive waste, although in practice the obligations of such a tenant with respect to making repairs are usually spelled out in the lease.

The subject of voluntary waste may become an important issue when a commercial tenant holding under a long-term lease undertakes to make major alterations to the leased premises and the tenant's right to do so is not defined by the terms of the lease. If the effect of the alteration is to diminish the value of the landlord's reversionary interest, the tenant's conduct amounts to waste and the landlord is entitled to injunctive relief and damages.[3] But when the effect of the change is to increase the economic value of the property (so-called ameliorating waste) despite a radical alteration of the premises, such as the demolition of an old building and its replacement with a more modern one, the answer is less clear.[4] Much will depend on the facts of the particular case such as the length of the unexpired term, the needs of the tenant, a change in the neighborhood, and the basis of the landlord's objections.[5] The

3. Statutes in about one-half of the states allow the landlord to recover double or treble damages for the commission of waste. Many of these statutes also allow the landlord to declare a forfeiture of the tenant's estate. These statutes are collected in Restatement (Second) of Property (Landlord & Tenant) § 12.2, Statutory Note (1977). Even apart from statute the landlord may have the remedy of terminating the lease when the tenant commits waste. *Id.* § 12.2(2)(a); Reporter's Note to § 12.2, p. 462.

4. In the leading case of Melms v. Pabst Brewing Co., 104 Wis. 7, 79 N.W. 738 (1899) the court held that a life tenant was not liable for waste even though the tenant pulled down a residential building on the land and lowered the grade of the land to street level. Due to changes in the surrounding area the property had ceased to be useable as a residence and, in fact, the changes made by the tenant increased the value of the property. *Compare* Brokaw v. Fairchild, 135 Misc. 70, 237 N.Y.S. 6 (1929), *aff'd,* 231 App.Div. 704, 245 N.Y.S. 402 (1930), *aff'd,* 256 N.Y. 670, 177 N.E. 186 (1931) (life tenant not entitled over the objection of remaindermen to demolish an unproductive "exceedingly fine house" on Fifth Avenue, New York city, and replace it with a thirteen story apartment building).

5. The Restatement, Second, adopts a flexible approach and states, in substance, that in the absence of a controlling provision in the lease the tenant is entitled to make such changes in the physical condition of the premises as are reasonably necessary for the tenant's

rights of the parties should be set out in the lease and usually are. An occasional statute regulates the respective rights of the parties in the absence of lease provisions.[6]

Unless required by the terms of the rental agreement, a tenant is not normally under a duty to occupy the rented premises. Yet in special situations, and by reason of economic factors, a commercial tenant may be obligated to occupy and use the premises.[7]

§ 6. Landlord's Remedies for Breach by Tenant

Since almost all leases provide for the payment of rent by the tenant, the most common default of tenants consists of non-payment of the agreed rent. If this occurs, what remedies are available to the landlord? It is obvious that landlord can maintain an action for breach of contract and recover for all past due rent. However, without more, landlord cannot sue for rents due in the future since there is no breach until the date of payment has past.[1] The landlord's right to recover damages beyond this is less clear when the term of the lease has not expired. For example, suppose the tenant has not only defaulted in the payment of rent or in the performance of some other covenant in the lease but has also repudiated the lease and abandoned the premises. In this case the landlord may wish to treat the conduct of the tenant as an anticipatory repudiation of the contract amounting to a total breach of the

reasonable use of the property. Restatement (Second) of Property (Landlord & Tenant) § 12.2 (1977).

6. Under N.Y. Real Prop. Acts, § 803 (McKinney 1979), a tenant having an unexpired term of at least five years may alter or replace a structure on the land if the change will not violate any term of the rental agreement, will not decrease the value of the landlord's reversion, and is, of a nature that a prudent owner in fee simple absolute of the property would be likely to make in view of existing conditions. The tenant is required to give the landlord prior written notice of the proposed change and may be required to give security for the completion of the project and for protection

of the landlord against responsibility for expenditures incurred incident to the alteration.

7. See, e.g., Ingannamorte v. Kings Super Markets, Inc., 55 N.J. 223, 260 A.2d 841, 40 A.L.R.3d 962 (1970) (lessee was key tenant in a small shopping center); Tooley's Truck Stop, Inc. v. Chrisanthopouls, 55 N.J. 231, 260 A.2d 845 (1970) ("economic interdependence" of business operations of lessor and lessee; lessor entitled to terminate the lease unless lessee resumed operation of the business).

§ 6

1. See, e.g., Jordon v. Nickell, 253 S.W.2d 237 (Ky.1952).

lease and seek to recover from tenant as damages the difference between the rent reserved and the fair rental value for the balance of the term, discounted to present value. Some courts allow this;[2] others do not.[3] Some leases also contain a "rent acceleration clause" to the effect that if tenant defaults in the payment of rent when due, all future rents payable under the lease (as distinguished from damages) become immediately due and payable. States are divided on the validity of such clauses.[4]

At common law landlord could not sue tenant for possession for nonpayment of rent unless the lease expressly empowered the landlord to do so.[5] Today, most states have statutes allowing the landlord to terminate the tenancy for non-payment of rent.[6] Moreover, it is the almost invariable practice of landlords to insert in leases a clause giving the landlord the right to terminate, or providing for automatic termination of the tenancy, on breach by the tenant of any of the covenants of the lease. If the lease is terminated, the tenant is no longer liable for rent for any future period because there is no existing relationship of landlord and tenant, but the tenant may be liable for damages either under the doctrine of anticipatory breach[7] or on the theory of a total present breach of the whole lease contract.[8]

2. See, e.g., Sagamore Corp. v. Willcutt, 120 Conn. 315, 180 A. 464 (1935); Harden v. Drost, 156 Ga.App. 363, 274 S.E.2d 748 (1980); Employment Advisors, Inc. v. Sparks, 364 S.W.2d 478 (Tex. Civ.App.1963), writ refused 152 Tex. 111, 254 S.W.2d 507 (1953). In California, the remedy of anticipatory breach is given to the landlord by statute in the case of a residential tenancy. Ann. Cal. Civ. Code § 1951.2 (West 1985). See Schoshinski, American Law of Landlord and Tenant, § 10.15.

3. See, e.g., People ex rel. Nelson v. West Town State Bank, 373 Ill. 106, 25 N.E.2d 509 (1940) (rejecting notion that doctrine of anticipatory breach applies to leases); Cooper v. Casco Mercantile Trust Co., 134 Me. 372, 186 A. 885 (1936); Maflo Holding Corp. v. S. J. Blume, Inc., 308 N.Y. 570, 127 N.E.2d

558 (1955). Cf. Long Island R.R. Co. v. Northville Industries Corp., 41 N.Y.2d 455, 393 N.Y.S.2d 925, 362 N.E.2d 558 (1977).

4. See Restatement (Second) of Property (Landlord & Tenant), § 12.1 cmt. j and reporter's notes (1977). If rent is accelerated, landlord should be unable to also obtain possession.

5. See § 3, note 8 supra.

6. Id. For a brief survey of statutes authorizing the landlord to terminate the tenancy for breach by the tenant of his obligations under the lease, see Schoshinski, American Law of Landlord and Tenant, § 6.3.

7. See supra note 2.

8. Hawkinson v. Johnston, 122 F.2d 724 (8th Cir.1941), cert. denied, 314 U.S.

Frequently, the lease will contain an indemnity clause providing in substance that on termination of the lease by the landlord for breach by the tenant, or on abandonment of the premises by the tenant, the landlord may relet the premises on behalf of the tenant and the tenant shall be liable for all damages sustained by the landlord after the reletting. Such a clause is valid, but unless it is so phrased as to entitle the landlord to maintain periodic actions for damages, the court may view the damages resulting from the reletting as "single and entire" and not ascertained until the end of the term.[9]

If the landlord does terminate the lease for non-payment of rent, pursuant to statute or a clause in the lease, and the tenant refuses to vacate the premises, the landlord can maintain a summary action to regain possession. In all jurisdictions statutes have been enacted providing a speedy remedy against tenants wrongfully retaining possession.[10] The existence of these statutes has strengthened the modern trend toward abolishing the landlord's old common-law remedy of self-help which gave the landlord the right to make a peaceable entry upon premises for the purpose of re-gaining possession on the termination of the tenancy. However, in an increasing number of jurisdictions, either by statute or judicial decision, a landlord is denied the right to retake possession, in the

694, 62 S.Ct. 365, 86 L.Ed. 555 (1941); Sagamore Corp. v. Willcutt, 120 Conn. 315, 180 A. 464 (1935); Novak v. Fontaine Furniture Co., 84 N.H. 93, 146 A. 525 (1929). Cf. Parker v. Russell, 133 Mass. 74 (1882).

9. Hermitage Co. v. Levine, 248 N.Y. 333, 162 N.E. 97 (1928). Accord, Woodbury v. Sparrell Print, 187 Mass. 426, 73 N.E. 547 (1905). The comment of Cardozo, C.J. in Hermitage Co. v. Levine, supra, is worth noting. "If the damage clause as drawn gives inadequate protection, the fault is with the draftsman." 248 N.Y. at 338, 162 N.E. at 98. For a case enforcing an indemnity clause giving the landlord, on the tenant's default, the right to recover damages on a monthly basis, *see* Vareka

Investments, N.V. v. American Investment Properties, Inc., 724 F.2d 907 (11th Cir.1984) (applying Fla. law).

10. These summary proceedings to recover possession supplement the old common-law action of ejectment. In some states they are called actions of forcible entry and detainer (*e.g.* Ill.Compiled Statutes Ann. ch. 735 (West 1992); in Connecticut and Massachusetts they are called actions of summary process (Conn. Gen. Stat. Ann. §§ 47a–23–42 (West 1994)), (Mass. Gen. Laws Ann. ch. 239, §§ 1–13 (West 1988) and in New York, summary proceedings (N.Y. Real Prop. Acts. Law §§ 701–767 (McKinney 1979). The statutes are listed in Restatement (Second) of Property (Landlord & Tenant, § 14.1, Statutory Note) (1977).

absence of abandonment of the premises by the tenant, other than through a judicial proceeding.[11]

§ 7. Termination of the Tenancy

There are numerous ways by which a tenancy may be terminated. A tenancy may end by mere lapse of time as in the case of a tenancy for a fixed period of time.[1] It may terminate by one of the parties giving the other party a proper notice to terminate as in the case of a periodic tenancy or a tenancy at will. It also may terminate on default of the tenant by reason of the exercise by the lessor of a power to terminate reserved in the lease; or on breach by the landlord of the covenant of quiet enjoyment amounting to a constructive eviction. Additionally, it may come to an end by surrender. Some of the legal problems generated by the termination of the tenant's estate, or its attempted termination, are now briefly considered.

11. *See, e.g.*, Mass. Gen. Laws Ann. ch. 184, § 18 (West 1991); Berg v. Wiley, 264 N.W.2d 145 (Minn.1978); Restatement (Second) of Property (Landlord & Tenant) § 14.2 (1977).

Moreover, at common law the landlord had the remedy of distress (also called distraint), that is, the right to seize any chattels of the tenant or of other persons on the land and hold them as security for the payment of overdue rent. The right of distress was not favored in this country and it exists today only in a few states. However, in several states the landlord's claim for rent is secured by a statutory lien on the tenant's chattels brought onto the premises. For a detailed treatment of these remedies, *see* Schoshinski, American Law of Landlord and Tenant, §§ 6.21, 6.22.

§ 7

1. A tenant of public housing or of publicly assisted or subsidized housing cannot be evicted without cause despite the expiration of the term specified in the lease, and is entitled to notice and hearing before eviction. The tenant is deemed to have "a property right or entitlement to continue occupancy until there exists a cause to evict other than the mere expiration of the lease." Joy v. Daniels, 479 F.2d 1236, 1241 (4th Cir. 1973). *See* Note, Procedural Due Process in Government–Subsidized Housing, 86 Harv.L.Rev. 880 (1973). For similar protection given to public housing tenants at the state level, *see* Mass. Gen. Laws Ann., Ch. 121B, § 32 (West 1986).

In New Jersey a residential tenant is given by statute a qualified right of continued occupancy of the premises. He can be evicted only for one of the causes set out in the statute. N.J. Stat. Ann. § 2A:18–61.1 (West 2000). The statute does not apply to owner-occupied premises having fewer than three rental units in certain circumstances. Puttrich v. Smith, 170 N.J.Super. 572, 407 A.2d 842 (1979). For an interesting comparison with French law, *see* Note, Landlord and Tenant in French Law: A Recent Statute, 3 Oxford J. of Legal Stud. 425 (1983).

A surrender is, in essence, a premature ending of the landlord-tenant relationship by mutual agreement of the parties. It involves a yielding up of the tenant's estate and an acceptance thereof by the landlord. Since a surrender requires mutual agreement, the unilateral action of the tenant in abandoning possession of the premises and repudiating the tenancy does not effectuate a valid surrender. But the landlord may by subsequent conduct manifest acceptance of the surrender. Whether the landlord has done so is usually a question of fact and one that is frequently litigated.[2] If the landlord has unqualifiedly resumed possession of the premises for the landlord's benefit, landlord, by such conduct, has accepted a surrender.[3]

The courts are not in agreement as to whether the landlord has a duty to attempt to mitigate the damage arising from the abandonment of the premises by the tenant. The traditional view is that because a lease is more of a conveyance than a contract, the general rule of contract law requiring the injured party to mitigate damages is not applicable. Courts adopting this view generally hold that the

2. For a collection of cases, *see* Schoshinski, American Law of Landlord and Tenant, § 10.11.

The remedies available to the landlord on abandonment by the tenant were summarized in Centurian Development Ltd. v. Kenford Co. Inc., 60 A.D.2d 96, 98, 400 N.Y.S.2d 263, 264 (1977)as follows: "When defendant (tenant) abandoned or surrendered these premises prior to expiration of the lease, the landlord had three options: (1) it could do nothing and collect the full rent due under the lease; (2) it could accept the tenant's surrender, re-enter the premises and relet them for its own account and under these circumstances the tenant would be released from further liability from rent; or (3) it could notify the tenant that it was entering and re-letting the premises for the tenant's benefit. * * * Any excess (of rent collected) would be payable to the tenant and the tenant would remain liable for any deficiency."

3. Thus, if the landlord unconditionally accepts the keys to the premises without protest and leases the property to another, he has accepted a surrender. Taylan Realty Co. v. Student Book Exchange, Inc., 354 Mass. 777, 242 N.E.2d 877 (1968). Similarly, if the landlord, after abandonment by the tenant, makes substantial alterations of the premises, without the tenant's assent, and changes the locks, the landlord has accepted the surrender. Guaranty Bank & Trust Co. v. Mid–State Ins. Agency, Inc., 383 Mass. 319, 418 N.E.2d 1249 (1981). *Compare* McGrath v. Shalett, 114 Conn. 622, 159 A. 633 (1932). Usually, the acceptance by the landlord of the keys to the premises when returned by the tenant does not, without more, constitute an acceptance of the surrender. *See, e.g.,* Cantor v. Van Noorden Co., Inc., 4 Mass. App.Ct. 819, 349 N.E.2d 375 (1976). Cf. Bove v. Transcom Electronics, Inc., 116 R.I. 210, 353 A.2d 613 (1976).

landlord, on breach and abandonment by the tenant, may allow the premises to remain idle and sue the tenant for rent as it falls due.[4] This view has been adopted by the Restatement.[5] The Restatement view is justified on the grounds that "abandonment of property is an invitation to vandalism, and the law should not encourage such conduct by putting a duty of mitigation of damages on the landlord."[6] Many courts, on the other hand, have held that the landlord has an obligation to make a reasonable effort to relet the premises for the remainder of the term.[7] Still other courts have imposed a duty to mitigate if the lease itself provides that the landlord may enter on abandonment by the tenant and relet for the latter's benefit.[8] At the present time, the trend is towards requiring the landlord to make a reasonable effort to relet the premises to a new tenant where there is an abandonment by the original tenant. This trend is particularly strong in the case of residential tenancies.[9]

The traditional concept of a lease as primarily a conveyance of an estate in land has also been influential in determining the rights of the parties where a building on the leased premises is destroyed or substantially damaged by fire or other casualty. With a few exceptions the courts have held that the lessee, in the absence of a so-called "fire clause" in the lease, continues to be liable to pay the reserved rent despite the destruction or damage. The lease is viewed as a sale of the term of years and the rent is regarded as the purchase price.[10] On this theory there has been no failure of

4. *See, e.g.,* Fifty Associates v. Berger Dry Goods Co., 275 Mass. 509, 176 N.E. 643 (1931); Gruman v. Investors Diversified Services, 247 Minn. 502, 78 N.W.2d 377 (1956); Centurian Development Ltd. v. Kenford Co. Inc., 60 A.D.2d 96, 400 N.Y.S.2d 263 (1977).

5. Restatement (Second) of Property (Landlord & Tenant) § 12.1(3)(1977).

6. *Id.* at cmt. i.

7. United States National Bank of Oregon v. Homeland, Inc., 291 Or. 374, 631 P.2d 761 (1981); Sommer v. Kridel, 74 N.J. 446, 378 A.2d 767 (1977).

8. Woodbury v. Sparrell Print, 198 Mass. 1, 84 N.E. 441 (1908). Contra,

tenBraak v. Waffle Shops, Inc., 542 F.2d 919 (4th Cir.1976) (no duty to mitigate).

9. *See, e.g.,* Sommer v. Kridel, supra note 7. The Uniform Residential Landlord and Tenant Act provides: "The aggrieved party has a duty to mitigate damages." § 1.105.

10. *See, e.g.,* Sigal v. Wise, 114 Conn. 297, 158 A. 891 (1932); Fowler v. Bott, 6 Mass. 63 (1809). The Restatement (Second)of Property rejects the common-law view and adopts the minority position that the tenant may terminate the lease if the leased property is made unsuitable for the use intended by the parties by reason of a sudden non-

consideration even though the lessee has lost the expected benefit of the transaction. The harshness of this result has led to the enactment of statutes in many states relieving the tenant of liability for future rent in the event of accidental sudden destruction or substantial injury to a leased building.[11] An exception to the common-law rule applies where the subject matter of the lease is a portion of a building, such as an apartment or suite of offices, as distinguished from a lease of land together with an entire building.

The termination of a tenancy often gives rise to the problem of the holdover tenant. When an estate for years, or a periodic tenancy, or a tenancy at will, comes to an end the tenant, instead of vacating the premises, sometimes continues in possession without the landlord's consent. In this situation the status of the occupant is that of a tenant at sufferance. The landlord has an election to bring a summary proceeding to recover possession[12] or to treat the continued occupancy of the former tenant as creating a new tenancy. The new tenancy, according to most courts, arises by operation of law and not from the implied consent of the tenant.[13] The courts are not in agreement as to the duration of the new tenancy. The majority of courts hold that a periodic tenancy with a base period

manmade force. Restatement (Second) of Property (Landlord & Tenant) § 5.4 (1977). *Accord* Albert M. Greenfield & Co., Inc. v. Kolea, 475 Pa. 351, 380 A.2d 758 (1977).

It would seem that in a jurisdiction accepting the doctrine of an implied warranty of habitability in all residential tenancies the tenant would be excused from the obligation to pay rent in the event of accidental destruction or substantial damage by casualty of the leased premises. *Cf.* Berman & Sons, Inc. v. Jefferson, 379 Mass. 196, 396 N.E.2d 981 (1979).

11. For a list of these statutes, *see* Restatement (Second) of Property (Landlord & Tenant), Statutory Note to ch. Five (2)(1977). The Uniform Residential Landlord and Tenant Act, § 4.106 permits the tenant to terminate the rental agreement if the premises are destroyed or damaged by fire or other casualty so that enjoyment of the unit is substantially impaired.

12. The landlord can also recover from the tenant holding over without his assent the fair rental value of the premises during the holdover period. Lonergan v. Connecticut Food Store, Inc., 168 Conn. 122, 357 A.2d 910 (1975); Gordon v. Sales, 337 Mass. 35, 147 N.E.2d 803 (1958). He may also recover any special damages caused by the holding over. Abbott v. McCoy, 208 Okl. 224, 254 P.2d 997 (1953). Restatement (Second) of Property (Landlord & Tenant) § 14.6 (1977).

13. *See* A. H. Fetting Mfg. Jewelry Co. v. Waltz, 160 Md. 50, 152 A. 434 (1930) (new tenancy imposed on tenant as a matter of policy to ensure "confidence in leasehold transactions").

determined by reference to the original tenancy is created and that the manner in which rent is computed is determined by the terms of the original lease. Thus, if the original tenancy was for one year or longer and the lease provided for an annual rent payable in monthly installments, the new tenancy is one from year-to-year.[14] No court seems to have imposed on the tenant a new term in excess of one year although in a few cases the tenant has been held to an additional fixed term of a year. Because of the harshness of the holdover rule, it has been abrogated or modified by statute in some jurisdictions.[15]

The lease may contain provisions that supercede the holdover tenancy doctrine. For example, in *Commonwealth Building Corporation v. Hirschfield*[16] the court held that because the lease provided that if the tenant held over tenant would be liable for double rent for the period of occupancy, the landlord could not elect to treat tenant as a year-to-year tenant.

§ 8. Transfer of the Interest of Landlord or Tenant

Usually, the lessor is the owner of an estate in fee simple in the premises prior to the execution of the lease. The effect of the lease is to carve an estate for years out of this fee and to leave the lessor with a reversion in fee simple. This reversion is freely transferable. A transfer of the reversion normally carries with it the right to future rents, although there can be an assignment of rent without an assignment of the reversion, as well as an assignment of the reversion without the rent.[1] Moreover, an assignment of the rever-

---

14. Id.

15. *See, e.g.,* Cal. Civ. Code Ann. § 1945 (West 1985); Conn. Gen. Stat. Ann. § 47a–3d (West 1994); N.J. Stat. Ann. § 46:8–10 (West 1989); N.Y. Real Prop. Law § 232–c (McKinney 1989); Uniform Residential Landlord and Tenant Act § 4.301(c). See also, Herter v. Mullen, 159 N.Y. 28, 53 N.E. 700 (1899)(holdover tenant not liable as year-to-year tenant where tenant's mother who lived with tenant was so ill that she could not be moved).

16. 307 Ill.App. 533, 30 N.E.2d 790 (1940).

§ 8

1. Where the lessor transfers "the within lease" to a third person the question arises whether the transfer is an assignment of the rent alone or also an assignment of the reversion. It is usually held that an assignment by the lessor of the "lease" without mention of the reversion operates as an assignment of the rent only. United States v. Shafto, 246 F.2d 338 (4th Cir.1957); Hunt v. Thomp-

sion transfers to the assignee the benefit of the lessee's covenants, as well as the burden of the lessor's covenants which run with the land.[2] At common law attornment by the tenant; that is, assent to the transfer, was necessary to make the assignment effective but the requirement of attornment no longer exists.

The interest of the lessee, being an estate for years, is normally transferable in the absence of a restrictive clause in the lease or a statutory provision forbidding transfer without the lessor's assent.[3] Most leases, in fact, contain a provision forbidding the lessee to assign or sublet without the written consent of the lessor. Such provisions, since they are restraints on alienation, are strictly construed by the courts. Thus, a provision against assignment without the lessor's consent does not prevent a subletting without his consent and vice versa. Most leases, if they bar an assignment, also bar a sublease.

An assignment made in violation of a restrictive clause is not void; the estate for years vests in the assignee until effective action

---

son, 84 Mass. (2 Allen) 341 (1861). *Cf.* Masury v. Southworth, 9 Ohio St. 340 (1859). *See* 2 ALP, § 9.45.

The common-law view is that rent due in the future is not a chose in action but an incorporeal interest in real property. The rent is deemed to issue out of the land. Accrued rent, however, is personal property, a chose in action.

Some jurisdictions require, by statute, that an assignment of rents under a lease be recorded in order to be effective against a subsequent bona fide purchaser of the reversion. *See, e.g.,* Mass. Gen. Laws Ann. ch. 183, § 4 (West 1991); N.Y. Real Prop. Law § 294–a(2) (McKinney 1989). In the absence of such a statute, an assignee of the rents prevails over a later purchaser of the reversion who had no notice of the prior assignment. *See* Winnisimmet Trust, Inc. v. Libby, 232 Mass. 491, 122 N.E. 575 (1919).

2. At earlier common law an assignee of the reversion could not enforce

against the lessee the covenants and conditions in the lease. A remedy was given to transferees of the reversion by the statute 32 Henry 8, c. 34 (1540). In some states this statute is deemed to be in force as part of the common law and in other states statutes having the same effect have been enacted. *See, e.g.,* Cal. Civ. Code § 821 (West 1982); N.Y. Real Prop. Law, § 223 (McKinney 1989).

3. Statutes forbidding transfers by the lessee without the lessor's assent are found in a few states. Occasionally, the interest of the lessee is held to be nontransferable, even in the absence of statutory provision or express restriction in the lease, on the ground that the lessor relied on the personal qualities or business efficiency of the lessee, the rent being fixed at a percentage of profits or sales. Nassau Hotel Co. v. Barnett & Barse Corp., 162 App.Div. 381, 147 N.Y.S. 283 (1914), *aff'd* 212 N.Y. 568, 106 N.E. 1036 (1914). *See also* Marcelle, Inc. v. Sol & S. Marcus Co., 274 Mass. 469, 175 N.E. 83, 74 A.L.R. 1012 (1931).

is taken by the lessor to avoid the transfer.[4] Usually, the lease will contain a clause giving the lessor the power to terminate the estate granted for breach of any covenant or condition and this forfeiture provision gives the lessor an effective remedy in case of an unauthorized assignment. The lessor may waive a breach of the nonassignment covenant and lessor's acceptance of rent from the assignee with knowledge of the assignment will normally be held to amount to a waiver.

Where the lease does contain a clause prohibiting assignment or subleasing without the consent of the lessor and does not provide that the lessor's assent shall not be unreasonably withheld, many courts have said that the lessor may arbitrarily refuse to consent to a transfer by the lessee although this view is rejected by the Restatement.[5] But if the lease stipulates that the landlord will not unreasonably withhold assent to an assignment or sublease and landlord breaches this covenant the tenant can terminate the lease, or go forward with the transfer, or sue for damages.[6]

If the lessor consents to an assignment by the lessee in a particular instance, it would seem that this would not deprive the landlord of the right to refuse to consent to any further assignment by the assignee. Yet in *Dumpor's Case*[7] the court held that a single license to assign operates to extinguish the condition against unauthorized assignments as to all future assignments. The court reasoned that "the condition could not be divided or apportioned by

4. People v. Klopstock, 24 Cal.2d 897, 151 P.2d 641 (1944).

5. The Restatement (Second) of Property (Landlord & Tenant)§ 15.2 (1977) takes the position that the landlord cannot unreasonably withhold his consent to a transfer by the tenant. *See also* Jacobs v. Klawans, 225 Md. 147, 169 A.2d 677 (1961); Gruman v. Investors Diversified Services, Inc., 247 Minn. 502, 78 N.W.2d 377 (1956); Dress Shirt Sales, Inc. v. Hotel Martinique Associates, 12 N.Y.2d 339, 239 N.Y.S.2d 660, 190 N.E.2d 10 (1963). *Contra* Cohen v. Ratinoff, 147 Cal.App.3d 321, 195 Cal. Rptr. 84 (1983); Fernandez v. Vazquez, 397 So.2d 1171 (Fla.App.1981).

In Alaska, Delaware and New York the matter of assignment or sub-lease by a residential tenant is regulated by statute. Alaska Stat. § 34.030.060 (1974); Del. Code Ann. Tit. 25, § 5512(b) (1974); N.Y. Real Prop. Law § 226–B (McKinney 1989).

6. *See, e.g.,* Homa–Goff Interiors, Inc. v. Cowden, 350 So.2d 1035 (Ala. 1977); Adams, Harkness & Hill, Inc. v. Northeast Realty Corp., 361 Mass. 552, 281 N.E.2d 262, 54 A.L.R.3d 673 (1972); Ringwood Associates, Ltd. v. Jack's of Route 23, Inc., 166 N.J.Super. 36, 398 A.2d 1315 (1979).

7. 4 Coke Rep. 119b, 76 Eng.Rep. 1110 (1603).

the act of the parties." The highly artificial nature of the reason assigned for the rule is apparent. Although the rule of *Dumpor's Case* was abrogated by statute in England in 1859 and has been criticized by some courts and many writers, it has found acceptance in some states.[8]

A transfer by the lessee may be either an assignment or a sublease. Since different legal consequences flow from the nature of the transfer it is important to distinguish between the two types. It is usually held that the transfer is an assignment when it conveys to the transferee the entire balance of the unexpired term so that there is no reversion or reversionary interest left in the lessee.[9] A sublease, on the other hand, is a transfer of an interest in the lessee's estate for a shorter period than the unexpired term, such that when the interest of the sublessee ends the remainder of the term reverts back to the lessee.[10] For example, suppose L leases Blackacre to T for a term beginning on January 1, 2001 and ending on December 31, 2010. Thereafter T transfers the property to A for a term ending on December 31, 2010. This would be an assignment because A's term ends at the same time that T's term would have ended. On the other hand, if T transfers to S for a term ending on October 31, 2008, this is a sublease since S's term ends short of the end of T's term. In this case, T has a reversion that becomes possessory on November 1, 2008. Of course, T's interest ends on December 31, 2010, and the fee reverts to L. Even if the difference in time in the duration of the lessee's estate and that of the transferee is as short as one day the transfer is classified as a

---

8. *See, e.g.,* Reid v. Weissner & Sons Brewing Co., 88 Md. 234, 40 A. 877 (1898); Aste v. Putnam's Hotel Co., 247 Mass. 147, 141 N.E. 666, 31 A.L.R. 149 (1923). *Contra* Leibowitz v. 18 East 41st St. Corp., 89 N.Y.S.2d 160 (1949). Courts have held that the rule is inapplicable where the lessor in consenting to a specific assignment has expressly reserved the right to require that no further assignment be made except with his consent. Rothrock v. Sanborn, 178 Cal. 693, 174 P. 314 (1918). *Cf.* Crowell v. Riverside, 26 Cal.App.2d 566, 80 P.2d 120 (1938). It has also been held inapplicable to a condition against subletting

without the lessor's consent. Seaver v. Coburn, 64 Mass. (10 Cush.) 324 (1852).

9. *See, e.g.,* Jaber v. Miller, 219 Ark. 59, 239 S.W.2d 760 (1951); Dayenian v. American Nat. Bank & Trust Co. of Chicago, 91 Ill.App.3d 622, 47 Ill.Dec. 83, 414 N.E.2d 1199 (1980); Anchor Holding Co. v. Michael's Coffee Shop, 81 A.D.2d 535, 438 N.Y.S.2d 104 (1981); Snow v. Winn, 607 P.2d 678 (Okl.1980).

10. *See* Restatement (Second) of Property (Landlord & Tenant) § 15.1 cmt. i; § 16.1 (1977).

sublease or sub-tenancy. If the transfer is of an interest in a physical portion of the leased premises for the entire balance of the lessee's term, it is usually classified as a partial assignment.

Much of the litigation over the nature of the transfer by the lessee has arisen in the situation where the transfer has been for the entire unexpired balance of the term but in the instrument of transfer the lessee has reserved a different rent from that in the main lease and has also reserved a right of re-entry in the event of non-payment by the transferee. It is commonly said that a reversion is necessary for the landlord-tenant relation. Even though the transfer by the lessee is for the full balance of the term does the reservation of the right of re-entry amount to a retention of a reversionary interest in the lessee? If so, the transfer is a sublease because of the landlord-tenant relationship between lessee and transferee. Most courts take the view that the reservation of a right of re-entry in the instrument of transfer leaves no part of the former estate in the transferor and conclude that the transfer operates as an assignment.[11] The right of re-entry is regarded as a new interest created by the instrument of transfer rather than part of the original estate of the lessee. A minority of courts hold that the reservation of a right of re-entry leaves in the lessee a "contingent reversionary interest" and that the transfer is, therefore, a sublease.[12] And, an occasional decision, rejecting the formalistic test of the presence or absence of a reversionary interest remaining in the lessee, gives effect to the intention of the parties.[13] The intention test is given considerable weight when the litigation is between the lessee and his transferee.[14]

There exists between lessor and lessee a dual legal relationship. With respect to the covenants or promises set out in the lease to be performed by either party there is said to be "privity of contract",

---

11. *See, e.g.,* Sexton v. Chicago Storage Co., 129 Ill. 318, 21 N.E. 920 (1889); Murray Hill Mello Corp. v. Bonne Bouchee Restaurant, Inc., 113 Misc.2d 683, 449 N.Y.S.2d 870 (1982).

12. Davis v. Vidal, 105 Tex. 444, 151 S.W. 290 (1912) is a leading case. See also, Dunlap v. Bullard, 131 Mass. 161 (1881). The Restatement (Second) of Property (Landlord & Tenant) adopts this view. § 15.1 cmt. i(1977).

13. Jaber v. Miller, 219 Ark. 59, 239 S.W.2d 760 (1951).

14. *See* Davidson v. Minnesota Loan & Trust Co., 158 Minn. 411, 197 N.W. 833, 32 A.L.R. 1418 (1924).

that is a nexus or relationship flowing from the lease. But there is also a nexus or relationship flowing from the ownership of property interests in the same land by each party, and this relationship is described as "privity of estate." In sum, there is between lessor and lessee both privity of contract and privity of estate.

When the lessee transfers his interest by assignment, the privity of contract between the lessor and lessee continues to exist, in the absence of a release by the lessor or a novation. Therefore, the lessee continues to be liable on all of his promises set out in the lease, including, for example, his promise to pay the reserved rent. However, the assignment has the effect of severing the privity of estate that previously existed between lessor and lessee. Rather, there is now privity of estate between the lessor and the assignee, and by reason of this privity of estate the assignee becomes liable, so long as he continues to own the leasehold, on all of the lessee's covenants that run with the land, including the covenant to pay rent. As between lessee and assignee, the latter is said to be primarily liable to the lessor, but the lessor may maintain an action against either of them.[15]

When the lessee transfers an interest in the leasehold by way of sublease instead of assigning his estate, there is neither privity of contract nor privity of estate between the lessor and the sublessee. Therefore, the sublessee is not liable to pay the rent reserved in the

15. The courts are not in agreement as to whether the assignment has the effect of making the assignee a surety for the lessee. In De Hart v. Allen, 26 Cal.2d 829 at 832, 161 P.2d 453 at 455 (1945) the court stated: "It has sometimes been said that the effect of an assignment is to make the lessee a surety for the assignee. This may be true in a limited sense as between the assignee and his assignor, the lessee, but as between the lessor and the lessee the latter remains a primary obligor under his express contract to pay rent." But in Hamlen v. Rednalloh Co., 291 Mass. 119 at 124, 197 N.E. 149 at 152–153 (1935) the court said: "Although the liability of the defendant lessee to pay rent under its covenant in the lease was not termi- nated by reason of its assignment, one effect of the execution of that instru- ment, to which the lessor was a party, was, as between assignee and lessee, the creation of the relationship of principal and surety as to the debts for rents thereafter coming due under the lease." See also Net Realty Holding Trust v. Giannini, 13 Mass.App.Ct. 273, 432 N.E.2d 120 (1982). If the position of the lessee is viewed as that of a surety, any agreement between the lessor and the assignee, not assented to by the lessee, which adversely affects the lessee, may have the effect of releasing the lessee from his obligations under the lease. Walker v. Rednalloh Co., 299 Mass. 591, 13 N.E.2d 394 (1938); Gerber v. Pecht, 15 N.J. 29, 104 A.2d 41 (1954).

main lease nor is he obligated to perform the other covenants of the lessee, in the absence of a contractual assumption of these covenants. The lessee, of course, continues to be liable for the rent by reason of both privity of contract and privity of estate.[16] If neither the lessee nor sublessee pays the lessor rent, the lessor will no doubt terminate the lease and sue both for possession.

The liability of the assignee arising from privity of estate with the lessor extends only to those covenants in the lease that "run with the land." When we say that the burden of a covenant runs with the land we mean that the obligation of performance of the promise passes to the succeeding owner of the interest of the promisor. In order for a covenant to run with the estate of the lessee, the original parties to the lease must have intended the covenant to run and the covenant must "touch and concern" the transferred interest. A covenant may be said to "touch and concern" the land when its performance directly affects the rights of the parties with respect to their interests in the land. A promise which is personal and collateral to the property interest, such as a promise to guarantee the payment of rent under a lease of different property, does not meet the touch and concern requirement.[17] The covenants ordinarily found in a commercial lease, such as a covenant to pay rent, to pay taxes on the leased property, to supply heat, to make repairs, to grant an option to renew the lease or to purchase, are held to run with respect to both benefit and burden. Covenants to pay money have given the courts the most difficulty.[18]

16. For a helpful discussion, see Schoshinski, American Law of Landlord and Tenant, §§ 8.10–8.13.

17. The "touch and concern" requirement for the running of a covenant had its origin in Spencer's Case, 5 Co. 16a, 77 Eng.Rep. 72 (1583). Although the phrase is quaint, it is in current use and expresses a concept that is generally accepted. See Restatement (Second) of Property (Landlord & Tenant) §§ 16.1, 16.2 (1977); 2 ALP §§ 9.1–9.7. A leading American case discussing Spencer's Case, supra, is Masury v. Southworth, 9 Ohio St. 340 (1859). It should be noted that the touch and concern requirement is applicable to the running of the benefit of a covenant, as well as to the burden, although in most cases if the requirement is satisfied as to one end of the covenant it will be met also as to the other end. 2 ALP § 9.4. For a valuable and influential analysis of the touch and concern aspect of covenants, see Bigelow, The Content of Covenants in Leases, 12 Mich.L.Rev. 639 (1914).

18. See Schoshinski, American Law of Landlord and Tenant, § 8.2.

The liability of the assignee of a lessee on "real" covenants, that is, on covenants running with the land, comes to an end (apart from any contractual assumption of liability) if the assignee assigns the estate to another person. This is true although the further assignment was made to a financially irresponsible transferee for the purpose of enabling the original assignee to escape liability for future rent.[19]

To illustrate some of the foregoing principles, consider each of the following examples:

1. L leases Blackacre to T for a period of ten years at a monthly rental of $500. T later assigns the balance of the term to A who now is in privity of estate with L. If A fails to pay L rent, L may sue T for the rent because they are in privity of contract and sue A for the rent because they are in privity of estate. Since, as between A and T, A should pay the rent because A benefitted from A's possession of Blackacre, if L sues T for the rent, T can recoup it from A. In other words, T is a surety for A.

Suppose A assigns the balance of the term to A-1. Here, L and A-1 are in privity of estate for the balance of the term assigned to A-1. L and T are in privity of contract. L and A have neither privity of estate nor contract and thus if A-1 defaults in the payment of rent, L can sue T or A-1 but not A.

2. L leases Blackacre to T for ten years. Thereafter T sublets to S who fails to pay rent. L has no privity of estate or contract with S and, thus, can sue T only for nonpayment of rent because L and T have both privity of estate and contract. Of course, L can also terminate the lease and sue both for possession.

In both of these examples, the transferee (A or S) could have promised T to pay rent directly to L. In some jurisdictions this creates privity of contract between L and A or S, as the case may be, because L is the third-party beneficiary of the contract between T and A or T and S.

---

19. *See* Reid v. Weissner & Sons Brewing Co., 88 Md. 234, 40 A. 877 (1898); Shoolman v. Wales Mfg. Co., 331 Mass. 211, 118 N.E.2d 71 (1954).

Chapter 4

FUTURE INTERESTS—THE REVERSIONARY INTERESTS

§ 1. The Nature of a Future Interest

The great genius of the common law, as previously seen, was the development of the concept permitting the ownership of land to be carved up into different successive slices or "estates" and that of these "estates" only one need be a presently possessory estate. Thus, O, owner of Blackacre in fee simple, may, by a single conveyance, convey Blackacre to B for life, then to C for life, then to D and his heirs. B has a present possessory life estate. C and D both have presently existing estates although they have no right to possession until some time in the future. C and D have what are called future interests. The phrase "future interest" is somewhat misleading (for which we apologize) inasmuch as these interests have a present existence even though enjoyment of possession is postponed. In fact, they can be quiet valuable, in fact, they can be more valuable than a present interest.[1] The interests of both C and

§ 1

1. To illustrate, suppose O deeds property to A for life, remainder to B. If A is age 88, A's life estate is not very valuable in relationship to B's future interest known as a remainder. If, on the other hand, A is age 10, B's remainder is much less valuable than A's inter- est. The value of the respective interests of A and B is a function of two things: life expectancy and assumed rates of re- turn. The younger the life tenant and the higher the rate of return, the more valuable the life estate; the older the life tenant and the lower the rate of return, the less valuable the life estate.

D can be transferred to third persons and D's interest (but not C's interest) is descendible or devisable.[2] Moreover, both C and D have a right that B, the holder of the present estate, shall not commit waste, and, if B does commit waste, they may be entitled to damages. In general, a legal future interest in land may be defined as a present right in relation to the land by virtue of which possession will be had, or may be had, in the future.[3]

Future interests can either be retained by the grantor or testator or created in a third person. There are three types of retained reversionary interests all of which were valid common-law estates:[4] the reversion, the possibility of reverter, and the right of entry for condition broken (also known as the power of termination). The future interest that could be created in a third person and recognized by the common-law courts was called a remainder.[5] There are four kinds of remainders: the vested remainder (also known as the indefeasibly vested remainder), the vested remainder subject to open (also known as the vested remainder subject to partial divestment), the contingent remainder, and the vested remainder subject to complete divestment.

There were other future interests that also could be created in third persons that prior to 1536 were recognized by the courts of equity and thereafter by the courts of law as well. These were the shifting and springing executory interests.[6]

§ 2. Reversions

Blackstone defined a reversion as "the residue of an estate left in the grantor, to commence in possession after the determination

2. C's interest is not descendible or devisable because it ends at C's death.

3. Future interests may also exist in personal property and in equitable interests in both real and personal property. In fact most of the modern law of future interests is concerned with beneficial interests in trusts the subject matter of which usually consists of stocks and bonds. *Importantly, the classifica-* *tion scheme of estates in land and most rules of law developed with respect to interests in land apply as well to future interests created in trust.*

4. This means they were recognized by the English courts of law as distinguished from the courts of equity.

5. *See* ch. 5, *infra.*

6. *See* ch. 8, *infra.*

of some particular estate granted out by him."[1] This definition remains generally valid. It assumes the quantum theory of estates and that theory determines whether there is any interest "left" in the transferor. If O, owner of Blackacre in fee simple absolute, conveys Blackacre to B and his heirs there can be no reversion in O since B's fee simple absolute represents the totality of ownership in Blackacre. But, if O conveys Blackacre to B for life or in fee tail, O has a reversion in fee simple.[2] Or, if T devises Blackacre to B for life, and no further disposition of Blackacre is contained in the will, there is a reversion in fee either in the residuary legatees under T's will or, in the absence of a residuary clause in T's will, then in T's heirs. So also, a person having a lesser estate than a fee simple will, upon the transfer of an estate smaller than his own, have a reversion. Thus, if B has an estate for life and transfers to C an estate for years (regardless of the number of years) B has a reversion. If C then transfers an estate for a lesser number of years to D, C also has a reversion. B and C have intermediate reversions and B's grantor has the ultimate reversion. In brief then, whenever a person has a vested estate and transfers to another a legally smaller vested estate the segment of ownership retained by the transferor is called a reversion.[3]

Under the common law no reversion resulted if the owner of a freehold estate created an estate for years since the termor did not have seisin. Thus, if O, owner of Blackacre in fee simple absolute, conveyed Blackacre to B for ten years, strictly speaking O had a present fee simple subject to a term for years rather than a reversion in fee expectant upon an estate for years. Today, however, O is said to have a reversion in fee subject to a term of years.

§ 2

1. 2 Bl. Comm. 275. A "particular" estate is any estate smaller than a fee simple. Thus, O owing Blackacre in fee simple absolute, conveys "to B for life, then to C and his heirs." B's life estate is a particular estate. The term "particular" is used in the sense (derived from the Latin) of meaning a portion of the whole.

2. O's reversion will become possessory at the termination of B's life estate or B's fee tail. If O is not then living, O's successors-in-interest then living will be entitled to possession of the property.

3. Can one life estate be deemed to be legally smaller than another life estate? It would seem not, according to the quantum theory of estates. If B has an estate for his own life and conveys to C for the latter's life, does B have a reversion? The Restatement affirms that B has a reversion. Restatement of Property, § 154 cmt. d (1936). *But see* Simes & Smith, The Law of Future Interests § 82 (2nd ed. 1956). If C predeceases B it is agreed that the property would revert to B.

Since a reversion was, by common-law standards, "vested" it amounted to an estate and was transferable inter vivos and, after the Statute of Wills, was devisable.[4] But the fact that all reversions are said to be vested does not mean that they will necessarily become possessory in the future. The reversion may be subject to defeasance. Thus, if O, owner of Blackacre in fee simple absolute, conveys Blackacre to B for life, then to such of B's children and their heirs as survive B, the state of the title is: life estate in B, contingent remainder in fee in B's surviving children,[5] reversion in O in fee. If B dies leaving no surviving children the land reverts to O, or if O is dead to O's heirs or his devisees.[6] But if B dies leaving surviving children O's reversion will be divested.

Review Problems

1.   O, the owner of Blackacre in fee simple absolute, conveys Blackacre to B for life. B has a life estate and O has a reversion. If O dies in B's lifetime and by his will bequeaths all of his property to Y, then Y has the reversion and upon B's death Y's reversion will become possessory. Y's interest is classified as a reversion even though Y is a transferee since Y did not acquire the interest simultaneously with the creation of the life estate in B.

2.   O, the owner of Blackacre in fee simple absolute, conveys Blackacre to B for life, the to B's surviving children and their heirs. O has a reversion which will become possessory if B dies without surviving children. If B dies with surviving children, O's reversion is divested. If O dies intestate in B's lifetime and B later dies without surviving children, the heirs of O who succeeded to O's reversion at O's death will acquire a fee simple absolute in Blackacre.

---

4.   When a reversion is transferred, it retains its character as a reversion in the transferee's hands. Thus, O, owner of Blackacre in fee simple, conveys to B for life. O later transfer the reversion in fee simple to C. C now has a reversion, not a remainder.

5.   See, ch. 5, *infra*.

6.   Since reversions are both descendible or devisable, if O bequeaths O's reversion by will, that devise trumps the interest of O's heirs. Thus, only if O dies intestate or dies with a will that fails to dispose of the reversion, will the reversion pass to O's heirs. If O's will contains what is known as a "residuary clause" (*e.g.*, I give the residue of my estate to___), the residuary beneficiary succeeds to all of O's property not otherwise specifically devised by O's will.

§ 3.   The Nature of a Possibility of Reverter

A possibility of reverter is the interest left in a transferor who creates a fee simple determinable.[1] Thus O, the owner of Blackacre in fee simple absolute, conveys it "to B and his heirs so long as the California redwoods stand and if they shall cease to stand, Blackacre shall revert to O and his heirs." B has a fee simple determinable. O's reversionary interest (which may never become possessory) is a possibility of reverter. If the redwoods fall, B's estate expires automatically and O (or O's successor-in-interest) becomes the owner of Blackacre in fee simple absolute.

A possibility of reverter, like the reversion, can exist only in the transferor or his heirs and cannot be created in a transferee. For this reason it is classified as a reversionary interest.[2] Technically, the fee simple determinable is not a legally smaller estate than a fee simple absolute; hence, the creator of a fee simple determinable cannot be said to have a reversion even though his retained interest is of a reversionary nature.

Review Problem

O, the owner of Blackacre in fee simple absolute, conveys it "to B and his heirs so long as the California redwoods stand and if they shall cease to stand, Blackacre shall revert to O and his heirs." B has a fee simple determinable and O has a possibility of reverter.

§ 4.   Characteristics of Possibility of Reverter

Under the English common law, contingent future interests were inalienable inter vivos except by fine or common recovery.

§ 3

1. See ch. 2, § 4, supra. A fee simple determinable is sometimes called a base fee. Thus, we have three terms any one of which may be used to describe the interest of a grantee in fee simple whose estate is limited to expire automatically on the occurrence of a state event: fee simple determinable, fee simple on special limitation, and base fee.

An owner in fee simple who grants an estate in fee simple conditional also retained a possibility of reverter. Re-

statement of Property, § 154 cmt. g (1936). But since the fee simple conditional is of significance only in a very few states (Iowa and South Carolina) this type of possibility of reverter will not be discussed further in this chapter. See ch. 2, § 6, supra.

2. The Restatement of Property defines a possibility of reverter as "any reversionary interest which is subject to a condition precedent." Restatement of Property § 154 (1936).

These interests were thought of as mere expectancies rather than as estates. This view influenced a number of American courts to hold that the possibility of reverter was not transferable inter vivos to a third person.[1] Today, however, there is a great preference for free transferability of all future interests, and the weight of authority upholds the alienability of the possibility of reverter.[2] In most states there are statutes providing for the transferability of future interests and these statutes are usually construed to include possibilities of reverter.[3] Moreover, it seems that the possibility of reverter can be transferred in equity by a specifically enforceable contract to convey and at law by virtue of the doctrine of estoppel by deed, in the sense that if the possibility of reverter becomes a possessory estate the contract or deed will be given effect.[4] And, the courts have agreed that the possibility of reverter is releasable to the owner of the determinable fee. In all but a few jurisdictions this type of future interest is held to be both descendible and devisable.[5]

§ 4

1. *See, e.g.,* Consolidated School Dist. No. 102 Washington County v. Walter, 243 Minn. 159, 66 N.W.2d 881, 53 A.L.R. 2d 218 (1954) (prior to Minnesota statute expressly making such interests alienable); Magness v. Kerr, 121 Or. 373, 254 P. 1012 (1927).

2. *See, e.g.,* Nichols v. Haehn, 8 A.D.2d 405, 187 N.Y.S.2d 773 (N.Y.App. Div.1959), 45 Corn. L.J. 373 (1960). The subject is now governed by statute in New York. The statute provides that possibilities of reverter (defined as "the residue of an estate left in the grantor or his heirs, or in the heirs of a testator, upon a conveyance or devise until the happening of a specified event") are "descendible, devisable and alienable, in the same manner as estates in possession." N.Y. Real Prop. Law, §§ 59, 59–a (McKinney, 1989), as *amended by* 1962 N.Y. Laws ch. 146. The act does not affect "any rights or interests existing prior to" September 1, 1962. The Restatement takes the view that possibili-

ties of reverter are alienable. Restatement of Property, § 159 (1936).

3. For a collection of these statutes, *see* 2A Powell, Real Property c. 21. In Illinois the possibility of reverter is by statute expressly made inalienable by inter vivos conveyance although it is releasable to the grantee or his transferee. Ill. Comp. Stat. Ann. § 330/1 (West 2001).

4. The doctrine of estoppel by deed is a conveyancing principle of broad application. If a grantor having no title to the land purports to convey it by a warranty deed he will be estopped to show that at the time of the deed he had no title to convey. If he later acquires the title, his after-acquired title passed to the grantee (without further conveyance) by way of estoppel.

5. *See, e.g.,* Brown v. Independent Baptist Church of Woburn, 325 Mass. 645, 91 N.E.2d 922 (1950). In Illinois, by statute, the possibility of reverter is non devisable but is descendible. Ill. St. Ann. ch. 30, ¶ 37b.

Because the possibilities of reverter can be unlimited in scope and duration, they tend to clog the marketability of land titles and impede the normal economic development of the land. As a result, in recent years there has been a growing hostility to possibilities of reverter as evident from the enactment in many states of statutes restricting the duration of possibilities of reverter to a specified period of years after the effective date of the statute[6] and requiring periodic re-recording of pre-existing possibilities of reverter.[7] And, a New York statute makes radical changes in the enforceability of possibilities of reverter restricting the use of land where the restriction is of no actual and substantial benefit to the person seeking enforcement "either because the purpose of the restriction has already been accomplished, or, by reason of changed conditions or other cause, its purpose is not capable of accomplishment, or for any other reason."[8]

§ 5. The Nature of the Right of Entry for Condition Broken

A right of entry for condition broken is a future interest retained by a transferor who conveys an estate on condition subsequent. It can be created only in the transferor or his successors in interest, never in a third person.[1] This right of entry is not, strictly

---

6. *See, e.g.,* Ill. Comp. Stat. Ann. § 330/4 (West 2001) (40 years) (applicable only to interests created after enactment of the statute); Mass. Gen. Laws Ann. ch. 184A § 7(1991) (30 years). Statutes limiting the duration of these interests also exist in Connecticut, Florida, Maine, Minnesota, Nebraska and Rhode Island.

7. *See, e.g.,* Iowa Code § 614.24 (1998) (constitutionally upheld as to pre-existing interests in Presbytery of Southeast Iowa v. Harris, 226 N.W.2d 232 (Iowa 1975)); Mass.Gen.Laws Ann. ch. 260, § 31A (West 1992); Minn.Stat. Ann. § 541.023 (2000) amended by 2001 Minn.Sess.Law Serv. ch.7, ch.50(West); Wichelman v. Messner, 250 Minn. 88, 83 N.W.2d 800 (1957). *See also* N.Y. Real Prop. Law § 345 (McKinney 1989) (un-

constitutional as applied to interests predating statute, Board of Education v. Miles, 15 N.Y.2d 364, 259 N.Y.S.2d 129, 207 N.E.2d 181 (1965).

8. N.Y. Real Prop. Law §§ 346–349 (McKinney, 1989) *repealed by* N.Y. Real Prop. Acts §§ 2111; N.Y. Real Prop. Acts. Art. 19, §§ 1951–1955, *added by* N.Y. Laws, 1962, c. 142. California has a similar statute. Cal. Civ. Code § 885.040 (West 1982). A change of conditions is generally held, in the absence of statute, ineffective to prevent enforcement of the possibility of reverter. *See* Simes & Smith, The Law of Future Interests, §§ 1991–1994 (2nd ed. 1956).

§ 5

1. This rule is as old as Littleton who stated that "no entry nor re-entry

speaking, a "right" in the sense of being a present legally enforceable claim. It is rather a power to terminate the granted estate on breach of the specified condition. On breach of the condition the transferor can elect to terminate the granted estate or not as the transferor pleases. Until the transferor manifests an election by making either an entry on the land or bringing an action to recover it, the grantee's estate continues. Because the option to terminate the granted estate for breach of the condition is the distinguishing characteristic of the right of entry it is sometimes called a "power of termination." It is so described in the Restatement of Property[2] but despite the accuracy of this term the courts continue to use the older terminology. Unhappily, they all too frequently refer to a right of entry as a "possibility of reverter." This designation is objectionable in that it tends to confuse a right of entry with the interest left in the creator of a fee simple determinable.

It is possible to attach a condition subsequent to an estate other than a fee simple. Thus, O, the owner of Blackacre in fee simple, conveys Blackacre to "B for life on the express condition that B reside on Blackacre and in the event that B does not do so O may re-enter and possess Blackacre as of his former estate." B has a life estate subject to a condition subsequent. O has a reversion in fee simple coupled with a right of entry. However, the fee simple

(which is all one) may be reserved or given to any person, but only to the feoffer [conveyor], or to the donor, or to the lessor, or to their heirs; and such re-entry cannot be given to any other person." Littleton, Tenures, § 347. But under modern law it is possible for the grantor to create in a third person an interest comparable to a right of entry. Thus, O conveys "to B and his heirs on condition that the land be used only for residential purposes and if during B's lifetime the land is used for non-residential purposes then to C and his heirs." C has a future interest called an executory interest. This executory interest, unlike the right of entry, is subject to the rule against perpetuities and frequently the gift over will be void because it violates that rule. See, e.g., Proprietors of

Church in Brattle Square v. Grant, 69 Mass. (3 Gray) 142 (1855); Edward John Noble Hospital of Gouverneur v. Board of Foreign Missions of Presbyterian Church in U.S., 13 Misc.2d 918, 176 N.Y.S.2d 157 (N.Y.Sup.Ct.1958). The subject of executory interests is treated in ch.8, infra.

2. Restatement of Property §§ 24,45 (1936). The term "power of termination" is also used in a recent New York statute; it is there defined as "a power reserved to the grantor or his heirs or to the heirs of a testator to enter for breach of a condition attached to an estate granted or devised." N.Y. Real Prop. Law § 59–b (McKinney 1989) amended by 1962 N.Y. Laws Ch. 146; now covered by N.Y. Est. Powers and Trusts Law § 6–4.6 (McKinney 1992).

and the estate for years are the estates most commonly created subject to a condition subsequent.[3]

Review Problem

O conveys Blackacre to B and his heirs but if the property is used for residential purposes then O may re-enter and take possession of Blackacre. B has a fee simple on condition subsequent. It is expressly subject to the condition subsequent of only using Blackacre for residential purposes. B's estate is alienable, devisable, and descendible. O has a right of entry for condition broken which O can exercise should Blackacre not be used by B or B's successors for residential purposes. This right of entry at common law was neither alienable or devisable, but it was descendible. Today, it is often alienable, devisable, and descendible such that the right is enforceable by O or O's successors. However, in some states a periodic recording of O's intent to enforce the power is required.

§ 6. Enforcement of the Right of Entry

At early common law it was usually necessary for the grantor to make an actual entry on the land in order to terminate the granted estate for breach of the condition. But the necessity of entry no longer exists in American law. Many courts hold that the bringing of an action of ejectment or its equivalent is a sufficient indication of the grantor's election to terminate, although some courts require that notice of the election be given prior to the commencement of the action. Since the grantor has an election to enforce a forfeiture for breach or not, the grantor may waive the privilege either by express agreement or by conduct. Thus, a lessor who accepts payment of rent by the lessee after knowledge of the breach of condition waives the right to terminate for such breach although the lessor may enforce a forfeiture for subsequent breaches.[1] Whether mere inaction without more by the grantor, short of

3. In practically all standard forms of lease a right of entry is created in favor of the lessor for nonpayment of rent or breach of other covenants and conditions set forth in the lease. In such cases the right of entry for condition broken is incident to the reversion in the lessor.

§ 6

1. *See* Whitehouse Restaurant v. Hoffman, 320 Mass. 183, 68 N.E.2d 686 (1946).

any applicable statute of limitations, will amount to a waiver of the privilege to enforce a forfeiture is a controversial point. On principle, it would seem that failure to declare a forfeiture within a reasonable time after the grantor knows, or reasonably should have known, of the breach of condition should be held to amount to a waiver of the particular breach.[2]

Courts of equity sometimes grant relief against enforcement of a forfeiture for breach of a condition subsequent as an application of the doctrine that equity will relieve against penalties and forfeitures. A large element of discretion is involved and normally relief will be confined to situations where money damages can put the grantor in the same position as if the breach has not occurred. Thus, a lessee who pays or tenders rent past due may be granted equitable relief against enforcement of a right of entry for breach of the covenant to pay rent but not where the lessor has changed his position by leasing to a third person after making a re-entry.[3]

§ 7. Alienability of Right of Entry for Condition Broken

Under the English common law a right of entry for condition broken was not transferable by an inter vivos conveyance to a third person. In the words of Lord Coke: "Nothing in action, entry or re-entry can be granted over" and he assigned as a reason the "avoiding of maintenance, suppression of right and stirring up of suits."[1] While the reason assigned by Coke may have been historically unsound[2] the rule itself was unquestioned and stood until changed by statute in the middle nineteenth century.[3] American

---

2. *Accord* Goodman v. Southern Pacific Co., 143 Cal.App.2d 424, 299 P.2d 321 (1956). *See* Jefpaul Garage Corp. v. Presbyterian Hospital, in New York, 61 N.Y.2d 442, 474 N.Y.S.2d 458, 462 N.E.2d 1176 (1984).

3. *See* Paeff v. Hawkins–Washington Realty Co., 320 Mass. 144, 67 N.E.2d 900 (1946); Dodsworth v. Dodsworth, 254 Ill. 49, 98 N.E. 279 (1912) (relief against forfeiture for non-payment of taxes).

§ 7

1. Co. Litt. 214.

2. Professor Thorne states that the true reason for the non-assignability rule was the lack of a remedy under medieval law to the assignee. Since neither the assignee nor his ancestor had ever had seisin no real action to recover the seisin was available to him. *See* Thorne, Sir Edward Coke 14–17 (Selden Society Lecture, 1957).

3. 7 & 8 Vict. c. 76, § 5 (1844).

courts accepted the rule and even today it represents the weight of authority where the right of entry is not accompanied by a reversion, such as in a lease. In a few states there are statutes expressly making the interest alienable;[4] and in some jurisdictions a general statute providing for alienability of future interests has been held to include rights of entry for condition broken but there appears to be no general movement in favor of alienability of these interests.[5] The non-alienability rule is held to apply to assignments before and after breach of the condition.

A few American jurisdictions have held not only that a right of entry not incident to a reversion is inalienable but that an attempted alienation has the effect of destroying the right of entry-thereby adding what Professor Powell has called "a monstrous excrescence on this anachronism."[6] This doctrine originated in the case of *Rice v. Boston & Worcester Railroad Corporation*[7] and has been followed in a handful of jurisdictions. The Restatement originally accepted the *Rice* case as stating American law but has since repudiated it.[8] Since most courts have not passed on the question the Restatement change may be influential in persuading them to reject a doctrine that had no English case law to support it and lacks justification both in logic and in policy. Courts which hold that a possibility of reverter is inalienable do not also hold that it is destroyed by an attempted alienation. There is no reason for applying a different rule in the case of a right of entry.

4. *See, e.g.*, Cal. Civ. Code § 1046 (West 1982); Conn. Gen. Stat.Ann. § 47–29 (West 1995); N.Y. Real Prop. Law § 59(McKinney 1989), *amended by* 1962 N.Y. Laws Ch. 146; now covered by N.Y. Est. Powers & Trusts Law § 6–5.1 (McKinney 1992).

5. In Illinois a statute provides that rights of entry are incapable of being alienated or devised. However they are descendible. Ill. Comp. Stat. Ann. § 330/1 (West 2001).

6. 2A Powell, Real Property, § 275[3] (f).

7. 94 Mass. (12 Allen) 141 (1866).

8. Restatement of Property § 160 cmt. c (1936); Restatement of the Law (Supp., 1948) p.415. Only six states (Colorado, Maine, Massachusetts, Michigan, New York and Oregon) have applied the destruction on transfer rule. Michigan has since abrogated it by statute and Iowa and Oklahoma have refused to apply it. An Ohio case rejects it. PCK Properties, Inc. v. Cuyahoga Falls, 112 Ohio App. 492, 176 N.E.2d 441 (1960). *Accord* Emrick v. Bethlehem Township, 506 Pa. 372, 485 A.2d 736 (1984). As to the present New York law, *see supra* note 4.

At early common law a right of entry incident to a reversion was not transferable with a grant of the reversion. But by a statute enacted in 1540[9] it was provided that a right of entry incident to a reversion resulting from a conveyance of a life estate or a term of years would pass with a transfer of the reversion. This statute, or adaptations of it, are in force in many American jurisdictions and in others the courts reach the same result as that attained by the statute. Therefore, an assignee of a lessor can enforce against the lessee a right of entry specified in the lease for breach of its conditions.[10]

All courts agree that a right of entry is releasable by the grantor (or his heirs) to the then owner of the estate on condition subsequent. And the prevailing view is that such an interest is both descendible and devisable.[11]

§ 8. Duration of Right of Entry Arising From Fee Simple on Condition Subsequent

In recent years legislation has been enacted in many states limiting the duration of rights of entry arising from the creation of fees simple on condition subsequent.[1] Like the possibility of reverter, the right of entry is not, in the view of American courts, subject to the Rule against Perpetuities and is, therefore, capable of indefinite duration. Statutes restricting to a specified number of years the duration of possibilities of reverter, or requiring re-recording of claims of such interests, usually include rights of entry within their coverage.[2]

---

9. 32 Hen. 7, c. 34.

10. That the subject matter of the condition must touch and concern the land. *See* Stockbridge Iron Co. v. Cone Iron Works, 102 Mass. 80, 84 (1869).

11. Restatement of Property, §§ 164, 165 (1936). New York had taken the anomalous position that a right of entry for condition broken is not descendible or devisable but does to the heirs "by representation." Upington v. Corrigan, 151 N.Y. 143, 45 N.E. 359 (1896). At the present time in New York all future estates, including possibilities

of reverter and rights of entry, are descendible, devisable, and alienable. N.Y. Est. Powers & Trusts law §§ 6–3.2, 6–5.1 (McKinney 1992).

§ 8

1. Rights of entry incident to a reversion, such as those contained in leases, are not affected by such legislation.

2. *See, e.g.,* Mass.Gen.Laws.Ann. Ch. 184A, § 7 (1991). Statutes limiting the duration of rights of entry based upon fees simple on condition subsequent also exist in Connecticut (30

§ 9. The Possibility of Reverter Distinguished From Right of Entry for Condition Broken

It is necessary to distinguish carefully between a determinable fee simple and a fee simple on condition subsequent. Both of these estates are frequently created for the purpose of controlling the use of the land granted in the future and in that respect they are functional equivalents.[1] Moreover only a slight verbal difference in the creating instrument results in the granted estate being labeled as of one type rather than the other. But the conceptual differences are important. The future interest retained by the grantor of a determinable fee simple is a possibility of reverter; the future interest arising in the grantor of a fee simple on condition subsequent is a right of entry for condition broken.[2] These two future interests have different characteristics.[3] The principal difference between them is that the possibility of reverter automatically becomes a present estate in the grantor in fee simple, without any election on the part of the grantor, on the occurrence of the event specified in the instrument of conveyance. But a right of entry for condition broken is a power to terminate the granted estate for breach of the condition and until that power is properly exercised

years), Florida (21 years), Kentucky (30 years), Illinois (40 years), Maine (30 years), Nebraska (30 years), and Rhode Island (20 years). As to New York, see § 6, supra note 9. The Florida statute is unusual in that it permits a possibility of reverter or right of entry which exceeds the maximum period of duration to be enforced as a covenant or equitable restriction. Fla.Stat.Ann. § 689.18 (West 1994).

§ 9

1. Both of these estates are the historical antecedents of modern-day techniques of controlling land use through deed covenants and zoning laws. See generally, Goldstein, Rights of Entry and Possibilities of Reverter as Devices to Restrict the Use of Land, 54 HARV. L. REV. 248 (1940).

Remainders created in third persons, following on the heels of a life estate, are typically used as part of the wealth transfer process and thus are more often used in deeds of gifts and will. Fee simple determinables and fee simple on condition subsequent with their associated reversionary interests are rarely used in the wealth transfer process.

2. At times courts have added to the confusion by referring to a right of entry as a "possibility of reverter." See, e.g., Taylor v. Continental Southern Corp., 131 Cal.App.2d 267, 280 P.2d 514 (1955); Nicoll v. New York and Erie Railroad, 12 N.Y. 121 (1854); see also Proprietors of Church in Brattle Square v. Grant, 69 Mass. (3 Gray) 142 (1855).

3. For an argument that the differences between the two interests are insubstantial, see Dunham, Possibility of Reverter and Powers of Termination—Fraternal or Identical Twins?, 20 U. CHI. REV. 215 (1953).

the grantee's estate continues despite the breach. Thus, O, the owner of Blackacre in fee simple absolute, conveys Blackacre "to B and his heirs on condition that if liquor is sold on Blackacre O shall have the right to reenter and repossess Blackacre." B has a fee simple on condition subsequent and O has a right of entry for condition broken. If B opens a liquor store on Blackacre B still owns a fee simple on condition subsequent and will continue to own such estate until O, if ever, enters to take possession or begins an action to regain possession. Suppose, however, that the conveyance had been "to B and his heirs so long as liquor is not sold on Blackacre and if liquor is sold on Blackacre, it shall revert to O and his heirs." Here, B has a fee simple determinable. If B sells liquor on Blackacre his fee simple automatically come to an end and reverts to O. Suppose that following the sale of liquor on Blackacre but prior to any action by O to recover the property the government condemns Blackacre under its power of eminent domain. O would be entitled to the whole condemnation award.[4] On the other hand, if B's interest had been a fee on condition subsequent, O's failure to exercise his power of termination within a reasonable time could result in the award being payable to B only.[5]

Suppose O conveys Blackacre to B and his heirs so long as liquor is not sold on the premises. Ten years later B sells liquor on the premises and, as a result, O's possibility of reverter automatically becomes possessory. If B fails to vacate Blackacre, O has a cause of action against B in ejectment which accrues at the very

4. See Proprietors of Locks and Canals on Merrimack River v. Commonwealth, 341 Mass. 631, 171 N.E.2d 146 (1961). It should be noted that in this case the reverter had occurred prior to the taking by the state. Where there is an eminent domain taking prior to the occurrence of the specified event, the majority of courts hold that the owner of the determinable fee takes the entire condemnation award and that the owner of the possibility of revert is not entitled to any part of the award. But in Ink v. City of Canton, 4 Ohio St.2d 51, 212 N.E.2d 574 (1965) the court allotted a share of the award to the holder of the possibility of reverter. See Comment,

The Effect of Condemnation Proceedings by Eminent Domain upon a Possibility of Reverter or Power of Termination, 19 VILL. L. REV. 137 (1973).

5. See City of Santa Monica v. Jones, 104 Cal.App.2d 463, 232 P.2d 55 (1951). In re Certain Premises in Block 4987 Bounded by Farragut Road, 291 N.Y. 501, 50 N.E.2d 645 (1943); City of New York v. Coney Island Fire Dept., 259 App.Div. 286, 18 N.Y.S.2d 923 (N.Y.App.Div.1940) aff'd, 285 N.Y. 535, 32 N.E.2d 827 (1941); Simes & Smith, The Law of Future Interests, § 258 (2nd ed. 1956). But cf. Restatement of Property, § 53, cmt. d (1936).

moment B sells liquor on the premises. Thus, if O fails to sue B in ejectment within whatever period state law provides, O's later suit may be barred.[6] On the other hand, suppose O conveyed to B and his heirs but if liquor is sold on the premises O may elect to reenter the property. Here, conceptually, O should have no cause of action for possession until liquor is sold on the Blackacre *and* O demands possession and B refuses; thus, O's cause of action for possession should not accrue until there has been a demand and refusal. However, there is a division of authority on this point with some courts holding the statute of limitations begins to run from the date of B's breach of the condition and others holding that it runs from the time of demand and refusal.[7]

§ 10. Constructional Problems

It is often difficult to ascertain whether a particular deed or will creates a fee simple determinable or a fee simple on condition subsequent. Whether it is one or the other depends on the intention of the parties. Normally, this intention is sufficiently manifested by the language in the deed or will, but an ambiguity may be clarified by resort to the circumstances of the transaction.[1] The mode of termination of the granted estate provided for in the governing instrument is the controlling test of the parties' intention. Generally, unless there is manifested an intent that the estate is to expire

6. *See generally* Dunham, Possibility of Reverter and Powers of Termination—Fraternal or Identical Twins, 20 U of Chi. L. Rev. 215 (1952). All states have statutes of limitations that provide that suits for possession must be brought within some stated period after the cause of action accrues. Common time periods are ten years, twenty years and twenty-one years. The effect of the running of such a statute against the holder of a cause of action can result in the possessor acquiring a good title to the land by adverse possession. A possessor can acquire a title by adverse possession if throughout the period the owner could have sued for possession, the possessor's possession was actual, open and notorious, exclusive, continuous, and hostile and under claim of right.

7. *See* Dunham, *supra* note 6.

§ 10

1. "If the four corners of the deed provide a coherent expression of the parties' intent, we need search no further, but if an ambiguity or a reasonable doubt appears from a perusal of the particular symbols of expression our horizons must be broadened to encompass the circumstances surrounding the transaction." Oldfield v. Stoeco Homes, Inc., 26 N.J. 246, 257, 139 A.2d 291, 297 (1958); *See also* Carruthers v. Spaulding, 242 App.Div. 412, 275 N.Y.S. 37 (N.Y.App.Div.1934).

automatically on the happening of the stated event, the transferee does not have a fee simple determinable.

No particular words are necessary to create either a fee simple determinable or a fee on condition subsequent, but historically certain words have come to indicate an intent to create one type of estate rather than the other. The words "while," during," "until" or the phrase "so long as" are typical words of limitation and are usually held to manifest an intent to create a fee simple determinable. Normally, no express words of reverter are necessary to create a determinable fee[2] although the absence of a reverter clause may lead to the court to construe the deed as not creating a determinable estate.[3] On the other hand, the presence in the deed of a statement that on the occurrence of the stated event the land shall "revert" to the grantor is not alone conclusive of the grantor's intention to retain a possibility of reverter, especially where the instrument also contains language of condition.[4]

The phrases "upon condition that," "provided that," "but if," "if it happen that" are typical phrases of condition subsequent[5] and when coupled with the provision for re-entry by the transferor, normally will be construed to manifest an intent to create a fee simple on condition subsequent.

The dislike of the courts for forfeitures is often enough to sway a court to have a constructional preference for the fee simple on condition subsequent in an otherwise ambiguous instrument.[6] This

2. Peters v. East Penn Township School District, 182 Pa.Super. 116, 126 A.2d 802 (1956). *But cf.* PCK Properties, Inc. v. Cuyahoga Falls, 112 Ohio App. 492, 176 N.E.2d 441 (1960).

3. *See* In re Copps Chapel Methodist Episcopal Church, 120 Ohio St. 309, 166 N.E. 218 (1929).

4. *See, e.g.,* Dyer v. Siano, 298 Mass. 537, 11 N.E.2d 451 (1937); Trustees of Union College v. New York, 173 N.Y. 38, 65 N.E. 853 (1903); Oldfield v. Stoeco Homes, Inc., 26 N.J. 246, 139 A.2d 291 (1958).

5. Restatement of Property, §§ 44, 45 (1936). *See* Simes & Smith, The Law of Future Interests, § 286 (2nd ed. 1956).

6. *See, e.g.,* Oldfield v. Stoeco Homes, Inc., n. 5, *supra*; Storke v. Penn Mutual Life Ins. Co., 390 Ill. 619, 61 N.E.2d 552 (1945). *Cf.* Charlotte Park and Recreation Commission v. Barringer, 242 N.C. 311, 88 S.E.2d 114 (1955), *cert. denied* 350 U.S. 983, 76 S.Ct. 469, 100 L.Ed. 851 (1956). But in Opinion of the Justices to the Senate, 369 Mass. 979, 338 N.E.2d 806 (1975) despite words of condition in a deed, the estate created was said to be a fee simple determinable because of an additional clause reciting that "if said grantee shall fail to

construction can be more favorable to the grantee, particularly if the grantor did not expressly retain a right of entry for condition broken and the court neither implies one nor construes the condition as creating either a trust or a covenant.[7]

keep and perform said Condition then and in such event this deed shall become and be absolutely null and void." *Compare* United Methodist Church in West Sand Lake v. Dobbins, 48 A.D.2d 485, 369 N.Y.S.2d 817 (N.Y.App.Div.1975) where the deed recited that the conveyance to a church was "upon the express condition" that the land be used for church purposes and the deed further stated that if the land was not so used it "shall then revert back to the form" of the grantor. The conveyance was held to create a fee simple on condition subsequent.

California and Kentucky have, with rare good sense, abolished the fee simple determinable. Ky. Rev Stat. Ann.

§ 381.218 (Banks–Baldwin 1955) provides; "The estate known at common law as the fee simple determinable and the interest known as the possibility of reverter are abolished. Words which at common law would create a fee simple determinable shall be construed to create a fee simple subject to a right of entry for condition broken. In any case where a person would have a possibility of reverter at common law, he shall have a right of entry. The California statute is substantially similar." Cal. Civ. Code West's Ann. § 885.020 (1982).

7. *See, e.g.*,President and Fellows of Middlebury College v. Central Power Corp. of Vermont, 101 Vt. 325, 143 A. 384 (1928).

Chapter 5

FUTURE INTERESTS—
THE REMAINDERS

§ 1. The Concept of a Remainder

A remainder is a future interest created in a transferee "in such manner that it can become a present interest upon the expiration of all prior interests simultaneously created, and cannot divest any interest except an interest left in the transferor."[1] Thus, O owning Blackacre in fee simple conveys it "to B for life and then to C and his heirs." B has a possessory life estate, called the particular estate, and C has a remainder in fee simple. Since the remainder was limited to C and his heirs," when it becomes possessory at B's death C will have a fee simple absolute. If the remainder had been limited to C and the heirs of his body," then, at common law, C would have a remainder in fee tail.

C's future interest was originally called a remainder because on the expiration of B's life estate the land "remained" away from O, the transferor, instead of reverting to O. At common law the number of remainders which can be created is unlimited.[2] Thus, O might convey to B for life, then to C for life, then to D for life, then

---

§ 1

1. Restatement of Property, § 156(1) (1936).

2. In a few states the number of successive life estates was formerly restricted by statute to not more than two. These statutes were patterned on N.Y.

Real Prop. Law §§ 43, 45 (McKinney 1989) as those sections stood prior to their amendment in 1959. Sections 43 and 45 were repealed in 1960. See 6 American Law of Property (hereinafter referred to as "ALP"), §§ 25.92–25.98 and Supp., 1977.

142

to E and the heirs of his body, then to F and his heirs. All of the transferees except B have remainders since the interest of each can become a possessory estate on the expiration of the prior estates.

According to the doctrine of estates, a fee simple represented the totality of ownership; there can be no remainder after a fee simple, whether it be a present estate in fee simple or a vested remainder in fee simple. Since a fee simple determinable was looked upon as having the same quality of duration as the fee simple absolute, there could be no remainder after a fee simple determinable.[3]

How does a remainder differ from a reversion? First, a reversion arises by operation of law apart from the intent of the transferor; a remainder is created in a transferee only by an express or implied limitation and by the same instrument which creates a present possessory estate in a transferee. Second, a reversion arises only in favor of the transferor (or his heirs) whereas a remainder can be created only in favor of a third person, and then only if created simultaneously with the creation of the present possessory estate.[4] Thus, if O transfers property to B for life, O has a reversion. If later O transfers this reversion to C, then C has a reversion and not a remainder.

---

3. Restatement of Property, § 156(2)(1936). This rule effectively is an exception of the definition of a remainder in section 156(1). If the future interest following the fee simple determinable becomes possessory it does not "divest" the interest of the prior transferee holding the fee simple determinable as such estate ends upon the happening of limitation, not a condition. Nonetheless, the Restatement continues to adhere to the common-law rule prohibiting a remainder to follow on the heels of a fee simple determinable.

The future interest limited to take effect on the expiration of a fee simple determinable is classified as an executory interest, not as a remainder. Thus, if O conveys "to B and his heirs so long as the land is used during B's lifetime for residential purposes and if during B's lifetime the land is not so used then to C and his heirs" B has a fee simple determinable and C has an executory interest. *Cf.*, First Universalist Society of North Adams v. Boland, 155 Mass. 171, 29 N.E. 524 (1892). *See* Restatement of Property, §§ 25.47, 156(2)(1936). Simes & Smith, The Law of Future Interests § 103 (2d ed. 1956).

4. Finally, at English common law there was tenure between the holder of the particular estate and the reversioner but there was no tenure between the holder of the particular estate and the remainderman. This last difference would, of course, be of no significance in modern law.

Prior to the Statute of Uses (1536) the remainder was the only future interest that could be created in favor of a person other than the transferor or his heirs. A future interest created in favor of a transferee which did not possess the characteristics of a remainder was void. A principal characteristic of a remainder is that it becomes a possessory estate only on the expiration, and not the divestment, of the preceding estates created by the same instrument. A remainder does not cut short a prior estate; it awaits the orderly termination of the preceding estate by the happening of a limitation. Thus, O, owning Blackacre in fee simple, conveys Blackacre "to B and his heirs but if B dies leaving no surviving children, then to C and his heirs." C does not have a remainder but a future interest that divests or displaces B's estate in fee. It divests B's estate because for B's estate to come to an end a condition (not a limitation) must occur.[5] At common law such a future interest— called an executory interest—was void, but after the Statute of Uses it was valid.[6]

To qualify as a remainder the future interest must be limited to take effect in possession *immediately* on the expiration of the prior interest simultaneously created. A remainder cannot be so limited as to become a possessory estate following a gap after the ending of the prior estate. Thus, suppose O, who owns Blackacre in fee simple, conveys Blackacre to B for life, and one year after B's death to C and his heirs. C does not have a remainder. Prior to the Statute of Uses C's interest was void but thereafter it could be created as a valid springing executory interest.[7]

The definition of a remainder[8] contemplates the possibility that the future interest labeled a remainder might or might not become possessory at the end of the particular estate. *It is not essential that it must become possessory.* Thus, merely because a remainder is subject to a condition precedent that might prevent it from become possessory in the future does not prevent that interest from being classified as a remainder. In fact, it is this distinction that largely distinguishes the vested remainder from the contingent remainder.

---

5. *But see* note 3, *supra* (fee simple determinable exception).

6. *See generally* ch. 8, *infra.*

7. *Id.*

8. *See* note 1 *supra* and accompanying text.

Likewise, under that definition the classification of a future interest as a remainder does not mean that if it becomes possessory it forever will remain possessory, a distinction relevant to the difference between a vested remainder and a vested remainder subject to complete divestment.

Review Problems

1. O, who owns Blackacre in fee simple, conveys Blackacre to B for life, and upon B's death, to C and his heirs. B has a life estate and C has a remainder in Blackacre. C's estate is capable of becoming possessory immediately upon the termination of B's life estate.

2. O, who owns Blackacre in fee simple, conveys Blackacre to B for life and one day after B's death, to C and his heirs. C cannot have a remainder because C's estate is incapable of becoming possessory *immediately* upon the termination of B's estate. Rather, one day must pass before C's estate can become possessory.

§ 2.   Historical Basis of Distinction Between Remainders

The notion that a tenant of land in fee simple could convey a present possessory estate in that land and simultaneously create a future estate in favor of a third person was not readily accepted by the early common law.[1] It is probable that remainders were not recognized as valid estates until shortly after the Statute De Donis (1285). Thereafter a remainder following a fee tail was given recognition and legal protection. Remainders following a life estate were then developed.[2] The common law, however, was not willing

---

§ 2

1. For a discussion of the historical development of remainders, *see* Percy Bordwell, The Common Law Scheme of Estates and the Remainder, 34 Iowa L.Rev. 401 (1949).

2. A freehold estate following on a term of years is classified as a remainder in modern law. Restatement of Property, § 156 (1936). The common law view was that such an interest was a present free-

hold estate rather than a remainder. Thus, O, owner of Blackacre in fee simple, conveys Blackacre to B for ten years, then to C and his heirs. Because C had seisin, the common law view was that C had a present estate in fee simple subject to a term of years in B. This type of conveyance was often used to repay B for money B loaned C to purchase Blackacre.

to recognize as a valid estate every future interest having some of the characteristics or the form of a remainder. If O, the owner of Blackacre in fee simple, conveyed "to B for life, and on B's death to C and his heirs" C was in a position to take the seisin on B's death and to discharge the feudal obligations due to the lord of the fee. C, therefore, had an estate in the land, a valid remainder. Suppose that O conveyed "to B for life and on B's death to C (a bachelor) and his heirs if, but only if, C marries." Here, there is an element of uncertainty attaching to C's interest, a condition precedent to C's right to take the land on B's death. C might or might not marry and until C did C had no right to the seisin. The common law took the view that C did not have an estate but the mere possibility of acquiring an estate. Not until the sixteenth century was C's interest recognized at law. It was then decided that if the condition precedent of marriage was satisfied during the continuance of the preceding estate C would be permitted to take the land on the expiration of B's life estate. C's interest was labeled a "contingent" remainder to distinguish it from a "vested" remainder. This distinction arose at a time when it was a rigid principle of the common law that on the termination of a possessory freehold estate there must be some ascertained person in existence capable of taking the seisin. There could be no gap in, or abeyance, of the seisin. Because of this principle, if C's contingent remainder could not become possessory when the life estate terminated because the condition had not yet occurred, it was destroyed.[3]

All remainders are either vested or contingent. A remainder is "vested" when it is limited in favor of a person who is both in existence and ascertained and is not subject to a condition precedent. For example, if O creates a remainder in C, a living person, and the remainder is not subject to any condition precedent, C's remainder is vested.

If, on the other hand, the remainder is limited to an unascertained person[4] or to a person who is not in existence, or it is limited

---

3. § 9, *infra.*

4. Thus a remainder limited to the first child of B who graduates law school by a conveyance made at a time when B is dead and has children none of whom

has yet graduated law school is contingent. It is contingent because the remainderman is not yet ascertained. Until it is determined which, if any, of B's children will be the first to graduate law

in favor of an ascertained living person but is subject to a condition precedent,[5] it is a "contingent" remainder.

The word "vested" when used by the common law referred to ownership of an estate—the vested remainder was an estate, the contingent remainder was only a possibility of an estate.[6] An estate may be vested in possession as well as in interest or it may be vested only in interest. If O, the owner of Blackacre in fee simple, conveys to B for life, remainder to C and his heirs, B has an estate vested both in possession and in interest; C has an estate vested in interest only. Of course, at B's death C's interest will vest in possession as well. All present possessory freehold estates are vested in both interest and possession.

Although the concept of a remainder, as well as of other future interests, had its origin in the land law, today future interests may be created in personal property, including intangibles, as well as in real property.[7] In fact, it is more likely today that a future interest (particularly remainders) will be created in property held in a trust than in a conveyance of real property. Since it is appropriate to speak of a remainder in personal property, the concept of a "vested" remainder as an estate and that of a "contingent" remainder

school we cannot ascertain which of B's children is the remainderman.

5. The condition may be expressed or implied. For example, a remainder limited to B if B survives A is a remainder subject to an express condition precedent. If a remainder is limited in favor of a class of persons, such as issue or descendants, it may be subject to an implied condition of survivorship.

6. This was the primary meaning of "vested" in property law. The word is also used in other senses, e.g., in the sense of being transmissible on death. The use of the term in the latter sense has led a court to speak of "a vested interest in a contingent remainder!" Clarke v. Fay, 205 Mass. 228, 235, 91 N.E. 328, 330 (1910). Fortunately, such use of "vested" is not common. For a discussion of the concept of "vested," *see*

5 ALP, §§ 21.5–21.8; Simes & Smith, The Law of Future Interests §§ 133–141 (2d ed. 1956).

7. The topic of future interests in personalty is not specifically covered in this book. For a comprehensive treatment, see Simes & Smith, The Law of Future Interests, §§ 331–371 (2d ed. 1956). It should be noted, however, that at the present time most future interests are created in personal property, not in land, and more particularly, personal property held in trust. This is because future interests today usually arise under a trust and trust property almost invariably consists of money, shares of stock, bonds and other kinds of securities. The interest of the trust beneficiaries is equitable, not legal. As a general matter, the classification scheme for future interests in realty applies as well to future interests in trusts.

as the possibility of an estate is now anachronistic. Today when we speak of a remainder as being "vested," we mean that it has certain definite characteristics, namely, that the remainderman is a presently identifiable person and that the remainder is not subject to a *condition precedent*.[8]

The word "vest," however, often takes on other meanings. For example, some courts—although we think inappropriately—use the word "vested" as synonymous with "transmissible" and "contingent" as synonymous with "non-transmissible." For example, if O, the owner of Blackacre in fee simple, conveys to B for life, then to C and his heirs, and C dies before B, C's interest passes through C's estate to the devisees of the interest under C's will or, if none, to C's heirs. Thus, C's interest (vested) is transmissible. Likewise, if O deeds Blackacre to A for life, then to B is B survives A and B dies before A, B's contingent interest is not transmissible because it expires by his death.

However, not all vested interests are transmissible and not all contingent interests are nontransmissible. For example, if O conveyed to B for life, then to C for life, then to D and his heirs and C died before B, C's estate (although vested) is not transmissible as it expired when the limitation attached to it occurred. Conversely, contingent interests can be transmissible. For example, suppose O deeds property A for life, then to B and his heirs if X marries Y. Suppose further that B dies before A leaving B's entire estate to Z. Even though B's interest was contingent on X marrying Y, if that event occurs before A dies (and today even after A dies), the property will pass to Z.

§ 3. The Classification of Remainders

Traditionally, remainders are divided into two main categories: vested and contingent. At common law, substantially different legal

---

8. It is almost impossible to define the word "vest" in a single sentence that will be accurate in all contexts. Generally speaking, the term has reference to the absence of a *condition precedent* to the future interest becoming possessory, other than the termination of the preceding estate or estates created by the same conveyance.

An interest subject to a *condition subsequent* as distinguished from a *condition precedent* can be vested. *See* § 5, *infra*.

consequences attached to these two types of interests because vested remainders were thought to be an estate while a contingent remainder had merely the possibility of becoming one.[1] As a result, a vested remainder was transferable; a contingent remainder was not transferable.[2] A vested remainder was indestructible; a contingent remainder was destructible.[3] A vested remainderman received greater protection against misuse of the land by the holder of the possessory estate than did a contingent remainderman. A vested remainder could generally accelerate whereas a contingent remainder could not.[4]

Today the differences between these two types of remainders are less important. Several of the common law consequences of being a contingent remainder, such as the rule of destructibility, as we shall see, have been eliminated or modified. In some situations it is immaterial whether the remainder is classified as vested or contingent since the end result is the same. But, there are still significant differences between the two types of remainders, and the classification of a particular interest as of one type or the other may dictate certain consequences in a given case. Of course, contingent remainders (unlike indefeasibly vested remainders[5] but not vested remainders subject to complete divestment[6]) can still fail if the contingency to which they are subject does not occur, thus exposing the holder of the estate to the risk of losing it. Furthermore, the Rule against Perpetuities[7] is generally applicable to contingent remainders but not to vested remainders. And, there is

§ 3

1. The modern definition of the word "estate" is sufficiently broad to include contingent remainders. See Restatement of Property, § 9 (1936).

2. In almost all American jurisdictions, today, both vested and contingent remainders are alienable.

3. See § 9, *infra*.

4. For example, if O conveyed Blackacre to B for life, then to C and his heirs and B's estate terminated prematurely as a result of a tortious feoffment (an attempted conveyance by B of more than B had) or B's conviction of a crime, C's interest could become immediately possessory. On the other hand, if C's remainder was conditioned on C surviving B, then upon the premature termination of B's interest, C's interest could not accelerate. In fact, if the rule of destructibility applied, C's interest in this case would be destroyed and would never become possessory. See § 8, *infra*.

5. See § 5(A), *infra*.

6. See § 5(C), *infra*.

7. See ch. 8, § 11, *infra*.

a greater likelihood that a contingent remainder will not accelerate if the particular estate prematurely terminates. For example, suppose O, the owner of Blackacre in fee simple, conveys Blackacre to B for life, then to C and his heirs if C marries X. Suppose further that three years after the conveyance B renounces the life estate in Blackacre. C's contingent remainder[8] is not likely to accelerate if C has not yet married X.[9]

To what extent does the classification of a remainder as vested or contingent depend on the intention of the transferor? In a donative transaction the intention of the transferor as expressed in the creating instrument is given effect, when possible, in determining the disposition of the property. Thus, if the transferor manifests an intent that a particular future interest shall be subject to a specified condition precedent the transferor's intention is given controlling weight. Where the manifestation of intention is not clear, or is absent, rules of construction are resorted to in order to ascertain the meaning of the language used.[10] For example, at common law, there was a presumption that a remainder was vested, not contingent. This construction necessarily made the property more marketable as contingent remainders were inalienable. Today, on the other hand, there may be tax reasons to prefer a contingent to a vested construction where the language in the instrument is ambiguous.[11]

8. The Restatement of Property discards the term "contingent remainder" because of the confusion that has arisen in its use and substitutes the term "remainder subject to a condition precedent." Restatement of Property, § 157(d) (1936). However, the courts continue to use the older terminology.

9. Although contingent remainders were not generally capable of accelerating, a court might avoid that rule by construing the instrument to determine whether any purpose would be served in light of the grantor's intent in denying acceleration.

10. Much of the modern law of future interests is concerned with prob-

lems of construction most of which are beyond the scope of this book. As to theories of construction, see Simes and Smith, The Law of Future Interests, §§ 461–473 (2nd ed. 1956); 5 ALP,§§ 21.1–21.4; Restatement of Property, §§ 241–242 (1940).

11. For a discussion of the constructional preferences, see In re Estate of Houston, 414 Pa. 579, 201 A.2d 592 (1964). With respect to remainders in a trust, the Uniform Probate Code evidences a constructional preference for contingent remainders. See Unif. Prob. Code § 2–707.

§ 4. The Definition of a Vested Remainder, Generally

It is difficult to formulate a simple but precise and comprehensive definition of a vested remainder. In general, it may be defined as a future interest limited to a person in existence and ascertained at the time the interest is created who is given the right to immediate possession whenever and however the preceding estate or estates terminate because the interest is not subject to a condition precedent.[1] This definition finds its basis in the common-law doctrine of the necessity of continuity of seisin.

However, the definition most often quoted by the courts is that given by Professor John Chipman Gray: "A remainder is vested if, at every moment during its continuance, it becomes a present estate, whenever and however the preceding freehold estates determine. A remainder is contingent [not vested] if, in order for it to become a present estate, the fulfillment of some condition precedent, other than the determination of the preceding freehold estates, is necessary."[2] A present unconditional right to possession in favor of an identified person on the termination of the preceding interests may be said to be the essence of a vested remainder. Some states have statutes defining vested and contingent remainders.[3] These statutes are patterned on the common-law concept but in a few jurisdictions they have been judicially construed to reach a result different from the common law in certain situations.[4]

The following cases are illustrations of vested remainders in C. In each case C's remainder is vested. In each case O, the grantor, owns Blackacre in fee simple and conveys Blackacre:

§ 4

1. A vested remainder cannot be subject to a condition precedent but may be subject to a condition subsequent in which case it is classified as a vested remainder subject to being divested. *See* § 5, *infra*.

2. Gray, Rule Against Perpetuities, §§ 9, 101 (4th ed. Little Brown & Co. 1942).

3. *See, e.g.*, N.Y. Est. Powers & Trust Law § 6–4.10 (McKinney 1992):

"A future estate subject to a condition precedent (the N.Y. statutory term for contingent remainder) is an estate created in favor of one or more unborn or unascertained persons or in favor of one or more presently ascertainable persons upon the occurrence of an uncertain event."

4. *See, e.g.*, Moore v. Littel, 41 N.Y. 66 (1869).

1. To B for life, then to C and his heirs.

2. To B and the heirs of his body, then to C and his heirs.[5]

3. To B for life, then to C for life.[6]

4. To B for life, then to X for life if X marries, remainder to C and his heirs.

5. To B for life, then to the children of X and their heirs (X being alive and having one child, C).

6. To B for life, then to C and his heirs but if C does not marry before B dies then to X and his heirs.[7]

7. To B for life and on his death to such of his children as B may by will appoint, and in default of appointment to C and his heirs.[8]

---

5. At common law B had a fee tail and C had a vested remainder in fee. C had a vested remainder because if B's estate terminates, the termination is the result of the happening of a limitation, namely, that B's line of lineal descendants became extinct. However, in a state having a statute abolishing the fee tail and substituting a different estate the future interest given to C would be a contingent remainder or an executory interest depending on the type of statute. *See* Simes & Smith, The Law of Future Interests, § 313.

6. Here, since O failed to convey away the entirety of O's fee simple, O retains a reversion.

7. Here, C has a vested remainder. It is a remainder limited in favor of an ascertained person—C—and it is not subject to the happening of any condition precedent. It is subject, however, to defeasance upon the happening of a condition subsequent. X does not have a remainder since to become possessory it must divest the interest of another transferee, namely C. It is a shifting executory interest. However, if C were to die in B's lifetime without ever having married, C's vested remainder would

be divested and X's interest would become a vested remainder. *See generally* § 5(C), *infra*.

8. A power of appointment is an authority one person (the donor) gives to another (the donee) which permits the donee to re-order a property disposition once made by the donor. In a well-drawn instrument creating a power of appointment the donor will generally designate the persons to take if the donee fails to exercise the power of appointment. These persons are called takers in default of appointment. Under the existing rules of construction, where an instrument creates a power of appointment and designates the takers in default, the exercise of the power is deemed to be a condition subsequent that divests the takers in default of their interest. Thus, in the conveyance in the text, courts construe the interests of C as if the instrument had read "to B for life, then to C and his heirs but if B exercises a power of appointment in favor of his children, then to such of B's children as B appoints. Here C has a vested remainder subject to divestment; B's children would have an executory interest.

§ 5. The Classification of Vested Remainders

There are three kinds of vested remainders: (1). Remainders absolutely vested (sometimes called the "indefeasibly vested remainder"); (2). Remainders vested subject to partial divestment (also known as "subject to open)[1]; and (3). Remainders vested subject to complete divestment.[2] Illustrations 1, 2, 3 and 4 in the preceding section are examples of indefeasibly vested remainders; illustration 5 exemplifies a remainder vested subject to partial divestment; and illustrations 6 and 7 typify remainders vested subject to complete divestment. Why? Read on.

A. Remainders Indefeasibly Vested

A remainder is indefeasibly vested when it is limited in favor of a born, ascertained, or identifiable person or persons and is *not* subject to any words of condition precedent or condition subsequent which might cause the interest to not vest, or if vested, to be divested. Thus, O, the owner of Blackacre in fee simple, conveys Blackacre to B for life, then to C and his heirs. C has an indefeasibly vested remainder. It is subject to no conditions of any kind.[3] In fact, this remainder is in fee simple[4] and it will become possessory in all events. Stated differently, there is no imaginable circumstances under which this remainder will not become possessory. But, what if C died before B? Because C's remainder is alienable, devisable, and descendible, if C dies before B, the remainder will

§ 5

1. *See* Restatement of Property, § 157(b)(1936).

2. The classification here adopted is similar to, but not identical with, the classification of vested remainders used in the Restatement of Property. The Restatement classifies vested remainders into: (a) remainders "indefeasibly vested;" (b) remainders "vested subject to open;" (c) remainders "vested subject to complete defeasance." Restatement of Property, § 157 (1936). The word "defeasance" is used in the Restatement as including both expiration and divestment. Under the Restatement terminology a vested remainder in fee simple determinable would not be indefeasibly vested since the remainder interest could expire by the occurrence of the stated event; however, the remainder would not be subject to divestment by reason of its being a determinable estate since it would expire but not be cut short on the happening of the stated event.

3. The termination of the particular estate preceding C's estate, i.e, B's life estate, is not a condition.

4. This means that when it becomes possessory, C will have a fee simple.

become possessory (no if, ands, or buts) in C's successors-in-interest. Thus, when we say C has a vested remainder we really mean that C has an interest in Blackacre and it is that interest that is classified as a vested remainder.

A remainder can be vested even though there is no certainty that the remainderman will ever enjoy actual possession. Thus, O conveys Blackacre to B for life, then to C for life. Here, C has a vested remainder, although it is possible that it will never become possessory. C will never, in fact, come into possession if C dies before B. However, it is the presence or absence of a condition precedent, not the certainty or probability of enjoyment of possession, that decides whether the remainder is vested or contingent.[5]

Words which are conditional in form but which express nothing more than the law implies will not make the remainder contingent. Thus, if T devises Blackacre to B for life and from and after B's death to C and his heirs in fee, it might be argued that B's death is a condition precedent to C's remainder. But the words "from and after" are construed to refer to the time of enjoyment of possession by C, not to the time of the vesting of C's interest. The courts usually apply a presumption in favor of construing a limitation as creating a vested rather than a contingent interest, and also a presumption in favor of early vesting rather than later vesting. Hence, when an instrument creates a life estate in B and then provides for a remainder in C "at B's death," or "when B dies," or "in the event of B's death" such language will not be construed as making the remainder contingent.[6]

5. If O conveys Blackacre to B for life, then to C for life if C survives B, is C's remainder vested or contingent? The remainder would seem to be vested on the ground that the condition of C's survivorship adds no additional element of uncertainty; since C has only a life interest he could not take in any event unless he survived B. Simes & Smith, The Law of Future Interests, § 142 (2d ed. 1956). If, on the other hand, the limitations were to B for life, then to C and his heirs if C survives B, the remainder in fee to C would be contingent because of the condition precedent of survivorship.

6. Another way of thinking of this is that the phrase "at B's death" is merely redundant of the limitation contained in B's estate which is an estate for life. But put more candidly, the termination of the life estate (an event which will happen as we are all going to die) is not a condition precedent to future interests following on its heels.

B. Remainders Vested Subject to Partial Divestment

A remainder is vested subject to being partially divested (or subject to open) when it is limited in favor of a group of persons, typically collectively described (such as A's children) *where there is at least one remainderman who is alive and ascertained.* The nature of this remainder is that the percentage size of each remainderman's interest is subject to diminution in favor of other members of the class who may later join the class. This type of remainder, frequently called a vested remainder vested subject to open, is illustrated by a common kind of class gift. Suppose T devises Blackacre to B for life, then to the children of B and their heirs. At the time of T's death B has one child, C. C's remainder is vested because C is alive and ascertained. C (or C's successors) is certain to acquire a possessory interest on the expiration of B's life estate. At common law, the seisin can pass to C immediately on B's death. However, during B's life, C's remainder is subject to open to let in after-born children of B because they also come within the terms of the gift. Thus, if after T's death two more children are born to B they take equally with C as remaindermen and C's interest is reduced to a one-third share.[7]

If, in the above example (T devises Blackacre to B for life, then to the children of B and their heirs), B has no children at the time of T's death, there is a contingent remainder in B's unborn children.[8] If a child is born to B that child's contingent remainder becomes a vested remainder subject to open, and the contingent remainder in any unborn children is changed into an executory

---

7. In Minnig v. Batdorff, 5 Pa. 503 (1847), the court summarized the rule thus: "When there is an immediate gift to children, those only living at the testator's death will take; but it is now settled, that where a particular estate or interest is carved out, with a gift over to the children of the person taking that interest, or of any other person, the limitation will embrace not only the objects living at the death of the testator, but all who shall subsequently come into existence before the period of distribution. Such a remainder vests in the objects to whom the description applies at the death of the testator, subject to open and let in others answering the description as they are born successively."

8. There is, of course, a logical difficulty in viewing any unborn person as owning a future interest. However, it is customary for courts and lawyers to conceptualize unborn persons as capable of owning such interests. What is really meant is that living persons having interests in the property will be compelled by the courts to respect the expectant interests of those who may acquire rights in the property on birth.

interest which will partially divest the vested remainder of the earlier born child or children.[9] On the death of B, the vested remainders become present possessory estates in fee simple in B's children.

In every class gift the question arises: At what point in time can no more children join in the class and share in the gift? In property talk, the question is generally stated: "When will the class gift *close?" This is a very important question because once it is determined a gift to a class of persons is closed, then no new members can join the class and share in the gift.*

In the last example (a remainder limited to B's children on B's death) the answer is pretty obvious. Under what is known as the physiological class closing rule, a class closes when the person who can produce the class members dies. Thus, the class clearly closes at B's death since B is the person who can produce members of the class.[10]

Suppose, however, that T devises Blackacre to B for life, then to the children of C and their heirs. Obviously, if C were to die in B's lifetime, the class gift to C's children would close physiologically at C's death. On the other hand, suppose both C and two of C's children survive B. Is the class closed at B's death? Yes, under what is known as the rule of convenience[11] which is an alternative way to close a class. Under the rule of convenience, a class that is still open physiologically closes whenever any member of the class (or such

---

9. It should be noted that some courts have referred to the interests of the unborn children in this situation as contingent remainders. *See* 1 ALP, § 4.34. In a jurisdiction that makes contingent remainders indestructible there will be little, if any, practical difference.

10. If at B's death, B is survived by four children and a spouse who is pregnant and she later gives birth to B's fifth child, that fifth child is also included in the class under the rule that a child conceived before the date of distribution (B's death) and born thereafter, is deemed to be alive on the date of distribution. *See generally* Restatement (Second) of Property, § 26.2, cmt. c

(1988). As we move into the 21st century, issues will arise whether children born as a result of assisted reproductive technologies after the death of their biological parents will also be included in the class gift. See, Woodard v. Commissioner of Social Security, 435 Mass. 536, 760 N.E.2d 257 (2002) (child conceived posthumously with father's sperm is father's heir for social security purposes). See also Unif. Parentage Act § 707.

11. Restatement (Second) of Property, § 26.2(1) (1988). The rule of convenience is a rule of construction and will give way to a contrary intent. *Id.* at cmt. p.

member's successor) is entitled to demand possession of his or her share. A class member is entitled to demand possession of his or her share so long as there is no outstanding present possessory estate, like a life estate, and the potential demandant's interest is not *subject to any conditions precedent*. Thus, in the preceding example, C's children during B's life had a vested remainder subject to open. It was subject to no conditions precedent. Once B died, either of them could demand possession of his or her share since B's outstanding life estate had come to an end and the interest of C's children was subject to no conditions precedent. This is enough to close the class. *And, don't forget, once the class closes, no new members can join the class.* Thus, if two years later C has a third child, that child does not share in the gift.[12]

The rule of convenience's requirement that a demandant's interest not be subject to any unfulfilled condition precedent does not affect vested remainder subject to open but can impact contingent remainders limited in favor of a class. Thus, suppose T devises Blackacre to B for life, remainder to the children of C and their heirs who attain the age of 21. If C survives B but C's oldest child is then only 14, the class does not yet close under the rule of convenience (and obviously not physiologically since C is living) because C's oldest child's interest is subject to the unfulfilled condition of reaching age 21. The class will close under the rule of convenience if that child reaches age 21 in C's lifetime. If that child does not reach 21, the gift will remain open until C dies or another child of C reaches age 21.[13]

C. Remainders Vested Subject to Complete Divestment

A remainder is vested subject to complete divestment when the remainderman is in existence and ascertained and the remainderman's interest is not subject to a condition precedent. But the remainderman's right to possession or enjoyment on the expiration of the prior interests is subject to termination by reason of the happening of a condition subsequent followed by an executory interest, or by the exercise of a power of appointment or a right of

---

12. *See* Restatement (Second) of Property, § 26.2 cmt. i (1988).

13. *See generally* Restatement (Second) of Property, § 26.2 cmt. m (1988).

entry for condition broken. Thus, O, the owner of Blackacre in fee simple, conveys Blackacre to B for life, then to C and his heirs but if C dies leaving no surviving children then to D and his heirs. C has a vested remainder subject to complete divestment if C dies without surviving children. D's interest is not a remainder but an executory interest. If C predeceases B leaving no surviving children, C's interest is divested and D's executory interest ripens into a vested remainder. Similarly, if C survives B and later dies without surviving children, C's fee simple is divested and D's executory interest becomes a fee simple.

Similarly, if O conveys Blackacre to B for life, remainder as B shall appoint, and in default of appointment to C and his heirs, C has a remainder vested subject to complete divestment.[14] Because of the strong preference for construing an interest as vested, C's remainder is viewed as being subject to divestment by the exercise of the power of appointment rather than as being contingent on the non-exercise of the power. If B exercises the power and appoints the property to X, X takes an executory interest. A third example of this type of remainder would be: O conveys Blackacre to B for life, remainder to C and his heirs on the express condition that if the premises are used for the sale of intoxicating liquor O shall have the power to re-enter and repossess Blackacre.[15]

Whenever in the same conveyance or devise future interests are created in two distinct transferees (whether as individuals or as separate class gifts) difficult problems of construction can arise in determining whether words of condition amount to a condition

---

14. A power of appointment may be generally defined as a power or authorization given by the owner of a property interest (the donor) to another person (the donee) to designate a transferee or transferees of that interest (the appointees) or the shares which the appointees are to take. Instruments creating powers of appointment usually make a gift over in default of appointment to take care of the situation where the donee of the power fails to exercise it. These persons are called "takers in default of appointment."

15. A further illustration of a remainder vested subject to complete divestment is where property is given in trust for the benefit of a person for life with power in the trustee to invade the principal for the benefit of the life tenant, followed by a remainder over. Thus, O transfers to T in trust to pay the income to B for life together with such portion of the principal as T may deem necessary for B's comfortable maintenance, remainder to C in fee.

precedent to the interest or a condition subsequent.[16] *If the conditional words amount to a condition precedent the remainder is contingent; if such words amount to a condition subsequent the remainder is vested subject to divestment.* Thus, if T devises Blackacre to B for life, then, if C (a bachelor) marries before B dies, to C and his heirs on B's death, but if C does not marry before B dies, then to D and his heirs, C's remainder is contingent. C's remainder is subject to a condition precedent. On the other hand, it T devises Blackacre to B for life, then to C (a bachelor) and his heirs but if C does not marry before B dies then to D and his heirs, C has a vested remainder subject to divestment. C's remainder is subject to a condition subsequent. It is true that the difference is principally one of form since C will not take in either case unless he marries during B's lifetime yet the distinction is usually adhered to by the courts with possible consequences.[17] Thus, form matters.

So how does one distinguish between a condition precedent and a condition subsequent. There are a number of tests that potentially help resolve the problem, all of which are merely rules of construction capable of giving way to a contrary intent. The starting point in making the classification is to understand that interests in a conveyance are classified in the order in which they are set forth in the governing instrument. If O conveys Blackacre to B for life, then to C and his heirs but if C fails to attain the age of 21, then to D and his heirs, first B's interest is classified (it is, of course a life estate), then C's interest is classified, then D's interest is classified. Next, the words of condition attached to the gift of the *first* future interest as it appears in the instrument are identified. Here, the words are: "but if C fails to attain the age of 21." Then, one determines whether those words come before or after the designation of the taker of that first future interest. Here, all the words of condition come after the designation of C as the remain-

---

16. If only one future interest is created in a deed or will in an individual or class and it is subject to a condition, the condition is invariably a condition precedent. For example, whether O deeds Blackacre to B for life, and if C reaches age 21, to C and his heirs or, alternatively, deeds Blackacre to B for life, then to C and his heirs if C reaches the age of 21, C has a contingent remainder. *See* § 6, *infra*.

17. For example, if B's estate ends before B's death, C's interest accelerates if it is vested; it may not accelerate if it is contingent.

derman. Thus, they come after (they are subsequent) to the designation of C as a remainderman; they are words of condition subsequent and C has a vested remainder subject to divestment. But, suppose, O conveys Blackacre to B for life, then if C attains age 21, to C and his heirs, but if C does not attain age 21, then to D and his heirs. Here there are two conditional phrases: "if C attains age 21" and "but if C does not attain age 21." However, because interests must be classified in the order in which they are set forth in the governing instrument, the first conditional phrase to be considered is "if C attains age 21" and it appears before the designation of C as the remainderman. They come before the name of C; they are words of condition precedent and C has a contingent remainder. Once C's interest is classified, it is easy to classify D's interest. If C has a vested remainder subject to complete divestment, then D must have a shifting executory interest;[18] if C has a contingent remainder, D must also have a contingent remainder.

The foregoing remember is merely a rule on construction. Sometimes it just doesn't work. For example, suppose T devises Blackacre to B for life, then to C and his heirs if C attains age 21 but if C fails to attain age 21, then to D and his heirs. Using the test set forth in the preceding paragraph, at first glance it appears C has a vested remainder subject to divestment because all the words of condition appear after the designation of C as the remaindermen. However, this would result in C's interest being classified in the same manner it would have been classified if T had devised Blackacre to B for life, then to C and his heirs but if C fails to attain age 21, then to D and his heirs. Nonetheless, that is how it might be classified if the court concluded such construction would be consistent with T's intent. However, such a construction does violence to another rule of construction which is that in construing instruments courts should try to give effect to all the words used by the grantor or testator. The suggested construction gives no effect to the phrase "if C attains age 21" but treats them as mere surplusage. In order to give effect to them a court could hold C has a contingent remainder just as if T had devised Blackacre to B for life, then if C attains age 21 to C and his heirs but if C fails to attain age 21, then to D and his heirs.

---

18.   *See* ch. 8, *infra.*

Problems of construction involving age contingencies have plagued courts for centuries. The test suggested by Professor Gray is often quoted and adopted by some courts: "Whether a remainder is vested or contingent depends upon the language employed. If the conditional element is incorporated into the description of, or into the gift to, the remainderman,[a possibility more likely to occur with class gifts as distinguished from gifts to an individual as in the preceding paragraph], then the remainder is contingent; but if, after words giving a vested interest, a clause is added divesting it, the remainder is vested."[19] Gray's test is helpful in many cases but it may be difficult to determine in some cases whether the conditional element is "incorporated into the gift to the remainderman."

If T devises Blackacre to B for life, then to such of B's children as shall attain the age of 21, and for want of any such children to X and his heirs, the remainder to B's children is contingent prior to the attainment of the specified age by a child.[20] The condition of age attainment is viewed as being incorporated into the description of the remaindermen. Yet if the limitations read: to B for life, then to B's children, if they attain 21 and for want of such children to X in fee, it is possible that the remainder to the children (assuming all are under 21) would be viewed as vested subject to divestment. The requirement of age attainment could be treated as not being a condition inherent in the designation of the remaindermen.

Review Problems

In each of the following O, who owns Blackacre in fee simple absolute, deeds Blackacre:

19. Gray, Rule Against Perpetuities, § 108 (4th ed. Little Brown & Co. 1942). In Howard v. Batchelder, 143 Conn. 328, 122 A.2d 307 (1956), the court quoted Gray and also stated: "The form of the limitation is of primary importance in solving the difficulty. If the form indicates that the condition is to happen before the remainderman is to take, the remainder is ordinarily held to be contingent. If the form is that of an unconditional gift followed by language to the effect that the remainder is to be taken away from the remainderman if a condition happens, then the remainder is generally construed as vested subject to complete defeasance." *Cf.* 1 ALP,§ 4.36.

20. The case given is basically that of Festing v. Allen, 12 M. & W. 279 (Ex. 1843). *See* 5 ALP, § 21.32; Simes & Smith, The Law of Future Interests, § 148 (2d ed. 1956).

1. To B for life, remainder to C and his heirs. B has a life estate and C has a vested remainder which is capable of becoming possessory immediately upon the termination of B's life estate. The termination of B's life estate is not a condition precedent; C's interest is vested because it is subject to no conditions.

2. To B for life, then to C for life. B has a life estate, C has a vested remainder for life, and O has a reversion. C's interest is not subject to any conditions. While C's interest may terminate if C predeceases B, that termination results from the limitation attached to the interest and not as the result of any condition.

3. To B for life, then to B's children and their heirs, and at the time of the conveyance B has one living child. B has a life estate; B's children have a vested remainder subject to open. If during his life B has more children, they will join in the class gift to B's children and as new children join the class the percentage interest of B's other children will be diminished. However, the interest of a child of B is never totally eliminated even if a child dies before B. In that case, the interest of B's deceased child passes through the deceased child's estate to the child's heirs or devisees. The class gift will close physiologically at B's death.

4. To B for life, then to C's children and their heirs, and at the time of the conveyance C has one living child. B has a life estate and C's children have a vested remainder subject to open. If C dies in B's lifetime, the class closes physiologically. If both C and a child of C survive B (or, because the interest of C's children is alienable, devisable and descendible, if C and a successor of C's child survive B) the class closes at B's death under the rule of convenience. Once the class closes no new members can join the class; thus if C has another child after B dies, that child is excluded from the class.

5. To B for life, then to C and his heirs but if C fails to graduate from law school before 2015, then to D and his heirs. B has a life estate; C has a vested remainder subject to complete divestment. If C graduates from law school before

2015 and B is still living C's interest becomes an indefeasibly vested remainder and D's interest terminates. If B dies before 2015 and C has yet to graduate from law school, then C has a fee simple subject to an executory interest. If C graduates law school by 2015, C's interest ripens into a fee simple absolute; if not, D has a fee simple absolute.

6. To B for life, then if C reaches age 21, to C and his heirs but if C dies before age 21, then to D and his heirs. B has a life estate and C has a contingent remainder. C's interest is subject to a condition precedent as the conditional words precede the gift to C. D has an alternative contingent remainder. If the conveyance had been to B for life, then to C and his heirs but if C dies before age 21, then to D and his heirs, C would have had a vested remainder subject to complete divestment and D an executory interest. C's interest is a vested remainder subject to complete divestment as it is subject to a condition subsequent. The words of condition follow and therefor are subsequent to the gift to C.

7. To B for life, then to C and his heirs if C survives B but if C dies before B then to D and his heirs. Here, C could have a vested remainder subject to complete divestment and D could have a shifting executory interest. On the other hand, C and D could have alternative contingent remainders. Which interest they have depends on whether the court simply construes their interests in the order in which they are set forth in the governing instrument, thus finding that C's interest is subject only to a condition subsequent with the phrase "if C survive B" being mere surplusage. Alternatively, the court could construe their interests as alternative contingent remainders to take account of the rule of construction that all the words used in the governing instrument must be given effect.

§ 6.   The Nature of a Contingent Remainder

A contingent remainder is a remainder which either is (1) created in favor of an ascertained person *but is subject to a condition precedent*; (2) created in favor of an unborn person (where the implied condition is being born); or (3) created in favor of an existing but unascertained person (where the implied condition is being ascertained). It was not, according to the English common-law definition, an estate but merely the possibility of an estate. In the medieval period, the law refused to recognize the validity of contingent remainders on the ground that the contingent remainderman had at the time of the conveyance no present capacity to take the seisin on the expiration of the preceding freehold estate, and the conveyance could not be effective to give the remainderman the seisin after a gap following the freehold estate. By the fifteenth century, if not earlier, a contingent remainder in favor of the heirs of a living person was recognized; other types of contingent remainders were gradually given recognition and the rules governing them were developed.

In each of the following conveyances by O, the owner of Blackacre in fee simple, there is a contingent remainder:

A. To B for life, then to C and his heirs if X marries Y. At the time of the conveyance X and Y are not married. This remainder is limited in favor of an ascertained person but is subject to the happening of a condition precedent. This contingent remainder can become a vested remainder if the condition of X marrying Y occurs before the termination of the preceding estate. If X marries Y in B's lifetime, C's remainder becomes vested immediately and all of the characteristics of a vested remainder attach thereto.[1] The vesting of C's remainder operates to divest O's reversion, and, since the condition precedent has been satisfied the seisin or possession will pass to C as soon as B's estate ends. If C dies before B, C's vested remainder passes to any devisees under C's will, or absent devisees, C's heirs.

B. To B for life, then to C's children and their heirs. At the time of the conveyance C has no children. Thus, the interest of C's children is impliedly conditioned on C having

---

§ 6

1. As this example illustrates, all future interest have the possibility of "changing colors." Contingent remainders can become both vested remainders and present possessory estates; executory interests can become vested remainders and present possessory estates;

vested remainders can become present possessory estates and so forth. When interests in property are being classified, they are being classified as of the date of classification (not necessarily for all time thereafter) based upon facts and circumstances at the time of the classification.

children. If C has a child in B's lifetime, the interest of C's children ripens into a vested remainder subject to open to admit more of C's children into the class before the class closes at B's death under the rule of convenience (assuming it has not closed earlier physiologically).[2] If C's child were to predecease B, that child's interest would pass through the child's estate to the child's heirs or devisees.

C. To B for life, then to B's heirs. B, the designated ancestor, is alive. Therefore, B's heirs are not presently ascertained because living persons have no heirs. Thus, the remainder limited to B's heirs is impliedly conditioned on B's death, the event that will ascertain B's heirs. While those persons who may ultimately be determined to be B's heirs at B's death may actually be living, until B's death, it cannot be finally determined that such persons in fact will be B's heirs. At B's death, B's heirs will be determined. That is when the implied contingency of being ascertained will occur.

§ 7. Remainders Subject to a Condition Precedent

A remainder subject to a condition precedent is a contingent remainder even though the remainderman is an ascertained person. This is because the remainderman has no right to immediate possession if the preceding estate should come to an end so long as the condition precedent remains unsatisfied. From the common-law perspective, this inability to take the seisin, should the freehold become vacant, made this interest contingent.

The most common type of condition precedent is one requiring the remainderman to survive the life tenant or to survive to a specified age. Thus, T devises Blackacre to B for life, and, if C survives B, to C and his heirs. Here, C has a contingent remainder expressly contingent on C surviving B. Or, T devises Blackacre to B for life, then to such of B's children as shall survive B and their heirs and B and B's two children are living. Here the contingent remainder is contingent on B's children surviving B, and, in the case of B's later born children, being born and then surviving B. Similarly, if T devises Blackacre to B for life, then to C and his

2.   See § 5(B), *supra.*

heirs, if C attains the age of twenty-one and C is under the age of 21 at T's death),[1] C has a contingent remainder conditioned on C attaining age 21.

Frequently, a deed or will contains alternative limitations each being subject to a condition precedent. Thus, T devises Blackacre to B for life, then to such of B's children and their heirs as survive B, but if no child of B survives him, then to C and his heirs. Here, the state of the title would be: Life estate in B, alternative contingent remainders in fee in B's children who survive B and in C, reversion in T's heirs in fee (assuming that there is no residuary clause in T's will).[2] If T's will had a residuary clause, T's reversion would pass to the named residuary legatees.

Review Problems

1. O conveys Blackacre to B for life, remainder to C and his heirs if C attains age 21. At the time of the conveyance, C is age 18. B has a life estate, C has a contingent remainder and O has a reversion. If C attains age 21 before B dies C's contingent remainder ripens into a vested remainder and O's reversion terminates.

§ 7

1. Remember, even though the words of condition follow the designation of C as remainderman, they are words of condition precedent as the rule of construction discussed in § 3, *supra* apply only where there are two or more transferees of a future interest.

2. Although the alternative contingencies are mutually exclusive and will exhaust all possibilities, T's heirs (T is, by hypothesis, dead as this devise appears in T's will) will be deemed to have a reversion because at common law contingent remainders were destructible. Hence, the reversion might take effect in possession. The doctrine of destructibility of contingent remainders is explained in § 8, *infra*. Even today, without destructibility, there is the remote possibility that T's heirs would be entitled to possession for some period of time because B might renounce the life estate

and a court might not accelerate the contingent remainders. In this case, T's heirs would be entitled to possession until such time as it is determined whether B had surviving children. See also notes 3–4, *infra* and accompanying text.

It will be recalled that in certain situations the strong preference for construing a remainder as vested may cause a court to construe the first limitation as creating a vested remainder subject to divestment by an executory interest. See § 3, *supra*. Thus, T devises Blackacre to B for life, then to the children of B in fee and if any child predeceases B his share to go to X in fee. B has one child, C. C's remainder is vested subject to divestment. The limitation to X is viewed not as an alternative limitation imposing a requirement of survival as a condition precedent to C's remainder but as a supplanting or divesting limitation if C does not survive the life tenant. See 2A Powell, Real Property, ¶¶ 329, 330.

2. T devises Blackacre to B for life, remainder to such of C's children who survive B. C predeceased T but has three children who survive T. B has a life estate, C's children who survive B have a contingent remainder and T's successors have a reversion. If any one or more of C's children survive B, those children will have a fee simple in Blackacre. If none of C's children survive B, the property reverts in fee simple to the successors of T's estate.

3. O conveys Blackacre to B for life, and if C survives B, then to C and his heirs, but if C dies before B, then to D and his heirs. B has a life estate and C and D have alternative contingent remainders. C's remainder is conditioned on C surviving B; D's contingent remainder is conditioned on C predeceasing B. O, of course, has a reversion.

Thoughtful students may ask: How can O have a reversion given that at B's death either C or D will succeed to Blackacre. Thus, O's reversion cannot become possessory. To answer this mystery, one must recall that the classification system we have is based on the English common law. Clearly both C and D have interests subject to a condition but at common law, O would also have had a reversion which, in light of the destructibility rule[3] could ripen into a fee simple. This might occur, for example, if during B's life B committed a tortious feoffment[4] or was imprisoned for a felony, with the resulting forfeiture of his life estate. Because neither remainderman would then be ready to take possession since at the time of forfeiture it would not be known whether or not C survived B, O's reversion would become possessory. Even today without forfeitures, B's life estate could terminate before B dies, say by B's renunciation making it possible for O to claim possession of the property at least until it is determined whether C survived B.

§ 8.   Remainders to Unascertained Persons

A remainder limited in favor of an unascertained person is necessarily a contingent remainder. This is so because until the remainderman is ascertained there is no one ready to take the

---

3. *See* § 9, *infra.*

4. This was an attempted conveyance by B of an estate greater than B had.

seisin or possession should the preceding freehold estate come to an end. Thus, the event that ascertains the remainderman is effectively a condition precedent.

Remaindermen may be unascertained because they are unborn. Thus, T devises Blackacre to B for life, then to the children of C, a bachelor, and their heirs. The remainder to C's children is contingent on being born. If a child is born to C during B's lifetime, that child has a remainder vested subject to open in favor of other children of C born before B dies. The concept of a remainder in favor of persons not yet in existence may seem strange. It is true, of course, that legal relations with respect to property can exist only between living persons. When we speak of a contingent remainder in unborn persons we mean that the law recognizes the possibility of a legal relationship arising in the future and that the recognition of this potential interest has present legal consequences, e.g. the inability of the life tenant to deal with the property as though no such potential interest had been created. In fact, this relationship is viewed as significant enough to be worthy of legal protection such that in many cases a guardian-ad-litem must be appointed to represent the potential takers of these interests.

Frequently, the remaindermen are in existence but their identity is uncertain until the happening of a future event. Thus, suppose T devises Blackacre "to my son B for life, then to B's widow." At the time of the conveyance B, age 55, is married to W. If we construe "widow" as meaning only B's present wife, W, then she has a vested remainder. On the other hand, if we construe "widow" as meaning whoever is B's wife at the time of B's death, then the remainderman is unascertained until B's death.[1]

Another common instance of a remainder contingent by reason of uncertainty of the remaindermen is found in a limitation of a remainder to the heirs of a living person.[2] It is obvious that a

§ 8

1. This problem illustrates that in classifying interests we must first construe the instrument to eliminate ambiguities.

2. Historically, heirs are those persons entitled to take real property under the statutes of descent upon the death of the owner thereof intestate; next of kin are those persons entitled to personal property under the statutes of descent upon the death of the owner intestate. In many states no distinctions are drawn between the intestate successors

person's heirs cannot be determined until the person dies because until then it cannot be known who those persons will be who will inherit his property. The common law expressed this thought in the maxim *"Nemo est haeres viventis"* (No one is the heir of the living.) A living person may have heirs apparent or heirs presumptive but not heirs. It follows, then, that if T devises Blackacre to B for life, remainder to the heirs of C (a living person), the remainder is contingent. If C dies in B's lifetime, C's heirs are then determined and the remainder vests in them.

Review Problems

1. O conveys Blackacre to B for life, then to B's widow and her heirs. If widow means that person who is B's surviving spouse whether that person is B's current spouse or another person to whom B may later marry, the remainder is contingent on that widow being ascertained. The latest that will occur is B's death.

2. O conveys Blackacre to B for life, then to C's heirs. C's heirs have a vested remainder if, at the time of the conveyance, C is dead. If C is alive, they have a contingent remainder. Even though the persons who may ultimately be determined to be C's heirs are living, until C dies their status as C's heirs cannot be finally determined.

§ 9. Destructibility of Contingent Remainders at Common Law

At common law the usual method of creating a freehold estate was by a transaction called a feoffment with livery of seisin. This involved a transfer or delivery of seisin and possession of the land. It became a fundamental rule of common-law conveyancing that there can be no livery of seisin to take effect in futuro. Livery of seisin was a present act and O could not convey a freehold estate to B on October 1, to take effect on the following November 1. From the nature of livery of seisin the rule was derived that there could be no conveyance, by feoffment or otherwise, of a freehold estate to

of real and personal property and such   "heirs."
successors are simply referred to as

commence in futuro.[1] The limitation of a remainder, however, did not violate this rule since a remainder follows after the present, particular estate created by the same conveyance. When O enfeoffed B to have and to hold to B for life, remainder to C and his heirs, B was invested with the seisin on his own behalf and on behalf of C, and upon B's death, or upon the termination of the life estate from any cause, the seisin would continue in C in C's own behalf. In this example C has a vested remainder and there is, therefore, no possibility of a lapse in the seisin. But suppose O conveyed to B for life, remainder to C's eldest son and his heirs and, at the time of the conveyance C is childless. The remainder is contingent since C's eldest son at the time of the conveyance had not yet been born. If B died before C had any children, what became of the contingent remainder? The seisin could not be suspended or put in abeyance. It must vest in somebody. The remainderman was not yet in existence, hence the seisin must be in O or if O is dead then in O's successors (O's heirs or devisees). If C later married and had a son, would the seisin then pass to the son? No, because it would take a new conveyance to get the seisin out of O. The result was that the contingent remainder was destroyed.

From the feudal doctrines of seisin there arose the well settled common-law rule that a freehold contingent remainder which did not vest at or before the termination of the preceding freehold estate was destroyed. Such termination of the preceding estate might result from the natural expiration of that estate, from forfeiture, or from merger.

A. Destructibility by Normal Expiration of Supporting Freehold Estate

A contingent remainder by its very nature is subject to the possibility of not becoming vested prior to the natural termination of the supporting freehold estate because of the happening of a limitation attached to that estate. If the supporting estate, usually a life estate, should come to an end while the remainder is contingent, the remainder must fail if the rule of destructibility applies. Thus, O, the owner of Blackacre in fee simple, conveys to B for life,

§ 9

1. *See* Roe d. Wilkinson v. Tranmer, 2 Wils. 75, 95 Eng.Rep. 694 (1757).

then to the heirs of C (a living person). B dies while C is still living. Since the remaindermen are not ascertained at B's death, the seisin must revert to O and the contingent remainder is destroyed. If, however, the remainder vests at the same time as, or before, the expiration of the supporting estate, the remainder is not destroyed. Thus, O conveys Blackacre to B for life, then to B's surviving children. Here the same event which marks the termination of the supporting freehold (B's death) also causes the contingent remainder in B's "surviving children" to become vested in possession in those of B's children who in fact survive B.[2] If the conveyance had been to B for life, then to C for life, then to the surviving children of C, the death of B during C's life would not cause the remainder in the surviving children to fail because it would be supported by C's life estate. The English courts admitted one exception to the strict logic of the common-law rule prohibiting a gap in the seisin and the creation of a freehold estate to commence in the future—a posthumous child may be considered as being in existence prior to his birth. Thus, in *Reeve v. Long*[3] T devised Blackacre to B for life, remainder to B's first son in fee tail, with remainders over. B died before any son was born to him but he left his wife "great with child." Six months later a son was born. The House of Lords, reversing the King's Bench, held that the son was entitled to take.[4]

Initially, some difficulty arose in connection with contingent remainders subject to an age contingency where some members of the class satisfied the contingency when the preceding estate terminated but others did not. For example, suppose O conveyed Blackacre to A for life, then to B's children who attain age 21. A dies survived by B's five children. Three of B's children are over age 21 but two are under age 21. Is the entire remainder valid or destroyed or is only the interest of B's two children under age 21 destroyed? In time, the courts resolved this issue by finding that

2. If B has no surviving children, then the remainder fails because there are no identifiable takers of the remainder.

3. 3 Lev. 408, 83 Eng.Rep. 754 (1695).

4. The reporter tells us that "all the judges were much dissatisfied with this judgment of the Lords" because it created an exception "where the law was so clear and certain." It should be noted that at the time lay members of the House of Lords voted on cases coming up on appeal. It may be presumed that they were not overly impressed by the nice technicalities of property law.

the entire remainder was valid. Two possible rationales could support this result. One merely treats the interest of the two children under 21 as severable from those over 21 and classifies that interest as an executory interest not subject to the rule of destructibility. The other merely views the entire remainder as vesting at A's death and the inclusion of the two children under age 21 in the class if they reach age 21 as merely a function of the class closing rules.[5]

B. Destructibility Arising From Forfeiture of Supporting Freehold Estate

The rule of destructibility also was applied in cases where the supporting freehold estate terminated prior to the time of its natural expiration. For example, at common law a premature termination would result from a forfeiture of the supporting life estate. A forfeiture would occur if a person having a life estate attempted to transfer a greater estate than he owned–a so-called "tortious feoffment."[6] As a consequence of B's act, B's life estate was forfeited and the reversioner or vested remainderman had a right of entry against X.[7] It followed that any extant contingent remainder dependent on the life estate for support was destroyed if the condition precedent had not occurred before or simultaneously with the termination of the particular estate.

5. *See* Simes and Smith, The Law of Future Interests § 205 (2nd ed. 1956).

6. This would also follow if the conveyance were made by fine or common recovery.

7. The reason usually given to explain the forfeiture of the life tenant's estate was that his conveyance was a breach of the feudal obligation of loyalty which he owed to his lord. The validity of this explanation is open to question. The law of reversions and remainders was not developed until the late thirteenth century and at that time feudalism was in its decline. It took a statute enacted in 1278 to give an heir an imme-diate right of action (equivalent to forfeiture) against a tenant in dower who wrongfully alienated her dower lands. A similar remedy was later extended to reversioners and remaindermen. It was not until 1310 that a writ of entry was available to the holder of a vested remainder against the alienee of an ordinary life tenant. Thus, the doctrine of forfeiture of a life estate for a tortious feoffment first emerges as an offshoot of a statutory remedy. *See* Plucknett, Concise History of the Common Law 362, 569–570 (5th ed. 1956); Bordwell, Common Law Scheme of Estates And the Remainder, 34 Iowa L.Rev. 400, 405–406 (1949).

C. Destructibility by Merger

A third situation in which a contingent remainder would fail by reason of the termination of the supporting life estate arose from the doctrine of merger. Under the merger doctrine, whenever successive vested estates are owned by the same person the smaller of the two estates is absorbed by the larger. Thus, if O, the owner of Blackacre in fee simple, conveys to B for life, then to B and his heirs, B has only one estate, a fee simple. By the doctrine of merger, the life estate merges in, or is swallowed by, the larger estate. So also if O, owning in fee simple, conveys to B for life and O subsequently transfers O's reversion to B. Here, B will also have a fee simple, not a life estate plus the reversion in fee. In order for a merger to take place the two estates must be both successive and vested. Therefore, a merger will not be effected where a vested estate intervenes between the two estates. Thus, O conveys to B for life, then to C for life, then to B and his heirs. B has both a life estate and a vested remainder in fee. C's vested remainder will prevent a merger of B's two estates. If C predeceased B, then B's estate would merge to give B a fee simple absolute. But, a contingent remainder, not being an estate according to common-law rules, would not prevent two estates owned by the same person from being treated as successive estates. Thus, O conveys to B for life, then to C for life if C marries. Before C marries O assigns the reversion to B. B's life estate merges in his reversion in fee and C's remainder is destroyed.

Since the merger of a life estate with another vested estate causes a premature termination of the life estate, any contingent remainder dependent on the life estate for support is destroyed. Thus, O, the owner of Blackacre in fee simple, conveys to B for life, then to C and his heirs if C attains age twenty-one. If at a time when C is ten years old O conveys O's reversion in fee to B, or B conveys B's life estate to O, or both O and B convey their estates to a third person, C's contingent remainder will be destroyed. Since C's contingent remainder failed to vest at or prior to the termination of the supporting life estate, it is extinguished.

The general rules of merger and destructibility of contingent remainders are subject to two qualifications: 1. a fee tail will not merge into a fee simple; 2. a contingent remainder will not be destroyed by a merger of a life estate and the next vested estate *if the two estates are created simultaneously with the contingent remainder.*

As to the first exception, the statute De Donis was thought to prevent the destruction of a fee tail by merger. It was true that once a tenant in tail acquired the power to convey a fee simple (at common law by suffering a common recovery) a contingent remainder following the fee tail would be destroyed by such a conveyance, but this had nothing to do with the doctrine of merger. Similarly, a vested remainder expectant on the fee tail would be eliminated by such conveyance.

As to the second exception if it were held that merger of the two estates destroyed the contingent remainder created simultaneously with them, the intention of the transferor would be completely defeated. Therefore, if O, the owner of Blackacre in fee simple, conveys Blackacre to B for life, then to C for life if C marries, then to B and his heirs, C's contingent remainder is initially valid. Likewise, if T devises Blackacre to B for life, then to C for life if C marries, and the reversion simultaneously descends to B as heir of T, the contingent remainder in C is not destroyed by merger of the life estate and the reversion.[8] If there is a later transfer by B to a third person of B's two estates there will be a merger in the transferee and C's contingent remainder will be destroyed.[9]

Likewise, suppose O conveyed Blackacre to B for life, the to B's first born daughter and the heirs of her body, then to B and his heirs. At the time of the conveyance B is childless. While B has both the life estate and the next vested estate[10] they would not merge to

---

8. Would it be correct to say that there is no merger here or to say that there is a merger but that it will not have the effect of destroying the contingent remainder? There are theoretical difficulties in either answer but there is no doubt about the rule itself. Perhaps we can say there is a merger subject to a split-up if the contingent remainder vests.

9. In Purefoy v. Rogers, 2 Wms. Saund. 380, 85 Eng.Rep. 1181 (1671) T devised to B for life, then if B should have a son and name him after T to such son in fee. The reversion passed to X. Before B had a son X conveyed the reversion to B. Later a son was born to B. It was held that B's life estate merged in the reversion, and the son's contingent remainder was destroyed.

10. Yes, a vested remainder could

destroy the contingent remainder in tail simultaneously created with B's life estate and vested remainder in fee simple. Again, if B conveyed both the life estate and vested remainder to D, they would merge in D's hands to destroy the contingent remainder in tail.

D. Trustees to Preserve Contingent Remainders

The destructibility of contingent remainders posed a threat to the stability of English family settlements of land and the conveyancing bar set to work to circumvent the destructibility rule. In the seventeenth century the conveyancers began to resort to the device of inserting in the settlement after the particular life estate an additional remainder to trustees "to preserve contingent remainders." Thus, O, the owner of Blackacre in fee simple, would convey to B for life, then to X and Y and their heirs for the life of B in trust for B and to preserve contingent remainders, then to B's first born son in fee tail male, remainders successively to B's other sons in fee tail male, with remainders over (B having no son at the time). It was held, partly for policy reasons, that the remainder to the trustees was vested.[11] Therefore, if B made a tortious conveyance in fee and thereby forfeited his legal life estate, the right of entry in the trustees would support the contingent remainders in the unborn sons. Thus, the estate of the trustees continued until B's death and protected the contingent remainders from being destroyed by a premature termination of B's life estate.

E. The Destructibility Rule in the United States

In the nineteenth century, American courts generally accepted the English doctrine of destructibility as a part of the common law. Because conveyance by feoffment was rare, only a few cases dealt with destructibility resulting from forfeiture of the supporting life estate; but, in several states destruction by merger and by failure to vest at or before the normal expiration of the preceding life estate was held to be in effect. Yet there was a growing dissatisfaction with the rule. The original reasons for the rule bore little relation to contemporary property concepts. The feudal doctrine of the

follow a *contingent remainder in fee tail.*   **11.** Dormer v. Packhurst, 6 Bro. P.C. 351 (1740); *see* Duncomb v. Duncomb, 3 Lev. 437 (1697).

necessity of continuity of seisin and the prohibition of the creation of a freehold estate to commence in the future were devoid of practical significance in the nineteenth and twentieth centuries. More importantly, the rule operated to defeat the intention of the grantor or testator. In England a series of statutes commencing in 1845 abolished the destructibility rule. In the United States approximately one half of the states have enacted statutes abrogating the rule in whole or in part.[12] In a few jurisdictions there are decisions rejecting the rule without the aid of legislation.[13] Only in Florida,[14] Oregon,[15] and Pennsylvania,[16] are there cases which do not appear to have been overruled or overturned by statutes recognizing that the rule continues to exist but it is difficult to assess the continued viability of these cases. Because it is no longer the law that a life tenant who purports to convey a fee simple forfeits his life estate,[17] destructibility in these latter states will usually arise only from merger or on a failure of the contingent remainder to vest at or before the natural determination of the supporting life estate.[18] In many states there are no decisions on the point and no legislation. The position taken by the Restatement of Property that contingent

12. The statutes are collected in 1 ALP, § 4.63, n. 1; Powell, Real Property, ¶ 314; Simes & Smith, The Law of Future Interests, § 207. Some of these statutes do not in terms cover the situation of failure of the remainder to vest prior to the normal termination of the prior freehold estate. The rule is expressly rejected by the Restatement. Restatement of Property, § 240 (1936).

13. See, e.g., Abo Petroleum Corp. v. Amstutz, 93 N.M. 332, 600 P.2d 278 (1979); Rouse v. Paidrick, 221 Ind. 517, 49 N.E.2d 528 (1943); Hayward v. Spaulding, 75 N.H. 92, 71 A. 219 (1908).

14. See, e.g., Blocker v. Blocker, 103 Fla. 285, 137 So. 249 (1931).

15. See, e.g., Love v. Lindstedt, 76 Ore. 66, 147 P. 935 (1915); Halleck v. Halleck, 216 Or. 23, 337 P.2d 330 (1959)

16. See, e.g., Jordan v. McClure, 85 Pa. 495 (1878).

17. In a few states forfeiture for tortious alienation is expressly abolished by statute. See, e.g., Mass.Gen.Laws Ann. ch. 184, § 9 (West 1991): "A conveyance by a tenant for life or years which purports to grant a greater estate than he possesses or can lawfully convey shall not work a forfeiture of his estate but shall pass to the grantee all the estate which such tenant can lawfully convey."

18. In some states there are statutes providing for forfeiture of the life estate where the life tenant commits waste. See, e.g., Mass.Gen.Laws Ann. ch. 242, §§ 1, 2 (West 1988). In a state retaining the destructibility rule contingent remainders dependent on the forfeited life estate would seem to be destroyed.

remainders are indestructible[19] may influence these uncommitted jurisdictions to reject the doctrine of destructibility.

The rule of destructibility rule was inapplicable to equitable contingent remainders and legal contingent remainders in terms for years or in personal property. These interests do not involve the concept of seisin.

§ 10. Implied Conditions of Survivorship

As previously noted, most contingent remainders are either conditioned either on survivorship or on an age contingency. With respect to the condition of survivorship more often than not the contingency is expressly set forth in the deed or will in such form as "if B survives me" or "to such of C's children who survive me." However, there are numerous instances where a condition of survivorship is implied, rather than expressed. To say that a condition is implied is to mean that in construing a deed or will, a court determines to "write into" the instrument words not set forth in it. In doing so, invariably courts rely either on the intent of the grantor or testator or, alternatively, well-established rules of construction.[1]

At common law, if the deed or will provided that upon the termination of the life estate, the property should be "divided and paid over to" multiple beneficiaries or a class of beneficiaries, only those beneficiaries who survive to the time of distribution (the termination of the preceding life estate) were entitled to share in the property. This so-called "divide and pay over" rule has been

---

19. Restatement of Property, § 240 (1936). The comments on this section of the Restatement set out the English and American historical background.

§ 10

1. In some cases, courts refuse to imply a condition of survivorship on the theory that such an implication would be inconsistent with the intent of the testator or grantor. *See, e.g.,* In re Estate of Houston, 414 Pa. 579, 201 A.2d 592 (1964)(testator bequeathed property in trust to pay income to his "surviving children" and upon death of survivor to his grandchildren. The court refused to imply a condition of survivorship with respect to grandchildren noting that testator knew how to express such a condition when he wanted to as evident from the gift to children. Thus, failure to include such a condition in the gift of the remainder suggests testator had no intent to do so).

rejected by the Restatement largely because the exceptions to the rule have largely swallowed up the rule.[2]

Conditions of survivorship are implied with gifts to classes where there is the potential that the class members could be of differing generations. For example, a remainder limited in favor of "issue" but not "children" implies a condition of survivorship because the class of issue could include children, grandchildren, great-grandchildren and so on[3] whereas, the class of children is limited only to the ancestor's immediate offspring.[4] In gifts to issue and descendants it is generally appropriate to imply a condition of survivorship because such class designation includes within the description of the class persons in a more remote generation who, under a per stripes method of distribution, can only take if their ancestor who would otherwise have been in the class was deceased. But, suppose the gift is to "issue per capita" and not "per stirpes." With a gift to issue per capita, all issue are entitled to share in the gift, including those of a more remote generation whose ancestors are living. Thus, in a gift to issue per capita, a condition of survivorship is not implied.[5]

A survivorship contingency is often implied where there are alternative remainders, at least with respect to the first remainder, not otherwise subject to an express condition of survivorship. For example, if O deeds Blackacre to B for life, and upon B's death, to C or to D, C's remainder is impliedly conditioned on C surviving B. If C predeceases B, then D takes. However, if both C and D predecease B, the property passes to D's estate as only C's interest is impliedly conditioned on survivorship.[6]

2. Restatement of Property, § 260 (1940). See also 1 ALP, 5, § 21.21.

3. Restatement (Second) of Property, § 28.2 (1988). A similar rule applies with gifts to descendants.

4. Other uni-generational classes include: "brothers and sisters" and "nieces and nephews." See also Halbach, Future Interests: Express and Implied Conditions of Survival, Part I, 49 Cal. L. Rev. 297 (1961); Part II, 49 Cal. L. Rev. 431 (1961), French, Imposing a General Survival Requirement on Beneficiaries of Future Interests: Solving the Problems Caused by the Death of A Beneficiary Before the Time Set for Distribution, 27 Ariz. L. Rev. 801 (1985).

5. Restatement of Property, § 249 (1940).

6. Restatement of Property, § 252 (1940). See also Simes and Smith, The Law of Future Interests, § 581 (2nd ed. 1956). But see Lawson v. Lawson, 267 N.C. 643, 148 S.E.2d 546 (1966) (holding that a contingent remainder expressly

Under the provisions of the Uniform Probate Code, when property is transferred *in trust* to pay the income to A for life, then to A's children, there is an implied condition of survivorship attached to the gift to A's children.[7] Thus, if any child of A predeceases A, that child's estate is not entitled to a share of the trust principal at A's death. Furthermore, the Code creates an alternative gift in the deceased child's surviving issue, if any, or, if none, in A's other surviving children. The effect of this provision to make apparently vested interests impliedly contingent on survivorship. This rule can give way to a contrary intent. For example, if the grantor of the trust provided that if any child of A predeceased A that child's share would pass to his or her estate, that provision would control.

The Code also provides that words of survivorship are not sufficient to avoid the alternative gift. Thus if O transfers property in trust to pay the income to A for life, and upon A's death to distribute the corpus to A's *surviving* children, there is still an implied gift over to the issue of any child of A who predeceased A. Only in the absence of such issue would the deceased child's share inure to the children of A who survived A.[8]

§ 11. Alienability of Remainders

A vested remainder has always been considered an estate and, therefore, is as transferable by deed or by will as any similar possessory estate. A remainder vested subject to partial or complete divestment is as freely alienable as a remainder absolutely vested but remains subject after alienation to the divesting condition.

It was the accepted view at English common law that a contingent remainder was inalienable inter vivos except by fine or common recovery. The argument of champerty, which for so long

conditioned on an event other than survivorship is impliedly conditioned on the remainderman being alive when the event occurs). This appears to be a very distinct minority rule.

7. This rule is inapplicable to legal as distinguished from equitable interests.

8. Under the common law, if the remainder were limited to "A's surviving children" the interest of any child of A who predeceased A would fail and only A's surviving children would take the gift. In other words, the issue of a deceased child of A would not share in the gift.

made choses in action nonassignable, was advanced as a reason for the non-transferability inter vivos of this interest which was looked upon as a mere possibility or expectancy. Yet it was held that a contingent remainder was releasable to the holder of the possessory estate or to the person whose interest would be divested by the happening of the contingency. In 1845 contingent remainders were made alienable in England by statute.

The earlier American cases followed the English rule of the non-alienability of contingent remainders. But, at the present time contingent remainders are freely alienable in the great majority of the states.[1] In more than half of the American jurisdictions this result is reached by statute. These statutes are not uniform in scope. Some of them provide that "expectant estates" are as alienable as estates in possession; others declare that "future interests" are alienable;[2] and others specify that certain types of contingent remainders are alienable.[3] Even in the absence of statute in all but a handful of jurisdictions the courts have held such interests freely transferable inter vivos.[4] It is probable that in all states contingent remainders are transferable by way of estoppel and specifically enforceable contract. Thus, if the owner of the contingent remainder conveys his interest by warranty deed, or other deed containing representations of title, and the contingency later happens, the after-acquired title of the grantor will inure to the grantee by estoppel.[5] Similarly, if the contingent remainderman contracts to convey his interest, courts of equity will grant specific performance of the contract when the remainder vests. The courts agree that contingent remainders are releasable, and they are

§ 11

1. The Restatement of Property declares that all remainders and executory interests are transferable by ordinary conveyance. Restatement of Property, § 162 (1936)

2. See, e.g., N.Y. Est. Powers & Trust Law § 6–5.1 (McKinney 1992): "Future estates are descendible, devisable and alienable, in the same manner as estates in possession." See Cal.Civ. Code § 699 (West 1982).

3. See, e.g., Mass.Gen.Laws Ann. ch. 184, § 2 (West 1991)(descendible contingent remainders made assignable).

4. For a full treatment of the topic of alienability, see 1 ALP, §§ 4.64–4.67; 2A Powell, Real Property, ch. 21; Simes & Smith, The Law of Future Interests, §§ 1852–1859.

5. See, e.g., Smith v. Groton, 147 Conn. 272, 160 A.2d 262 (1960) (estoppel based on quitclaim deed).

devisable and descendible subject to the contingency attached to the interest.[6]

§ 12.   The Rule in Shelley's Case

A.   *Statement of the Rule*

The Rule in Shelley's Case may be stated in its simplest form as follows: If a freehold estate is conveyed by deed or bequeathed by will to a person and in the same conveyance or will a remainder is limited to the heirs or to the heirs of the body of that person, that person takes both the freehold estate and the remainder.[1] The Rule takes its name from Shelley's Case,[2] the report of which contains the argument of counsel wherein the Rule was stated as follows: " * * * it is a rule in law, when the ancestor by any gift or conveyance takes an estate of freehold, and in the same gift or conveyance an estate is limited either mediately or immediately to his heirs in fee or in tail; that always in such cases, 'the heirs' are words of limitation of the estate, and not words of purchase."

The effect of the Rule is to convert what would otherwise be a remainder in the heirs or heirs of the body into a remainder in the named ancestor. Thus, suppose O, the owner of Blackacre in fee simple, conveys or devises Blackacre to B for life, and after B's death to the heirs of B. If there were no Rule in Shelley's Case the state of the title would be: life estate in B, contingent remainder in fee simple in B's heirs, reversion in O in fee. However, by virtue of the Rule the state of the title is: life estate in B, vested remainder in B in fee simple. At this point, another rule—the doctrine of merger—causes B's life estate to coalesce with B's remainder such that B has a fee simple absolute. Similarly, if O grants or devises Blackacre to B for life, remainder to the heirs of B's body, by virtue of the Rule, coupled with the operation of merger, B, at common

---

6. For a discussion of other characteristics of remainders, such as protection against conduct of the life tenant and third persons, creditors' rights, partition, and representation in proceeding affecting the title, *see* 1 ALP, §§ 4.78–4.117.

§ 12

1. For other statements of the Rule and a thorough discussion of its opera-

tion, *see* 1 ALP, §§ 4.40–4.52; 3 Powell, Real Property, §§ 378–380; Simes & Smith, The Law of Future Interests, §§ 1541–1572 (2d ed. 1956); Restatement of Property, §§ 312, 313 (1940).

2. 1 Co.Rep. 93b (1581).

law, gets a present estate in fee tail. Under the Rule the limitations are treated as though they read: to B for life, remainder to B and the heirs of his body.

B. Origin and Development of the Rule

It may seem strange that the origin of, and the reasons for, one of the most famous rules in the entire field of real property law are not definitely known, yet the beginnings of the Rule are hidden in the obscurity of legal history. It is certain that the Rule did not originate in Shelley's Case. It was applied as early as 1366 in the *Provost of Beverley's Case*[3] and there are indications of its earlier existence. When the law of remainders was in its early stage of development, a conveyance to B for life, then to the heirs of B would not seem greatly dissimilar from a conveyance to B and his heirs. Perhaps for that reason both kinds of conveyance were held effective to give B a fee simple. However that may be, the Rule had from the beginning a close connection with feudal tenure. It will be recalled that when an owner of land in fee simple died the lord of the fee was entitled to profitable incidents of tenure deriving from the descent to the heir. Depending on the type of tenure, the lord was entitled to primer seisin, relief, or wardship and marriage. These incidents would not attach if the heir took by purchase, that is as a remainderman. The Rule in Shelley's Case served to protect the feudal rights of the lord by taking the remainder away from the heir and giving it to the ancestor, thereby forcing the heir to take by descent if he was to take at all.[4]

The Rule had such vitality that it survived in full force for many centuries after the conditions which gave it birth were only dimly discernible in history. It became "part and parcel of the law of England." When feudal conditions could no longer justify its existence, its continuance was assured by the inertia of precedent and the fact that it tended to increase the alienability of land. It was extended in scope to include equitable interests in land. The Rule did not have a peaceful existence. A mass of literature grew up

3. Y.B. 40 Ed. 3, f9, 18.

4. The strong policy of the law in favor of protection of the lord's feudal dues is evidenced by a statute of 1267 making ineffective against the lord a feoffment to his eldest son by an owner in fee simple. 52 Hen. 3, c. b.

on the subject and a legion of cases, containing many fine distinctions, filled the reports. Lord Macnaghten eloquently described the situation as it existed about the beginning of the nineteenth century: "Things were not going well with the rule. Its feudal origin was a disgrace. Its antiquity was a reproach. Some judges thought that on those grounds it ought to be discountenanced. Then it was constantly made a matter of complaint that the rule disappointed the intention, as if that were not its very end and purpose—as if it had not been at the outset 'levelled against the views of the parties.' It was always being disparaged, and what was perhaps worse, it was always being explained. It led to profound discussions and some very pretty quarrels."[5] Yet the Rule persisted in England until abolished by the Law of Property Act, 1925.[6]

In the United States the Rule was almost universally accepted by the courts as an integral part of the common law, although it has been rejected by the courts of some states.[7] The great majority of the courts held, in accordance with the English view, that it was a positive rule of law, not a rule of construction, that is, that its operation did not depend on the intention of the conveyor or testator but would apply, if its requirements were satisfied, regardless of the transferor's intention. Indeed, an express declaration in the instrument that no more than a life estate is intended to be given to the ancestor, or that the heirs shall take as purchasers, will not prevent the ancestor from also taking the remainder under the Rule.[8] In one respect a few of the American courts extended the

5. Van Grutten v. Foxwell, (1897) App.Cas. 658. One of these "pretty" quarrels arose between Lord Mansfield, Chief Justice of the King's Bench, and the conveyancing bar over Mansfield's decision (1770) in the famous case of Perrin v. Blake, 1 Coll.Jur. 318 (1791). Mansfield held that the Rule would not apply where the testator made it clear that he intended the devisee to take only a life estate even though there was a further limitation of a remainder to the heirs of his body. His decision was reversed in the Exchequer Chamber. 1 W.Bl. 672, 96 Eng.Rep. 392 (1772). It thus became settled that the intention of the grantor or testator that the ancestor

should take no more than a life estate would not prevent the application of the Rule. Charles Fearne, a conveyancer, published the first edition of his work on Contingent Remainders for the purpose of exposing the "heresies" in the opinion of Lord Mansfield.

6. 15 & 16 Geo. 5, c. 20, § 131.

7. See, e.g., Thurston v. Allen, 8 Hawai'i 392 (1892), Crawford v. Barber, 385 P.2d 655 (Wyo.1963) and Smith v. Hastings, 29 Vt. 240 (1857).

8. Bishop v. Williams, 221 Ark. 617, 255 S.W.2d 171 (1953); Wilson v. Harrold, 288 Ill. 388, 123 N.E. 563 (1919);

scope of the Rule beyond its English boundaries—they applied it to interests in personal property. Occasionally, the Rule was said to apply to chattels by analogy as a rule of construction. Most state courts, however, have confined its application to interests in land.[9] The nineteenth century witnessed the Rule's period of ascendancy. As we shall see, however, legislation in the great majority of states has made the Rule a doctrine of declining importance in American law.

C. Operation of the Rule

The Rule in Shelley's Case operates only on the remainder given to the heirs of the ancestor. It in no way affects or disturbs the freehold estate given to the ancestor. It does not affect executory interests.[10] Thus, in the simple case of O conveying Blackacre to B for life, then to the heirs of B, the Rule leaves undisturbed the life estate given to B but converts what would be a contingent remainder in B's heirs into a vested remainder in B himself.[11] A freehold estate in the ancestor is an indispensable pre-requisite for the application of the Rule but in the application of the Rule the remainder alone is affected.

The application of the Rule may or may not result in a merger of the freehold and the remainder. The effect of the Rule may be to create a situation to which the doctrine of merger will apply (as in the case of a devise to B for life, remainder to B's heirs) but the Rule itself is entirely independent of the merger doctrine. It will apply even though a vested estate is interposed between the freehold and the remainder. Thus, in the *Provost of Beverley's Case* the Rule was applied where the limitations were to B for life, remainder to B's son and his wife in fee tail, remainder to the heirs of B. While the remainder is deemed limited to B by virtue of the Rule, the interposition of the vested estate in tail, however, prevents a

Sybert v. Sybert, 152 Tex. 106, 254 S.W.2d 999 (1953).

9. The Restatement asserts that the Rule applies only to transfers of interests in land. § 312(3) cmt. b. For a collection of cases, see Simes & Smith, The Law of Future Interests, § 367.

10. *See generally* ch. 8, *infra*.

11. The Rule of Shelley's Case standing alone does not give B a fee simple absolute. For that to occur, B's life estate and remainder must merge. Merger will not occur if there is another vested estate intervening between B's life estate and B's remainder.

merger of the freehold and the remainder. Likewise, if a contingent remainder is interposed between the ancestor's freehold and the contingent remainder to the heirs, there will be no merger even though the Rule applies. Thus, T devises Blackacre to B for life, and if C marries D, then to C and his heirs, but if C does not marry D, then to B's heirs. The state of the title would be: life estate in B, contingent remainder in C and, if the Rule in Shelley's Case applies, alternative contingent remainder in B. B's life estate does not merge into B's contingent remainder. If C predeceases B without having married D, then B's contingent remainder ripens into a vested remainder and it merges with B's life estate to give B a fee simple absolute.

In order for the Rule to apply the following requirements must be satisfied: 1. there must be a freehold estate given to the ancestor; 2. by the same instrument a remainder must be limited to the heirs or to the heirs of the body of the ancestor; 3. the freehold and the remainder must be of the same quality, that is, both legal or both equitable.

As to the first requirement, in the American cases the freehold is invariably a life estate although under the classic English view the freehold estate could be a fee tail. The life estate may be one pur autre vie as well as for the ancestor's own life. And, it may be a defeasible life estate. Thus, O conveys Blackacre to B for life or until she remarries, then to the heirs of B. By the operation of the Rule plus the effect of merger B gets a present estate in fee simple. The life estate need not be one in possession.[12] Thus, T devises to B for life, then to C for life, remainder to the heirs of C. The Rule operates to convert the remainder in the heirs of C into a vested remainder in C. There will be a merger and the end result will be: life estate in B, vested remainder in C in fee.

---

12. If the life estate limited to the ancestor expires before the instrument takes effect does the Rule apply? Thus, T devises to B for life then to the heirs of B. B predeceases T and the life estate lapses. In Illinois the Rule applies, hence the heirs of B do not take under the will. Lydick v. Tate, 380 Ill. 616, 44 N.E.2d 583, 145 A.L.R. 1216 (1942); Belleville Savings Bank v. Aneshaensel, 298 Ill. 292, 131 N.E. 682 (1921). The Restatement takes the position that since there is no life estate in the ancestor the Rule does not apply. Restatement of Property, § 312 cmt. c. For arguments pro and con, see Simes & Smith, The Law of Future Interests, § 1561 (2d ed. 1956).

The requirement of a life estate in the ancestor is satisfied where the life estate is one held in co-tenancy with another. Thus, O conveys Blackacre to B and C for their lives as tenants in common, remainder to the heirs of B. The Rule operates on the remainder so as to give B a remainder in fee simple. The cases seem to hold that B takes the whole remainder in fee simple.[13] The Restatement, however, takes the position that where B has only a one half interest in the estate for life he should be held to take only a one half interest in the remainder, the other half interest in the remainder going to B's heirs as purchasers.[14] Under this view, the Rule operates on the remainder only to the same extent as the fractional interest of the ancestor in the life estate.

The second requirement for the operation of the Rule, that the same instrument which creates the life estate must also limit a remainder to the heirs or heirs of the body of the life tenant, prevents the Rule from applying when the future interest given to the heirs is an executory interest. Thus, O conveys to B for life, and one year after B's death to the heirs of B. Because of the gap following B's life estate the interest limited to the heirs of B is a springing executory interest,[15] not a remainder, and the Rule is not applicable.

Most of the difficulties arising in the application of the Rule involve the question whether the remainder which has been limited in the instrument is a remainder to the heirs or heirs of the body of the ancestor. Where the conveyance or devise gives a life estate to B and then a remainder "to the heirs of B" or "to the heirs of B's body" and the quoted words are used without qualification it is clear enough that the Rule applies. Frequently, however, the conveyor or testator, instead of using the standard formula, will use

13. The leading case is Bails v. Davis, 241 Ill. 536, 89 N.E. 706 (1909). The conveyance was to B and C "during their natural lives and after their death to the heirs of said" B. The court said that B and C took an estate as tenants in common during their joint lives with a remainder in fee in B. Thus, C had a life estate in an undivided half interest and B had a present fee simple in an undivided half interest plus a remainder in fee in the other half interest. *Cf.* Powell, Real Property, ¶ 379.

14. Restatement of Property § 312 cmt. r (1940). The Restatement agrees that the Rule operates on the entire remainder where the life estate is limited to B and C as joint tenants or tenants by the entirety since each tenant is seised of the whole life estate.

15. *See* ch. 8, *infra.*

language which may or may not be substantially equivalent. The court, therefore, is confronted with a preliminary problem of construction. Before it can determine the applicability of the Rule, it must first construe the language of the particular limitation to ascertain its meaning.

The English courts took the view that in order to satisfy the requirements of the Rule the remainder must be limited to heirs or heirs of the body of the ancestor as a class taking in succession from generation to generation. It was not sufficient that the remainder be limited to that person or persons who at the moment of B's death would be his heir. This view was undoubtedly a product of the English system of descent under which there could be only one heir in each generation. Primogeniture cast the descent on the eldest male; where the descent was to females they took together as one heir. It was natural, therefore, to view the requirement of a remainder to "heirs" as meaning something more than a remainder to the individual or individuals who would inherit in the first generation. Thus, in *Archer's Case*[16] the Rule was held not to apply when land was devised to B for life, with remainder to the next heir male of B and the male heirs of the body of such next heir male. Here the remainder was not limited to heirs generally.

Some state courts have adopted the English view that the remainder must be limited to heirs or heirs of the body of the ancestor from generation to generation in an indefinite line of succession. Under this view the Rule does not apply if the remainder is limited to those persons who on the death of the ancestor intestate will inherit his real property.[17] But, the weight of American authority rejects this technical meaning given to the words "heirs" or "heirs or the body" by the English courts and holds that the Rule operates where the remainder is limited to those persons who would be the heirs of the life tenant at the time of his death.[18]

---

16. 1 Coke 66b, 76 E.R. 146 (1597).

17. *See, e.g.,* Taylor v. Cleary, 29 Gratt. (70 Va.) 448 (1877). The conveyance was to B for life and after his death to such person or persons as shall at that time answer the description of heir or heirs at law of said B "and such person or persons shall take the said

land under that description as purchasers under and by virtue of this deed, and not by inheritance as heirs of the said" B.

18. *Accord* Restatement of Property, § 312 cmt. f, g (1940). The Restatement calls this the "American rule". For

Thus, O conveys land in State X to B for life, and after B's death to such person or persons as may be entitled to inherit real estate from him by virtue of the statutes of State X. B takes a fee simple.[19] Similarly, in *Pugh v. Davenport*,[20] T devised property to A for life, then to the bodily issue of A. The court applied the rule on the theory that the phrase "bodily issue" was the equivalent of heirs.

Whichever view is adopted as to the meaning of the requirement that the remainder must be one to the heirs or heirs of the body of the life tenant, difficult problems of construction may arise when the draftsman of the instrument substitutes other words for the standard formula or adds words to it. The following illustrations are suggestive of some of the problems: 1. to B for life, then to his heir during its life;[21] 2. to B for life, then to his children and their heirs;[22] 3. to B for life, remainder to his heir;[23] 4. to B for life, then to his heirs in fee simple;[24] 5. to B for life, then to his heirs of blood;[25] 6. to B for life, then to the heirs of his body, their heirs and assigns;[26] 7. to B for life then to his issue.[27]

an extensive discussion, see Simes & Smith, The Law of Future Interests, § 1548.

19. *See, e.g.,* People v. Emery, 314 Ill. 220, 145 N.E. 349 (1924). But compare the language of the same court in Bails v. Davis, 241 Ill. 536, 89 N.E. 706 (1909).

20. 60 N.C.App. 397, 299 S.E.2d 230 (1983).

21. The Rule does not apply. *See,e.g.,* Bennett v. Morris, 5 Rawle 9 (Pa.1835).

22. The Rule does not apply unless from the context it appears that the word "children" was used in the sense of heirs. *Cf.* Hough v. Farmers Bank & Trust Co. of Lancaster County, 359 Pa. 555, 60 A.2d 11 (1948) (to B for life, then to her children, share and share alike or heirs at law; Rule applies).

23. The Rule applies, apparently on the theory that the singular word includes the plural.

24. Most courts hold that the Rule applies. For a collection of cases, *see*

Simes & Smith, The Law of Future Interests, § 1549, n. 77.

25. The Rule has been held inapplicable. *See, e.g.,* Cahill v. Cahill, 402 Ill. 416, 84 N.E.2d 380 (1949). The court based its decision on the ground that the remainder was not to heirs generally of the life tenant but to a restricted class of heirs which would not include all persons who would inherit as heirs under the statute of descent, for example, a widow or adopted child of the life tenant.

26. There are decisions both ways in this situation. *See, e.g.,* Sybert v. Sybert, 152 Tex. 106, 254 S.W.2d 999 (1953) (to B for life only and after his death to vest in fee simple in the heirs of his body; Rule applies); Aetna Life Insurance Co. v. Hoppin, 214 Fed. 928 (7th Cir.1914) (to B for life, then to the heirs of the body of B, their heirs and assigns; Rule does not apply).

27. It is usually held that the Rule applies, the word "issue" being construed as meaning "heirs of the body."

At times the question has arisen whether the Rule applies when the remainder to the heirs or heirs of the body is subject to a condition precedent in addition to the contingency arising from the fact that the remaindermen are unascertained. Thus, O conveys Blackacre to B for life, and after B's decease to his wife, C, and her heirs if C survives B, and if she does not survive B then to the heirs of B. The Rule is generally held to apply. The state of the title is: life estate in B, contingent remainder in C in fee, alternative contingent remainder in B in fee, reversion in O in fee. There will be no merger of B's life estate and his contingent remainder. But if C predeceases B the remainder in B will vest and there will then be a merger of B's two estates.

The third requisite for the operation of the Rule, that the life estate in the ancestor and the remainder to the heirs or heirs of the body must both be legal or both equitable, may create a problem when the conveyance is in trust. If O transfers property to T to hold for the life of B in trust, and on B's death the property to belong absolutely to the heirs of B, the Rule will not apply. Here there is an equitable life estate in B and a legal remainder in B's heirs since the duration of the trust is limited to B's life. Suppose that the conveyance is to T in trust for B for life, and on B's death the trustee to convey to the heirs of B. Is the remainder legal or equitable? The majority of courts have held that the direction to the trustee to convey to the heirs imposes an active duty on him so that the trust continues until the conveyance. Therefore, the remainder as well as the life estate is equitable and the Rule applies.[28]

D. The Rule in Modern Law

Mr. Justice Holmes once said: "It is revolting to have no better reason for a rule of law than that so it was laid down in the time of

Restatement of Property, § 312, cmt. g (1940). Cf. Baker v. Forsuman, 15 Ill.2d 353, 155 N.E.2d 24 (1958). As to the effect on the Rule of statutes abolishing the fee tail and substituting some other estate, see Simes & Smith, The Law of Future Interests, § 1569 (2nd ed. 1956) For a rare case involving a remainder to the heirs of the body of the life tenant,

see Evans v. Giles, 83 Ill.2d 448, 47 Ill.Dec. 349, 415 N.E.2d 354 (1980).

28. Restatement of Property, § 312 cmt. h (1940). See City Bank and Trust Co. in Dixon v. Morrissey, 118 Ill.App.3d 640, 73 Ill.Dec. 946, 454 N.E.2d 1195 (1983); Burnham v. Baltimore Gas & Electric Co., 217 Md. 507, 144 A.2d 80 (1958).

Henry IV. It is still more revolting if the grounds upon which it was laid down have vanished long since, and the rule simply persists from blind imitation of the past."[29] This criticism is strikingly applicable to the Rule in Shelley's Case. The Rule is a troublesome anachronism that has no substantial justification for its continued existence. The only argument that can be advanced in favor of its retention is that it makes land more freely alienable but it does this by defeating the intention of the conveyor or testator. Moreover, the argument of freer alienability in this context would seem to be inconsistent with the present trend of the law towards making contingent remainders indestructible. The Rule has produced a mass of litigation. It operates as a trap for the unwary testator or attorney. A skilled draftsman can easily circumvent the Rule by creating a non-freehold estate in the ancestor or by giving to the life tenant's heirs an executory interest instead of a remainder. Thus, T devises to B for 100 years if B so long live, then to the heirs of B; or, T devises to B for life, and one day after B's death to the heirs of B.

Such considerations as these have led the legislatures in most states to abrogate the Rule.[30] In some states the wording of the statute is such as not to cover explicitly all situations to which the Rule might be applicable and a question may arise as to the scope of the statute.[31] Normally, the effect of a statute abolishing the Rule is to give a life estate to the ancestor and a contingent remainder to the heirs but this is not universally true.[32] Typically, statutes abolishing the Rule apply only prospectively to interests

---

29. Holmes, The Path of the Law, 10 Harv.L.Rev. 457, 469 (1897).

30. For a collection of these statutes, *see* 1 ALP § 4.51; 3 Powell, Real Property, ¶ 380; Simes & Smith, The Law of Future Interests, § 1563.

31. *See, e.g.,* Fla.Stat.Ann. § 689.17 (West 1994). The Illinois and Iowa statutes are a model of effective simplicity. Illinois provides: "The rule of property known as the rule in Shelley's Case is abolished." Ill. Comp. Stat. Ann. § 345/0.01 (West 2001). Similarly Iowa provides that: The rule or principle of the common law known as the rule in

Shelley's case is hereby abolished and is declared not to be a part of the law of this state. Iowa Code § 557.20.

It is said that Mr. Justice Holmes as a young man sought the advice of Ralph Waldo Emerson in connection with a paper he was writing on a difficult subject. Emerson cautioned him: "When you shoot at a king you cannot afford to miss." Illinois and Iowa took no chance of missing. The Rule was indeed a king in the realm of property law.

32. *See* Moore v. Littel, 41 N.Y. 66 (1869).

created after the statute's enactment. Thus, even in jurisdictions that have abolished the Rule, it applies to older instruments such that interpretative problems continue to surface in the courts from time to time.[33] Of course, in states where the legislature has not afforded relief the courts and the profession must continue to struggle with the intricacies of the Rule.[34]

Review Problems

1. O conveys Blackacre to B for life, remainder to B's heirs. Under the Rule in Shelley's Case the remainder limited in favor of B's heirs is deemed limited in favor of B. Then, under the doctrine of merger, B's life estate and vested remainder merge to give B a fee simple absolute.

2. O conveys Blackacre to B for life, remainder to C for life, then to B's heirs. Under the Rule B has a vested remainder but it does not merge with B's life estate to give B a fee simple because B's remainder is not the next vested estate.

3. O conveys Blackacre to B for life, then to C's surviving children, or if C dies childless, then to B's heirs. At the time of the conveyance C is childless. Under the Rule B has a remainder but it is contingent on C dying childless. Thus B's life estate and B's remainder do not merge. However, if during B's life C dies childless then B's remainder vests and merges with B's life estate to give B a fee simple absolute.

§ 13.　The Doctrine of the Worthier Title

A.　*Statement of the Doctrine*

At English common law a man could not either by conveyance or by devise limit a fee simple to his own heirs. The heirs of the transferor were not permitted to take as purchasers under the conveyance or will and the attempted limitation was void. Let us

---

33. *See, e.g,* Society National Bank v. Jacobson, 54 Ohio St.3d 15, 560 N.E.2d 217 (1990); In the Matter of the Estate of Hendrickson, 324 N.J.Super. 538, 736 A.2d 540 (Sup.Ct.1999).

34. The rule appears to apply in Arkansas, Colorado, Delaware, Indiana, Louisiana (as to wills), New Hampshire (as to wills), North Carolina, and Oregon (as to wills).

consider this statement first with respect to wills, and then with respect to inter vivos conveyances.

Where a will devised to the heirs of the testator an estate of the same kind and quality as the heirs would have taken by descent if the testator had died intestate the heirs were required to take by descent instead of by purchase. Thus, T, owner of Blackacre in fee simple, devises it to B for life, then to the heirs of T. The remainder to the heirs of T is void as such, and they take the reversion by descent. Likewise, if land was devised to a designated person who turned out to be the testator's heir that person took by descent, not by devise. Thus, T devises land "to my son John and his heirs." At T's death John is his only heir. John takes the land by descent, not as purchaser under the will. It will be noted that the rule in its application to wills determined the character or manner in which the heir took the land; *it did not affect who actually took.*

The rule in its application to inter vivos transfers was that: a conveyor cannot create a remainder in his own heirs. Lord Coke expressed it as follows: "If a man makes a gift in taile or a lease for life, the remainder to his own right heirs, this remainder is void, and he hath the reversion in him * * * "[1] In the case of a conveyance the effect of the rule is to convert what would otherwise be a contingent remainder in the heirs of the conveyor into a reversion in the conveyor himself. Thus, O conveys Blackacre to B for life, and after B's death to the heirs of O. By virtue of the rule the state of the title is: life estate in B, reversion in fee simple in O. In its application to conveyances the rule prevents the heir from taking under the conveyance. In fact, the heir may never take because of the ancestor's power to transfer the reversion to a third person by a later conveyance or by devise.

This rule, or combination of rules, became known in American law as the doctrine of worthier title. The rule in its testamentary aspect required the heir to take by descent rather than by devise as

<hr>

§ 13

1. Co.Litt. 22b. Coke went on to give a specious explanation for the rule: "for the ancestor during his life beareth in his body (in judgment of law) all his heirs, and therefore it is truly said that

haeres est pars antecessoris." Professor Thorne has pointed out that Coke was adept at inventing a maxim to fit the occasion. Thorne, Sir Edward Coke 7 (Selden Society Lecture, 1957).

title by descent was said to be "worthier" or better than a title derived by purchase for the reason that a descent of lands from a disseisor to his heir barred the right of entry of the person disseised (but not the right of action), whereas if the title were acquired by purchase the disseisee's entry was not barred.[2] At times it has been objected that it is inappropriate to label as the worthier title doctrine the rule prohibiting a conveyor from creating a remainder in his own heirs on the ground that in this situation the rule does not force the heir to take by descent but prevents him from taking at all unless, perchance, the conveyor later dies intestate still owning the land.[3] But both aspects of the rule, or the two rules if you prefer, had a common origin and a common purpose in feudal society, and modern courts and writers usually apply the same term to both types of transactions. The two aspects of the rule are often differentiated by referring to one as the testamentary branch of the worthier title doctrine and to the other as the inter vivos branch of the doctrine.

B. Origin of the Doctrine

It is highly probable that the same considerations which led to the development of the Rule in Shelley's Case also shaped the doctrine of worthier title in both its testamentary and inter vivos

---

2. In the leading case of Ellis v. Page, 61 Mass. (7 Cush.) 161 (1851) the court said: "It is a well settled rule of real property, that a limitation to an heir in a devise is void, and that the heir cannot be a purchaser; Co.Litt. 22b; or, to state the rule more fully, if a man devises by his will his land to his heir at law and his heirs, in such case the devise, as such is void and the heir will take by descent and not by purchase, for the reason that the title by descent is the worthier and better title, by taking away the entry of those who might have a right in the land."

Professor Plucknett tells us that for a long time the early common law did not allow a claimant to land to maintain a writ of right, the most solemn of the real actions, unless he could show that he acquired seisin by descent from his ancestor. T. F. Plucknett, Legislation of Edward I 39–40 (1970). In later times, the real plaintiff in an action of ejectment could not maintain the action if his right of entry to the land had been lost by reason of descent of the land from the disseisor to his heir. See J. H. Baker, An Introduction to English Legal History 255 (2d 1979).

3. See Warren, Remainder to the Grantor's Heirs, 22 Tex.L.Rev. 22 (1943). In the fifteenth and earlier centuries inter vivos transfers of land were much less frequent than in later centuries; and land was devisable only in a few areas by special custom. Therefore, under those conditions the rule forbidding a remainder to the heirs of the conveyor would normally result in the heir taking by descent on the later death of his ancestor.

aspects. Feudal policy dictated that the incidents of tenure accruing to the lord on the death of the tenant should not be evaded. At the time, feudal policy was public policy and the feudal estate tax (the relief) had to be paid. The incidents of relief, wardship and marriage accrued to the lord on the descent of the fee but not where the fee was acquired by purchase; hence, the necessity of rules requiring the heir to take by descent and not by purchase. A thirteenth century statute made void, as against the lord of the fee, a feoffment (conveyance) by the tenant to his eldest son, who was his heir apparent.[4] In the next century when the law of remainders was being developed, a rule prohibiting the limitation of a remainder to the heirs of the conveyor would seem a natural corollary. Furthermore, a devise by a tenant to his own heir would be too obvious an evasion of the lord's seignorial rights to be tolerated.

The doctrine survived and flourished long after wardship and marriage had been abolished and the incidents of tenure had become inconsequential. The cases applied the doctrine in both of its branches as a positive rule of law but restricted its application to real property only.[5] By the nineteenth century it was felt that the doctrine had outlived whatever utility it formerly had and it was totally abrogated by Parliament in 1833.[6]

C. The Doctrine in American Law

In a substantial number of states the worthier title doctrine has been recognized and accepted as a part of the common law. However, the two branches of the rule have had a different course of development in American law and, therefore, must be considered separately.

---

4. This was the Statute of Fraudulent Feoffments. 52 Hen. 3, c. 6 (1267). For the text of the statute, see Pickering, Statutes at Large 59–60. With the abolition of wardship and marriage by the Tenures Abolition Act (12 Car. II, c. 24) in 1660 the statute became a dead letter although it was not formally repealed until 1863. 26 & 27 Vict. c. 125. For Tudor legislation designed to prevent evasion of the tenurial incidents, see 34 & 35 Hen. 8, c. V, § 15 (1542–3).

5. The earliest cases thus far uncovered are from the second half of the sixteenth century but it is highly unlikely that the doctrine originated at that relatively late time. The English cases are collected in Morris, The Inter Vivos Branch of the Worthier Title Doctrine, 2 Okla.L.Rev. 133 (1949); Morris, The Wills Branch of the Worthier Title Doctrine, 54 Mich.L.Rev. 451 (1956).

6. 3 & 4 Will. 4, c. 106, § 3.

1.　*The Testamentary Branch of the Doctrine*

Most of the cases applying the testamentary or wills branch of the doctrine arose in the nineteenth century and in the early part of the twentieth century. As usually formulated by the courts, the rule was stated to be that where a devise to the heirs purports to give them an estate of the same quantity and quality as they would have taken by descent in the absence of a will then the heirs must take by descent and not under the will. The rule applied whether the estate given to the heir was a present or a future interest and whether given to the heir by name or under the form of a limitation to the heirs of the testator. The English concept of quantity referred to the type of estate devised to the heir but some United States courts refused to apply the rule where the heir would have taken by descent a different share or proportion of the testator's estate.[7] The rule was held to be applicable where the devise gave the heir an equitable interest under a trust. In a very few jurisdictions the doctrine was expanded to include bequests of personal property to the next of kin.[8]

At the present time it will usually make no difference whether the person who takes an interest in the estate of the testator takes in the capacity of heir or of devisee. Therefore, the instances in which the question of the applicability of the wills branch of the doctrine can arise are relatively rare.[9] On principle, there should be

7. For an excellent discussion of the "same quantity and quality" concept in American law, *see* Morris, The Wills Branch of the Worthier Title Doctrine, 54 Mich.L.Rev. 451, 488–491 (1956).

8. *See, e.g.,* In re Warren's Estate, 211 Iowa 940, 234 N.W. 835 (1931), overruled, In re Estate of Kern, 274 N.W.2d 325 (Iowa 1979) and In re Estate of Grulke, 546 N.W.2d 626 (Iowa Ct.App.1996); Parsons v. Winslow, 6 Mass. 169 (1810).

9. In some states there are still a few situations where under the local statutes the course of descent of property depends upon whether it was acquired by the decedent by inheritance or

by purchase. *See* Morris, The Wills Branch of the Worthier Title Doctrine, *supra* note 5 at 470. A second area of possible significance of the wills branch of the doctrine exists in connection with the marshaling of assets of the estate of a decedent. If the assets are not sufficient for the payment of debts, legacies and expenses, intestate realty and personalty must be sacrificed before resorting to the property passing under the will. Hence, if a devise to the heir is void and he takes by intestacy his interests may be adversely affected. Ellis v. Page, 61 Mass. (7 Cush.) 161 (1851); *cf.* Biederman v. Seymour, 3 Beav. 368, 49 Eng. Rep. 144 (1840). See Restatement of Property, § 314(2) cmt. j (1940).

no difference in legal consequences in any case. The Restatement of Property takes the position that the wills branch of the doctrine should no longer a part of American law.[10]

2. The Inter Vivos Branch of the Doctrine

If the wills branch of the doctrine is a moribund rule (with the Restatement administering the *coup de grace*), the inter vivos branch, by contrast, plays a vigorous and important role in modern law.[11] The earlier American cases, following the English precedents, applied the doctrine as a positive rule of law applicable normally only to conveyances of realty. From the relatively simple rule that a grantor cannot limit a remainder to his own heirs the doctrine has evolved into a rule of construction applicable to the limitation by inter vivos transfer of an interest in real property to the heirs of the transferor or of an interest in personal property to his next of kin. The point of departure came in the landmark case of *Doctor v. Hughes*.[12] In that case O conveyed real property to T in trust to pay the income therefrom to the settlor (O) for life, and upon his death "to convey the said premises (if not sold) to the heirs at law of" O. The settlor, who was still living, had two daughters one of whom conveyed to her husband all of her interest in the trust property. A judgment creditor of this daughter and her husband brought an

A third situation in which it may be important to determine whether an heir takes by descent or under the will is where the heir attempts to renounce or disclaim the interest given him. At common law an heir lacked the power to renounce an inheritance but a person taking property as devisee or legatee could renounce the interest given him under the will. The power to renounce or disclaim could have important estate and gift tax consequences and also could affect the rights of creditors of the disclaimant. The latter point is well illustrated by the recent case of City National Bank of Birmingham v. Andrews, 355 So.2d 341 (Ala.1978). The court repudiated the testamentary branch of the worthier title doctrine and held that an heir could renounce the devise and thereby prevent her creditors from reaching the property. Many states have enacted statutes allowing an heir or next of kin to renounce the right of succession to any property. *See, e.g.*, Iowa Code § 633.704; Mass. Gen. Laws Ann. ch. 191 A (West 1990); N.Y. Est. Powers & Trust Law § 2–1.11 (McKinney 1998); Unif. Prob. Code § 2–801.

10. Restatement of Property § 314(2)(1940).

11. For an able exposition of the rule in modern American law, *see* the opinion of Leventhal, J. in Hatch v. Riggs National Bank, 361 F.2d 559 (D.C.Cir.1966) (refusing to apply the rule).

12. 225 N.Y. 305, 122 N.E. 221 (1919).

action to reach the interest alleged to have been given the daughter under the trust. The court held that the limitation to the heirs of the settlor operated as a retention of a reversion in the settlor, not as a remainder to the heirs, and, therefore, the daughter took no interest under the trust. Although the court, speaking through Judge Benjamin Cardozo, applied the doctrine of worthier title it did so on the basis that the settlor actually intended to retain a reversion and thereby control the disposition of the principal of the trust property rather than to create a remainder and confer an interest on his heirs apparent. In the course of his opinion Judge Cardozo stated: "We do not say that the ancient rule survives as an absolute prohibition limiting the power of the grantor. At the outset, probably, like the rule in Shelley's Case, it was a rule, not of construction, but of property * * * But at least the ancient rule survives to this extent: That, to transform into a remainder what would ordinarily be a reversion, the intention to work the transformation must be clearly expressed. Here there is no clear expression of such purpose."

The decision in *Doctor v. Hughes* gave new strength and a new direction to the doctrine in American law. The importance of the court and the eminence of the judge who wrote the opinion gave the rule a prominence it had previously lacked[13] and changing the rule from a positive rule of law to one of construction appeared to have the merit of effectuating the intention of the grantor. As a consequence, most courts have since followed the lead of New York and have accepted the doctrine as a rule of construction.[14] In substance, then, the rule has the effect of creating a rebuttable presumption that when a conveyor limits a remainder to his own heirs, in the case of realty, or to his heirs or next of kin in the case of

13. Prior to Cardozo's opinion in Doctor v. Hughes there were few instances where courts dealt with limitations to the heirs of the grantor and referred to the worthier title doctrine. For instance, the lower New York court's opinion in Doctor v. Hughes gives no indication that the court was aware of the applicability of the doctrine. 174 App.Div. 767, 161 N.Y.S. 634. Another example is Sands v. Old Colony Trust Co., 195 Mass. 575, 81 N.E. 300 (1907).

14. *See* Restatement of Property, § 314(1) (1940); Restatement (Second) Trusts, § 127 cmt. b. (1959). The influence of Doctor v. Hughes is evident in such cases as National Shawmut Bank of Boston v. Joy, 315 Mass. 457, 53 N.E.2d 113 (1944) and McKenna v. Seattle–First Nat. Bank, 35 Wash.2d 662, 214 P.2d 664 (1950).

personalty, he intends to retain an indefeasible reversion and not to create a remainder in the heirs or next of kin. This presumption, however, will yield to the manifestation of a contrary intent.[15]

In its modern form the rule has not had a happy existence in the state of its origin. As a rule of construction it has proved difficult of application and the numerous New York cases involving the doctrine have been marked by inconsistency and confusion.[16] The problem most frequently has arisen in connection with transfers in trust. Thus, O transfers stocks and bonds to a bank or trust company in trust to pay the income to B for life, and at B's death to distribute the principal to O's heirs. The question whether O has retained a reversion or has created a contingent remainder can become important in several situations.[17] For example, O may later change his mind and desire to revoke the trust even though no power to revoke was reserved in the trust instrument. It is well established that the settlor (creator) may revoke the trust with the consent of all persons beneficially interested therein.[18] If the limitation to O's heirs amounts to the retention of a reversion in O there is no one beneficially interested except O and B and together they can revoke the trust. If it is found that O intended to create a remainder in his heirs their consent to the revocation will be necessary and O's heirs cannot be determined until O dies. As a result the trust cannot be revoked during O's lifetime even though O and B consent.[19]

15. The Restatement of Property states the modern rule as follows: "When a person makes an otherwise effective inter vivos conveyance of an interest in land to his heirs, or of an interest in things other than land, to his next of kin, then, unless a contrary intent is found from additional language or circumstances, such conveyance to his heirs or next of kin is a nullity in the sense that it designates neither a conveyee nor the type of interest of a conveyee." § 314(1). The justification for the rule is stated to be that "it represents the probable intention of the average conveyor" who in making a gift in remainder to his own heirs "seldom intends to create an indestructible interest

in those persons who take his property by intestacy, but intends the same thing as if he had given the remainder 'to my estate'." Cmt. a.

16. 3 Powell, Real Property, ¶ 381.

17. If it is found that O has a reversion his creditors can reach this interest; and O can transfer his reversion by deed or will.

18. Unif. Trust Code § 411.

19. Where the settlor of a trust creates a remainder in favor of his heirs or next of kin the remaindermen are necessarily unascertained until the death of the settlor. Even living persons who are heirs presumptive, or presumptive next

Although in *Doctor v. Hughes*[20] Judge Cardozo spoke of the
necessity of a "clear expression" of an intention by the grantor "to
transform into a remainder what would ordinarily be a reversion,"
later New York cases indicated a readiness to find an intent to
create a remainder in circumstances where the grantor's intention
is at best doubtful. The strong presumption in favor of a reversion
formulated by Judge Cardozo was gradually diluted into a rather
weak constructional preference for a reversion.[21] In *Whittemore v.
Equitable Trust Co. of New York*[22] the court held that the trust
could not be terminated by the settlor because of a found intent to
create a remainder. In that case three settlors transferred certain
bonds in trust, the income to be paid to B and C during their lives
and at the death of the surviving life beneficiary the property to be
returned to the settlors in equal shares if living; but if any be dead
his share to be paid to such persons as such deceased settlor should
by his will appoint, and in default of appointment to such persons
as would be entitled thereto if the settlor had been the owner
thereof at his death and had died intestate. In finding an intention
of the settlors to create a remainder in the heirs the court seems to
have relied on the fact that the settlors made a "rather full and
formal disposition of the principal of the trust estate" in case they
died before the life beneficiaries, and also on the fact that they

of kin, may not survive the settlor. If the
settlor desires to terminate a trust
which is not by its terms revocable, the
contingent interest of the unborn and
unascertained remainderman cannot be
destroyed. It will be necessary for the
court to appoint a guardian *ad litem* to
represent such persons. Hatch v. Riggs
National Bank, *supra* note 11. In New
York, by statute, such contingent remaindermen are not deemed to be persons beneficially interested in the trust
property, for purposes of revocation of
the trust, N.Y. Est. Powers & Trusts
Law § 7–1.9 (McKinney 1992) The statute applies only to trusts created on or
after September 1, 1951.

20. *Supra* note 12.

21. "It is clear from the cases in
this state since *Doctor v. Hughes*, supra,

* * * that, despite that the language in
that opinion that a reversion exists unless there is clear evidence to the contrary, the rule has been less limited in
application * * * While we have not yet
adopted a rule, either by statute or judicial construction, under which language
limiting an interest to heirs is unequivo-
cally given its full effect, the presumption which exists from the use of the
common law doctrine as a rule of construction has lost much of its force since
Doctor v. Hughes, supra." Matter of
Burchell's Estate, 299 N.Y. 351, 359, 87
N.E.2d 293, 297 (1949). As to the present law of New York, *see* N.Y. Est. Powers & Trusts Law § 6–5.9 (McKinney
1992)(abolishing the doctrine of worthier title).

22. 250 N.Y. 298, 165 N.E. 454
(1929).

reserved a power of disposition "only by will."[23] In later cases the New York Court of Appeals has attempted, with qualified success, to state the factors deemed to be significant in determining the intention of the settlor.[24] Not the least of the factors indicating an intention to create a remainder, according to the court, is the reservation by the settlor of a testamentary power of appointment of the principal without the retention of any other power of disposition over the corpus of the trust estate.[25] Perhaps the clearest conclusion to be drawn from these cases is that there is no reliable standard of predictability of the court's action in the reversion-remainder situation. At least in New York, the legislature has afforded relief.[26]

Litigation in other states involving the doctrine has been much less extensive than in New York, but, as previously stated, the doctrine, in the form of a rule of construction based on the presumed intent of the transferor, has won general acceptance. In

23. *But see* City Bank Farmers Trust Co. v. Miller, 278 N.Y. 134, 15 N.E.2d 553 (1938). In this case the trust agreement provided for weekly payments to the settlor of specified amounts from income and principal until the principal was reduced to $5000 and in that event the principal was to be returned to the settlor. On the settlor's death the trust property was to be paid as the settlor should by her will appoint, and in default of appointment to the persons entitled to take as her intestate successors. The court held the trust agreement gave rise to a reversion, not a remainder.

24. In Richardson v. Richardson, 298 N.Y. 135, 81 N.E.2d 54 (1948) the court stated: "To summarize, therefore, we believe that the settlor evidenced her intention to give a remainder to her next of kin because she (1) made a full and formal disposition of the principal of the trust property, (2) made no reservation of a power to grant or assign an interest in the property during her lifetime, (3) surrendered all control over the trust property except the power to make

testamentary disposition thereof and the right to appoint a substitute trustee, and (4) made no provision for the return of any part of the principal to herself during her lifetime."

25. Matter of Burchell's Estate, 299 N.Y. 351, 360, 87 N.E.2d 293, 297 (1949). For an excellent summary and discussion of the New York cases, *see* Verrall, The Doctrine of Worthier Title: A Questionable Rule of Construction, 6 UCLA L.Rev. 201 (1959).

26. The N.Y. legislature abolished the doctrine in 1967: "Where a remainder is limited to the heirs or distributees of the creator of an estate in property, such heirs or distributees take as purchasers." N.Y. Est. Powers & Trusts Law § 6–5.9 (McKinney 1992). Section § 7–1.9(b) of the N.Y. Est. Powers and Trusts Law (McKinney 1992) provides that, with respect to revocation of trusts, a disposition of property in favor of persons described only as the heirs, next of kin or distributees of the creator of the trust does not create a beneficial interest in such persons.

order to invoke the doctrine the conveyance must limit a future interest to the intestate successors of the transferor, that is, to his heirs in the case of land, and to his next of kin in the case of personal property. Therefore, the rule is not applicable where the gift is to "children" or "issue" of the transferor or where the persons to take are to be determined as of a time other than the transferor's death.[27] Nor does the rule apply where the gift is limited to named persons who later turn out to be the heirs or next of kin of the transferor. Although the limitation must be to the heirs or next of kin, the use of the words "heirs" or "next of kin" in the instrument is not necessary and any equivalent words are sufficient to satisfy this requirement of the rule.[28] Almost invariably the interest given to the heirs or next of kin is in the form of a remainder, but on principle the doctrine, as a rule of construction, should also be applicable where the limitation to them is an executory interest instead of a remainder.[29] In both situations it may be presumed, in the absence of a manifested contrary intention, that the transferor intended to retain a reversion or reversionary interest in himself rather than to create an interest in his intestate successors.

At times the doctrine is confused with the Rule in Shelley's Case.[30] Both rules involve a problem of remainders, but they are separate and distinct rules despite their probable common origin. The worthier title doctrine, in its inter vivos aspect, is concerned only with remainders to the heirs of the conveyor, whereas the Rule in Shelley's Case is concerned with remainders to the heirs of any person to whom a life estate has been given by the same conveyance. Thus, if O conveys to B for life, then to the heirs of B, the Rule in Shelley's Case will apply but not the worthier title doctrine. If O conveys to B for life, then to the heirs of O, the worthier title

---

27. Restatement of Property, § 314 cmt. c (1940). *But see* Bottimore v. First & Merchants Nat. Bank of Richmond, 170 Va. 221, 196 S.E. 593 (1938).

28. *See, e.g.,* Richardson v. Richardson, 298 N.Y. 135, 81 N.E.2d 54 (1948) ("to such persons as would be entitled to the same under the intestacy laws of the State of New York.")

29. The Restatement takes this view. § 314 cmt. f(1940). *See also,* 1 ALP §§ 4.20, 4.57.

30. *See, e.g.,* Sutliff v. Aydelott, 373 Ill. 633, 27 N.E.2d 529 (1940); Loring v. Eliot, 82 Mass. (16 Gray) 568 (1860).

doctrine will apply but not the Rule in Shelley's Case. In one situation the possible application of both rules must be taken into consideration. Assume that O conveys land to T in trust for O for life, and on O's death in trust for the heirs of O. It is sometimes said that in this situation both rules are applicable.[31] However, before the Rule in Shelley's Case can apply it must first be determined that the conveyance limits a remainder to the heirs of the life tenant. If the worthier title doctrine is accepted as a positive rule of law its effect, when applied to this conveyance, is to eliminate the remainder in the heirs of O and there is nothing on which the Rule in Shelley's Case can operate. If, taking the modern view, the worthier title doctrine is accepted as a rule of construction expressing the intention of the conveyor, we reach the same result. There is no remainder in the heirs of O because, presumably, O did not intend to give them a remainder. Again, there is nothing on which the Rule in Shelley's Case can operate. Only if, as a matter of construction of the conveyance, it is first determined that the worthier title doctrine does not apply because of a manifested intention of the conveyor to create a remainder, does the Rule in Shelley's Case come into operation. On the bare facts of the case given above, however, the conveyor has not manifested an intention to create a remainder in his heirs and, therefore, the limitation to the heirs will operate as a reversion in O and the Rule in Shelley's Case will not be applicable.

C. Statutory Modification of the Doctrine

In recent years there has been a trend in the direction of statutory abrogation of the worthier title doctrine in both of its branches. As a rule of construction the inter vivos aspect of the doctrine has been productive of litigation and confusion; and it has been questioned whether the modern rule does in fact express the intention of the normal settlor of a trust.[32] As a consequence, statutes abolishing the doctrine have been enacted in many states.[33]

---

31. Simes & Smith, The Law of Future Interests, § 1607. *Cf.* Restatement of Property, § 314 cmt. g (1940).

32. Verrall, The Doctrine of Worthier Title: A Questionable Rule of Construction, 6 UCLA L.Rev. 371 (1959). The leading case repudiating the doctrine without the aid of legislation is Hatch v. Riggs National Bank, 361 F.2d 559 (D.C.Cir.1966).

33. Ark. Code Ann. § 220 (Michie 1987); Cal. Civ. Code § 1073 (West 1982); Ill. Comp. Stat. Ann. § 350/1

Review Problems

O conveys Blackacre to B for life, and upon B's death to O's heirs. Under the Doctrine of Worthier Title, O has a reversion in fee simple. Thus, upon B's death Blackacre reverts to O in fee simple absolute. If O had conveyed the reversion to X, or, alternatively, had died testate leaving the reversion to X, or, alternatively, had died intestate leaving X as O's sole heir, then upon B's death, X would take a fee simple absolute. Most importantly, since O had a reversion, if O bequeathed the reversion to Y and left X as O's sole heir, Y would take the reversion to the exclusion of X and ultimately, at B's death, the fee simple absolute in Blackacre.

On the other hand, if the Doctrine did not apply then O's heirs would have a contingent remainder which would not be defeated by a bequest or lifetime conveyance to a stranger. Of course, in this case if B died survived by O and the rule of destructibility applied, the interest of O's heirs would be destroyed and the property would revert to O. If O, however, predeceased B, O's heirs would be ascertained as of O's death and their interest would ripen into a vested remainder.

(West 2001) Ind. Code Ann. § 30–4–2–7 (West 1994) (as to trusts only); Mass. Gen. Laws Ann. ch. 184, § 33 A (West 1991)(abolishing wills branch of the rule); ch. 184, § 33 B (West 1991) (abolishing the inter vivos branch); Minn. Stat. Ann. § 500.14(4) (West 1990); Neb. Rev. Stat. § 76–115; N.Y. Est. Powers & Trusts Law § 6.5–9 (McKinney 1992); Tex. Prop. Code Ann. § 5.042 (Vernon 1984); W. Va. Code, § 36–1–14(a)(1966). In Illinois the statute has been given a narrow scope. See Stewart v. Merchants National Bank of Aurora, 3 Ill.App.3d 337, 278 N.E.2d 10 (1972). See also Unif. Prob. Code § 2–710 (abolishing doctrine of worthier title as rule of law and construction).

Chapter 6

COMMON LAW METHODS OF CONVEYANCING

§ 1. Creation and Transfer of Present Freehold Estates

Prior to the seventeenth century the typical form of conveyance of a present freehold estate in land was the feoffment with livery of seisin. A feoffment was the grant of a fief or feudal tenement and livery of seisin was the means by which the grant was effected. At a time when seisin was tantamount to ownership[1] it was logical enough that the law should take the position that a transfer of seisin was essential to the creation of a freehold estate. If O was seised of Blackacre in fee simple and wished to convey his estate to B, it was necessary that O invest B with the seisin. This was done by means of a feoffment with livery of seisin, or more shortly, a feoffment. O and B, or their agents, would go upon the land and O would formally "give" or "deliver" the seisin to B in the presence of witnesses from the neighborhood. O would usually hand over to B a branch, twig or piece of turf as a symbol of the land itself although this ceremonial act was not essential. What was essential was the investiture of B with the seisin. Thus, O, the feoffor, must declare that he gives the seisin to the feoffee, B; and having installed B in occupancy of the land, O must completely relinquish the possession. The feoffor would declare at the time of the livery what estate he gave to the feoffee. Livery of seisin could

§ 1
1. *See* ch. 1, §§ 11–13, *supra.*

also be made in view of the land without the parties actually going on it, but in that case it was necessary for the feoffee to make an entry on the land during the lifetime of the feoffor, otherwise the feoffment was void.

Until the enactment of the Statute of Frauds in 1677[2] no writing was necessary to make the feoffment valid. The estate conveyed passed to the feoffee solely by virtue of the transfer of the seisin. From the thirteenth century onward it was, in fact, customary for the feoffor to deliver to the feoffee a deed or charter of feoffment but the function of the charter was to furnish evidence of the livery of seisin and of the nature of the estate given, as well as to set forth the covenant of warranty. The language of the charter, written in the past tense, indicated its purpose: it recited that the feoffor had "given and granted" the land and had delivered the seisin to the feoffee. The operative act in the transaction was the delivery of seisin, not the giving of the charter or deed. Over time and, of course today, the reverse of this became true; the deed becoming essential and livery of seisin obsolete.

The enactment in the sixteenth century of the Statute of Uses[3] gave rise to new modes of conveying freehold estates which took effect through the execution and delivery of deeds, and the medieval conveyance by feoffment with livery of seisin fell into disuse. The Real Property Act of 1845[4] provided that a present freehold estate could be transferred by a simple deed of grant. Yet conveyance by feoffment, evidenced by a deed, continued to be theoretically possible in England until the twentieth century when the Law of Property Act, 1925,[5] finally made it invalid as a mode of conveyance.[6]

2. 29 Car. 2, c. 3, § 1. The statute provided that an estate "made and created by livery and seisin only, or by parol, and not put in writing, and signed by the parties so making or creating the same, or their agents * * *" should have the effect of an estate at will only.

3. 27 Hen. 8, ch. 10 (1536).

4. 8 & 9 Vict. ch. 106.

5. 15 & 16 Geo. 5, ch. 20, § 51.

6. Feoffments were occasionally used to convey land in colonial times in America. In Massachusetts, a provincial act of 1697 provided that a deed of lands, signed, sealed and acknowledged by the grantor and recorded "shall be valid to pass the same, without any other act or ceremony in the law whatsoever." At the present day valuable land in Ipswich, Massachusetts is owned by a charitable corporation bearing the ancient name "The Feoffees of the Gram-

Livery of seisin was by its very nature a present act which operated to take the seisin out of the feoffor and put it in the feoffee. Therefore, a feoffment with livery of seisin could not be made to take effect at a future date. O could not enfeoff B of Blackacre with the feoffment to take effect on B's subsequent marriage or upon O's death. The transaction was deemed void and the seisin continued in O. Herein lies the probable reason for the common-law rule that a freehold estate could not be created to commence *in futuro*.[7] Since seisin passed to the feoffee at the time of the feoffment, or not at all, there could be no springing freehold estate to arise in the conveyee out of the estate of the conveyor at a future time. Nor could seisin be suspended or put in abeyance for any period of time since under the medieval law there must always be a tenant to answer to the lord's demand for the feudal dues and · to the plaintiff's writ in a real action.

Although conveyance by feoffment was the usual method of creating and transferring a present freehold estate, it was not the only method available. Conveyance by fine was also rather widely used in the medieval period. A fine was the compromise of a feigned action, usually an action begun by writ of covenant, between the parties to the conveyance.[8] The compromise set forth the terms of the conveyance and a copy of this compromisé became an official record of the court and was preserved as such. Thus, conveyance by fine had the great advantage of giving the conveyee an official record of his title, a title which, unlike the charter of feoffment, was subject neither to theft nor forgery. Yet, the fine was incomplete until seisin had been delivered to the conveyee.

Another mode of conveying land through the use of the judicial machinery was the common recovery. Unlike the fine, the common recovery was a real action prosecuted to a final judgment ordering

mar School in the Town of Ipswich." The land was conveyed to the Feoffees at some time between 1650 and 1660 "for the use of school-learning in the said town forever."

7. The effect of this rule on the destructibility of contingent remainders has been discussed in ch. 5, § 8, *supra*.

8. The word "fine" is derived from the Latin term *"finalis concordia"*, meaning final concord or agreement of the parties. The whole process was called "levying a fine."

the "recovery" of the lands by the plaintiff. In its classical form, as developed in the late fifteenth and in the sixteenth centuries, the collusive common recovery became an effective means whereby a tenant in tail could alienate in fee simple and destroy reversions and remainders expectant on the estate tail, as well as the rights of his issue.[9] The Fines and Recoveries Act (1833)[10] abolished both of these methods of conveyancing. There are a few instances of the use of fines and recoveries in early American law, but they were never an important factor in this country and were supplanted by conveyance by deed.

§ 2. Creation of Non–Freehold Estates

Because the tenant for years and the tenant at will did not have seisin, such estates were not created by a feoffment. An agreement between the parties that the transferee should have a specified estate for years or a tenancy at will followed by an entry into possession by the tenant was sufficient to create the estate. Prior to the Statute of Frauds (1677) a lease for years need not in any case be in writing, although as a practical matter a leasehold estate for any substantial period would be evidenced by a writing under seal in order that the parties might maintain an action of covenant for breach of the promises set forth in the lease. Until the lessee entered into possession, he had no estate in the land. The lessee had the peculiar interest called an *interesse termini*. This interest was assignable even before the doctrine of assignability of contract rights in general had evolved. The insistence of the common law on the taking of possession by the lessee before his position as tenant was recognized is analogous to the necessity of the conveyee of a freehold estate obtaining seisin to acquire the status of a freehold tenant. This curious concept of *interesse termini* is now obsolete.[1]

---

9. For an excellent discussion of fines and recoveries, see Plucknett, Concise History of the Common Law 619–622 (5th ed. 1956); A.W.B. Simpson, A History of the Land Law 123–137(2d ed. 1986).

10. 3 & 4 Will. 4, ch. 74.

§ 2

1. As to *interesse termini* under modern law, *see* ch. 3, § 2, *supra*.

§ 3. Creation of Future Interests

Since a reversion arises by operation of law and not by agreement of the parties, no manifestation of an intention by the conveyor to create a reversion was necessary to produce that result. A conveyance by the conveyor of a legally smaller estate than his own automatically resulted in the retention of a reversion.[1] If the conveyor wished to reserve a right of entry for condition broken (power of termination) it was necessary to manifest such intention by appropriate language in the charter of feoffment or other conveyance. Similarly, a possibility of reverter arose from the words of express limitation creating a determinable fee in the conveyee.

Prior to the Statute of Uses (1536), the only two types of future interests that could be created in a conveyee were the vested remainder and the contingent remainder. Both of these interests were created by appropriate language in the feoffment, or in the conveyance by way of fine. Thus, if O, the owner of Blackacre in fee simple, wished to give B a present possessory life estate in Blackacre and a remainder to C in fee tail followed by a remainder to D in fee simple, O would enfeoff B by delivering the seisin to him and as part of the transaction would declare, orally or in writing, that B should hold the land for life and that on B's death it should go to C and the heirs of his body and on failure of such issue to D and his heirs. B received the seisin in his own right and also on behalf of both the remainderman in fee tail and the remainderman in fee simple. Therefore, on B's death the seisin would automatically pass to C. The necessity of seisin passing to the remainderman delayed the recognition of the validity of a contingent remainder. If O enfeoffed B for life, remainder to the heirs of C, a living person, who was the remainderman and where did the seisin of the inheritance go at the time of the feoffment? If seisin of the fee remained in O it would take another conveyance to get it out of him. Not until the middle of the fifteenth century were these theoretical difficulties overcome, or ignored, by acceptance of the view that if

§ 3

1. It will be recalled that, strictly speaking, an owner of a freehold estate who created an estate for years did not by common law standards have a rever-sion; he retained a present freehold estate subject to the term of years. Under modern law, the transferor has a reversion expectant upon the estate for years. *See* ch. 4, § 2, *supra*.

the remainder vested at or prior to the termination of B's estate seisin could pass to the remainderman on B's death.[2]

It was permissible for O, seised in fee simple, to give a term of years to B and by the same transaction to give to C a fee simple subject to B's term. In other words, it was possible for the conveyor to create what we would now call an estate for years followed by a remainder in fee simple. This was done by having O deliver the seisin to B on behalf of C; at the same time O would declare the grant of the term of years to B and of the fee simple to C. In receiving the seisin B was acting as though he were C's agent and the seisin vested immediately in C. As Littleton puts it: "But if he (the feoffor) maketh livery of seisin to the lessee, then is the freehold, together with the fee to them in the remainder, according to the form of the grant and the will of the lessor."[3] Because, under the medieval law, the term of years was not an estate, C's interest was regarded as a present fee simple, not a remainder in fee simple. The present freehold was in C subject to B's term for years. It has become customary to describe these limitations as creating an estate for years in B, with a remainder in fee simple in C.

§ 4.   Common Law Rules Restricting the Creation of Future Interests

It may be helpful at this point to summarize and recapitulate some of the restrictive rules at common law governing the creation of future interests in transferees:[1]

A.   No freehold estate could be created to commence *in futuro*. This was a consequence of the concept of livery of seisin as a presently operative act.

2. *See* ch. 5, § 9, *supra* (rule of destructibility).

3. Littleton, Tenures, sec. 60 (c. 1481).

§ 4

1. The most important rule restricting the creation of future interests, the Rule against Perpetuities, is discussed in

Simes & Smith, The Law of Future Interests, §§ 1211–1439 (2nd ed. 1956). *See also* ch. 8, § 11 Two other rules limiting the creation of (2nd ed. 1956)some future interests, *infra* (the Rule in Shelley's Case and the Doctrine of Worthier Title) have been treated in ch. 5 *supra*.

B.   A freehold contingent remainder could not be supported by a term of years. Thus, if O conveys Blackacre to B for ten years, then to the heirs of C, a living person, the attempted remainder to C is void and O has an estate in fee simple subject to B's term of years. B receives possession but not seisin and since C's heir will not be ascertained until C's death there is no one capable of taking the seisin. Inasmuch as the seisin cannot be in abeyance it must remain in O. It cannot pass to C's heir when the latter is ascertained since this would violate the rule forbidding the creation of a freehold to commence in the future.

C.   A limitation operating to shift the seisin from one transferee to another transferee by cutting short or divesting a precedent estate was void. A grantor could reserve a right of entry in favor of himself but there could be no cut-off in favor of a stranger. Thus, suppose O enfeoffs B and his heirs but if B dies without having married then to C and his heirs. The limitation to C is void. Likewise, if O enfeoffs B for life but upon C paying B a sum of money then to C and his heirs, again the limitation to C is void. C's interest is not a remainder because a remainder, by its very nature, awaits the termination of the preceding estate before becoming a possessory estate. It does not displace or cut off a prior estate. Since the common law did not permit the creation of a springing or a shifting interest in a conveyee, it follows that the only future interest which could be limited in favor of a conveyee was a remainder.

D.   A future interest limited to take effect after an interval of time following the termination of the preceding estate was void. There could be no gap between the preceding estate and the remainder. Thus, O enfeoffs B for life, and one year after B's death to C and his heirs. The limitation to C is void. The seisin cannot be suspended during the year following B's death, thus, on B's death, seisin revert to O. Once the seisin has come back to O it will take a new conveyance to transfer it to C. The original conveyance is not effective to give the seisin to C because of the rule forbidding the creation of a freehold estate to take effect *in futuro*. A gap for even a short interval of time was not permitted. As we shall see in a later chapter,[2] after the enactment of the Statute of Uses (1536) it was possible for a conveyor to give an estate to one person and to provide that upon the occurrence of a specified event that estate should be cut short and an estate should arise in a third person. It also became possible at that later period of time to create a freehold estate to commence *in futuro*; that is, a freehold estate could be created to become effective at a future date without any precedent estate being limited, or after a gap following the termination of the precedent estate. In none of these cases would the future interest take effect by way of remainder.

§ 5.   Transfer of Future Estates

A reversion or remainder expectant upon a freehold estate could not be transferred by livery of seisin for the simple reason that the seisin was in the holder of the particular estate. Thus, O, the owner of Blackacre in fee simple, enfeoffs B for life. Since B and not O has the seisin, if O wishes to transfer the reversion to C he cannot do so by livery of seisin. He could do so by the type of conveyance called a grant. A grant was effectuated by the execution and delivery of a deed from the transferor to the transferee.[1] Although the term "grant" is, in its modern usage, practically synonymous with "conveyance" and is used generically without reference to a particular type of conveyance, in its technical common-law meaning it referred to a special type of conveyance. It was the appropriate method of transferring reversions, remainders and other incorporeal interests. The notion that certain interests in land were transferable by livery of seisin and other interests by grant was summed up in the maxim that "all lands lie in livery or in grant."[2]

2. Ch. 8, *infra*.

§ 5

1. The term "grant" derives from the language of the deed which recited that the conveyor "gives and grants" to the conveyee.

2. Doe v. Cole, 7 B. & C. 243, 108 Eng.Rep. 714 (1827). This distinction between conveyance by livery and conveyance by grant continued to exist as a matter of legal theory until 1845 when, by statute, present freehold estates became transferable by deed of grant. 8 & 9 Vict. ch. 106, § 2.

The owner of a freehold estate subject to a term of years could transfer his estate by grant. For example, suppose O, the owner of Blackacre in fee simple, leases Blackacre to B for ten years. The present freehold and seisin are in O but because of B's possessory estate O could not transfer his reversion by livery of seisin to C unless B temporarily surrendered the possession to O.[3]

A grant of a reversion or of a remainder was not effective until the holder of the present particular estate assented to the transfer. This assent was known as attornment. The requirement of attornment by the tenant probably finds its origin in the personal relation existing between lord and tenant in feudal times. The necessity of attornment was abolished in England in 1705 and is an obsolete doctrine in all American jurisdictions at the present time.

If the holder of a possessory estate for life or years desired to transfer it to the person having the immediate reversion or next vested remainder he could do so by surrender. Lord Coke described a surrender as "a yielding up an estate for life, or years, to him that hath an immediate estate in reversion or remainder, wherein the estate for life, or years, may drown by mutual agreement between them."[4] The estate surrendered would merge in the estate of the surrenderee. Prior to the Statute of Frauds no writing was necessary but under the provisions of that Statute the surrender had to be by deed or note or "by act and operation of law."[5]

A release was the converse of a surrender. As in the case of the surrender, the release could be used only when both parties to the transaction already had estates or interests in the land. It could, as between holders of successive estates in the same parcel of land, be given only by a person out of possession to a person in possession. Thus, if B has a life estate in land, followed by a remainder in C in fee simple, C could convey his remainder to B by means of a release. A release, being an instrument in writing under seal, was a species of grant. It was also the appropriate type of conveyance

3. Doe v. Cole, n. 2, *supra*. The practice was, prior to the Statute of Uses, for the lessee to give up possession for a moment to the lessor to enable the lessor to make livery of the seisin subject to the lease.

4. Co.Litt. 337b.

5. As to surrender in the modern law of landlord and tenant, *see* ch. 3, § 7, *supra*.

where the joint tenant of a freehold estate desired to transfer his estate to the other joint tenant or where a disseisee wished to convey his right of entry to the disseisor.

It was possible for an owner of land in fee simple to convey his estate without livery of seisin by means of a lease and release. Thus, O, the owner of Blackacre in fee simple, wishes to convey it to B in fee simple. O could, by agreement and entry, create in B an estate for one year and upon B's entry into possession give B a deed of release of the reversion "to have and to hold to B and his heirs," thereby putting the whole fee in B. This method seems not to have been in common use prior to the Statute of Uses (1536) but thereafter it became the established practice to convey land by means of a bargain and sale of a term of years followed by a common law release of the reversion.

Today, no particular form of deed is required for a valid inter vivos conveyance of an interest in land although a testamentary transfer must satisfy the requirements of the applicable wills act.[6] It is generally held to be sufficient if the written instrument of conveyance is signed by the grantor or his duly authorized representative, identifies the grantee and the land being conveyed, and manifests an intent to make a present transfer of an interest in the land.[7] Local usage determines the form of the deed and frequently the conveyancing portion of the instrument is expressed in terms of "grant" or "bargain and sell". In many states, statutes provide for the optional use of a specified form and spell out the legal effect of the language used with respect to covenants for title.[8] In all

---

6. While state laws differ, at a minimum a will must be in writing, signed by the testator and witnessed by at least two witnesses. *See generally*, Unif. Probate Code § 2–502(a)(imposing only minimal requirements). Many states, however, impose additional requirements such as the requirement that testator declare the instrument to be the will, the requirement that testator request the witnesses to act as such, and the requirement that testator sign the will at the end. Some states also permit holographic wills (wills entirely in a tes-

tator's handwriting). *See, e.g.*, Unif. Probate Code § 2–502(b).

7. *See* Unif. Simplification of Land Transfers Act § 2–201 (1977).

8. *See, e.g.*, Cal. Civ. Code §§ 1053, 1092, 1113 (West 1982); Mass. Gen. Laws Ann. ch. 183, §§ 8–11 (West 1991). The Massachusetts statutes further provide: "In a conveyance of real property the word 'grant' shall be a sufficient word of conveyance without the words, give, bargain, sell and convey, and no covenant shall be implied from the use of the word 'grant'." Mass. Gen. Laws

jurisdictions the deed must be delivered in order to be an effective conveyance of a legal estate in the land.

Ann. ch. 183, § 12 (West 1991). For a brief description of the various statutes, *see* 6A, Powell, Real Property ¶ 885 (Rohan ed. 1984).

Chapter 7

USES AND THE STATUTE OF USES—VALIDATING EXECUTORY INTERESTS AT LAW

§ 1. The Nature of a Use

Thus far we have been discussing estates and interests in land from the viewpoint of the common law. We now consider English land law from the viewpoint not only of a court of law but also of a court of equity. Until 1875 there existed in England a separate court, called the Court of Chancery, which dispensed justice in a way that was designed to afford a remedy where none was available under the rigid, formulary common-law procedure. The Chancellor, as keeper of the king's conscience, sought to give relief as justice and equity required even though, or rather because, the petitioner could obtain no redress for his grievance in the king's common-law courts. Over the course of time, the principles applied by the Chancellor in deciding cases coming before him became integrated into a system of jurisprudence called by the distinctive name "equity". The law of real property of today is a result of the application of both common-law and equitable doctrines, and it was by means of the institution of "uses" that equity came into contact with the land law.

In the fourteenth century there became prevalent a practice whereby land owners conveyed their lands to friends to hold for the use and benefit of the feoffors or of third persons.[1] The person for whose use or benefit the land was held was called *cestui que use*.[2] The purpose of such conveyances frequently was to enable the landowners to deal with their lands in a manner not countenanced by the common law or to evade the liabilities incident to legal ownership, such as the rule of destructibility. Thus suppose O, the owner of Blackacre in fee simple, wished to dispose of Blackacre by will at a time when disposition by will was not recognized by the law courts, i.e, prior to 1540. To accomplish this goal, O would enfeoff B in fee simple to hold to O's use during O's lifetime and after his death to transfer the land according to O's will. Upon O's death, B, the owner of Blackacre in fee simple, would then carry out the terms of O's will and transfer Blackacre to O's intended beneficiaries. Likewise, a dying land owner could by a conveyance to several feoffees to uses (who would take as joint tenants) deprive the lord of the fee of the important incidents of wardship, marriage or relief. For these and other reasons men sought to rid themselves of the legal title to land and yet retain the beneficial ownership. A feoffment to uses or in trust was generally adequate to accomplish this purpose.

It is obvious that the success of a feoffor's attempt to put the legal ownership of his land in someone else and retain the beneficial ownership in himself depended on the feoffee keeping his promise to deal with the land according to the agreement made at the time of the feoffment. Unless some way could be found to enforce the feoffee's promise the feoffor's position was indeed precarious. In the law courts the feoffee was recognized as the true owner; the cestui que use in possession was only a tenant at will. Seisin had vested in the feoffee by virtue of the feoffment and the

---

§ 1

1. The "use" as a device for putting the beneficial enjoyment of land in a person other than the owner was resorted to as early as the Domesday Book but the practice was not widespread until the thirteenth and fourteenth centuries. For an account of the origin and development of the use, *see* Plucknett, Concise History of the Common Law 575– 587 (5th ed. 1956); 2 Powell, Real Property §§ 265–267; 1 American Law of Property [hereinafter referred to as "ALP"], §§ 1.17–1.25; 4 Holdsworth, History of English Law 409–443 (1924).

2. The term "cestui que use" is a corruption of the law French phrase *"cestui a que use le feoffment fuit fait"* (he to whose use the feoffment was made).

law courts were not at all concerned with the feoffee's promise to deal with the land for the benefit of the feoffor or his nominees. That promise in no way affected the legal estate in the land and beyond the legal title the common law would not inquire.[3] The situation was one naturally calling for the exercise of the extraordinary jurisdiction of the Court of Chancery, and the Chancellor accepted jurisdiction in the early fifteenth century.

The principle upon which the Chancellor decided to give protection to the cestui que use against faithless feoffees to uses was a simple one: a man ought to keep his promises, and should not be allowed to profit by his own breach of faith. The Court of Chancery, therefore, began to apply its peculiarly powerful sanctions of fine and imprisonment to force feoffees to uses to perform their undertakings. The Chancellor did not interfere with the legal title of the feoffee to uses. He recognized the legal title as being in the feoffee but compelled the latter to refrain from making use of that legal title in a manner inconsistent with the promise under which he had received it.[4] As a consequence of Chancery's protection of cestui que use there was a dual ownership of land, the legal title of the feoffee to uses, or trustee, and the equitable title of cestui que use—an equitable title that is transferable, inheritable, and devisable.

Having decided to enforce the use against the feoffee to uses, would the Chancellor also enforce it against others who were transferees from that feoffee? The answer ultimately formulated was that those who took legal title with notice of the use and those who took without notice but paid no value for the transfer were bound by the use. Thus, heirs of the feoffee to uses, donees, and

3. When the remedy of assumpsit had developed it would have enabled the feoffor to recover damages against the feoffee to uses for breach of his undertaking but by then far more effective relief was obtainable in Chancery.

4. Did the Chancellor recognize an *in rem* right on the part of the cestui que use, a right in the land itself, or only an *in personam* right against the feoffee? That is a theoretically debatable point, but the rights of the cestui que use were so similar to in rem rights that for practical purposes we may treat those rights as being rights in the land itself—a species of ownership.

No doubt, in its origin and later development the use did not bind the land; it bound only the conscience of the person acquiring the legal ownership. But the extensive, although not complete, protection given by Chancery to the cestui que use amounted to a type of equitable "ownership." *See* 1 Scott, The Law of Trusts, § 1 (4th ed. 1987).

purchasers with notice took subject to the use but bona fide purchasers for value, without notice, from the feoffee to uses took the legal title unencumbered by the equitable title of the cestui que use. A person taking the legal estate under a title independent of that of the feoffee to uses, such as a disseisor, was not bound by the use. The only remedy of the cestui que use in such a case would be to petition the Chancellor to compel the trustee to institute an action to recover possession of the land.

As to the duties imposed on the feoffee to uses, these depended for their details on the terms of the particular feoffment. In general, however, those duties were as follows:

1. The feoffee to uses must permit the cestui que use to occupy the land or to take the rents and profits thereof;

2. He must convey the legal estate according to the instructions of the cestui que use;

3. He must take all necessary proceedings to defend the legal title against the claims of third persons.

In turn, the feoffee could compel the cestui que use to indemnify him for the costs and expenses incurred in discharging these duties. In some instances, the feoffee to uses demanded and got compensation for his services.[5]

§ 2. Use Estates and Interests Including Springing and Shifting Uses

We have thus far spoken chiefly of feoffments to the use of the feoffor or to the uses to be declared by the will of the feoffor, but a use estate could be and frequently was created in favor of third persons. Thus, O, the owner of Blackacre in fee simple, enfeoffs B and his heirs to the use of C for ten years, then to the use of D for life, then to the use of E and his heirs. B has the legal estate in fee

---

5. When one of the feoffees to uses was a lawyer, as was often the case, he was generally compensated. Holdsworth points out that it was most unusual to have only one feoffee to uses. If only a single feoffee was availed of, his death would entitle the lord of the fee to the feudal incidents. Hence, the feoffment was normally made to as many as six or more feoffees to uses. When their number became dangerously low there would be a re-enfeoffment to a larger group. 4 Holdsworth, History of English Law 421–422 (1924).

simple but C, D and E have equitable or use estates. In recognizing uses, the Chancellors in a general way, followed the common-law pattern of estates as their model. There could be equitable possessory estates, and equitable remainders, for years, for life, in fee tail and in fee simple corresponding to legal estates and remainders. As the Chancellors were not in any way dealing directly with the legal title they were not bound by the rigid categories of interests in land emanating from the common-law doctrine of seisin. Hence, a degree of flexibility was permissible in the limitation of equitable interests which did not obtain in the creation of common-law estates. These differences require examination.

We have in our discussion of conveyancing at common law pointed out four restrictions on the creation of future estates:[1]

1. No freehold estate could be created to commence in futuro. Thus, O enfeoffs B and his heirs, the feoffment being declared to go into effect the following Christmas. B takes nothing.

2. A freehold contingent remainder preceded only by a term of years is void in its inception as an attempt to create a freehold to commence in futuro. Thus, O conveys to B for ten years, then to the heirs of C, a living person. The heirs of C take nothing.

3. A limitation providing that on the happening of a specified event a freehold estate should be cut short and an estate commence in a third person was void. Thus, O enfeoffs B and his heirs but if B dies childless then to C and his heirs. C takes nothing.

4. There could be no gap between the particular freehold estate and a freehold future interest or between two freehold "remainders." Thus, O enfeoffs B for life and one year after B's death to C and his heirs. C takes nothing.

None of these restrictions applied to the creation of equitable interests. To illustrate:

1. On July 1, O enfeoffs Blackacre to B and his heirs to the use of C and his heirs beginning on August 1. The legal

§ 2
1. *See* ch. 6, § 4, *supra.*

estate in Blackacre is in B before and after August 1. There is a resulting use[2] in O in fee for the period of a month and on August 1 the use springs up in favor of C. Thus a use could be created to commence in futuro, and it was called a "springing use."

2. O enfeoffs Blackacre to B and his heirs to the use of C for ten years then to the use of the heirs of D, a living person. The heirs of D have a valid equitable contingent interest.[3]

3. O enfeoffs Blackacre to B and his heirs to the use of C and his heirs but if C dies unmarried then to the use of D and his heirs. B has the legal estate in fee simple. C has an equitable estate in fee simple, but if C dies unmarried that use estate is cut short and the use shifts to D in fee. The use limited in favor of D was called a "shifting use." A shifting use is one which cuts short a prior use estate in a person other than the conveyor upon the happening of a condition; a springing use is one which cuts short a use estate in the conveyor.

4. O enfeoffs Blackacre to B and his heirs to the use of C for life and one year after C's death to the use of D and his heirs. B has the legal estate in fee simple. C has an equitable life estate followed by a resulting use to O in fee simple subject to a use in D in fee simple commencing one year after C's death. This use in D cutting short the resulting use in O was also a springing use. Thus, there could be a gap between the use estates limited in favor of strangers.

In brief, by virtue of the doctrine of uses it was possible to create equitable interests, in the nature of springing and shifting uses, that had no counterpart in the common-law scheme of estates.

§ 3. Methods of Creating or Raising a Use

While a use was typically created or raised by a feoffment to uses, it could also be created in connection with any other common-law type of conveyance such as a fine, common recovery, lease,

---

2. The concept of a resulting use is explained in § 4, *infra*.

3. If D is still living at the end of C's term, the interest given to the heirs of D would not fail but would take effect as a springing use which would divest the resulting use in O on D's death.

release or grant. Broadly speaking, a use could be created with or without a transfer of possession. A use was raised with a transfer of the possession where it was created upon an actual transfer of the seisin as in the case of a feoffment to uses. No technical words were necessary to create a use, and the declaration of the use could be oral or written. The word "use" was frequently employed but it was not essential.[1] Any words expressing the feoffor's intention that the legal estate should be held for the benefit of another person were sufficient. A declaration that the feoffee should hold the land upon trust or confidence for C and his heirs, or that he should permit C and his heirs to take the profits, was sufficient to raise a use.

At the beginning of the sixteenth century it was settled that a use could be raised without a transfer of the seisin by means of a bargain and sale. A bargain and sale was an agreement whereby the owner of land for a pecuniary consideration paid to him promised to sell the land to, or to hold it for the benefit of, the promisee. Thus, in 1530 (before the Statute of Uses) O, the owner of Blackacre in fee simple, orally or in writing promises B, in consideration of the payment of the purchase price by B, to sell Blackacre to B in fee simple, or promises to hold the land for the benefit of B and his heirs. Since no legal conveyance has been made, O was still the legal owner of the land but in equity B was protected by treating him as the beneficial owner of the property. The Chancellor would compel O to allow B to have the use of the land, the rents and profits thereof, and to convey the legal title at B's request. A bargain and sale, therefore, raised a use in the bargainee.[2]

§ 3

1. When the use was declared by written instrument the medieval Latin phrase *"ad opus"* (to the use of) was commonly inserted in the earlier documents.

2. Here again the underlying reason for recognizing a use in the bargainee was that it would have been unconscionable for the seller, after receiving the purchase price, to violate the trust imposed in him by the buyer. Although the doctrine of a use arising from a "bargain and sale" of lands seems to have originated in the situation where the bargainee had paid the agreed purchase price, it was later extended to cases where the bargainee had paid any valuable consideration for the bargainor's promise to convey. Ultimately, a mere recital of consideration in a deed of bargain and sale was sufficient to raise a use. Jackson ex dem. Hudson v. Alexander, 3 Johns. 484 (N.Y.1808).

§ 4. Resulting Uses

So common had become the practice of conveying lands to uses that the Chancellor would sometimes imply a use where none had been expressed. For example, where O enfeoffed B in fee simple and no use was expressly declared and B gave no value for the conveyance, the Court of Chancery presumed that it was O's intention not to make a gift to B but to retain the beneficial ownership in himself. This was a wholly reasonable construction to put upon the transaction at a time when feoffments to uses were so numerous. The use was said, therefore, to result or come back to O. An express declaration of the use in the feoffee or in a third person, or the giving of consideration for the feoffment, negated any resulting use. There would be no resulting use in the case of a conveyance of a smaller estate than the conveyor had since the tenure existing between conveyor and conveyee was held to be sufficient, by reason of the obligation consequent thereon (such as fealty), to rebut the presumption of a resulting use. Thus, O holding land in fee simple enfeoffs B for life. B has a legal life estate unencumbered by any use in favor of O, and O has a legal reversion in fee.[1] It should be noted that there would be no question of a resulting use on a bargain and sale since that transaction was, prior to the Statute of Uses, essentially a transfer of the use estate only.[2]

§ 5. The Statute of Uses

The system of divided ownership of land that resulted from the practice of conveying lands to uses undoubtedly resulted in much inconvenience, litigation, and fraud. As abuses crept in, Parliament felt it necessary from time to time to enact remedial legislation. In 1377 a statute was passed to prevent frauds on creditors, and in 1392 one to prevent evasion of the statutes of mortmain (which forbade conveyances of land to religious houses and corporations).

---

§ 4

1. In fact, prior to the Statute of Uses it was not possible to create even an express use on a feoffment for life or in tail because of the tenure between feoffor and feoffee. Only a feoffee in fee simple could hold to the use of another.

4 Holdsworth, History of English Law 429 (1924).

2. The ancient doctrine of resulting uses is the progenitor of the concept of resulting trusts in the modern law of trusts. See 5 Scott, The Law of Trusts, § 404 (3d Ed. 1967).

The culmination of legislative attempts to control conveyances to uses came in 1535 with the famous Statute of Uses.[1]

The Statute of Uses is probably the most important piece of legislation dealing with the English land law, and its far-reaching consequences are still felt today. The causes which led to its enactment are to be found in an English King's need of money. The Statute was primarily designed to restore to the Crown the feudal revenues that were lost because of the conveyance of lands to uses. In the sixteenth century the incidents of tenure, such as wardship, marriage, relief, primer seisin, and escheat, were burdensome exactions on the tenant and, correspondingly, a profitable source of revenue for the lord of the fee. Because the king "alone was always lord and never tenant" he lost heavily when landowners by conveyances to joint feoffees to uses rid themselves of the incidents of tenure by retaining only the beneficial ownership. Henry VIII by means of the Statute of Uses sought to put an end to this drainage of the royal revenues.

The long preamble to the Statute sets forth in detail the real and fancied grievances flowing from uses but the true purpose of the Statute is to be found in that clause which recites as one of the reasons for its enactment "to the intent that the king's highness * * * shall not in any wise hereafter by any means of inventions be deceived, damaged or hurt, by reason of such trusts, uses or confidences."

The abolition of uses was not looked upon with favor by the land owning class who feared the loss of the power to devise their lands, but Henry was able to enlist the support of the common-law lawyers in Parliament in putting through the Statute because of their deep-rooted jealousy of the Court of Chancery. As Maitland well puts it, the Statute "was forced upon an extremely unwilling Parliament by an extremely strong-willed king."[2]

§ 5

1. 27 Hen. 8, ch. 10. The Statute became effective in 1536. Statutory developments prior to the Statute of Uses are traced in 4 Holdsworth, History of English Law 443–449 (1924). That Parliament was gradually tightening control over uses is evidenced by a statute of 1489 making the heir of the cestui que use of lands held by knight service liable to wardship or relief where the cestui que use died intestate.

2. Maitland, Equity 35 (1909). The classic exposition of the causes leading

Strictly speaking, the Statute of Uses was aimed at the control of the creation of uses rather than at their abolition. It did not declare presently existing uses to be void; it did not forbid the creation of uses in the future. It sought to accomplish its purpose by uniting the legal and equitable title in the cestui que use. Its operating principle was to convert the equitable title of the cestui que use into a legal estate by drawing the seisin and legal title from the holder thereof and vesting it in the cestui que use. The essence of the Statute is to be found in these words:

> "[W]here any person or persons stand or be seised, or at any time hereafter shall happen to be seised, of and in any * * * lands * * * to the use, confidence or trust of any other person or persons * * *, by reason of any bargain, sale, feoffment, * * * that in every such case, all and every such person and persons * * * that have or hereafter shall have any such use, confidence or trust * * * shall from henceforth stand and be seised, * * * of and in the same * * * lands * * * of and in such like estates as they had or shall have in use, confidence or trust of or in the same; and that the estate, title, right and possession that was in such person or persons that were, or hereafter shall be seised of any lands, * * * to the use, confidence or trust of any such persons * * * be from henceforth clearly deemed and adjudged to be in him or them that have, or hereafter shall have, such use, confidence or trust * * *."

In substance, the Statute provides that where one person stands seised of land to the use of another person, that other person shall be seised of a like estate as he had in the use. Thus, in cases to which the Statute is applicable, its effect is to convert an equitable or use estate into a corresponding legal estate. Use estates or interests thus converted or changed into legal estates or interests are said to be "executed". For example, in 1540 O, the owner of Blackacre in fee simple, enfeoffs B to have and to hold to B and his heirs to the use of C and his heirs. By virtue of the Statute, C has a legal estate in fee simple absolute. The use declared in favor of C is executed into a legal estate by drawing to it

to the enactment of the Statute is set forth in 4 Holdsworth, History of English Law, 450–461 (1924).

the legal title and seisin which momentarily vested in B by virtue of the feoffment. B in reality serves merely as a conduit for the passing of the seisin to C. So also, if O in 1540 for value received, bargains and sells land to B and his heirs by a deed duly enrolled, B gets a legal estate in fee simple absolute. The use raised by the bargain and sale in favor of B is executed into a legal estate. To spell this out more fully: O, by virtue of the bargain and sale, stands seised to the use of B; since the Statute of Uses provides that where one person is seised to the use of another, the seisin shall be deemed to be in the one having the use to the extent of the use estate, O's legal estate is vested in B and united with B's use estate thereby giving B a legal estate in fee simple. Similarly, where O enfeoffs B and his heirs to the use of C and his heirs, B stands seised to the use of C and the Statute takes B's fee simple estate from B and vests it in C.

It should be noted that the legal estate vested in the cestui que use would usually be of the same duration and quality as the use estate declared in him, but in any event the person to whom the use estate was given would get no larger legal estate than that given to the feoffee to uses since it was the estate of the feoffee which was taken from him and vested in the person to whom the use estate was given. Thus, O enfeoffs B for life to the use of C and his heirs. C gets only a legal life estate since B's life estate was all that could be vested in C. The state of the title would be: estate pur autre vie in C, reversion in O in fee simple.[3]

3. *See* Megarry & Wade, Law of Real Property 157 (4th ed. 1975). The old rule that a use could not be raised on a feoffment for life disappeared after the Statute of Uses.

Chapter 8

THE EFFECT OF THE STATUTE OF USES

The effect of the Statute of Uses upon the law of real property was threefold: First, it introduced new methods of creating and transferring estates; second, it permitted the creation of new types of legal future interests; and third, it gave rise to the modern trust in the form of an unexecuted use.

§ 1. The Effect of the Statute on Conveyancing

The older common-law methods of conveyancing were not abrogated by the Statute of Uses. A freehold estate could still be conveyed by livery of seisin; a term of years could be created by agreement and entry; a reversion or vested remainder could be transferred by grant. Unless a use was in some way declared or raised on such a conveyance the Statute had no application and the validity and efficacy of the transaction depended exclusively on common-law principles. The rigid rules of the common law, such as the prohibition of an attempt to create a freehold to commence in futuro, continued to be applicable to common-law conveyances. The Statute, however, gave rise to new methods of conveyancing in addition to the still existing common-law methods and also made possible a combination of the new and old methods.

§ 2. Feoffment to Uses

Both before and after enactment of the Statute of Uses, an owner of land could convey it to a feoffee to hold to such uses as were declared at the time of the feoffment. The Statute would convert the use estates thus raised into legal estates by uniting the seisin of the feoffee with the use in the cestui que use. Thus, O enfeoffs B and his heirs to the use of A for life, then to the use of the eldest unborn son of A and the heirs of the body of that son, then to the use of C and his heirs. The state of the legal title immediately after the use in B was executed would be: life estate in A, contingent remainder in fee tail in A's unborn son and vested remainder in fee simple in C.

At common law, a man could not convey to himself or his wife but after the Statute this could be done by raising a use estate in favor of himself or his wife which would be executed into a legal estate. After the rise of the newer methods of conveyancing in the seventeenth century feoffments to uses were rarely used in practice.

§ 3. Resulting Uses After the Statute

If, prior to the Statute of Uses, O seised of land in fee simple, enfeoffed B and his heirs and no uses were declared and no consideration was paid, there would be a resulting use in fee simple so that B would hold the legal title to the use of O. What would be the result of such a transaction after the Statute of Uses? A literal application of the Statute would execute the resulting use in the feoffor so as to vest in him the entire estate, thereby rendering the transaction nugatory. Although such a conveyance was undoubtedly due to ineptness on the part of the conveyancer, the courts applied the Statute rigorously and held that the resulting use was executed.[1] The danger of a common-law conveyance being made ineffective by reason of an executed resulting use led to the practice of inserting in such conveyances an express declaration of a use in the conveyee in order to rebut a resulting use.[2]

§ 3

1. Armstrong dem. Neve v. Wolsey, 2 Wils. 19, 95 Eng.Rep. 662 (1755).

2. Older types of deeds in use in the United States guarded against a resulting use by declaring that the land was conveyed to the conveyee "and his heirs to have and to hold to his and their own use and behoof forever." An occasional statute deals explicitly with the problem. Mass.Gen.Laws Ann. ch. 183, § 14 (West 1991) provides: "If no use is declared in a conveyance or devise of real estate, the same shall take effect as if it

A resulting use would also arise in the case of a partial declaration of a use as well as in the case of a common-law conveyance of an estate in fee simple with no declaration of a use. Thus, O enfeoffs B and his heirs to the use of C for life, or in tail, or for years. The undeclared residue of the use results to O thereby giving O a legal reversion in fee simple, expectant upon the particular legal estate given to C. B takes nothing, because the Statute of Uses divests B of the seisin momentarily vested in B by the feoffment. A use will not result to the feoffor, however, where by the terms of the conveyance a use is expressly limited to him for life or for years. Thus, O enfeoffs B and his heirs to the use of O for life. There is no resulting use and the state of the title (legal and equitable) is a life estate in O, remainder in B in fee simple. The reason for such construction is this: if a resulting use were implied in favor of O, the life estate expressly limited to O would merge in the reversion in fee simple thereby vesting the entire estate in O, contrary to his declared intention to give himself a life estate.[3]

§ 4.   Conveyance by Bargain and Sale

Since before the Statute of Uses a use could be raised by a bargain and sale, after the Statute a legal freehold estate could be created or transferred by means of a bargain and sale. The use raised by the bargain and sale would be executed by the Statute into a legal estate. Thus, an entirely new method of conveying freehold estates was made possible by the Statute, dispensing with the necessity of livery of seisin. The Statute itself operated to vest the seisin of the bargainor in the bargainee. Prior to the Statute no writing was required for a valid bargain and sale. The framers of the Statute of Uses foresaw that, unless supplementary legislation were enacted, it would be possible to convey a freehold estate in

were expressed to be for the use of the grantee or devisee." Since modern deeds almost invariably contain a recital of consideration the question of a resulting use is not a matter of practical importance at the present time. It will be recalled that in a conveyance by bargain and sale there could be no resulting use because the transaction raised a use in the bargainee.

3. There could be a resulting use where a use estate in tail was declared in the feoffor. Thus, O enfeoffs B and his heirs to the use of A and the heirs of his body. The state of the title would be: estate in fee tail in O, reversion in fee simple in O. The statute De Donis would prevent a merger of the fee tail in O's reversion in fee simple.

land by an oral bargain and sale without the presence of witnesses. Such a secret conveyance, if permitted, would contravene the long established policy of the law. To avoid this situation the same Parliament which passed the Statute of Uses also enacted the Statute of Enrolments.[1]

The Statute of Enrolments provided in substance that no conveyance of an estate of *inheritance* or *freehold* by means of a bargain and sale should be effective unless the bargain and sale was in writing, under seal, and enrolled in certain public offices mentioned therein. These requirements for the public recording of a deed of bargain and sale made secret oral transfers of estates of freehold impossible.[2]

§ 5. Conveyance by Lease and Release

The requirement of registration resulting from the Statute of Enrolments displeased large landowners who desired to make family settlements without rendering the transaction a matter of public record but still wished to make use of the newer methods of conveyancing introduced by the Statute of Uses. The ingenuity of conveyancers eventually found a loophole whereby the Statute of Enrolments could be evaded and yet advantage taken of the Statute of Uses. The Statute of Enrolments was by its express terms applicable only to a bargain and sale of a freehold estate. A non-freehold estate, such as a term for years, might still be created by an oral or written bargain and sale which need not be recorded. The conveyancers hit upon the device of creating a term for years by means of a bargain and sale and then transferring the reversion by means of a common-law release to the bargainee, thereby vesting the complete estate in the bargainee. Thus, O, seised of Blackacre in fee simple, wishes to convey it to B. O would by a written instrument of bargain and sale, reciting a consideration of five shillings paid to him in hand by B, create an estate for one year

§ 4

1. 27 Hen. 8, ch. 16 (1536).

2. The Statute of Enrolments is the historical antecedent of modern-day recording statutes providing for the filing in county land records offices of instruments affecting land titles. These recorded instruments, as well as other publicly recorded legal documents, provide constructive notice to all would-be purchasers of land or other claimants having an interest in the land.

in B. Then O would, by a common-law release, convey the reversion to B and his heirs. The estate for a year would merge in the fee simple and B would then have a present estate in fee simple. The bargain and sale would, by force of the Statute of Uses, vest the term of years in B without the necessity of B's entering into possession and he was, therefore, in a position to accept a release of the reversion.[1] Had the estate for years been created by the common-law method of agreement and entry, B could not have validly accepted a release until after making an actual entry.

From approximately 1620 until 1845 the conveyance by lease and release was the most commonly used method of conveying land in England. It had the advantage (from the viewpoint of the parties) of transferring the title by means of a secret conveyance without involving the inconveniences of the common-law methods. It was not necessary for the parties to go upon the land as in the case of a transfer by feoffment, nor was it necessary for the conveyee to make an actual entry as in the case of a transfer of an estate for years by agreement and entry. Moreover, the requirement of recording and payment of a fee therefor under the terms of the Statute of Enrolments was circumvented. In actual practice the bargain and sale, in the form of a deed, and the release would be drawn up on the same paper with the bargain and sale being dated the day before the release. It was customary to insert a consideration of five shillings in the deed of bargain and sale, although in fact it was rarely ever paid. The mere recital of consideration, without actual payment, was considered sufficient to raise a use.[2] Another advantage of conveyance by lease and release was that it could be used to effectuate family settlements of land by declaring uses on the release. Thus, O, seised in fee simple, would bargain and sell a term of one year to B. Then O would release the reversion to B and his heirs to the use of O for life, then to the use of O's eldest son in fee tail, with further remainders by way of use.

§ 5

1. Lutwich v. Mitton, Cro.Jac. 604, 79 Eng.Rep. 516 (1621).

2. As later stated by Chancellor Kent: "The rule requiring a consideration to raise a use, has become merely nominal, and a matter of form; for if a sum of money be mentioned, it is never an inquiry whether it was actually paid, and the smallest sum possible is sufficient; nay, it has been solemnly adjudged, that a pepper corn was sufficient to raise a use." Jackson ex dem. Hudson v. Alexander, 3 Johns. 484 (N.Y.1808).

All of the uses would be executed by the Statute of Uses into legal estates or interests.

§ 6. The Covenant to Stand Seised

In addition to the bargain and sale, another entirely new method of conveying a legal estate which originated in the Statute of Uses was the covenant to stand seised to uses. Normally, the Chancellor would not enforce a use unless there was "good" consideration—that is, a sound or worthy reason for doing so. The equitable doctrine of consideration was not confined to the notion of recompense or value. It was clear enough that where there had been a feoffment to uses the Chancellor's intervention was warranted. So also, in a bargain and sale the payment of the purchase price or, in the sixteenth century, a recital of consideration, was sufficient to raise a use. But a gratuitous agreement to hold land to the use of another was not sufficient to persuade the Chancellor to enforce the use. Nevertheless, in the middle of the sixteenth century it was held that if a landowner by written instrument under seal promised to hold the land to the use of a relative in consideration of natural love and affection, or to the use of another in consideration of marriage, the covenant was effective to raise a use.[1] And the use thus raised would be executed by the Statute of Uses, thereby transferring the legal estate to the covenantee.

The covenant to stand seised, therefore, became valid as a method of conveyance where the parties thereto were related by blood or marriage. Because it could not be used for the purpose of conveying to a stranger, its principal use was in effectuating family settlements of land. Unlike the bargain and sale of a freehold estate, the covenant to stand seised was not required to be recorded under the Statute of Enrolments and, therefore, had the advantage of a private family arrangement. However, its usefulness was somewhat impaired after the device of a limitation to trustees to preserve contingent remainders had been invented in the seventeenth century because of the necessity that such trustees be relatives.

§ 6

1. Sharrington v. Strotton, Plowden 298 (1566).

No technical words were required to have the conveyance operate as a covenant to stand seised, nor was a formal recital of a covenant or promise necessary. Indeed, the word "grant" was held to be a sufficient expression of intention to stand seised to the use of the conveyee.[2] Although the required degree of relationship between covenantor and covenantee was probably a close one in the early development of the doctrine, it was later somewhat relaxed. A covenant in favor of a wife, brother, nephew, or spouse of a blood relation was valid.

§ 7. The Effect of the Statute on Future Interests— Executory Interests

The principal effect of the Statute of Uses on the law of future interests was that it made the creation of two new types of *legal* future interests possible. The rigid rules of the common law forbade the limitation of a freehold estate to begin in the future and forbade the cutting short of the estate of one grantee in favor of another grantee. As a consequence, the one type of future interest that could be created in a conveyee was a remainder. As we have seen, however, it was permissible in equity to create future interests in the form of springing and shifting uses that were not subject to these common-law restrictions.[1] By virtue of the Statute of Uses, such equitable future interests became converted into legal future interests and acquired the name "executory interests."

These new types of legal future interests made possible a variety of limitations that were unknown to the common law and imparted to the land law a much needed flexibility. To illustrate:

2. Roe dem. Wilkinson v. Tranmer, 2 Wils. 75, 95 Eng.Rep. 694 (1757). In Jackson ex dem. Wood v. Swart, 20 Johns. 85 (N.Y.1822) it was said: "It is scarcely necessary to observe that in such a conveyance no technical words are required; such as that the grantor covenants to stand seised, to the use of A etc.; but any other words will create a covenant to stand seised, if it appears to have been the intention of the party to use them for that purpose." *Accord* Gale v. Coburn, 35 Mass. (18 Pick.) 397 (1836).

§ 7

1. The extent to which, in fact, the Chancellor, prior to the Statute of Uses, recognized springing and shifting uses is far from clear but it is commonly assumed that such uses were then enforced. Shifting and springing uses were recognized at law in the middle of the sixteenth century and it is hardly likely that they were given legal recognition so soon after the Statute of Uses without prior chancery precedent. *Cf.* A.W.B. Simpson, A History of the Land Law 181, 196–198 (2d ed. 1986).

1. By means of a springing use, a freehold estate could now be limited to commence in futuro. Thus, O bargains and sells land to B and his heirs to have and to hold from and after the marriage of B to C. The state of the title is: estate in fee simple in O subject to a springing executory interest in B in fee simple taking effect in possession on B's marriage. Or, O enfeoffs X and his heirs to the use of B and his heirs from and after the marriage of B. The state of the title is: estate in fee simple in O (by means of an executed resulting use) subject to a springing executory interest in B in fee simple.

2. There could now be a gap between the limitations of freehold estates to successive grantees. Thus, O bargains and sells land to B for life, and one year after B's death to C and his heirs. The state of the title is: life estate in B, reversion in fee simple in O subject to a springing executory interest in C in fee simple to take effect in possession one year after B's death. The interest of C which is now executory will become a possessory estate by means of the execution of a springing use which will cut short O's resulting use.

3. There could now be a valid limitation of a future interest taking effect by cutting short a prior estate in another grantee. Thus, O bargains and sells land to B and his heirs but if B becomes a bankrupt then to C and his heirs. The state of the title is: fee simple in B subject to a shifting executory interest in fee simple in C. The interest of C which is now executory may become a possessory estate by means of the execution of a shifting use cutting short B's fee simple.

4. An owner of land could now validly create a contingent future interest preceded by a term of years. Thus, O bargains and sells land to B for ten years, then to the heirs of C, a living person. The state of the title is: estate for years in B, springing executory interest in the heirs of C in fee simple, reversion in O in fee simple. The interest of C's heirs takes effect by means of an executed springing use. It was, at first, doubtful whether a contingent use preceded by an estate for years was good but later decisions seem to have settled the point.

In each of the situations above, the executory interest could be created by a conveyance in the form of a bargain and sale, a covenant to stand seised (assuming that the parties were related by blood or marriage), or, except in the fourth illustration, a feoffment to uses.

§ 8. The Statute of Wills and Executory Devises

An immediate consequence of the Statute of Uses was the loss of the power to transmit a use estate by will. The common law, apart from special custom in certain localities, did not permit a devise of a freehold estate. Instead, landowners were able to circumvent this restriction by means of a feoffment to the uses declared in the feoffor's will. After the Statute of Uses this device was no longer effective because the Statute united the legal title and the use in the same person. The loss of the power to devise caused such deep resentment and discontent on the part of the land owning class that Henry felt compelled to restore that power and did so in 1540 by the Statute of Wills.[1]

The Statute of Wills gave a limited power to tenants in fee simple to devise their lands by a will in writing.[2] Because livery of seisin was not required, the courts construed this statute as permitting the creation of future interests which were not subject to the restrictions pertaining to the common-law forms of conveyance. There could be a devise of a freehold estate to begin in the future, and an estate could be devised to take effect in defeasance of a prior devised estate. No declaration of a use was necessary, although devises could be limited by way of a use. These new types of legal

§ 8

1. 32 Hen. 8, ch. 1 One of the grievances of the rebels in the rising known as the Pilgrimage of Grace (1536) was that the Statute of Uses had deprived men of the power to devise their lands. Primogeniture had little appeal for Tudor England. "The Englishman would like to leave his land by will. He would like to provide for the weal of his sinful soul, and he would like to provide for his daughters and younger sons. That is the root of the matter." Maitland, 3 Collect-ed Papers 335 (Fisher, ed. Cambridge Univ. Press 1911).

2. The landowner was empowered by the Statute of Wills to devise all of his lands held in socage tenure and two-thirds of his lands held by knight service. Moreover, those taking by devise were liable for the feudal dues as though they took by descent. The Tenures Abolition Act (1660) removed the restriction on the power to devise.

future interests, originating in the Statute of Wills and analogous to springing and shifting uses, were called executory devises. In common usage, the term "executory interest" includes executory devises as well as springing and shifting uses. The term "conditional limitation" is sometimes used as synonymous with "executory interest."[3]

§ 9. Characteristics of Executory Interests

The addition of executory interests to the category of permissible future interests imparted a desirable elasticity to the land law but at the same time it made that law much more complex. Inasmuch as executory interests had some legal attributes different from those possessed by the common-law future interests (reversions, possibilities of reverter, rights of entry for condition broken, and remainders) it frequently became necessary to decide whether a limitation in a conveyance or a will created an executory interest or a common-law type of future interest.

The type of conveyance used to create a future interest would not in all cases determine the nature of that interest. An executory interest, by its very nature, could not be created by a common-law conveyance on which no uses were raised. Thus, if O, after the Statute of Uses, enfeoffed B for life and one year after B's death to C and his heirs, C's interest would be void. The rule prohibiting the creation of a freehold estate to take effect in futuro still applied to common-law conveyances. It does not follow, however, that every future interest created by a conveyance operating under the Statute of Uses, or by a will, is an executory interest. Common-law types of future interests could be, and usually were, created by such conveyances as well. A remainder, for example, could be limited by the newer methods of conveyancing as well as by a common-law conveyance. Thus, O bargains and sells to B for life, then to C and his heirs. C has a legal remainder in fee simple expectant upon B's

---

3. *See, e.g.*, Proprietors of the Church in Brattle Square v. Grant, 69 Mass. (3 Gray) 142 (1855). To make matters slightly more confusing the Massachusetts court has, at times, used the term "conditional limitation" in the sense of special limitation, that is, language in an instrument creating a determinable estate. *See, e.g.*, Markey v. Smith, 301 Mass. 64, 16 N.E.2d 20 (1938).

legal life estate. C's interest is nonetheless a remainder although created by means of an executed use.

An executory interest, like a remainder, can be created only in a transferee, never in the transferor. There is, therefore, usually no difficulty in determining whether a limitation creates an executory interest or gives rise to a reversion, a possibility of reverter, or a right of entry for condition broken.[1] The principal difficulty comes in determining whether a future interest in a transferee created under a will or by a conveyance operating under the Statute of Uses is a remainder or an executory interest. This difficulty can only be resolved by examining the characteristics of the particular limitation. In resolving this difficulty consider the following definitions of the shifting and springing executory interests today:

> A. The shifting executory interest is a future interest limited in favor of a transferee that to become possessory must, upon the occurrence or non-occurrence of an event or contingency, divest either a present possessory estate of another transferee or a vested interest of another transferee.[2]

§ 9

1. This is not invariably true. Suppose that T devises land to a church to have and to hold so long as the land is used for church services, and if the land ceases to be used for such church services, then to C and his heirs. T also devises the residue of his estate to C. The devise to the church with the gift over to C creates a determinable fee in the church and a shifting executory devise in C. The gift over to C violates the Rule against Perpetuities and is, therefore, void. See, § 11, *infra*. This would normally leave a possibility of reverter in the transferor. Does the gift of the residue to C give C a possibility of reverter or a void executory interest? Under American law a possibility of reverter is not subject to the Rule Against Perpetuities. This, in substance, was the problem in Brown v. Independent Baptist Church of Woburn, 325 Mass. 645, 91 N.E.2d 922 (1950). The court held that under the residuary clause C received a possibility of reverter.

In some respects, an executory interest that divests an estate in a prior grantee resembles a common-law right of entry but a right of entry could be created only in favor of the transferor. Thus, T devises to B and his heirs but if B dies leaving no surviving children then to C and his heirs. C has an executory interest, not a right of entry. C's interest vests automatically on the happening of the specified event and no entry or election by him is necessary to cause the fee to shift to him.

2. Restatement of Property, §§ 25(1), 158 (1936). Although it is a characteristic of an executory interest that it normally takes effect in possession by divesting a prior freehold estate in another grantee (shifting executory interest) or a vested freehold estate in the grantor (springing executory interest), there is an exception in the case of

B. A springing executory interest is a future interest limited in favor of a transferee that to become possessory must divest the transferor of a retained interest after some period of time during which there is no transferee entitled to a present possessory freehold estate.³

In light of these definitions what is immediately obvious is that remainders, unlike executory interests, can take effect in possession only at the expiration of the preceding estate in another grantee⁴ and not by divesting another transferee's interest. By contrast, an executory interest can take effect only by divesting a preceding estate in another grantee (except where the preceding estate is a fee simple determinable), or by divesting a freehold estate in the transferor or his successors in interest after some period of time during which no transferee is entitled to a present possessory freehold estate.⁵ Put another way, a remainder is a successive interest; an executory interest is, normally, a divesting interest. Thus, T devises Blackacre to B for life, then to C and his heirs but if C dies before B leaving no issue surviving him then to D and his heirs. D's interest is an executory interest because it takes effect by divesting or cutting short C's vested remainder. But suppose that the limitations were as follows: to B for life, and if C survives B, then to C and his heirs, but if C dies before B, then to D and his

an executory interest limited after a fee simple determinable. There can be no remainder after a determinable fee; therefore, any interest limited to succeed such an estate is called an executory interest even though it will take effect on the expiration of, not the divestment of, the determinable fee. Thus, O bargains and sells land to B and his heirs so long as the land is used only for residential purposes, and if, during C's lifetime, the land is not so used, then to C and his heirs. B has a determinable fee followed by an executory interest in C in fee. *Id.* at § 25(2).

3. *See* ch. 1, § 11, *supra.*

4. The expiration occurs by the happening of a limitation, not a condition.

5. If O conveys to B (a bachelor) to have and to hold to B and his heirs from and after B's marriage to C, the future interest given to B is an executory interest which takes effect in possession by divesting a fee simple in O. The estate in O is not a reversion because it is not a future interest. The state of the title is: fee simple in O subject to an executory interest in B in fee simple. A contingent remainder can divest a reversion by becoming vested. Thus, if O conveys to B for life, then to the heirs of C (a living person), the death of C during B's lifetime will cause the remainder to C's heirs to become vested in fee simple thereby extinguishing O's reversion.

heirs. The limitations to C and D in this illustration are alternative contingent remainders. D's interest is not an executory interest because it does not divest the interest of another transferee. Only vested interests can be divested; C's interest is not vested because it is subject to a condition precedent which must occur before that interest can vest, thus making C's interest contingent.[6]

§ 10. Contingent Remainders and Executory Interests[1]

At common law contingent remainders could be destroyed by a tortious alienation by the owner of the supporting freehold estate.[2] When executory interests were first recognized in the middle of the sixteenth century it was generally thought that they were as destructible as contingent remainders. However, this view was repudiated in *Pells v. Brown*[3] and by virtue of that case it became settled that an executory interest was indestructible by an act of the owner of the preceding estate. The quality of indestructibility attaching to executory interests then became the principal characteristic of such interests and set them apart from contingent

---

6. See also, ch. 5, § 5 C, supra.

§ 10

1. At this point the student may be interested in knowing that England's great legal historian, Frederic W. Maitland, once asked: "For who shall interest us in contingent remainders or the Statute of Uses, while Chinese metaphysics remain unexplored?" 1 Collected Papers 190 (Fisher, ed. Cambridge Univ. Press 1911). But this rhetorical question was put to laymen, not to law students.

2. See ch. 5, § 8B, supra. The doctrine of forfeiture of a life estate on a tortious alienation was confined to common-law conveyances, that is, conveyance by feoffment, fine or common recovery. It was not extended to conveyances operating under the Statute of Uses. Thus, if B having a life estate bargained and sold the land to X and his heirs, X would get only an estate for the life of B, not a tortious fee sim-

ple. Any contingent remainders dependent on B's life estate would not be destroyed.

3. Cro.Jac. 590 (1620). The limitations in Pells v. Brown were these: A devised land to Thomas and his heirs; and if Thomas died without issue "living William, his brother," then to William and his heirs. After entering into possession Thomas suffered a common recovery to the use of himself and his heirs. Thomas later died without issue and William claimed the land. The court held: 1. the phrase "if he (Thomas) died without issue" meant definite failure of issue because the failure of issue on which the gift over was to take effect was failure in the lifetime of William; therefore, Thomas had a fee simple, not a fee tail; 2. the gift over to William was valid as an executory devise which would divest the fee in Thomas; 3. the executory devise in William was not destroyed by the common recovery.

remainders. The courts continued to hold that contingent remainders were destructible by forfeiture, merger or other termination of the supporting freehold estate. The courts also refused to draw a distinction between contingent remainders created by way of use or by will and those created by means of a common-law conveyance. This refusal to treat contingent remainders created by way of use or by will differently from common-law contingent remainders was due to the judges' concern that a consequence of holding such remainders indestructible would be to permit the creation of "perpetuities" and thereby impede the free alienability of land. At that time, the basis for the modern Rule against Perpetuities had not yet been formulated. Thus, it is a matter of some surprise that they ruled executory interests to be indestructible,[4] not that early seventeenth century judges held all contingent remainders destructible.

The rule that a contingent remainder created by way of use or by will was as destructible as a common-law contingent remainder was given additional importance by the refusal of the courts to allow a contingent remainder to take effect as an executory interest in order to save it from being destroyed as a contingent remainder. It became firmly settled that a future interest which, at the time of its creation, could take effect as a contingent remainder must take effect as such or fail. This rule, frequently called the rule of *Purefoy v. Rogers*[5] because of its application in that case, was stated by Hale, C.J. as follows: "where a contingency is limited to depend on an estate of freehold which is capable of supporting a remainder, it shall never be construed to be an executory devise, but a contingent remainder only, and not otherwise." In applying the rule to future interests created by way of use Lord St. Leonards said: "Now, if there be one rule of law more sacred than another, it is this, that no limitation shall be construed to be an executory or shifting use, which can by possibility take effect by way of remainder."[6] To

---

4. The holding in Pells v. Brown, *id.* that an executory interest could not be destroyed by a common recovery did not meet with general acceptance at the time. Indeed, it was later remarked that it "went down with the Judges like chopped hay." Scattergood v. Edge, 12 Mod. 278, 281, 88 Eng.Rep. 1320, 1322 (1697). As to the law prior to Pells v. Brown, *see* Plucknett, Concise History of the Common Law 594 (5th ed. 1956).

5. 2 Wm. Saunders 380, 85 Eng. Rep. 1181 (1671).

6. Cole v. Sewell, 4 Dr. & War. 1, 27, 4 Ir.Eq.Rep. 66, 68–69 (1843).

illustrate: T devises land to B for life, and after B's death to such of his children as shall attain the age of twenty-one. It is possible that the children of B will reach twenty-one before B dies. The limitation to the children could, therefore, at the time of its creation, take effect as a contingent remainder. Because that is so, the limitation must, regardless of subsequent events, take effect as a remainder or not at all. If, at the time of B's death, all of his children are under twenty-one their interest is destroyed and will not be preserved by treating it as an executory interest.[7]

The rule of *Purefoy v. Rogers* was a rule of law, not a rule of construction.[8] Thus, it cannot give way to a contrary intent; it is fixed and immutable. It undoubtedly operated to defeat the intention of the conveyor or testator in most of the cases in which it was applied. In the illustration given above, for example, (to B for life, then to such of B's children as shall attain twenty-one) it is almost certain that the testator intended that all of B's children who attained the age of twenty-one should take, whether they attained the specified age before or after B's death. But the rule implemented a concept of public policy. Because contingent remainders were destructible and executory interests were indestructible, it was thought desirable to classify future interests, where possible, as contingent remainders and thereby avoid the danger of permitting

7. Festing v. Allen, 12 Mees. & W. 279, 152 Eng.Rep. 1204 (1843). Contra, Bass River Savings Bank v. Nickerson, 303 Mass. 332, 21 N.E.2d 717 (1939). Suppose that at B's death he left surviving a son over twenty-one and a daughter under twenty-one. Would the daughter take on attaining twenty-one after B's death? Under the English view the daughter's interest would be classed as a contingent remainder and it would fail. But it is arguable that when the son reached twenty-one during B's lifetime he then had a vested remainder subject to open in favor of younger children who might later attain twenty-one and, therefore, the interest of such younger should be classed as an indestructible executory interest. There is some slight American support for this second view. *See* Simonds v. Simonds, 199 Mass. 552, 85 N.E. 860 (1908). The problem is discussed in 1 ALP, § 4.62; Simes & Smith, The Law of Future Interests, §§ 204, 205 (2nd ed. 1956).

8. White v. Summers, (1908) 2 Ch. 256. Two American cases have taken the opposite view and held that a limitation will not be treated as a contingent remainder if to do so would defeat the intention of the transferor. Simonds v. Simonds, 199 Mass. 552, 85 N.E. 860 (1908); Hayward v. Spaulding, 75 N.H. 92, 71 A. 219 (1908). *See* Simes & Smith, The Law of Future Interests § 204 (2nd ed. 1956).

the creation of remotely contingent interests. In truth, the rule was an aspect of the doctrine of destructibility.

Until contingent remainders were made indestructible by statute in England in the latter half of the nineteenth century it was necessary for the conveyancer to guard against their destruction.[9] The device commonly used in the English family settlement of lands was the limitation of a remainder (after the life estate) to trustees to preserve contingent remainders. Another device available to the draftsman was to create limitations of future interests which could never take effect as contingent remainders, thereby avoiding the rule of *Purefoy v. Rogers*. Thus, O by lease and release conveys to X and his heirs to the use of B for one hundred years if he so long live, then to the use of B's first son who shall attain the age of twenty-one and the heirs of his body. Since B has a determinable estate for years, not a life estate, the interest limited to B's first son is necessarily an executory interest; it could never have been a contingent remainder. Alternatively, O could convey to B for life, and one day after B's death, to B's first son who shall attain the age of twenty-one in fee tail. Again, the interest given to B's first son is an executory interest because it follows a gap after the life estate and can take effect only as a springing use.

Moreover, it became possible to avoid the rule of *Purefoy v. Rogers* by couching the gift of the future interest in the form of alternative limitations one of which could take effect only as an executory interest. An example of such alternative limitations in a gift to a class is found in the case of *In re Lechmere & Lloyd*.[10] In that case, T, in substance, devised land to B for life, and after B's death to such of her children living at her death as either before or after her death shall attain the age of twenty-one years. B died

---

9. Contingent remainders were made indestructible in England by forfeiture or merger of a preceding freehold estate in 1845 but they continued to be destructible by failure to vest before the natural termination of the supporting freehold estate until 1877. 8 & 9 Vict. ch. 106, § 8 (1845); 40 & 41 Vict. ch. 33 (1877). The latter statute applied only to instruments executed after the enactment of the statute. It should be remembered that the destructibility doctrine was not applicable to equitable contingent remainders in land or to interests in personal property analogous to contingent remainders. The concept of seisin was inapplicable to equitable interests in land, and to personalty.

10. 18 Ch.Div. 524 (1881).

leaving seven children, of whom five had attained the age of twenty-one and two had not. The question arose whether the two minor children would take if they lived to the age of twenty-one. The court held that they would take with the other five children on meeting the age requirement. The court treated the "before or after" death clause as creating "two distinct classes as the objects of the devise," one class being children who attained twenty-one before B's death, and the second class being children who reached majority after B's death. The court then stated: "But to enable the second class to participate it is necessary to read the gift to them as an executory devise. The rule is that you construe every limitation, if you possibly can, as a remainder, rather than as an executory devise. It is a harsh rule: why should I extend it? Why should a gift which cannot possibly take effect as a remainder not take effect as an executory devise? I see no good reason why it should not."[11]

Although the alternative limitations in *In re Lechmere & Lloyd* were contained in a gift to a class, it is also possible to phrase a gift to an individual in the form of alternative limitations, one of which is a contingent remainder and the other an executory interest. In a dictum in *White v. Summers*[12] it was said by Parker, J.: "Thus, in case of a devise to A for life, and after his death to B. if he shall have then attained twenty-one years, but if B shall not have then attained twenty-one years, then to B if and when he attains that age, there would be alternative gifts to B, one being a remainder and the other an executory devise, and which ultimately took effect would depend on whether B had or had not attained the age of twenty-one at the death of A."[13]

11.   *Accord* Dean v. Dean [1891] 3 Ch. 150.

12.   [1908] 2 Ch. 256.

13.   The rule of *Purefoy v. Rogers* was generally accepted by American courts as an integral part of the doctrine of destructibility of contingent remainders although the number of cases applying the rule was not large. The rule, as well as the destructibility doctrine itself, is of diminishing importance in modern times not only because of the prevalence of statutes making contin-gent remainders indestructible but also by reason of the fact that most future interests created today are interests created under a trust (equitable interests) or are interests in personal property, *e.g.* stocks and bonds. Nonetheless, because of the rule of *Purefoy v. Rogers*, in the United States we classify future interests in the same manner as they would have been classified prior to the adoption of the Statute of Uses even though the consequences of such classification may not be as important as they once

§ 11. The Rule Against Perpetuities

A common theme of the land law has been to thwart attempts to limit the marketability of land. For example, one consequence of the rule of destructibility was that whatever impediment existed to the alienability of land because of the presence of a contingent remainder following a life estate was removed at the life tenant's death if the contingent remainder was not ready to become possessory when the life tenant's died. Thus, the impediment to alienability lasted no longer than the life of the life tenant. However, because the rule of destructibility did not apply to executory interests, it was possible to magnify the impediments to alienability by creating an executory interest following either a life estate or a fee simple estate. In part, the Rule Against Perpetuities was designed to invalidate executory interests (and ultimately contingent remainders once they were no longer subject to the rule of destructibility) that might vest or fail to vest in a timely manner, and thus remove the impediments to alienability created by these interests.

The Rule Against Perpetuities provides that "no interest is good, if it must vest, if at all, not later than twenty-one years after some life in being at the creation of the interest."[1] Perhaps an easier way to understand the Rule is to recast it as follows: *A nonvested interest is good (meaning valid) if it is absolutely certain to vest, or fail to vest, not later than twenty-one years after the death of some life in being at the creation of the interest.* If such a life existed at the time the nonvested interest was created, such life would be a "validating life." The Rule, applied with mathematical precision, has confounded lawyers and law students for generations.[2] The Rule has been used to invalidate nonvested interests

were. For an extensive treatment of the subject matter of this section, *see* 1 ALP, §§ 4.53–4.63; Simes & Smith, The Law of Future Interests, §§ 191–209 (2nd ed. 1956).

§ 11

1. J. Gray, Rule Against Perpetuities § 201 (4th ed. 1942).

2. It may be some consolation to the practicing lawyer (but not to the law student) to know that the Supreme Court of California at one time held that an attorney who drafted a will containing a limitation that violated the Rule against Perpetuities was not liable for negligence to the intended beneficiaries who sustained a loss by reason of the invalidity of the limitation. Lucas v. Hamm, 56 Cal.2d 583, 15 Cal.Rptr. 821, 364 P.2d 685 (1961), *reversing* Lucas v. Hamm, 11 Cal.Rptr. 727 (1961). After quoting Professor Leach's description of the Rule as "a technicality-ridden legal

which actually vest within the life in being plus twenty-one years period merely because there was the possibility, however remote, that it might either vest or fail to vest in a timely manner viewed from the moment of the nonvested interest's creation.

For purposes of the Rule, the nonvested interests are limited to contingent remainders, executory interests, and remainders (vested or contingent) limited in favor of a class of persons if the class is open at the time of its creation. A contingent remainder or shifting executory interest can vest either by becoming a vested remainder or becoming possessory, a springing executory interest vests only by becoming possessory, and a class gift vests when both the class closes and all conditions precedent for each and every member of the class has occurred.

Perhaps a simple illustration would help your understanding of the Rule. Suppose O conveys Blackacre to "the first child of A and his heirs to graduate law school." A is alive at the time of the conveyance but A has no children. This springing executory interest is invalid under the Rule because there is no person living at the time of the conveyance, including A, the most likely candidate, with respect to whom it could be said that with absolute certainty the springing executory will vest or fail to vest within twenty-one years of that person's death. While more likely than not A's first child will graduate law school by being born and graduating law school in A's lifetime, it is also possible (if not necessarily probable) that A could have a child, die one year later, and then that child not graduate law school for another 25 years. Since it is possible that A's child could graduate law school more than twenty-one years after A's death (and the death of any other person alive at the time of the conveyance) the gift is invalid.

On the other hand, suppose O had conveyed the real property to "A's first born child and his heirs if that child graduates law school." At the time of the conveyance A and his three children, B, C and D (born in that order) are living. This conveyance is valid because it is limited in favor of B, that is, the only person who can

nightmare" and "a dangerous instrumentality in the hands of most members of the bar" (67 Harv.L.Rev. 1349) the court concluded that "it would not be proper to hold that defendant failed to use such skill, prudence, and diligence as lawyers of ordinary skill and capacity commonly exercise."

potentially take this gift is B as B is the only person meeting the description of "first born child of A." The gift is valid because B will either graduate law school in B's own lifetime or fail to graduate law school before dying. Thus it can be said with absolute certainty that the gift to B will vest (because B graduates law school), or fail to vest (because B does not graduate law school), no later than B's death.[3]

The common law fostered a number of pernicious subrules that were used to invalidate nonvested interests. Perhaps the worst of them was the "all or nothing rule" which applied only to class gifts. Under this rule, if a gift was bad as to one member of a class it was bad as to all. Make sure you understand this. If a gift was limited in favor of a class of persons and the interest of any one member of the class might vest too remotely, the interest of those class members that could only vest in a timely manner was also invalid. To fully appreciate the consequences of this, first consider a class gift that is valid. Suppose O conveys Blackacre to A for life, then to A's children who reach the age of twenty-one. At the time of the conveyance, A and two children of A, namely B and C, are living. The gift to A's children is valid because there is no way any of A's children, including a child of A born after the date of this conveyance, could reach, or fail to reach, the age of 21 more than twenty-one years after A's death. Thus, A is a validating life.

However, suppose O conveys Blackacre to A for life, then to A's children who reach the age of twenty-five, and, at the time of the conveyance A and A's two children, B and C, are then living. While in all likelihood all of A's children will either reach 25 in A's lifetime or within twenty-one years of A's death, there is some probability that they might not. Consider what might happen. One year after this conveyance, A could have a third child, D. The following year A could die survived by D, age 1, and B and C, ages 25 and 14, respectively. Since there is no possibility that D could reach age twenty-five within twenty-one years of A's death (or within twenty-one years of the death of B or C or anyone else alive at the time of the conveyance) his interest is not guaranteed to vest, or fail to vest, in a timely manner. But worse yet, even though

---

3. An additional twenty-one years is not necessary to even consider.

the interest of B and C would timely vest, under the "all or nothing rule," if the gift is bad as to one potential member of the class it is bad as to all. Thus the entire remainder gift, even to B and C, is invalid under the Rule.

With respect to gifts to classes, it is important to remember how a nonvested gift vests. The gift vests by both the class closing and all conditions precedents occurring for each and every member of the class. Thus, suppose O conveys Blackacre to A for life, remainder to A's grandchildren and their heirs. If, at the time of the conveyance A has no living grandchildren the gift to them is invalid. Consider the following. One year after the conveyance, A could have a child, B. One year later A could die. Without the rule of destructibility the remainder limited in A's grandchildren does not fail. Rather the class gift remains open until it is known whether or not B has a child (who would be a grandchild of A). Because that might not be determined until more than twenty-one years after A's death, the gift is invalid. On the other hand, suppose at the time of the conveyance A had one living grandchild. Here, A is a validating life because the gift to grandchildren will vest in all events at A's death because at that time the class gift will close and all grandchildren then living or their estates if they died in A's lifetime will share in the gift. Furthermore, once A dies no later born grandchildren of A will be able to join the class.[4]

As earlier noted, the Rule also applied to executory interests. For example, suppose O conveyed Blackacre to B and his heirs but if liquor is ever sold on Blackacre then to D and his heirs. Here, B has a fee simple subject to a shifting executory interest. However, the executory interest is void under the Rule because of the possibility that it might vest too remote. It might vest too remotely[5] because it is possible that liquor will be first sold on the premises more than twenty-one years after the death of B and D (who were alive on the date of the conveyance) and in fact after the death of any other person who was alive on that date. Because that remotely occurring event is the event that otherwise would cause D's interest

---

4. See ch. 5, § 5B, supra.

5. D's executory interest in this example could vest for purposes of the Rule only by becoming possessory. Thus,

to say it might vest too remotely means that it might become possessory too remotely.

to become possessory and vest, D's interest is void. To illustrate, suppose both B and D both die leaving an only child as their respective heir and thirty years later B's heir sells liquor on Blackacre. That event would cause B's estate (now held by B's heir) to be divested and shift to D's heir but, because that event might occur too remotely, D's heir estate is void.[6]

Likewise, suppose O conveys Blackacre to the X Church so long as the premises are used for church purposes and if not so used then to B and his heirs. B's interest is classified as a shifting executory interest. As such, it is void under the Rule because of the possibility that the premises might not be used for church purposes more than twenty-one years after the death of B and anyone else alive on the date of the conveyance.

A more comprehensive analysis of the rule is beyond the scope of this book[7] but any discussion of the rule would be incomplete without mentioning four reforms that have substantially ameliorated the harsh effects of the common law. These form reforms are:

1. The "wait-and-see" rule. Under this rule, which has been endorsed in the Restatement of Property,[8] if a nonvested interest actually vests or fails to vest in a timely manner, it is good even though there was the possibility, based upon facts that might have happened but which didn't that it could have vested too remotely. Thus, if O conveys Blackacre to A for life, remainder to A's children who attain age twenty-five and all of A's children are at least four years of age or older at A's death, the gift is good because it will vest or fail to vest no later than twenty-one years after A's death.

2. The "cy pres" doctrine. Cy pres means to reform as nearly as possible to accomplish the grantor's intent. Under this doctrine, if the terms of a nonvested interest could be

---

6. Typically under the Rule, the void interest is excised from the instrument. This would leave B with a fee simple absolute because there is no enforceable shifting executory interest.

7. The Rule is discussed comprehensively in Simes & Smith, The Law of Future Interests §§ 1211–1439 (2nd ed. 1956). *See also*, Leach, Perpetuities in a

Nutshell, 51 Harv. L. Rev. 638 (1938); Leach, Perpetuities: The Nutshell Revisited, 78 Harv. L. Rev. 973 (1965); Dukeminier, A Modern Guide to Perpetuities, 74 Cal. L. Rev. 1867 (1986).

8. Restatement (Second) of Property, § 1.3 (1983).

reformed (changed) to assure a timely vesting of the interest, a court can reform the terms to validate the gift. For example, suppose O conveys to A for life, then to A's children who attain age twenty-five. A dies survived by a child, age 2. Obviously such child cannot reach age twenty-five within twenty-one years of A's death; thus waiting to see if the interest will timely vest serves no purpose. However, if the age contingency were reduced from twenty-five to twenty-three by both reforming the gift over and then using wait-and see, the gift will timely vest or fail to vest.

3.   The "90–year rule." The 90–year rule is incorporated in the Uniform Statutory Rule Against Perpetuities Act which has been adopted in 26 states[9] and the District of Columbia. Under this Act, if the nonvested interest that would otherwise violate the common-law rule actually vests within 90 years of its creation it is valid. Interests valid under the common-law rule, of course, remain valid.

4.   Lastly, some states have abolished the Rule.[10]

Review Problems

1.   T devises Blackacre to A for life, remainder to A's children who attain age twenty-one. The gift to A's children is valid as it vests or fails to vest no later than A's death plus twenty-one years. If all of A's children are twenty-one or over at A's death, it vests at A's death. If any one or more of A's children is under age twenty-one at A's death, it vests or fails to vest in all of A's children no later than A's death plus twenty-one years.

2.   O conveys Blackacre to B for life, then to B's surviving children for their lives, and upon the death of the survivor of B's children, to B's surviving grandchildren. The gift of B's children

---

9.   Arizona, California, Colorado, Connecticut, Florida, Georgia, Hawaii, Indiana, Kansas, Massachusetts, Michigan, Minnesota, Montana, Nebraska, Nevada, New Mexico, North Carolina, North Dakota, Oregon, South Carolina, South Dakota, Tennessee, Utah, Virginia, Washington and West Virginia.

10.   *See* Alaska Stat. § 34.27.075 (Michie 2000); NJ Stat. § 46:2F–9 (West 1999); Idaho Code § 55–1522 (michie 1965); S.D. Codified Law, § 43–5–8 (Michie 1983).

vests no later than B's death. It is good. However, the gift to B's grandchildren is invalid under the common-law Rule. Four years after the conveyance B could have a child and B could die three years later survived by that child whose life estate would then vest. Thirty years later that child could have a child (who is a grandchild of B) and then twenty years later that child could die. But for the Rule, the gift to B's grandchild would then vest but, of course, because of the Rule it is invalid.

3. O conveys Blackacre "to B thirty years from now." B's springing executory interest is void under the common-law Rule because it could vest (i.e, become possessory) more than twenty-one years after the death of B or any one else alive at the time of the conveyance. To illustrate, B could have a child one year after the conveyance and then die leaving that child as B's only heir. Then B's interest would become possessory in B's successor more than twenty-one years later.[11] If the conveyance had been to "B thirty years from now if B is then living" the gift is good because it either vests in B's lifetime or fails if B dies. Thus, B is a validating life.

§ 12. Executory Interests in Modern Law

In the modern law of future interests, executory interests play an important role. By employing the device of shifting and springing interests it is possible for the property owner to exercise more flexible control in the disposition of his property by will or by deed. For example, a property owner can create a vested remainder in one person subject to divestment on a specified contingency in favor of another person. Or, the property owner may give a life estate to one person and make a gift over to take effect later than the termination of the life estate.[1]

---

11. B's interest can pass to B's successors because future interests are alienable, devisable, and descendible unless a condition is attached to the gift that prevents it from being so.

§ 12

1. For example, in Loats Female Orphan Asylum of Frederick City v. Essom, 220 Md. 11, 150 A.2d 742 (1959) T devised property to B for life or until she marries, then to a charitable corporation to be organized within twenty years from B's death. B married and thereafter the corporation was organized. The court held that after B's marriage the title was in T's heirs subject to an executory devise in the corporation. When the corporation was organized the fee automatically vested in the corporation.

Although executory interests came into the law originally in the form of shifting and springing uses that were converted into legal interests by force of the Statute of Uses, it is no longer necessary to employ the machinery of the Statute of Uses in order to create valid executory interests. The Statute of Uses, it is true, is deemed to be in force in many of the states, and, therefore, the modern deed can be given effect as a deed of bargain and sale. Occasionally, a court will expressly label a deed as one of bargain and sale or covenant to stand seised and discuss the doctrine of uses.[2] Even in jurisdictions where the Statute of Uses is not deemed to be in force, the modern deed is capable of creating any type of future interest which could be created by a conveyance operating under the Statute of Uses.[3] Because every state has a statute authorizing the transfer of property by will, the creation of executory devises is clearly permissible.

The distinction between contingent remainders and executory interests is one of diminishing importance.[4] In most states there are statutes abolishing the destructibility doctrine[5] and abrogating the Rule in Shelley's Case,[6] the doctrines that apply to contingent remainders but not executory interests. In such jurisdictions contingent remainders and executory interests are practically indistinguishable. On the other hand, where a contingent remainder remains destructible by merger or by failure to vest at or prior to the natural termination of the supporting freehold estate the distinction between these two types of interests continues to be of some importance.[7] And, whether successive future interest are properly

2. Ricker v. Brown, 183 Mass. 424, 67 N.E. 353 (1903) (covenant to stand seised); Bass River Savings Bank v. Nickerson, 303 Mass. 332, 21 N.E.2d 717 (1939) (bargain and sale).

3. Abbott v. Holway, 72 Me. 298 (1881).

4. See Dukeminier, Contingent Remainders and Executory Interests: A Requiem for the Distinction, 43 Minn. L.Rev. 13 (1958).

5. See ch. § 8, supra.

6. See ch. § 11, supra.

7. At times, the question may arise whether a future interest is an executory interest or a vested remainder. Thus, O conveys to B to have and to hold to B and his heirs from and after the death of O. Normally, O has a fee simple subject to an executory interest in B in fee but it is not uncommon for the courts to describe O's interest as a life estate with a remainder in B in fee. Basically, the question of the nature of O's estate should depend on his manifested intention. Usually, it will make no difference which labels are attached to the interests created; but if O's interest is classi-

classified as alternative contingent remainders or a vested remainder subject to divestment followed by a shifting executory interest can affect the validity of an interest under the Rule Against Perpetuities.[8]

At the present time, executory interests are, in the great majority of jurisdictions, freely transferable inter vivos, devisable by will, and descendible on the death of the owner intestate. The power to devise, or to have the interest devolve on intestacy, may, of course, be affected by a provision in the creating instrument making the executory interest subject to the contingency of survivorship to a specified time. In most of the states transferability of executory interests is made possible by statute but even in the absence of statute some jurisdictions have reached the same result.[9]

§ 13. Unexecuted Uses

To return to our discussion of the Statute of Uses, it should be observed that the Statute neither prohibited the creation of uses nor did it provide for the conversion of all uses into legal estates or interests. In most cases, it is true, existing uses and uses created in the future were converted or executed into corresponding legal interests; but in some situations the Statute was held not to be applicable and in those situations the uses created existed as purely equitable interests. Uses that were not converted into legal estates or interests were called unexecuted uses. The principal types of unexecuted uses were the following: (1). A use raised on a term of

fied as a life estate his liability for waste could be more extensive than if he is deemed to have a fee simple subject to an executory interest.

8. Suppose O transfers Blackacre to A for life, then to A's children and their heirs but if none of them reach age 25, then to B and his heirs. Here the vested remainder subject to divestment in A's children is valid under the Rule as it vests or fails no later than A's death when the class closes. B's interest is invalid, of course, because it could vest or fail to vest more than twenty-one

years after the death of A and B and any of A's children living at the time of the conveyance. However, had O conveyed to A for life, then if any of A's children reach age 25, to A's children and their heirs, but if none of them do, then to B and his heirs, both the interest of A's children and B are invalid under the Rule.

9. See 1 ALP, §§ 4.64–4.76; Simes & Smith, The Law of Future Interests, §§ 1852–1859, 1883, 1902 (2nd ed. 1956); 2A Powell, Real Property, ch. 21.

years or other chattel interest; (2). A use on a use; (3). An active use.[1]

1. A Use Raised on a Term of Years or Other Chattel Interest

By virtue of its own terminology, the Statute of Uses operates to convert a use into a like legal interest only where one person is "seised" of land to the use of another person. The word "seised" was used in its technical meaning of possession of a freehold estate in land.[2] If, therefore, a person was possessed of a non-freehold estate to the use of another, the Statute of Uses was inapplicable. Because a term of years was a non-freehold estate, a use raised thereon was unexecuted. Thus, A, having an estate for ten years in Blackacre, conveys his estate to B to the use of C. C's use is unexecuted. B holds the legal title to the term in trust for C. C's interest is purely equitable. Although a use raised on a term of years is unexecuted, it does not follow that all use estates for years are unexecuted. A use raised on a freehold estate for a term of years is clearly within the application of the Statute. Thus, O, being seised of an estate in fee simple, enfeoffs B and his heirs to the use of C for ten years, then to the use of D and his heirs. C has a legal estate for years.

A use raised on personal property in the nature of chattels or choses in action is clearly beyond the scope of the Statute and, therefore, unexecuted.

2. A Use on a Use

Prior to the Statute of Uses, the Chancellors held that a use could not be limited on a use, that is, a use could not be given to one person to be held to the use of another person. If O, for value received, bargained and sold land to B and his heirs to the use of C and his heirs, the use declared in C was held void on the ground that it was repugnant to the use raised in B by virtue of the consideration paid by him. Likewise, if O enfeoffed B and his heirs

§ 13

1. There were also other situations where a use would not be executed, e.g. a use raised on a conveyance of copyhold lands and a use raised on a conveyance in fee tail.

2. See ch. 1, § 11, supra.

to the use of C and his heirs to the use of D and his heirs, the use declared in favor of D was deemed void as being repugnant to C's use.

After the Statute of Uses, the courts of law, when called upon to consider the validity of a use limited on a use, applied the Chancery doctrine and held that the second use was unexecuted. Thus, in *Tyrrel's Case*,[3] O, in consideration of four hundred pounds paid by B, bargained and sold land to B and his heirs to the use of O for life, and after her decease to the use of B and the heirs of his body, and in default of issue, to the use of the heirs of O. The court held that the limitation of the uses was void "because an use cannot be engendered of an use." Because the use declared in O was not executed by the Statute, and was invalid in equity as a use on a use, no interest whatsoever passed to O by virtue of the conveyance.

It may be asked why such a conveyance as that in *Tyrell's Case* would have been drawn in that form. The most probable answer is that it was due to a mistake on the part of the conveyancer; that he intended the uses to be executed but overlooked the point that because a bargain and sale creates an implied use, the further limitation of the second use would be a use on a use. The Statute of Uses was a complex act attended by much uncertainty and confusion. Misunderstanding of its operation was common. Yet, if the Chancellor were to grant relief against such mistakes there would be the danger of reviving uses. And, as Holdsworth reminds us,[4] the Chancellor was a great officer of state as well as an equity judge; he would not risk defeating or impairing the policy behind the Statute. Nevertheless, when in 1634 another case involving the limitation of inconsistent uses arose, application was made to the Chancellor for relief against the mistake and relief was granted by ordering the holder of the legal title to convey to the second cestui que use.[5] This was not a holding that a use on a use would be enforced in

3. Dyer, 155a (1557).

4. Holdsworth, Historical Introduction to the Land Law 160–161 (1927).

5. Sambach v. Dalston, Tothill 188. For an account of this case, *see* Strathdene, Sambach v. Dalston; an Unnoticed Report, 74 L.Q.Rev. 550 (1958); Yale, The Revival of Equitable Estates in the Seventeenth Century: An Explanation by Lord Nottingham Cambridge L.J. 72, 78 (1957).

Chancery in the same way that uses were protected before the Statute of Uses. It was still too early for the Chancellor to recognize the second use as an equitable interest. With the enactment of the Tenures Abolition Act in 1660, however, there came a change of attitude. The economic purpose of the Statute of Uses had ceased to be a relevant consideration after the abolition of feudal dues. No reason of state now stayed the Chancellor from recognizing the use on a use as an equitable interest in land. By a process not altogether clear, it became established in the late seventeenth century that although a use on a use was not executed into a legal estate it would be protected in Chancery as an equitable estate.[6] By 1676 the great Chancellor, Lord Nottingham, could state: "If an use be limited upon an use, though the second use be not good in law nor executed by Statute (of Uses), it amounts to a declaration of trust and may be executed (enforced) in Chancery."[7]

With the recognition of the use on a use in Chancery, the law had come full circle. It was again possible for the landowner to split the ownership into a legal and equitable title by deliberately creating a use on a use. The unexecuted use became known as a trust, and so it is known today. Prior to 1536 the terms "use" and "trust" were synonymous and in the Statute of Uses itself the phrase "use, confidence or trust" appears repeatedly. But with the renascence of equitable interests in the form of the use on a use, the term "use" was restricted to a use executed by the Statute and the term "trust" was applied to an unexecuted use or equitable interest. Such trusts became common in the eighteenth century. The standard form of limitation to create a trust in a conveyance by lease and release was: "to X and Y and their heirs, unto and to the use of X and Y and their heirs, in trust for C."[8] The trustees

---

6. For an excellent account of the evolution of the use on a use, see A. W. B. Simpson, A History of the Land Law 198–207 (2d ed. 1986).

7. Grubb v. Gwillim, Selden Society, vol. 73, p. 347. A use on a use must be distinguished from a use after a use. The former is a contradictory or conflicting use; the latter is a successive use. Thus, O enfeoffs B and his heirs to the use of C for life, then to the use of D and his heirs. D's use is a use after a use, not a use on a use, and is executed by the Statute. The state of the title is: life estate in C, vested remainder in D in fee.

8. This was the basis of Lord Hardwicke's famous crack that the Statute of Uses "has had no other effect than to add at most three words to a convey-

obtained the legal title by force of the common-law conveyance, not by an executed use, but the declaration of a use to the trustees had the effect of making the second use in favor of C a use on a use.[9]

The recognition and protection accorded to the use on a use in Chancery marks the beginning of the modern law of trusts. In essence, the trust was the old use in a new form but in dealing with trusts the Chancellors were not bound by ancient doctrine and were free to fashion the trust into an effective instrument for the management and disposition of property. In course of time the trust acquired its own distinctive characteristics but the underlying concept remained the same—the holder of the legal title to property is under a duty enforceable in equity to deal with the property for the benefit of the cestui que trust, the designated beneficiary.

Today, the trust is a primary vehicle for the transfer of wealth to successive beneficiaries.[10] It is often used to provide management of property passing beneficially to minors, immature adults and incompetent adults. It is a common feature in interspousal estate planning, particularly with second marriages where the spouses wish to assure that children from a prior marriage will be protected. In certain cases, albeit less so than in the past, the trust is used to achieve tax savings available to trusts under either federal or state law.

ance." The three words, apparently, are "in trust for." Hopkins v. Hopkins, 1 Atk. 581 (1738). The statement is a witty exaggeration.

9. Doe v. Passingham, 6 B. & C. 305 (1827).

10. The classification scheme for future interests, as we have seen, developed in the context of conveyances for legal interests in real property. But the same scheme applies as well to equitable future interests held under the terms of a modern day trust. Typically, the holder of the future interest—remainder or executory interest, is said to have an interest in the trust "corpus" or the trust "principal." If classified as a remainder, then typically it is also classified as either "vested," "vested subject to open" "vested subject to complete divestment" or "contingent" Often the latter classification inappropriately is merely a surrogate for the legal conclusion that the future interest in the trust is devisable or descendible. However, whether the interest is transmissible, a very important question, often depends on other factors. And, rules of construction or of property law, such as the Rule in Shelley's Case, the Doctrine of Worthier Title, and most importantly, the Rule Against Perpetuities apply to a future interest in trust. Therefore, while it is likely true that future interests are infrequently created as legal estates today, the knowledge you acquire about legal future interest is transportable to equitable future interests.

The statement is sometimes made that the Statute of Uses failed to accomplish its purpose of abolishing dual ownership of land because, by the doctrine of unexecuted uses, a separation of the legal and equitable interests was effected. Such a statement is open to the criticism that it mistakes the purpose of the Statute and ignores its subsequent history. It is true that the object of the Statute was to prevent the separation of legal and equitable interests in land but this was merely a means to the end and that end was to put a stop to the drainage of royal revenues by the evasion of feudal dues through the practice of conveying to uses. The Statute did effectually put a stop to this drainage.[11] It was not until one hundred years after the Statute that Chancery gave protection to the use on a use and by that time feudal dues were no longer an important source of revenue to the Crown. By the time the use on a use was protected in equity the Statute of Uses had already accomplished its primary purpose. Active uses and uses raised on terms for years were held to be beyond the reach of the Statute but they were, at that time, neither numerous nor important.

3. Active Uses

An active use exists wherever duties are imposed on the grantee to uses over and above those to which the feoffee to uses was subject before the Statute of Uses. Prior to the Statute, such a feoffee had the passive duty to allow the cestui que use to take the rents and the profits, and also the affirmative duties to protect the estate against disseisors and to convey the legal title at the direction of the cestui que use. If the grantee to uses was directed by the terms of the conveyance to collect the rents and profits and pay them over to the holder of the use, the imposition of such additional affirmative duties was said to make the use an active use. Within ten years after the enactment of the Statute, it was held that an

---

11. As noted previously (ch. 1, § 7, note 1, *supra*), in 1540 a special court, The Court of Wards and Liveries, was set up to supervise the collection of the feudal dues to which the King was entitled. Under the efficient operations of this court (a combination of Tax Court and Internal Revenue Service) collections rose to a new high. *See* Bell, The Court of Wards and Liveries 190 et seq. (1953); Hurstfield, The Profits of Fiscal Feudalism, 1541–1602, 8 Econ. Hist.Rev.2d 53 (1955).

active use or trust was unexecuted and this decision was steadily followed.

There is nothing in the wording of the Statute of Uses that would make it inapplicable to active uses and the doctrine that such uses are unexecuted may be a questionable piece of judicial construction. It is true that to hold an active use to be executed would defeat the intention of the grantor by preventing the grantee to uses from performing the administrative duties assigned to him. However, the Statute was not designed to operate only in the case where the grantor's intention would not be thwarted. The probable reason for exempting active uses from the operation of the Statute was that such uses did not involve some of the evils against which the Statute was directed inasmuch as the feoffee to uses was in possession of the land and the ostensible owner. In any event, active uses or trusts were not common until the eighteenth century.

§ 14.　The Statute of Uses in the United States

Prior to the Revolution, the Statute of Uses was deemed to be in force in the American colonies and following the revolution the statute was incorporated into the states' legal systems as a part of the received common law. As stated by Chief Judge Parsons, in *Marshall v. Fisk:*[1] "The statute of uses being in force in England when our ancestors came here, they brought it with them, as an existing modification of the common law, and it has always been considered a part of our law." Some states, New York for example, later abrogated the Statute by legislation and enacted substitute statutes to deal with conveyancing and trusts. Other states substantially re-enacted the Statute of Uses. At the present time the Statute of Uses, or a statutory substitute therefor, can be said to be in force in the great majority of the states.[2]

As a result of the Statute of Uses being in force in the several states, transfers of estates in land by means of a bargain and sale or a covenant to stand seised were, and are, valid methods of conveyancing. Because the Statute of Enrolments, by reason of its local

§ 14

1.　6 Mass. 24, 31 (1809).

2.　As to the situation in the several states, *see* Bogert, Trusts, § 206 (rev. 2d ed. 1979). Incidentally, the Statute of Uses was repealed in England in 1925.

nature, was never deemed to be in force in America, land could be conveyed by a simple deed of bargain and sale and there was no need to resort to the more cumbersome English device of lease and release.[3] Conveyances by way of bargain and sale were, therefore, in frequent use. In practically all states there are statutes authorizing the conveyance of land by a simple form of deed that greatly resembles the old common-law "grant" but, unlike the common-law grant, the modern deed of grant can be used to transfer both present and future estates. The statutory deed is, in reality, a substitute for the common-law conveyance by way of feoffment.

The doctrine of unexecuted uses is recognized in jurisdictions where the Statute of Uses is in force. In such states, a use on a use creates an equitable interest only; and an active use or trust must be distinguished from a passive use or trust. In those states where land can be conveyed either by bargain and sale or by statutory deed equivalent to a feoffment, it sometimes becomes necessary to determine the mode in which the conveyance operates. Thus, for value received, O "gives, grants, bargains and sells" land to B and his heirs "in trust for, and to the use of" C and his heirs. If the deed is considered as one of bargain and sale, the use declared in favor of C is a use on a use and, therefore, unexecuted. The legal title is in B and the equitable title in C. If the deed is held to be a statutory substitute for feoffment, B stands seised to the use of C and C's use will be executed by the Statute of Uses so as to vest in him the legal title. In passing on a question of this nature the courts seek to effectuate the intention of the parties and will treat the deed as operating under that type of conveyance which will accomplish the result intended by the parties.[4]

3. Conveyances by lease and release were common in New York in the eighteenth century. See, e.g., Van der Volgen v. Yates, 9 N.Y. 219 (1853). This was due to the practice of lawyers following English form books on conveyancing.

4. Carr v. Richardson, 157 Mass. 576, 32 N.E. 958 (1893); Eckman v. Eckman, 68 Pa. 460 (1871). See also Burnham v. Baltimore Gas & Electric Co., 217 Md. 507, 144 A.2d 80 (1958). Occasionally, a statute clarifies the situation.

Mass.Gen.Laws Ann. ch. 183, § 14 (West 1991) provides: "When a conveyance or devise of real estate is made to a grantee or devisee to a use intended to be executed by the statute of uses, the word 'use' shall be employed in declaring the use; and provisions introduced by the words 'in trust' or other expressions that might otherwise create uses, shall be deemed to create trusts and not uses."

In the modern law of trusts, the terms "active trust" and "passive trust" are generally employed instead of "active use" and "passive use." Because an active trust is not executed by the Statute of Uses but a passive trust is executed, meaning legal title passes through the "trustee" to the beneficiaries, a determination whether in a particular case the "trust" is active or passive may become important. Thus, in *Burnham v. Baltimore Gas & Electric Co.*[5] O conveyed land to B and her heirs "in trust for the use and benefit of" B's two minor daughters, C and D, during their joint lives and for the life of the survivor, then to their heirs in fee simple. The question arose, after the death of the two daughters, as to the nature of the estates created. Because no active duties were imposed on the trustee in respect of the remainder interest, the remainder was a legal remainder. The central problem was whether the life estates given to the two daughters were legal or equitable. This in turn depended on whether the trust during the life of the daughters was active or passive. If passive, it was executed and because the life estates and the remainder would be legal interests the Rule in Shelley's Case would apply.[6] However, if the trust was active, the life estates given to the daughters were equitable and the Rule in Shelley's Case would not be applicable because the life estates and the remainder to the heirs would not be of the same quality. The court held that the trust for the daughters was passive (hence executed) and the Rule applied.[7]

5. 217 Md. 507, 144 A.2d 80 (1958).

6. The deed had been executed prior to the enactment of the Maryland statute abrogating the Rule in Shelley's Case.

7. For an excellent summary of the law with respect to active and inactive trusts, *see* Restatement (Second) of Trusts, § 69 (1959).

Chapter 9

CONCURRENT OWNERSHIP

From an early date the common law recognized the capacity of two or more persons to own concurrent interests in the same estate in land. In time, the various kinds of concurrent interests were classified under four headings: joint tenancy, tenancy in common, coparcenary, and tenancy by the entirety. With the exception of coparcenary, these types of concurrent interests form the basis of the modern law of co-ownership of real and personal property.[1]

§ 1. The Concept of Joint Tenancy

Joint tenancy is a form of co-ownership existing between two or more persons having an interest in real or personal property[1]

1. Two additional types of co-ownership of considerable importance in American law are community property and tenancy in partnership. Community property is a system of marital property rights derived from the Spanish law and exists in eight states: Arizona, California, Idaho, Louisiana, Nevada, New Mexico, Texas and Washington. Under this system husband and wife are co-owners of all real and personal property acquired by either or both during the marriage other than by gift, bequest, devise or inheritance. For details, see 2 American Law of Property [hereinafter referred to as "ALP"], §§ 7.1–7.36.

Tenancy in partnership is, as the name indicates, a unique form of co-ownership by which specific partnership assets, both real and personal, are held by partners. The concept of tenancy in partnership is a creation of the Unif. Partnership Act, § 25. The Act has been adopted in all states. See 6 U.L.A. 7 (Supp.1987).

As to the nature of condominiums and cooperatives, see, 1 Rohan & Reskin, Condominium Law and Practice (1987).

§ 1

1. The following discussion relates almost exclusively to joint tenancies in real property. While there are significant analogies to the joint tenancy in personal property, particularly bank accounts,

260

whereby they own the one interest together with each person having exactly the same rights in that interest. The unity of ownership of the joint tenants differentiates a joint tenancy from other types of co-ownership. Blackstone[2] in a frequently quoted passage, described this quality as a four unities test: "the unity of interest, the unity of title, the unity of time and the unity of possession; or in other words, joint tenants have one and the same interest, accruing by one and the same conveyance, commencing at one and the same time, and held by one and the same possession."[3] Blackstone's description is helpful in that it emphasizes the factor of identity of interest and enumerates the requisites for the creation of a joint tenancy; it describes the attributes of joint tenancy instead of analyzing the concept itself. That concept is the rather metaphysical one of a fictitious unity of persons as co-owners.[4] Put more simply, this amounts to saying that for some purposes the joint tenants are viewed as a unity but for other purposes they are recognized as having individual rights in respect of the property.

§ 2.   Creation of a Joint Tenancy

A joint tenancy is always created by act of the parties, never by descent or operation of law. At common law a conveyance or devise to two or more persons (other than husband and wife) was held to create a joint tenancy in the absence of a clear expression of the transferor's intention to create a tenancy in common. This constructional preference in favor of joint tenancy with its quality of survivorship arose from a desire to avoid splitting the feudal services due to the lord of the fee. After the decline of feudal tenure as a significant factor in the land law, the courts showed a disposition to seize upon any words that could be construed to indicate an intention to create a tenancy in common rather than a joint

---

there are some important differences with respect to the rights of joint tenants in personalty between themselves.

2. 2 Bl.Comm. 180. The requirement of unity of possession does not mean actual possession. There may be a joint tenancy in a future interest, such as a remainder. A unity of right to possession is sufficient.

3. Courts, in discussing the creation of joint tenancies, usually refer to the four unities. *See, e.g.,* Palmer v. Flint, 156 Me. 103, 161 A.2d 837 (1960).

4. For a discussion of the nature of joint tenancy, *see* 2 ALP, § 6.1; Hines, Real Property Joint Tenancies: Law, Fact, and Fancy, 51 Iowa L. Rev. 582 (1966).

[handwritten marginalia: tenants in common v. joint tenancy— latter, surviving tenant takes over deceased tenant's estate/interest]

tenancy. This judicial hostility to joint tenancy arose from the view that in the absence of a clear intention to that effect the ultimate ownership of the property should not depend on the accident of survivorship. This view has been reflected in legislation. In a few states joint tenancies have been abolished by statute.[1] In a minority of states there are statutes abolishing the characteristic of survivorship of joint tenancy.[2] In most states joint tenancies continue to exist in real and personal property as at common law but the common-law presumption favoring the creation of a joint tenancy has been abrogated by statute.[3] These latter statutes usually provide that a conveyance or devise to two or more persons (except fiduciaries such as trustees or executors) shall create a tenancy in common unless the creating instrument expressly declares that such persons shall take as joint tenants with right of survivorship and not as tenants in common or otherwise clearly manifests an intention to create a joint tenancy. Considerable litigation has arisen under such statutes in cases where the conveyance has not followed closely the statutory language but it is claimed that the language used manifests an intention to create a joint tenancy. Thus, if O conveys Blackacre to "B and C and to the survivor of them, his heirs and assigns" do B and C take as joint tenants in fee, or do B and C take a life estate as tenants in common with vested cross-remainders for life, with a contingent remainder in fee in the survivor? Or, O may convey Blackacre "to B and C as joint tenants and to the survivor of them, his heirs and assigns." Do B and C take as joint tenants in fee, or as joint tenants for life with a contingent remainder in fee in the survivor? Different answers have been given by the courts to these questions.[4] The language of the

§ 2

1. *See* Alaska Stat. § 34.15.130(Michie 1998)(as to real property)

2. *See, e.g.,* Tenn. Code Ann. § 66–1–107 (Vernon 1980); Fla.Stat.Ann. § 689.15 (West 1994); Tex. Prob. Code § 46 (Vernon 1980) (although joint tenants can agree in writing to a survivorship feature). For a hybrid type of statute, *see* Conn. Gen. Stat. Ann. § 47–14a (West 1995).

3. For a collection of these statutes, *see* 4A Powell, Real Property, ¶ 602[2].

4. In Michigan, for example, a conveyance to B and C or survivor has been held to create a life estate in B and C with a contingent remainder in fee in the survivor. Rowerdink v. Carothers, 334 Mich. 454, 54 N.W.2d 715 (1952). An opposite result was reached in Coffin v. Short, 82 R.I. 132, 106 A.2d 262 (1954). In Ames v. Cheyne, 290 Mich. 215, 287 N.W. 439 (1939), the court held

applicable statute may be controlling;[5] but in the absence of controlling statutory language the principal issue is whether the provision for survivorship in the conveyance expresses an intention to create a joint tenancy or a contingent remainder in the survivor.

Another situation which has given rise to a diversity of opinion among the courts is where the property owner attempts to convey directly to a third person and himself as joint tenants. Thus, O conveys Blackacre "to O and B and their heirs as joint tenants with right of survivorship and not as tenants in common." At common law a man could not convey to himself; thus, the effect of the conveyance would be to give B an undivided half interest as tenant in common with O. Since the unities of time and of title are lacking, no joint tenancy results. In the absence of statute, some courts apply the common-law rule;[6] others, however, have refused to be bound by the "outmoded unities rule."[7] In about half the states there are statutes permitting a direct conveyance to the grantor and other persons as joint tenants. In a jurisdiction where there is no such statute and no judicial decision clarifying the law, it is still necessary for O to convey to a straw man and then have the straw reconvey to O and B as joint tenants.

In states that recognize the traditional common-law joint tenancy, it is safe to assume that a conveyance from O to "B and C and their heirs as joint tenants with right of survivorship and not as tenants in common" creates the common-law joint tenancy with the survivorship feature.

that a deed to B and C "as joint tenants and not as tenants in common, and to the survivor thereof" creates a joint life estate with a contingent remainder in fee to the survivor, not a joint tenancy in fee. *Contra* Palmer v. Flint, 156 Me. 103, 161 A.2d 837 (1960). For a good analysis of the problem, *see* Comment, Joint Tenancy, 38 Mich.L.Rev. 875 (1940).

5. In some states (*e.g.* Massachusetts, New Mexico and Utah) the statutes regulating the creation of joint tenancies expressly provide that a transfer to two or more persons and "the surviv-

or of them" is sufficient to create a joint tenancy.

6. A leading case applying the old common-law rule is Deslauriers v. Senesac, 331 Ill. 437, 163 N.E. 327 (1928). The rule in Illinois has since been changed by statute. 765 Ill. Comp. Stat. Ann. 1005/1b (West 2001).

7. Therrien v. Therrien, 94 N.H. 66, 46 A.2d 538 (1946); Matter of Horler's Estate, 180 App.Div. 608, 168 N.Y.S. 221 (1917). The cases are collected in 44 A.L.R.2d 595 (1955).

§ 3. Characteristics of a Joint Tenancy

The most important characteristic of a joint tenancy is the right of survivorship. On the death of one of the joint tenants his interest does not descend to his heirs or pass under his will; the entire ownership remains in the surviving joint tenants. The interest of the deceased joint tenant disappears and the whole estate continues in the surviving tenants or tenant.[1] Thus, the widow of the deceased joint tenant has no common-law dower rights[2] and the creditors of the deceased joint tenant have no claim against the enlarged interest of the surviving tenants.[3]

The incident of survivorship attaching to the joint tenancy explains the popularity of this form of co-ownership, particularly with respect to certain types of personal property such as bank accounts, stocks, and bonds.[4] A property owner who desires to have

§ 3

1. The problem of the simultaneous deaths of all the joint tenants is taken care of by the Unif. Simultaneous Death Act, adopted in nearly all states. Section 3 of the Act provides: "Where there is no sufficient evidence that two joint tenants or tenants by the entirety have died otherwise than simultaneously the property so held shall be distributed one-half as if one had survived and one-half as if the other had survived. If there are more than two joint tenants and all of them have so died the property thus distributed shall be in the proportion that one bears to the whole number of joint tenants." 8A U.L.A. 164 (1985).

Kansas and Massachusetts in their version of the Act substitute for the second sentence in the quotation the following: "Where more than two joint tenants have died and there is no sufficient evidence that they died otherwise than simultaneously the property so held shall be divided into as many equal shares as there were joint tenants and the share allocable to each shall be distributed as if he had survived all the others."

2. By statute, a surviving spouse may be entitled to reach joint tenancy property held by the deceased spouse and another in satisfaction of an elective share. *See, e.g,* Unif. Probate Code § 2–202 (b)(2)(iv)(C).

3. The right of a creditor having an attachment, mortgage or other lien on the interest of a joint tenant may be preserved, by statute, despite the death of the debtor tenant. *See, e.g.,* Conn. Gen.Stat.Ann. § 47–14f (West 1995); Wis.Stat.Ann. § 700.24 (West 2001).

4. A number of different theories, including that of joint tenancy, have been advanced by the courts in the so-called "joint" bank account cases. But even where a court purports to apply the concept of joint tenancy to such cases, not all of the normal incidents of joint tenancy are held to govern the relations of the co-tenants. *See* Kepner, The Joint and Survivorship Bank Account—A Concept Without a Name, 41 Calif.L.Rev. 596 (1953); Kepner, Five More Years of the Joint Bank Account Muddle, 26 U. Chi.L.Rev. 376 (1959). *Cf.* Unif. Prob. Code §§ 6–101–113.

the property pass on her death to a particular person (usually a spouse or close relative) frequently creates a joint tenancy in the property as a substitute for a will. The reasons for so doing may be a distrust of wills, or a desire to avoid the delay and expense of probate proceedings, or an erroneous belief that the property will not be subject to estate taxes.[5] While the joint tenancy may well serve a useful purpose, particularly in the case of small estates, it is the subject of considerable misunderstanding among lay persons and the danger of such misunderstanding has led to legislation in a few states eliminating the right of survivorship as an incident of joint tenancy.

A joint tenant may freely alienate his interest in the jointly held property and such a transfer results in a severance of the joint tenancy. If A and B are joint tenants and A conveys his interest to C, the joint tenancy terminates and B and C hold as tenants in common. The transfer destroys the unities of title and of time since the transferee (C) acquires his interest by a different title and at a different time than did B. Since B and C own the property as tenants in common, there is no survivorship feature and at the death of either the decedent's interest passes to the decedent's heirs or beneficiaries under her will.

Suppose A, B and C are joint tenants and A conveys his interest to D. In this case, B and C remain joint tenants with respect to an undivided two-thirds interest and, as a unity, hold as tenants in common with D who has a one-third interest in the property. The survivorship feature is not terminated as between B and C such that at B's death survived by C, C owns two-thirds and D one-third of the property. Likewise, if A, B and C are joint tenants and A conveys his interest to B, the latter becomes a tenant in common with respect to the one-third interest conveyed by A but B and C remain joint tenants of a two-thirds interest. On B's death a one-third interest will pass under his will but a two-thirds interest will accrue to C as surviving joint tenant.[6]

5. Under I.R.C. § 2040, joint tenancy property under certain circumstances is subjected to the federal estate tax.

6. Jackson v. O'Connell, 23 Ill.2d 52, 177 N.E.2d 194 (1961).

The problem frequently arises as to what acts or conduct by a joint tenant in relation to his interest in the property, other than an absolute conveyance of that interest, severs the joint tenancy.[7] A joint tenant's mortgage of his undivided interest severs the joint tenancy in a jurisdiction adhering to the common-law rule that a mortgage transfers the legal title to the mortgagee.[8] In a state following the lien theory of mortgages, however, the mortgage creates a partial severance: the mortgage itself is effective against the surviving joint tenant but the equity of redemption accrues to the survivor.[9]

A contract by a joint tenant to convey his interest affects a severance on the theory that in equity the purchaser becomes the owner of the seller's undivided interest.

Whether a lease of a joint tenant's undivided interest completely severs the joint tenancy or leaves the reversion of the lessor-tenant subject to the joint tenancy is not clear.[10] Logically, it would seem that the execution of the lease destroys the unity of interest and causes a total severance. The commencement of a suit for partition will not cause a severance but the entry of a judgment for partition will have that effect even prior to the execution of the

---

7. *See* Swenson and Degnan, Severance of Joint Tenancies, 38 Minn.L.Rev. 466 (1954).

8. *See* Van Antwerp v. Horan, 390 Ill. 449, 61 N.E.2d 358 (1945); Tracy–Collins Trust Co. v. Goeltz, 5 Utah 2d 350, 301 P.2d 1086 (1956).

9. *See* Wilken v. Young, 144 Ind. 1, 41 N.E. 68 (1895). Contrary to Wilken v. Young, it has been held in California, that the lien of the mortgage expires on the death of the mortgagor-tenant and the surviving tenant takes the entire property free of the mortgage. People v. Nogarr, 164 Cal.App.2d 591, 330 P.2d 858 (1958). *Accord* Harms v. Sprague, 105 Ill.2d 215, 85 Ill.Dec. 331, 473 N.E.2d 930 (1984). In Connecticut and Wisconsin, the lien of the mortgage is preserved by statute when the mortgagor-tenant predeceases his co-tenant. *See* note 3, *supra*.

The "equity of redemption" is the right of the mortgagor to redeem the property subject to a mortgage following a breach of a condition in the mortgage by paying the debt within whatever period is provided by law.

10. In the leading case of Tenhet v. Boswell, 18 Cal.3d 150, 133 Cal.Rptr. 10, 554 P.2d 330 (1976), the court held that a lease by one of two joint tenants of his interest did not sever the joint tenancy either during the period of the lease or permanently, and that on the death of the lessor tenant during the term of the lease, the lease terminated and the entire ownership accrued to the surviving joint tenant. *Contra* Alexander v. Boyer, 253 Md. 511, 253 A.2d 359 (1969). *See* Comment, Consequences of a Lease to a Third Party Made by One Joint Tenant, 66 Cal.L.Rev. 69 (1978).

judgment.[11] A judgment lien on the interest of one of the joint tenants obtained by his creditor during the existence of the joint tenancy will not, prior to sale, sever the joint tenancy.

The courts are not in agreement as to the effect on the joint tenancy of a contract by all of the cotenants to sell the jointly held property to a third person. It is difficult to see why the contract should be held to create a severance with respect to the legal title but some courts have reached that result.[12] A conflict also exists as to whether the purchase money itself is held by the cotenants as joint tenants or tenants in common.[13]

It is possible for the cotenants to terminate the joint tenancy by a contract or agreement to sever the tenancy or by an agreement to deal with the property in a way inconsistent with their interests as joint tenants.[14]

At common law, neither a joint tenant nor a tenant in common could compel a partition, that is a division of the land into separate parcels and the allocation of one or more parcels to each tenant. The remedy of the writ of partition was made available to joint tenants and tenants in common by a statute in the reign of Henry VIII.[15] Later, Chancery assumed jurisdiction of suits for partition. At the present time, the availability of the remedy and the proce-

---

11. See Minnehan v. Minnehan, 336 Mass. 668, 147 N.E.2d 533 (1958); Sheridan v. Lucey, 395 Pa. 306, 149 A.2d 444 (1959).

12. See Compton v. Compton, 128 Ariz. 148, 624 P.2d 345 (App.1981); In re Baker's Estate, 247 Iowa 1380, 78 N.W.2d 863, 64 A.L.R.2d 902 (1956); Buford v. Dahlke, 158 Neb. 39, 62 N.W.2d 252 (1954). Contra Simon v. Chartier, 250 Wis. 642, 27 N.W.2d 752 (1947). Cf. Watson v. Watson, 5 Ill.2d 526, 126 N.E.2d 220 (1955).

13. Cases holding that the proceeds of the sale are owned in joint tenancy in the absence of an agreement to the contrary are: Teutenberg v. Schiller, 138 Cal.App.2d 18, 291 P.2d 53 (1955); Hew-

itt v. Biege, 183 Kan. 352, 327 P.2d 872 (1958); Lawrence v. Andrews, 84 R.I. 133, 122 A.2d 132 (1956); Contra, Illinois Public Aid Comm. v. Stille, 14 Ill.2d 344, 153 N.E.2d 59 (1958); Greenberg v. Greenberg, 141 Me. 320, 43 A.2d 841 (1945); In re Cossitt's Estate, 204 App. Div. 545, 198 N.Y.S. 560 (1923), aff'd 236 N.Y. 524, 142 N.E.2d 68 (1923).

14. The cases are collected in 64 A.L.R.2d 918 at 941 (1959); 39 A.L.R.4th 1068. In Minonk State Bank v. Grassman, 95 Ill.2d 392, 69 Ill.Dec. 387, 447 N.E.2d 822 (1983), the court held that a joint tenant could sever the joint tenancy by deeding her interest directly to herself as a tenant in common.

15. 31 Hen. 8, ch. 1 (1539).

dures governing it are universally covered by statute.[16] Voluntary partition by the cotenants was always permissible.

§ 4. Tenancy in Common

Tenancy in common is a type of concurrent co-ownership of real or personal property whereby each of the cotenants has a distinct and separate interest in the property but the right to possession and enjoyment is common to all of the cotenants. The only unity essential to a tenancy in common is the unity of possession. As Blackstone put it: "For indeed tenancies in common differ in nothing from sole estates but merely in the blending and unity of possession."[1] Unity of possession means that each of the tenants is entitled to possession and enjoyment of the whole property and every part thereof subject to the same right in the other tenants.[2] Since the unities of time, title, and interest are not required for a tenancy in common, such tenants may acquire their respective shares by different conveyances and at different times, their shares may be unequal,[3] and the quantum of estate held by each may be dissimilar. Because there is no unity of interest, there is no right of survivorship. On the death of a tenant in common in fee simple his share descends to his heirs or passes to the devisees under his will subject, at common law, to the rights of a surviving spouse.

Under modern law, the common-law presumption favoring the creation of a joint tenancy on a conveyance to two or more persons no longer exists. Therefore, at the present time the normal effect of a conveyance or devise to two or more persons is the creation of a

16. For details, see 4A Powell, Real Property, ¶ 607.

§ 4

1. 2 Bl.Comm. 180.

2. Thus, if A and B are tenants in common of Blackacre it is not correct to say that A is entitled to possession of one half of the parcel and B is entitled to possession of the other half. A has a right to possess all of Blackacre, and so does B.

3. A transfer of property to two or more persons presumptively creates equal undivided interests in each of the transferees. Suppose, however, that A and B acquire title to land as tenants in common, that the purchase price is $15,000, and A contributes $5,000 and B $10,000. The presumption of equal interests would be rebutted; A and B would have undivided interests proportionate to their contributions—one-third in A, two-thirds in B. See 2 ALP, § 6.5.

vs. joint tenancy

tenancy in common in the absence of a manifested intention that the transferees should hold under a different form of concurrent ownership.[4]

§ 5. Relations of Cotenants Inter Se

[handwritten margin note: owed bet'n the parties, not anyone else]

Apart from matters involving the right of survivorship, the mutual rights and duties of joint tenants and tenants in common are the same. They are, therefore, treated together.

Since each of the tenants is entitled to possession of the entire property subject to a reciprocal right in his cotenants, if one of the tenants excludes the others from the possession or enjoyment of the whole or any part of the land his conduct amounts to an ouster and an action of ejectment will lie in favor of the excluded tenants. Sole possession by the occupying tenant or appropriation of all of the rents and profits, without more, is not an ouster. There must be a repudiation of the rights of the cotenants and a claim of sole ownership; otherwise, the cotenants may properly assume that the possession of the occupying tenant is not hostile to their interests. The occupying tenant may acquire sole title by continuous adverse possession[1] for the statutory period but the courts demand clear proof of the hostile character of the possession and of notice of the adverse claim to the other cotenants. Actual knowledge by the non-occupying tenants of the repudiation of their ownership is not necessary but the conduct of the occupying tenant must be such as to give adequate notice to his cotenants of the occupant's claim of sole ownership before the occupant can acquire exclusive title by adverse possession. The courts are understandably reluctant to allow the title of the non-occupying tenants to be extinguished by the presumptively permissive possession of the occupying tenant.[2]

4. Where the grantees or devisees are husband and wife they may, in some jurisdictions, take as tenants by the entirety. See §§ 6, 7, *infra*.

§ 5

1. A person without title to real property may acquire a good title as against the true owner of the property by adverse possession. This occurs where the true owner fails to sue the wrongful possessor within that period of time provided by statute (typically between 10 and 20 years) and the character of the possession has been actual, open and notorious, exclusive, continuous and hostile. See generally H. Hovenkamp and S. Kurtz, The Law of Property, ch. 4 (5th ed. 2000).

2. See, e.g., Williams v. Fulton, 4 Ill.2d 524, 123 N.E.2d 495 (1954); McKnight v. Basilides, 19 Wash.2d 391,

The question of the liability of a tenant who assumes sole possession of the whole or a portion of the premises to account to his cotenants for the economic benefits derived from such sole occupancy is somewhat complex. We must distinguish between the liability of an ousting occupant and the liability of one whose possession is not in defiance of the rights of his cotenants; between liability for use and occupancy and liability for rents collected from third persons; between use of the land that depletes its value and use that does not involve substantial exploitation of the natural resources of the land.

When the occupying tenant's possession is held under such circumstances as to amount to an ouster of his cotenants, but he has not gained title by adverse possession, he is liable to account to his cotenants for their share of the fair rental value of the property. If the sole occupancy is not accompanied by an ouster, the occupant is not accountable to his cotenants for either use and occupancy or for profits derived from his use of the land, according to the majority of courts.[3] This view would seem to be a logical consequence of the proprietary nature of the interest of the occupant. All of the cotenants are free to enjoy their ownership and the nonoccupying co-owners should not, by abstaining from the exercise of their right to possession, be able to convert the status of the occupying tenant from that of co-owner to rent paying tenant.

At common law, the cotenants had no remedy against a tenant who assumed sole charge of the property and collected rents from third persons for its use, in the absence of an agreement by such tenant to act as manager of the property. A remedy was provided

143 P.2d 307 (1943). But a long continued exclusive and uninterrupted possession without any claim for profits being made by the non-occupying tenant is evidence from which the fact finder may infer an actual ouster. See, e.g., Allen v. Batchelder, 17 Mass.App.Ct. 453, 459 N.E.2d 129 (1984) (exclusive possession by plaintiff and her forebears for over ninety years; the fact that a tobacco-chewing sheep named Sebastian resided on the locus gave local notoriety to the farm.)

3. Larson v. Thoresen, 36 Cal.2d 666, 226 P.2d 571 (1951); Howland v. Stowe, 290 Mass. 142, 194 N.E. 888 (1935); Bennett v. Bennett, 193 Misc. 553, 81 N.Y.S.2d 653 (N.Y.Sup.Ct.1948). *Contra,* Cohen v. Cohen, 157 Ohio St. 503, 106 N.E.2d 77 (1952); McKnight v. Basilides, 19 Wash.2d 391, 143 P.2d 307 (1943).

by the *Statute of 4 and 5 Anne*[4] which gave an action of account to a joint tenant or tenant in common against his cotenant "as bailiff, for receiving more than comes to his just share or proportion." In a few states this statute is deemed to be in force as a part of the received common law; in most states a similar statute has been enacted. The majority of American courts have followed the interpretation placed on the Statute of Anne by the English courts and have restricted its application and the application of similar statutes to the situation where rents and profits have been received from third persons. They have refused to treat the statutes as imposing liability on an occupying tenant for the reasonable rental value of the land or for profits derived from the nondepleting use of the land.[5] Where the occupying tenant depletes the land by developing its natural resources, such as mineral deposits, oil and gas, he is accountable to his cotenants for their proportionate share of the net profits.[6]

Troublesome questions arise as to the respective rights and obligations of the parties where one tenant pays more than his proportionate share of the cost of improvements, repairs, taxes, and carrying charges on the property. Involved in these problems is the matter of available remedies. It is well settled that a tenant who causes improvements to be made to the property owned in joint tenancy or in common, without the express or implied agreement of his cotenants, cannot maintain an action against his cotenants to compel them to contribute to the cost of such improvements. The reason generally given is that a man cannot be improved out of his estate. If the cotenants cannot agree as to the necessity or desirability of making the improvements the appropriate remedy is partition. This does not mean, however, that the tenant who bore the cost of the improvements is entirely without right of reimbursement. In a partition proceeding or in an action for a final accounting of rents and profits an equitable adjustment will be made where possible. Thus, on partition of the land by physical division the improver may have the improved part assigned to him where this can be done without prejudice to the others. Where the property is

---

4. 4 & 5 Anne, ch. 16, § 27 (1705).
5. For a collection of cases, *see* 51 A.L.R.2d 388 (1957).

6. *See* 2 ALP, §§ 6.14–6.15.

ordered sold in the partition suit, the improver is entitled to receive that part of the proceeds attributable to the improvements, over and above the share otherwise due him.[7] And in a suit for accounting of rents and profits the improver is credited with any increase realized from the improvements.

The common law denied the tenant who paid the cost of necessary repairs to the common property a right of action for contribution against his cotenants and this view is still followed by some courts where the cotenants had not agreed to share the costs.[8] Other courts, perhaps a majority, allow contribution where the cotenants were requested to join in the making of reasonably necessary repairs but refused.[9] It is generally agreed, however, that the tenant causing such repairs to be made will be credited with their cost in adjusting the amounts due to the co-owners in an accounting for rents or in a partition suit.

A co-tenant is entitled to contribution from his co-tenants when he pays more than his share of the taxes, interest on a mortgage encumbering the property, or the principal of the mortgage. The usual remedy given to the tenant making such expenditures is to credit him with the overpayment in adjusting the rights of the co-owners in distributing the proceeds of a partition sale or in an accounting for rents and profits. An equitable lien on the shares of his cotenants may be given him to enforce his right of contribution. In some jurisdictions the tenant making the payment is allowed to enforce his right of contribution by a direct action at law against his cotenants.[10]

In dealing with the common property, joint tenants and tenants in common owe a duty of good faith to one another. In some respects they stand in a fiduciary relationship and are not free to

---

7. *See, e.g.*, Batchelder v. Munroe, 335 Mass. 216, 139 N.E.2d 385 (1957); Rainer v. Holmes, 272 Wis. 349, 75 N.W.2d 290 (1956). Cf. Cosgriff v. Foss, 152 N.Y. 104, 46 N.E. 307 (1897).

8. A leading case is Calvert v. Aldrich, 99 Mass. 74 (1868).

9. This is the view taken by the Restatement of Restitution, § 105

(1936). But compare 2 ALP, § 6.18. Where the tenant making the repairs has received the benefit of them through sole possession of the property he will normally be denied the right of contribution.

10. *See, e.g.*, Howland v. Stowe, 290 Mass. 142, 194 N.E. 888 (1935).

act with respect to the property as though they were strangers. This fiduciary concept is usually invoked where one of the cotenants acquires an outstanding encumbrance on the common property for himself, such as a mortgage or tax lien. The tenant acquiring an outstanding title or encumbrance will be compelled to hold it for the benefit of all of the cotenants if the others offer to contribute their proportionate share of the acquisition cost within a reasonable time. Most courts apply the same rule when one of the co-owners purchases the property at a mortgage foreclosure sale or at the foreclosure of a tax lien.[11]

§ 6. Tenancy by the Entirety—The Common–Law Concept

For many purposes the common law treated husband and wife as one legal person. This concept of the legal unity of the spouses resulted in the recognition of a peculiar kind of co-ownership between husband and wife—the tenancy by the entirety. In most respects this form of tenancy resembled the joint tenancy. It was characterized by the four unities of time, title, interest and possession. Yet the manner of holding the estate was said to be different—joint tenants were seized of a share and of the whole (*per my et per tout*), but tenants by the entirety were seised of the whole and not of a share (*per tout et non per my*).[1] As in the case of a joint tenancy, the incident of survivorship attached to a tenancy by the entirety but it was an indestructible right of survivorship. Both

---

11. *See* Salter v. Quinn, 334 Mass. 220, 134 N.E.2d 749 (1956) (delay of seventeen years did not necessarily preclude cotenant from asserting claim to an interest in the property); Beers v. Pusey, 389 Pa. 117, 132 A.2d 346 (1957) (delay of twelve years not fatal to claim of cotenants where wife of one of the tenants acquired title at sale of property for unpaid taxes). Cases holding that any of the cotenants may purchase at a public sale for his own benefit are: Starkweather v. Jenner, 216 U.S. 524, 30 S.Ct. 382, 54 L.Ed. 602 (1910); McNutt v. Nuevo Land Co., 167 Cal. 459, 140 P. 6 (1914).

§ 6

1. If you find this concept difficult to grasp, you are not alone. In his dissenting opinion in King v. Greene, 30 N.J. 395, 413, 153 A.2d 49, 60 (1959) Chief Justice Weintraub had this to say: "The estate by the entirety is a remnant of other times. It rests upon the fiction of a oneness of husband and wife. Neither owns a separate distinct interest in the fee; rather each and both as an entity own the entire interest. Neither takes anything by survivorship; there is nothing to pass because the survivor always had the entirety. To me the conception is quite incomprehensible."

spouses could join in a conveyance of the property to a third person but neither alone could create a severance of the tenancy or by any act defeat the right of survivorship of the other spouse. No right of partition existed. The right of survivorship was an attribute of the ownership by each spouse of the entire estate from the time it was conveyed to them; it was not a contingent future interest in the surviving spouse, superadded to a joint life estate.

At common law, a conveyance to grantees who were husband and wife created in them an estate by the entireties. It was not necessary that they be described as husband and wife or that the conveyance manifest an intention that they take as tenants by the entirety. Indeed, it would seem that under English common law the spouses were incapable of holding as joint tenants or as tenants in common.[2] Upon the creation of the tenancy the rights of the spouses were not equal during coverture. The husband alone was entitled to possession, use and enjoyment of the property. This superior right of the husband, however, would seem not to be a peculiar attribute of the tenancy by the entirety but rather a consequence of the husband's position as guardian of his wife. The analogy to the husband's estate *jure uxoris* in lands solely owned by the wife is apparent.

§ 7. The Tenancy by the Entirety in Modern Law

As might be expected, the tenancy by the entirety has met with a mixed reception in the United States. Its underlying concept of an artificial unity of husband and wife is repugnant to modern views of the status of married women. It is incompatible with the basic theory of the community property system of a conjugal partnership in acquisitions and gains and, therefore, was never recognized in the eight community property states. Among the common-law states, some have held that the Married Women's Property Acts, by granting to wives the right to own and control property as though single, abolished this unique type of co-ownership. Others have reached the same result by construing statutes relating to conveyances to two or more persons as eliminating the entirety estate.

---

2. Green v. King, 2 Wm. Blackstone 1211, 96 Eng.Rep. 713 (1777); Co.Litt. 291; 2 Bl.Comm. 181. But cf. Challis, Real Property 305 (1887). Tenancy by the entirety was abolished in England by the Law of Property Act (1925).

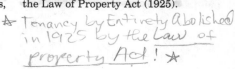

The net result is that at the present time the tenancy by the entirety exists in some twenty-two states.[1] In those jurisdictions which recognize this tenancy as a permissible type of concurrent ownership, it usually exists in a modified form, shorn of some of its common-law attributes.

In all of the states recognizing the tenancy by the entirety, the spouses are also allowed to hold property as tenants in common; and except in those states where joint tenancy has been abolished, they may hold as joint tenants. In many of these states a conveyance to husband and wife creates a tenancy by the entirety in the absence of a manifested intention that the grantees take as tenants in common or as joint tenants.[2]

The estate by the entireties is viewed as essentially a joint tenancy modified by the common-law doctrine of the unity of husband and wife. At common law, a conveyance to husband and wife and a third person gave to the husband and wife a one-half interest as tenants by the entirety, and to the third person the other one-half interest as a joint tenant with the spouses. This

§ 7

1. The following jurisdictions have retained the tenancy by the entirety in real property: Alaska, Arkansas, Delaware, District of Columbia, Florida, Hawaii, Indiana, Kentucky, Maryland, Massachusetts, Michigan, Missouri, New Jersey, New York, North Carolina, Oregon, Pennsylvania, Rhode Island, Tennessee, Vermont, Virginia and Wyoming. Not all of these jurisdictions recognize a tenancy by the entirety in personal property. The tenancy does not exist generally in personal property in Indiana, Michigan, New Jersey, New York, North Carolina, Oregon and Wyoming. See Annot. Estates by Entirety in Personal Property, 64 A.L.R.2d 8 (1959).

2. See, e.g., Matthews v. McCain, 125 Fla. 840, 170 So. 323 (1936); Mosser v. Dolsay, 132 N.J.Eq. 121, 27 A.2d 155 (1942); Roberts v. Roberts, 206 Misc. 779, 134 N.Y.S.2d 877 (1954). But in some jurisdictions retaining the tenancy

by the entirety, a conveyance to husband and wife without specifying the manner of their holding presumptively creates a tenancy in common. See, e.g., D.C. Code Ann. 1961, § 45–816 (1961); Mass. Gen. Laws An. ch. 184, § 7 (West 1977).

It was formerly held in Massachusetts that a conveyance to a husband and wife "as joint tenants in joint tenancy" created in the grantees a tenancy by the entirety unless expressly stated in the deed that they were not to take as tenants by the entirety. Hoag v. Hoag, 213 Mass. 50, 99 N.E. 521 (1912). This ruling has been abrogated by statute. Mass. Gen. Laws Ann. ch. 184, § 7 (West 1977) provides: "A conveyance or devise of land to a person and his spouse which expressly states that the grantees or devisees shall take jointly, or as joint tenants, or in joint tenancy, or to them and the survivor of them shall create an estate in joint tenancy and not a tenancy by the entirety."

resulted from a logical application of the theory that husband and wife were one legal person. At the present time, such a conveyance would, presumptively, create the same estate in the spouses but the third person would hold his half interest as a tenant in common.[3]

Since the tenancy by the entirety is necessarily predicated on the legal unity of husband and wife, it cannot be created in grantees who are not lawfully married at the time of the conveyance. The courts are not in agreement as to the effect of grant to two persons, who are not husband and wife, to hold "as tenants by the entirety." Some courts, perhaps a majority, find in the declaration that the grantees are to take as tenants by the entirety an expression of an intention to create a right of survivorship and hold, therefore, that a joint tenancy, rather than a tenancy in common, results.[4] Where husband and wife hold by the entireties and the marriage is ended by divorce, the tenancy also comes to an end and is normally converted into a tenancy in common.

At common law a man could not convey a legal estate to himself, to himself and his wife, or to himself and another person jointly. A tenancy by the entirety, therefore, could not be created by a direct conveyance from a husband to himself and his wife. In most of the states permitting tenancies by the entirety this rule has been changed by statute and a direct conveyance by either spouse to both spouses as tenants by the entirety is effective to create the intended estate. In the absence of a controlling statute, the courts are divided on the question.[5] Where the spouses hold property by

---

3. *See, e.g.,* Fulton v. Katsowney, 342 Mass. 503, 174 N.E.2d 366 (1961) (deed to A, H and W, his wife, as joint tenants and not as tenants in common held to give A a one half interest as tenant in common and the other half to H and W as tenants by the entirety. But under the current Massachusetts statute all of the grantees would take as joint tenants Mass. Gen. Laws Ann. ch. 184, § 7 (Supp. 1987) provides in part: "In a conveyance or devise to three or more persons, words creating a joint tenancy shall be construed as applying to all of the grantees, or devisees, regardless of marital status, unless a contrary, intent appears from the tenor of the instrument." *See also* note 2, *supra*.

4. *See, e.g.,* Coleman v. Jackson, 286 F.2d 98 (D.C.Cir.1960); Bove v. Bove, 394 Pa. 627, 149 A.2d 67 (1959). *Contra,* Fuss v. Fuss, 373 Mass. 445, 368 N.E.2d 276 (1977). Perrin v. Harrington, 146 App.Div. 292, 130 N.Y.S. 944 (1911).

The holding in the *Fuss v. Fuss* case, *supra*, was changed by statute. Mass. Gen. Laws Ann. ch. 184, § 7 (Supp. 1987).

5. For a collection of cases, *see* Annot., 44 A.L.R.2d 595 (1955).

the entireties, either spouse can, by the majority view, release his or her interest directly to the other spouse.[6]

The characteristics of the modern tenancy by the entirety differ substantially in most jurisdictions from the common-law attributes of the tenancy. While the indestructible right of survivorship is universally retained, the rights of the spouses during the marriage have been radically altered. In the great majority of jurisdictions the husband and wife have equal rights with respect to the possession, use and revenues of the property.[7] The exclusive right to possession and profits which the common law gave to the husband is usually held to have been abolished by the Married Women's Property Acts, although those statutes do not, in terms, purport to deal with tenancies by the entirety. In a few jurisdictions the rights of the spouses remain the same as at common law, with the husband having the exclusive right to possession, enjoyment and income.[8]

The courts are not in agreement as to the capacity of one of the spouses to transfer to a third person his or her interest in the property during the marriage, or as to the power of a creditor of one of the spouses to subject the debtor-spouse's interest to satis-

6. See Hale v. Hale, 332 Mass. 329, 125 N.E.2d 142 (1955); Howell v. Davis, 196 Tenn. 334, 268 S.W.2d 85 (1954).

7. See, e.g., Columbian Carbon Co. v. Kight, 207 Md. 203, 114 A.2d 28 (1955); King v. Greene, 30 N.J. 395, 153 A.2d 49, 75 A.L.R.2d 1153 (1959); Hiles v. Fisher, 144 N.Y. 306, 39 N.E. 337 (1895); Lindenfelser v. Lindenfelser, 396 Pa. 530, 153 A.2d 901 (1959).

8. Massachusetts was a leading exponent of this view. Licker v. Gluskin, 265 Mass. 403, 164 N.E. 613 (1929). Accord Arrand v. Graham, 297 Mich. 559, 298 N.W. 281 (1941); Lewis v. Pate, 212 N.C. 253, 193 S.E. 20 (1937). In each of these jurisdictions recent legislation has equalized the rights of the spouses with respect to the rents, income or profits of the property held by them as tenants by the entirety and each spouse is equally entitled to the

control, management and possession of the property. Mass. Gen. Laws Ann. ch. 209, § 1 (Supp. 1987); Mich. Comp. Laws Ann. § 557.71 (Supp. 1985); N.C. Gen. Stats, ch. 39, § 39–13.6 (1983). The Massachusetts statute was held not to be retroactive in Turner v. Greenaway, 391 Mass. 1002, 459 N.E.2d 821 (1984). Therefore, in Massachusetts there are now two kinds of tenancies by the entirety, depending on when they were created, with respect to the rights of the individual spouses and their individual creditors. The Massachusetts Supreme Judicial Court has refused to hold unconstitutional the older common-law type of tenancy by the entirety created prior to the statutory modification made by Mass. Gen. Laws Ann. ch. 209, § 1, (Supp. 1987), supra, effective February 11, 1980. West v. First Agricultural Bank, 382 Mass. 534, 419 N.E.2d 262 (1981).

faction of his claim. All courts agree that the right of the surviving spouse to the entire estate cannot be defeated by any transfer, voluntary or involuntary, made by the other spouse,[9] but diversity of opinion exists as to the ability of one of the spouses to convey his or her right to share in the possession and income of the property together with the contingent right of survivorship. On this point the courts may be classified into three main groups. The largest group holds that neither spouse can individually transfer his or her interest during the marriage or alienate his or her contingent right of survivorship.[10] These courts adopt the view that although the rights of the spouses are equal neither has a separate interest capable of alienation. A second group of four states[11] treats the modern tenancy by the entirety as essentially a tenancy in common with an indefeasible right of survivorship and permits either spouse to transfer his or her right to possession, income and profits together with his or her contingent right of survivorship. A third group of states, three in number,[12] adheres to the common-law view and allows the husband, but not the wife, to alienate his interest, including therein his contingent right of survivorship.

The question has been raised whether the tenancy by the entirety serves a justifiable social purpose in modern times. Admittedly, this tenancy is an anomaly based on an anachronism. In situations where the marriage relationship is unstable, the tenancy can operate to the disadvantage of one or both of the spouses. The inability of either spouse to compel partition or to effectuate a severance, or in some states to convey a separate interest to a third person, can create a deadlock with respect to the property. The legitimate claims of creditors can be defeated in those jurisdictions which do not permit a levy of execution on the interest of the

9. But by statute in Oklahoma a creditor of either spouse may force a sale of the debtor spouse's interest and thereby compel a severance of the tenancy. Okla.Stat. Ann. tit. 60, § 74 (West 1994).

10. In this group are: Delaware, District of Columbia, Florida, Indiana, Maryland, Missouri, Pennsylvania, Rhode Island, Vermont, Virginia and Wyoming. For a summary of the law of

the several states, see Phipps, Tenancy by Entireties, 25 Temp.L.Q. 24 (1951).

11. Arkansas, New Jersey, New York and Oregon.

12. Massachusetts, Michigan and North Carolina. As to the rights of creditors, see Huber, Creditors' Rights in Tenancies by the Entireties, 1 B.C. Int'l & Comp. L. Rev. 197 (1960). This rule, however, likely is unconstitutional.

debtor spouse. Despite these objections, however, the tenancy by the entirety continues to be a popular form of co-ownership in several states[13] and it is unlikely that appeals for its abolition will be heeded.[14] In a sense, this peculiar form of marital co-ownership operates as a substitute for a community property system in the common-law states which still retain it.

§ 8.   Tenancy in Coparcenary

An estate in coparcenary existed at common law where lands descended from the ancestor to two or more females, in default of a male heir, or where, by special custom in certain localities, lands descended to two or more males. Coparceners, or parceners as they were frequently called, constituted together but one heir and had but one estate. The name "parcener" is derived from the fact that apart from statute such a tenant had the right to compel a partition at a time when joint tenants and tenants in common had no such right. In many respects a tenant in coparcenary occupied a position intermediate between a joint tenant and a tenant in common. Like joint tenants, coparceners had a single estate, they could sue and be sued jointly in respect of the land, and one parcener could convey her share to her cotenants by a release. As in the case of tenants in common, no right of survivorship existed among coparceners, the share of a deceased parcener going to her heir who would hold in coparcenary with the surviving parceners. "And so long as the lands continue in a course of descent, and united in possession, so long are the tenants therein, whether male or female, called parceners. But if possession be once severed by partition, they are no longer parceners but tenants in severalty; or if one parcener aliens

13. In Massachusetts, for example, the greater portion of residential property, apart from large multi-unit apartment buildings, is held by husbands and wives as tenants by the entirety. The popularity of this tenancy was due in the past to special tax advantages under the state inheritance tax law (advantages that no longer exist), the immunity of the wife's interest to claims of her separate creditors, and a desire to avoid probate proceedings on the death of either spouse.

14. For criticisms of the tenancy by the entirety, see, Report of Committee on Changes in Substantive Real Property Principles, in Report of Proceedings of the Section of Real Property, Probate and Trust Law Division, A.B.A. (1944); Ritter, A Criticism of the Estate by the Entirety, 5 Fla.L.Rev. 153 (1952).

her share, though no partition be made, then are the lands no longer held in coparcenary but in common."[1]

The doctrine of estates in coparcenary was correlative to the rule of primogeniture prevailing in England whereby lands descended to the eldest male only, when there were two or more males related in equal degree to the deceased owner. This rule was never in force in this country and as a consequence estates in coparcenary were not generally recognized. In nearly all states heirs take as tenants in common. Although the term "coparceners" or "parceners" is sometimes used in statutes or decisions to describe persons taking land by descent,[2] the tenancy itself as a separate type of co-ownership is generally obsolete and only the name survives.[3] The ancient tenancy in coparcenary has been absorbed in the tenancy in common.

§ 8

1. 2 Bl.Com. 188, 189.

2. *See, e.g.,* Fla.Stat.Ann., § 66.04 (West 1943); W.Va.Code § 3640 (1955).

3. But cf. Gilpin v. Hollingsworth, 3 Md. 190, 56 Am.Dec. 737 (1852) (doctrine of worthier title not applicable to devise to heirs as tenants in common because their estate as tenants in common is different in quality than the estate they would take by descent as coparceners).

Table of Cases

281

*

Index

References are to Pages

289

†